MW01098525

"John Morrison's *Has God Said?* rightly identifies the central issue in an Evangelical doctrine of Scripture. It's all about the meaning of 'is,' as in 'the Bible is the Word of God.' Carefully distinguishing Barth's own position from 'Barthian' pretenders, Morrison analyzes various contemporary options, Evangelical and non-Evangelical, and then offers his own constructive proposal. Morrison's new position builds on Barth's (not Barthian!) Christocentric insights even as it reclaims the Scripture principle in a manner that even Calvin could applaud."

Kevin Vanhoozer
Research Professor of Theology
Trinity Evangelical Divinity School

"For those who want to think deeply about what it means to say that the Bible is the word of God, John Morrison brings wide-ranging resources and careful reflection. Reading this book is a challenging but rewarding task."

Millard Erickson
Professor of Theology
Baylor University

"Bravo to John Morrison for addressing a weighty issue in philosophical theology that is seldom even proposed, let alone faced squarely in recent academic discussions. Far from avoiding the general trend in recent critical thought, Morrison is to be commended for his affirmation that Scripture is an intricate component of God's redemptive self-revelation to a needy world. This volume places front and center God's work through Jesus Christ and in the very text of Scripture. I highly recommend this rigorous intellectual investigation and subsequent call to reaffirm Scripture as a crucial element in the revelation of God's loving actions to a needy creation."

Gary R. Habermas
Research Distinguished Professor
Liberty University

Has God Said?

Scripture, the Word of God, and the Crisis of Theological Authority

John Douglas Morrison

Pickwick *Publications*

An imprint of *Wipf and Stock Publishers*

199 West 8th Avenue • Eugene OR 97401

HAS GOD SAID?
Scripture, the Word of God, and the Crisis of Theological Authority

The Evangelical Theological Society Monograph Series 5

ISBN: 1-59752-581-2

Cataloging-in-Publication data:

Morrison, John Douglas

Has God said? : scripture, the word of God, and
    the crisis of theological authority / John Douglas
    Morrison.

Eugene, Ore.: Pickwick Publications, 2006
Evangelical Theological Society Monograph Series 5

xiv + 306 p. ; 23 cm.

ISBN: 1-59752-581-2

1. Bible—Inspiration. 2. Bible—Evidences, authority, etc.
3. Bible—Hermeneutics. 4. Barth, Karl (1886–1968). I. Title.
II. Series.

BS480 .M67 2006

To

My wife
Ellen

My children
Heather and Shawn

My son and daughter-in-law
Philip and Meghan

My new granddaughter
Charity Faith

My new grandson
Shawn Calvin

and
All our grandchildren
and the generations
to come

Thanks to

Sarah Pisney, Meredith Piper,
Sean Turchin, David Pensgard, Sharon Cohick, Phillip Hines
and
Gary Habermas
For his encouragement

Contents

Acknowledgments

The writing of this book has been a long if steady process. The concerns which gave rise to it, the dualistic separation of "the Word of God" from the language/text of Holy Scripture goes back to my doctoral dissertation on T. F. Torrance (since published as *Knowledge of the Self-Revealing God in the Thought of Thomas Forsyth Torrance*), and the lingering question of the "Barthian" ambiguities about divine disclosure, Christ the incarnate Word, and the prophetic-apostolic Scriptures. This concern was cross-pollinated by the works of evangelicals who, for seemingly inadequate reasons, finally, and often deceptively rejected the classical Scripture principle, the identity thesis that Holy Scripture is, under Christ the Word, the written and authoritative Word of God (cf. chapter seven).

From that point, this issue of the nature of Scripture became a matter of personal focus and, hence, research, writing, presentation and publication. By original design and long term engagement the chapters of *Has God Said?* were first manifested as lectures presented in such contexts as the Wheaton College Theology Conference and the national meetings of the Evangelical Theological Society (ETS) in such locations as Atlanta, Toronto, San Antonio, San Francisco, and Colorado Springs. I remain thankful to those who first heard the products of these interrelated researches, analytical, critical and constructive, and thereby the questions and comments, as well as many encouragements, which have led to the further clarification and the final deliberative product here.

To, into, and through these long processes many colleagues have been positive channels of simultaneous stimulation and encouragement—persevering with me over the long haul. T. F. Torrance of Edinburgh, now in his ninety-second year, has been and remains (through continued correspondence) a significant and formative theological source on the God-world-human relation (even where we differ). Kevin Vanhoozer is a scholar with an amazing theological mind, extraordinarily fruitful, and whose work on Scripture as God's illocutionary speech-acts is, in my opinion, far and away the best in the field. I am most privileged to know and be theologically "discipled" by him. Millard Erickson remains for me *the* evangelical theologian *par excellence*, a man of such mind and heart that I am simultaneously humbled and encouraged to follow in his faithful and fruitful theo-logical way as he follows Christ. He is the gold standard of evangelical theologians. These three stand out, among others God has brought into my life, as Christian brothers, men of great theological acumen, and as caring teacher-mentors who variously, directly and indirectly, have given to me and to whom I am so thankful.

Others near and far have likewise had much ongoing influence on and within the process of research and writing, notably Gary Habermas, thinker, apologist, man of God; Elmer Towns, who is thankfully on the mend even as I am writing this; the members of my department (including Don Fowler *ex officio*), and Carlos Eire of Yale University. As reflected in the "dedication," it is my wonderful and growing family which has, through the years of preparation, been so supportive and interested—even in my overly weighty explanations: Ellen, my patient wife, has been an unmovable, rock of support, believing in me and the project when I would lose heart. Heather, my daughter (and now Philip her husband), and Shawn, my son (now with Meghan and precious Charity and Shawn Calvin), have likewise seen this through with me from day one—and then some. To them there ever remains my heartfelt love and grateful thanks. Who knows? One of my children or grandchildren may have the nerve to read this material—I pray with blessing and profit. So too many others. Amen.

John Douglas Morrison
October 2005

Sight is intentional while sound is largely involuntary . . . in seeing we are the subject, the ones in control, those at the centre of our universe. . . . Sound comes to us and we receive it immediately. . . . We are the ones addressed whether we like it or not. . . . Sight is largely effortless whereas sounds are demanding. Sights and images are more to do with appearances while sound and words take us into meaning. . . . The paradox is that sight which we think is so certain is far less certain than we realize, whereas words with all their mystery, irony, and ambiguity, appearing to be fragile and fleeting, are the primary means whereby we can deal with things that are true and sure.

Jacques Ellul
The Humiliation of the Word

We are part of the generation in which the image has triumphed over the word, when the visual is dominant over the verbal and where entertainment drowns out exposition. We may go so far as to claim that we live in an age of the image which is also the age of the anti-word and which potentially is the age of the lie.

Os Guinness
"The Word in the Age of the Image"

The canon, a divinely initiated covenant document, is quite unlike other human constitutions. Whereas human constitutions are indeed situated social constructs, Scripture is essentially theo-dramatic discourse whose authority originates not in a corporate will-to-power on the part of Israel or the church but in a *divine-will-to-promise* . . . it plots the historical fulfillment of a singular promise.

Kevin Vanhoozer
The Drama of Doctrine

[in the "Scripture Principle" we find that] Scripture not only calls for subsequent performance but is itself a divine performance, a mode of divine communicative action whereby the Triune God furthers his mission and creates a new covenant people. . . . First, there is the material of the theo-drama: God's word-acts from creation to consummation. This is the material principle of the drama of redemption, and the subject matter of Scripture. Second, there is the script, the formal principle of the drama of redemption, its normative specification. As covenant document, Scripture is itself a revelatory and redemptive word-act of the Triune God. To speak of divine canonical discourse is to highlight the role of God as divine playwright who employs the voices of human authors of Scripture in the service of his theo-drama.

Kevin Vanhoozer
The Drama of Doctrine

"Then God spoke all these words . . . "

—Exodus 20:1
NRSV

———·———

"Thus says the LORD, Your Redeemer, the Holy One of Israel. . . ."

—Isaiah 43:14
NRSV

———·———

"But [Jesus] answered, 'It is written, One does not live by bread alone, but by
every word that comes from the mouth of God.'"

—Mathew 4:4
NRSV

———·———

"You are wrong, because you know neither the scriptures nor the power of
God. . . . [H]ave you not read what God said to you . . . ?

—Matthew 22:29, 31
NRSV

———·———

"And the Word became flesh and lived among us. . . .It is God the only Son,
who is close to the Father's heart, who has made him known."

—John 1:14, 18
NRSV

———·———

"Long ago God spoke to our ancestors in many various ways by the prophets,
but in these last days he has spoken to us by a Son. . . ."

—Hebrews 1:1-2
NRSV

———·———

"So also our beloved brother Paul wrote to you according to the wisdom given
him, speaking of this as he does in all his letters. There are some things in
them hard to understand, which the ignorant and unstable twist to their own
destruction, as they do the [other] scriptures."

—2 Peter 3:15-16
NRSV

1

Has God Said?

An Introduction

"Has God said?" Disguised as inquiry, this deceptive and diverting probe by the tempter early in the Genesis narrative, has real power. In the Synoptic Gospels, the narratives of Matthew and Luke present the parallel of the Second Adam, Jesus, in the wilderness, facing the temptor whose approach is again, in essence, "has God said?"

The Christian faith has always faced political, philosophical, cultural and religious attacks whose primary force and edge have been the antagonistic rejection of any notion of the authoritative self-disclosure of the covenant God of Abraham, Isaac, and Jacob, supremely revealed in Jesus the Christ. But the shifts in Western culture in the past three centuries have created a supreme crisis for the classical Christian understanding of divine authority as not only faithful but as truly historical. The reasons for these shifts, and so for this crisis in historical divine authority, are manifold. But Thomas Torrance is surely correct when he points especially to the pervasively injurious effects of the modern re-introduction of cosmological and epistemological dualisms into Western culture as a whole, and notably into the physical sciences, philosophy and, thereby, into Christian theology.[1]

1

As we will see in the chapters that follow, the profound influence of Rene Descartes (Cartesian dualism), Benedict Spinoza, and especially the cosmological dualism of Isaac Newton, which "shut God out" of the world and so from all spatio-historical action and objective self-declaration, through the epistemological dualism of Immanuel Kant, has variously permeated modern and postmodern Christian theology and its entire understanding of the God-world, God-human relationship. From the end of the "Enlightenment" the destructive effects of this dualism, this disjunctive thinking, this "thinking apart" what ought to be thought unitarily together, has affected every Christian doctrine, but most notably the classical Christian doctrine of revelation. This dualism has led to what Martin Buber has called "the conceptual letting-go of God."[2]

A highly problematic result of this renewed intrusion of dualism, cosmological and epistemological, is the loss of true objectivity. In the physical sciences the loss of the proper object led to the positivistic outcomes of the nineteenth and early twentieth centuries, and the clamping down of an alien notion of "*the* scientific method" upon all branches of human inquiry, no matter what the field or focus. Only with the efforts of such reflective scientists as Albert Einstein and Michael Polanyi, among others, has there been a faith-ful turning back to the proper object *as* it "gives" itself to be known. Faithful turning to the object in the physical sciences means that each proper field of inquiry (e.g., biology) must study its own proper object (*bios*/life) in the way that the proper object "gives itself" to be known. For each of the physical sciences the proper way, "the" scientific method, will be distinctive, dictated by the distinctive nature, and so self-disclosure, of the proper object. Thus recognition of differences between inanimate and animate objects, impersonal and personal objects, is of critical importance for true, objective knowing of the proper object as it makes itself known.

Given the destructive effects of modern (and much postmodern) dualism upon Christian theology, with its claim to gracious, covenantal and content-ful divine revelation, the redemptive truth of God, the call back to true objectivity, is of preeminent concern. Christian theological science must think after or "follow after" (*Nachdenken*) the way God has actually redemptively and objectively taken to disclose himself and truth about himself, about his relation to the world and to humanity, as well as his redemptive kingdom purposes, above all in Jesus Christ the Word made flesh (John 1:14 ff.), and in, under, of and from Christ the Word by the Holy Spirit, in Holy Scripture, the written Word of God.

It is the purpose of this book first to critically analyze the various sources of the destructive dualisms that have intruded into Western thinking, and their effects which have led to both the radical "transcendentalizing" and, even more often, the radical "immanentizing" of God in relation to the world. These problematic bases and outcomes have led to the rejection of the classical Christian understanding and affirmation of God's lordly, dynamic interactive relation to, and in, and for the world as Creator, Sustainer and Redeemer who reveals himself objectively in the world. In this way we will clear the path for the re-affirmation and fresh re-formulation of our understanding of the objective, content-ful self-revelation of God. That being so, we will therein affirm as well that a critical aspect of that redemptive self-revelation is the text, the canon of Holy Scripture. The God of Abraham, Isaac, and Jacob is a God who speaks, speaks graciously, speaks content-fully, speaks redemptively, and Holy Scripture is, in all of its historical textuality, the inspired record of what Nicholas Wolterstorff calls "divine discourse." Thus, against all who, contrary to the entire history and doctrinal confession of the Christian church, dualistically reject the possibility and actuality of God's self-revelation taking objective, historical, linguistic, textual form, we will endeavor to re-affirm what almost *all* Christians affirmed until two centuries ago: that under Jesus Christ the Word and by the Holy Spirit, the text of Holy Scripture *is as text* the written/enscripturated Word of God, and hence a crucial aspect of God's larger redemptive self-revelation to and for the world, as centered in Jesus Christ. Consequentially, to the skeptical question "Has God Said?" which, in our context here, denies the Christocentric, objective, content-ful *and textual* self-disclosure of God in space-time, we again confess that Yes, God has spoken; he has condescended in love to declare himself and his truth in human terms for human redemption in Jesus Christ, and, in his Name and by the Holy Spirit, in the canonical text of Holy Scripture.

By means of both critical analysis and constructive formulation, we will initially examine the "headwaters" of the modern separation of the "Word of God" from the text of Holy Scripture by unfolding the socio-political agenda of Benedict (Baruch) Spinoza, for whom such separation was important for personal freedom and, through Spinoza, the similar exegetico-theological concerns of Johann Semler and Johann Gabler.

Next we will inquire into and draw out the contemporaneous (to Spinoza et al.) and interrelated developments in philosophy and physics, thereby clarifying the reintroduction of destructive, dualistic thought forms into Western culture, and so into the Enlightenment and post-Enlightenment views of God and the God-world relation. As we will see, this dualism was then embodied in the influential theologies of such representative notables as Friedrich Schleiermacher, Rudolf Bultmann and Paul Tillich, among many others. Constructive Protestant evangelical responses will also be analyzed in the search of effective contemporary, constructive power in the face of such theological dualism.

From the conceptual groundwork of Enlightenment dualism, much of biblical/historical criticism of Holy Scripture ("higher criticism") rose to prominence with its plurality of presuppositions and critical methodologies. When such historical-critical methods have been coupled with broad dualistic assumptions, many practioners have falsely claimed that the "assured results" of biblical criticism have swept away any possible claims to the divine authority of Scripture. Such "critical" studies are said to show Scripture to be merely a human text. We will show why this is illogical and a grotesque *non sequitur*. Rather, we will point out first that, within their own proper and strict methodological boundaries, many of the biblical-critical approaches to Scripture can potentially be of significant help in finding what may well have been the human processes involved in Scripture's production. But for one to conclude from such analyses that Scripture cannot also be the written Word of the God who, by the Spirit, used these processes to declare/reveal his truth, is false, illogical and usually self-serving.

In chapter five, we will examine historical-theological developments relating to Holy Scripture and the Word of God in Roman Catholic thought from Trent to the present. Roman Catholicism, like all branches of Christianity East and West, has historically affirmed the "identity thesis," i.e., that Scripture is the written Word of God. Beginning from the documents on the matter at the Council of Trent, we will examine subsequent developments in Roman Catholic views on biblical criticism, the inspiration of Scripture, and modernism to and through Vatican I and then Vatican II (*Dei Verbum*) to the *New Catechism of the Catholic Church*. Therein, we will also critically examine the influential views of four prominent Roman Catholic scholars on the question of Holy Scripture and the Word of God: Karl Rahner, Raymond Brown, Avery Dulles, and Richard Swinburne.

In chapter six, we are concerned especially with Karl Barth and his effects upon Protestant orthodoxy. For Karl Barth, God's revelation or self-disclosure, centrally, above all, and fully so in Jesus Christ, the Word of God made flesh, is the center, circumference, and basis of every Christian doctrine. Barth's Christocentrism (or Christomonism, as some would claim) was applied consistently and very influentially on Christian theology after the First World War at multiple levels. As a result, "Barthians" of many stripes have widely promulgated what they understood or took to be Barth's view of revelation/Word of God and so the transcendent separation of such Word from the text of Holy Scripture. But Barthians have often proved to be among Barth's worst interpreters. In fact, recent studies have shown Barth's mature views of Scripture to be largely orthodox and, despite his readily misunderstood dynamic forms of expression, that Holy Scripture, in all its textuality, *is* the written Word of God. Yet the dualistic "Barthian" view of revelation has had increasing influence on Protestant orthodox and evangelical thinkers. Here the instructive case of theologian Bernard Ramm is considered.

What chapter six describes as the "Barthian" (contra Barth) separation of Holy Scripture from the transcendentalized Word of God, coupled with the claim that at crucial moments Scripture can adoptionistically "become" what it is not, the Word of God, forms a theological position that has had and continues to have growing influence among evangelical theologians. Here we will analyze the understanding of the nature of Scripture in relation to "the Word of God" in the thought of three prominent evangelical theologians: Clark Pinnock, Gabriel Fackre, and Donald Bloesch, each of whom accepts a form of this dualistic separation of the text of Scripture from a transcendent and essentially "wordless Word," which yet somehow has a positive transforming effect upon human lives. With these dualistic approaches to divine revelation we will examine contemporary evangelical thinkers who variously and constructively affirm the church's historical "identity thesis," i.e., that Holy Scripture is the written and authoritative Word of God: Paul Helm, Nicholas Wolterstorff, and J. I. Packer. This will prepare for the final chapter and its re-affirmation and reformulation of the "identity thesis."

Chapter seven is wholly constructive. Here we seek to positively respond to and build upon contemporary concerns and questions while again giving fresh presentation and affirmation of the church's historical confession that Holy Scripture is the written Word of God. To this end, we will formulate a new model of Scripture as written Word of God, a multileveled, interactive model, which makes use of Karl Barth's biblical Christocentricity and his Christocentric emphasis on biblical authority, as well as Thomas Torrance's energetic concern for theological and revelational objectivity. Also, importantly, we will employ Albert Einstein's interactive, dynamic portrayal of the nature of objective truth as interactively multileveled, top-down and bottom-up. Therefore we will conclude thereby that in, under, of, and from Jesus Christ, the divine Word of God made flesh (the ontological Word of God), and by the Holy Spirit, Holy Scripture is, by the processes of revelation and inspiration, the written Word of God (derivative Word of God). Reflecting remarkable similarity to this multileveled, interactive model of the Word of God, John Calvin's own understanding of the nature and authority of Holy Scripture above and within the Church and under Christ by the Holy Spirit, is briefly presented as an effective illustration (*mutatis mutandis*) of my model.

May God use this book in the church of Jesus Christ as it endeavors to minister the Word of God within the contemporary cultural context. And may the authoritative text of Holy Scripture, and therein Jesus Christ, the Word, the Lord, and Head of the Church be heard afresh with much Kingdom effect in the power of the Holy Spirit.

Endnotes

[1] T. F. Torrance has, for half a century, been a leading figure in the significant ongoing dialogue between Christian theology and contemporary physics. In that setting, he has been a major and active opponent of the modern intrusion or re-introduction of cosmological and epistemological dualism into Western culture generally, and into the physical and theological sciences in particular. Works by Torrance where such issues are variously dealt with are *Theological Science, God and Rationality, Space, Time, and Incarnation, Space, Time, and Resurrection, Theology in Reconstruction, The Ground and Grammar of Theology, Reality and Scientific Theology, Transformation and Convergence in the Frame of Knowledge*, and *Divine and Contingent Order*.

[2] Martin Buber, The Eclipse of God: Studies in the Relation Between Religion and Philosophy (New York: Harper, 1952).

2

Spinoza, Semler, and Gabler

Headwaters of the Modern Disjunction
of Holy Scripture from the Word of God

The June 2000 Southern Baptist Convention was, like many recent SBC conventions, steeped in controversy. One of the centerpiece discussions related to the revised "Baptist Faith and Message" and specifically to the nature of Holy Scripture. In what was in fact an attempt to separate the historical text of Scripture from divine revelation/Word of God, the amendment was offered which read, "The sole authority for faith and practice among Baptists is Jesus Christ, whose will is revealed in the Holy Scripture."[1] In commenting, the author of this defeated amendment responded, "[W]e are indeed people of the book, but we are also people who bow only before Jesus Christ our Savior."[2] The problem is that no Christian disagrees with that comment as such, but it actually misses the point while piously camouflaging the real intent: the separation of Holy Scripture from the Word of God. Given the "disclosure levels" or interactive means of God's redemptive-Kingdom revelatory acts and speech to make himself objectively known in the world, how can Holy Scripture be separate from the Christ revealed therein, and to whom Scripture points? How can this either-or be legitimate given the participative unitariness of both within the revelatory purposes of God in Christ to humanity? Yet, since the Enlightenment, this tendency toward a dualistic, rationalistic disjunction of the historical text of Holy Scripture (regarded as essentially a human product) from an ahistorical, trancendentalized Divine Truth/Word of God or "Christ" (a realm of unchanging ideas in some "upper story") has been basic to mainstream modern and postmodern theological emphases with regard to the possibility of content-ful knowledge of God. This is increasingly the case even in confessing evangelical circles (cf. chapter seven).

It is with the purpose of examining this question by means of influential modern sources of this dualistic separation that this book is written.

While Western thinking has long been plagued by dualistic, disjunctive tendencies, the same bifurcational inclinations have repeatedly arisen in the history of the Church's theological thinking with dire results. Dualism was at the heart of the Marcionite and Gnostic challenge, the Arian controversy, and on through the recurring periods of destructive controversy, when faith-ful thinking after the unitary, asymmetrical, interactive God-world relation, in all of its creative redemptive facets, has been disrupted by alien thought forms. It is this very concern, this kind of disjunctive thinking in modern philosophico-theological circles, which has led to the entrenchment of a perceived "gulf" between the historical text of Holy Scripture and a transcendentalized ahistorical "Word of God." Of particular significance to this modern and postmodern tendency has been work of Baruch Spinoza and then, from Spinoza, Johann Semler,and, as a transitional figure into the nineteenth century, J. P. Gabler (cf. chapter three).

Baruch Spinoza's Politico-Theological Intention to Separate the Word of God from Holy Scripture

Spinoza's Background

Baruch (Benedict) de Spinoza was born in Amsterdam in 1632 to a Portuguese Jewish family which had apparently left Portugal for religious reasons. In Holland they were able to be open in their Judaism and raised their son in accordance with Jewish traditions. He also became versed in cabalistic speculations, which were influenced by Neo-Platonism, and in the thought of Jewish philosophers such as Moses Maimondes. He pursued his interests in Latin, mathematics and Cartesian philosophy, and some Greek, from sources outside of his Jewish school setting.[3]

Though taught in the Jewish tradition, Spinoza soon found himself at odds with orthodox Jewish thought and interpretation of Scripture, and at the age of twenty-four was excommunicated from the Jewish community. Having been trained in lens grinding, he was able to provide for himself while leading the life of scholar and philosopher, producing many works and engaging in much correspondence. In 1673, he refused the chair of philosophy at Heidelberg, probably to maintain freedom of thought and life. He died of consumption four years later. [4]

Only two of his works were published during his lifetime, and only one of these appeared under his own name. His *Tractatus, Theologico politicus* (*Theologico-Political Treatise*), which will be the focus of our concern, was published anonymously in 1670, selling many copies across Europe and going through many editions and translations. It created a storm of controversy, being prohibited by the States-General in 1674 and placed on the Index by the Roman Catholic Church.[5]

Bases of Spinoza's Metaphysical System

Before giving focus to the *Theologico-Political Treatise*, an exceedingly brief overview of Spinoza's metaphysics is in order. Several features should be noted. First of all, Spinoza was, among other things, a rationalist, a determinist, and a developer of Cartesian philosophy. He also saw truth "geometrically" in terms of clear and distinct ideas and of propositions logically derived from self-evident axioms. He was also a pantheistic monist.[6] Beginning with this last element, because of its formative significance for all of his thought, Spinoza systematically emphasized the idea that there is only one substance—the infinite divine substance— which is identified with Nature: *Deus sive Natura*, God or Nature. This metaphysical perspective is presented in geometrical form in his *Ethics*. Infinite Nature or Substance or God displays itself in an infinite number of attributes. Of these, only extension and thought are knowable by human beings.[7] It is possible that Spinoza was inclined toward his pantheistic monism and his use of the word "God" for ultimate reality by his early study of certain Jewish writers, though not from the Old Testament where no such identity is made.[8] Indeed, while still a youth, Spinoza concluded that belief in a personal transcendent God, free creator of the universe, was philosophically untenable. Copleston notes, as a result of this perspective, that Spinoza came to conclude that:

> . . . theological language expressing this belief has a valuable function to perform for those who cannot appreciate the language of philosophy; but he regarded its action as being that of leading people to adopt certain lines of action rather than as that of conveying true information about God.[9]

Such a conclusion was to be central to his argument in the Treatise. Against Maimonides and traditional Judeo-Christian religion as a whole, Spinoza argued that truth is not to be found in Scripture or in religion (except for simple truths), but only in philosophy. It is not that Scripture and religion are contradictory but rather that faith deals in the pictorial, the imaginative and in piety, while philosophy, specifically rationalist philosophy, gives the truth in purely rational form. The two realms speak different languages. Each must go its own way.

Then as philosophy proves that the ultimate reality or God is infinite, this reality must contain all being within itself. Thus God cannot be something other than or distinct from the world. The concept of God as infinite Being expressing itself, but yet comprising within itself the totality of reality—pantheistic monism is basic (sometimes covertly so) to all of Spinoza's philosophical expression. All of this, as the development of the logical implications of Cartesian rationalism in the direction of monism and determinism, was presented and argued in his typical, careful, geometrical form of expression, i.e., that true philosophy was, for Spinoza, "the logical deduction of propositions from definitions expressing clear and distinct ideas and from self-evident axioms."[10] For Spinoza, this method was true philosophy, for it infallibly resulted in the truth, a coherent and comprehensive explanatory account of the world as we experience it.

Also pertinent to our larger analysis of Spinoza's view of divine revelation/the Word of God and the nature of (Judeo-Christian) Scripture is his view of understanding or perception. In his *Treatise on the Correction of the Understanding*, he distinguishes four levels of understanding; in his Ethics he gives three (minus the first). The first and lowest is opinion (*opinio*) or imagination (*imaginatio*). This level alone is the cause of error. It is the perception of knowledge but from vague or confused experience. It is significant that, for the most part, Spinoza links "true religion" with this sense of "imagination."

The second level of perception given in Spinoza's *Ethics* consists in adequate ideas of particular properties of things and in inferential and general concepts—yet without any clear idea of essences. This is the level of sense perception, the physical senses, and abstract ideas. The third level, the highest level of understanding, Spinoza calls "intuitive knowledge." It proceeds from the second level, from an adequate idea of some attribute of God to the adequate knowledge of particular things.[11] The point seems to be that Spinoza conceived of the logical deduction of the essential and eternal structure of Nature from the divine attributes as providing the necessary framework for seeing all things. The whole of Nature is concretely one great system expressing, and at the same time causally dependent on, infinite Substance. If so, then, at the third level of knowledge, the mind returns to perceive individual things in their essential relation to God and not, as at the first level, as isolated phenomena. "The more we understand individual things (in their essential, determined nature) the more we understand God."[12] We find here something of a mystical transformation of our knowing processes, and so the (incomplete) vision of all things in God.

This is of utmost importance. This third level of knowledge, this understanding of the relation of all things to God, is said to be the way to freedom from servitude to passions. This "knowledge of God" is the greatest virtue. So far as we conceive all things as following necessarily from the divine nature, from the infinite causal system of Nature, we conceive such "under the species of eternity" (sub specie aeternitatis). Such knowledge of ourselves and all things is to know God, and the pleasure accompanying the idea of God is the intellectual love of God who cannot be expected to love in return. This love of God is "our salvation, blessedness, or liberty."[13] Yet such religious, indeed Judeo-Christian, language containing even something akin to piety, is a holdover of Spinoza's Jewish upbringing and has no real connection to his system.

The Theologico-Political Treatise

Spinoza's Purpose. In terms of Spinoza's purpose for writing the *Treatise*, he rarely, if ever, puts all of his "cards" out on the table, i.e., there is Spinoza's stated purpose and his real purpose. He says he wants to rid true religion of the effects of superstition and credulity. He also wants to define and then distinguish this true religion from all philosophy. He says he wants to show that, as such, true religion and true philosophy never overlap, the one (religion) dealing only in morality and piety, the other (philosophy) in questions of truth. Indeed, it is *his own* form of both true religion and philosophy that is found to be most conducive to an ordered, peaceful state, and thus most pleasing to rulers.

Hence, Spinoza is in fact waging an aggressive apologetic against both Christian and Jewish orthodoxy, which he equates with "superstition," while seeking political freedom for his own philosophical pursuits.[14] Thus, he presents orthodoxy as not only fearful, godless superstition, but as "wicked and dangerous to the state."[15] It is possible that Spinoza used such *ad hominem* argumentation because something similar had been used against him and his own speculative rationalistic philosophy.

In light of such apologetic goals, it was necessary for Spinoza to carefully orchestrate numerous strands of argumentation. True religion must alter its bases, nature, and goals. It must be cut off from all relation to other endeavors. While often seemingly encouraged and affirmed by Spinoza, religion must in fact be devalued, effaced, shown to be the result of inferior human capacities. To this end, Spinoza reformulates and reduces the true, universal, "Catholic" faith to Jesus' precept to love one's neighbor as oneself. This, he says, is the one standard of faith.[16] Throughout the Treatise, Spinoza goes to great lengths to present himself as the real champion of "true piety" and "true religion." Such a covert method of actual attack is hardly new with Spinoza (e.g., the Trojan horse), but he refines it, and his approach has been a constant stratagem of heterodoxy ever since (making good evil and evil good). If this is so, then Spinoza's central target must have been the basis of authority in matters of the faith, of theology, and of truth and falsehood, as understood by Judeo-Christian orthodoxy. Therefore, the nature of miracles, "prophecy," "revelation," and Holy Scripture, and the relation of each of these to the Word or Truth of God as understood according to orthodoxy, are of great concern for Spinoza. Indeed, very early in the *Treatise,* this point of our particular focus and concern surfaces when he says despairingly, "I pass on to indicate the false notions (of the 'multitude') . . . ever prone to superstition, and caring more for the shreds of antiquity than for eternal [rationalist] truths—pays homage to the books of the Bible, *rather than* to the Word of God."[17] Given his purpose, he must strip Scripture of all divine authority while somehow portraying himself as one who is faithful to Scripture. Such a dualist, disjunctive approach, such "transcendentalizing," is basic to Spinoza's approach, and to all who continue to find it necessary to disjoin "the Word of God" from the tainting effects of history and the very textuality of the historical text of Holy Scripture.

Spinoza's Reconceptualization of Revelation

Spinoza approaches his reconceptualization and redefinition of "revelation" from his reductionist view of true religion, i.e. as related only to obedience and morality, and thus to "imagination," and not to truth (which is the domain of philosophy alone). Through all such claims, Spinoza's repeated refrain is "adaptation," i.e., the adaptation of the nature of miracle and of "revelation" to the times and presuppositions of the prophet. Prophecy, then, is said to be an imaginative, evocative, pictorial manifestation intended only to stir the piety of the uneducated populace, and then the apostolic writings (NT) are said to be mere *ad hoc* teachings, not prophecies, and with no claims to inherent authority. These views, coupled with the previously mentioned issues, and related to his metaphysical bases, are key to Spinoza's separation of the eternal, transcendent "Word of God" from the text of Holy Scripture.

While we can only mention the point in passing, it must be noted that Spinoza's response to any miracle claims inside or outside of Scripture is instructive for our larger question. Contrary to what many critics say about him, there is a sense in which Spinoza does not deny miracles. He does not deny that the Red Sea parted, or that many other "miraculous" events probably took place. Rather, as a pantheistic monist and determinist, and as one whose view of the physical operations of the world was essentially the same as Isaac Newton's (cf. chapter three), Spinoza's point is that these occurrences were not, as was often said by contemporary defenders of miracles, the contravention of the "fixed and immutable" laws of nature. Given his "God or Nature," the power of God is the power of nature and "God" does not work against himself. Divine law is natural law. All things work as they are "determined" to work according to strict cause-effect, mechanistic laws and rules. So while the direct physical cause of those "miraculous" events may not be known, there was a natural cause and that is all. "Miracle," then, is taken to be a hermeneutical issue, i.e., someone *regarding* an event as a "miracle." "Nothing happens in nature which does not follow from her laws . . . miracles were wrought according to the understanding of the masses, who are wholly ignorant of the working of nature."[18] In this way, Scripture can excite the wonder and devotion of the masses. This "fixing" of the world system and the identification of the divine power with nature is obviously foundational for Spinoza's adapted understanding of prophecy and revelation.

In an early aside in his discussion of prophecy and revelation, Spinoza very selectively argues from Scripture, that "the Spirit of God," "the Holy Spirit," etc., is a reference to the human spirit made holy in devotion to God. It is not a reference to God acting directly to or through the human being.[19] Again, given his identification of God and Nature, there can be no special, direct divine action in the world at all. "God" acts equally in all things.[20] Therefore, according to Spinoza, if we are to properly reckon with the nature of prophecy, with the notion of "God speaking" and so with "revelation" in the Old Testament, we must realize that the "imagination" of the prophets was that faculty whereby the "decrees of God" or "the mind of God" was "revealed." While "the mind of God," his "eternal thoughts," are said to be impressed on all human minds, yet in some special sense this is particularly true of the prophets. What distinguished the Old Testament prophets was the role of "imagination"; they only perceived God's "revelation" by the "aid of imagination," i.e., by real or imaginary words, figures and pictures. Spinoza then says that one could claim that this process occurs by the power of God, but that would be redundant, since all takes place equally by the power of God (*Deus sive Natura*). Yet this, he says, is the only means of "divine action" referred to in Scripture.[21]

> As the prophets perceived the revelations of God by the aid of imagination, they could indisputably perceive much that is beyond the boundary of

the intellect, for many more ideas can be constructed from words and figures than from the principles and notions on which the whole fabric of reasoned knowledge is reared. . . . [The] prophets perceived nearly everything in parables and allegories and clothed spiritual truths in *bodily* forms, for such is the usual method of imagination. We need no longer wonder that Scripture and the prophets speak so strangely and obscurely.[22]

Thus, in sharp contrast to sure and certain knowledge via the pure principles of reason, Spinoza links prophecy with vivid "imagination" which he is concerned to separate from that real, eternal truth (laws of reason) which he calls "the Word of God." It is then not "prophecy," "revelation," or finally Scripture which directs his argument to its outcome and the casting of prophetic, revelational words in a "pious" but negative light, but rather Spinoza's hermeneutical reductionism, as rooted in his rationalism, pantheistic monism and his ascription of all events equally to "God."

Thus prophets, as persons of "unusually vivid imagination," were not men of clear thinking, not fitted or given to logical or abstract reasoning. But, says Spinoza, they were given wholly to what is moral. Again, prophecy is not directed to the truth and the intellectual certitude Spinoza required, but to obedience and moral certitude. But always the "revelation" varied, was accommodated to the prior opinions and temperament of the prophet. Since God, as identified with nature, does not actually or directly speak, what is usually taken as "God speaking" through the prophets is simply the eternal Truth of the divine, accommodated, adapted to and expressed according to the prior views, imagination, education, style, disposition, cultivation, and moral context of the prophet. But, again, such "revelation" does not result in any knowledge of God as such. Spinoza says:

[T]he prophecies varied according to the opinions previously embraced by the prophets and that the prophets held diverse and even contrary opinions and prejudices [i.e., no knowledge of God]. . . . From thence I shall conclude that prophecy never rendered the prophets more learned . . . we are therefore, not at all bound to trust them in matters of intellect [i.e., eternal, national, divine truth].[23]

The prophets did not receive special divine truth content from God. Indeed, they only passed on common views of God and his nature and purpose. All prophecy conformed to previously held opinions (and to their context). The only special qualities possessed by the true prophets, along with their vivid imaginations, was their piety, their faithfulness to God, and their capacity to stir up such in others. Yet for all this, Spinoza continues to claim that his views create no detriment or harm to Scriptural authority.

Something of an anomaly in all of this is Spinoza's portrayal of Moses' prophetic vocation as actually unique in almost every way[24]—with the apparent exception of Jesus, whom he seems to compare to and even esteem beyond Moses (as the Messiah, *if* he is to be taken seriously).[25] To Moses, somehow, the "real voice of God" was revealed, in contrast to the highly imaginary, pictorial and obscure nature of "revelation" to other prophets. With Moses it is as though one has an instance of the prophetic equivalence to the clear and distinct ideas of rationalism. Yet here, too, Spinoza is finally able to find the same basic fault, i.e., the necessary fault of all that is merely historical and tangible and contingent. If Moses was given the "real voice of God" then, given God's nature, such a voice would be merely a divine use of created media in some yet unknown way, and so finally not the real voice or real word of God such as exists eternally and nondiscursively in the "Mind of God."[26]

Additionally, Spinoza seeks to tear down the historical, orthodox Judeo-Christian view of Scripture by adding to his argument a critical analysis of the (nonMosaic) Divine Law/Torah,[27] a studied negation of all traditional authorship of the Old Testament books (e.g., all historical books are by Ezra),[28] carefully stated ridicule of the canonization process and a claim that while the apostles were surely prophets, their approach, style, and the *ad hoc* nature of most epistles show clearly that the apostles wrote not as prophets, but merely as teachers (i.e., nonauthoritatively) to encourage only the original recipients. Further, he says, the apostles were never "commanded" to write and, like the prophets, these adapted what they wrote to their own wills, styles, and contemporary opinions.[29] In all, Spinoza subjects the whole of Scripture to very selective, creative, but systematic and destructive higher criticism (of which he is often said to be "the Father"). All such he strategically develops, while repeatedly emphasizing that he is thereby strengthening true piety and faithfulness and, most significantly and centrally, that he is in no way disparaging the true "Word of God." Indeed, the true "Word of God" is said to remain now and forever wholly faultless and perfect.[30]

Spinoza's Separation of "Word of God" from Scripture. Spinoza's point on Holy Scripture has now been almost fully stated. But in anticipated response to critics he says:

> Those who look upon the Bible as a message sent down by God from Heaven to men will doubtless cry out that I have committed the sin against the Holy Ghost because I have asserted that the Word of God is faulty, mutilated, tampered with and inconsistent . . . but the expressed opinions of prophets and apostles openly proclaim that God's eternal Word and covenant, no less than true religion, is Divinely inscribed in human hearts, that is, the human mind [i.e., not in writing]. . . . Those, therefore, who reflect, will find nothing in what I have written repugnant either to the Word of God or to true religion and faith . . . contrariwise . . . I have strengthened faith.[31]

This clear dualistic separation, later variously and influentially developed by both G. E. Lessing and especially Immanuel Kant, is crucial for Spinoza's direct and indirect purposes, and so for the separation of religion from all effect and constraint on the pursuit of philosophy. For such reasons he claims to be the true defender of the Word of God.

Yet, according to Spinoza, this does not negate the legitimacy of referring to Scripture as "Sacred" if one recognizes that all such speaking is functional and metaphorical and not ontological in nature. Like all inanimate things which can be called "sacred," so too Scripture, to the extent that it teaches what is necessary for obedience and promotes piety. If so, then it continues to be "sacred." But even if Scripture ceases to so function, or if it is ever used to promote evil and injustice, then it is no longer properly sacred.[32] Objectors to these claims, who would emphasize not only the divine authority of the eternal Word and of the Word as written upon the human heart but also of Holy Scripture as the written Word of God, are branded as purveyors of dangerous superstition, "worshiping paper and ink in place of God's Word."[33]

Spinoza's dual conclusion, then, is that while the text of Scripture has been mutilated, fragmented, and corrupted in multitudinous ways (as most of his *Treatise* endeavors to prove), yet "we must not say that the Word of God has suffered in like manner."[34] Scripture is but "paper and ink," while the True Word of God, true religion, the eternal, rational Truth/Mind of God can never be directly affected because it is not directly historical. It can only be mediated to the human situation, e.g., by or through Scripture. "I will show wherein the (true) law of God consists, and how it cannot be contained in a certain number of books."[35] Making much of "New Covenant" language from both testaments (e.g. Jeremiah 31, Ezekiel 34, 36; 2 Corinthians 3), Spinoza then concludes that the Word of God truly relates to each person only as "written upon the heart."[36] Therefore, the true Word of God lies beyond the historical text of Scripture, though there can be some mediational and functional relation between the two. It can even be said that God is the "Author" of Scripture "because of the true religion therein contained, and not because He wished to communicate to men a certain number of books" (indeed, how can Spinoza's God consciously communicate anything?).[37] Therefore he concludes that no modification, mutilation, or destruction of Scripture can deprive persons of the "Word of God" or "of true religion." As Spinoza influentially portrays the relation of the Word of God to Scripture, Scripture is said to "contain" the Word of God. And that transcendentalized "Word" which Scripture "contains" in order to effect piety and true religion remains, then, uncorrupted.[38] Therefore, according to Spinoza, Scripture is not itself the revelation of God's truth; it is not the written Word of God, and it does not give knowledge of God but is only (when used "rightly") useful for imagination, piety, and the stirring of "true religion" (i.e., of the true Word of God upon the human heart). Again, Scripture does not (except in a few simple doctrines[39]) have or teach truth but only morality and piety. Rational truth is the proper and distinct domain of philosophy alone. Thus Spinoza has labored to show "that between faith or theology and philosophy there is no connection. . . . Philosophy has no end in view but truth; faith is . . . nothing but obedience and piety."[40] Only when philosophy and theology are separated properly can each endeavor be rightly pursued as every person wills and without any constraint from the other. Only when such a separation has occurred can a properly ordered society be the result.[41]

Johann Semler's Historico-Scientific Intent to Separate Word of God from Holy Scripture

Biblical-Theological Developments after Spinoza

As noted, Spinoza's pseudonymous *Theologico-Political Treatise* was widely read, going through many editions and, in a time of intellectual ferment, it had much formative influence on contemporary and later Enlightenment thought. From Spinoza, numerous cultural and scholarly movements and efforts began to develop, advancing Spinoza's own ideas. With regard to the nature of Scripture, the thinking of Richard Simon, the rise of textual criticism and English Deism were of special importance here in developing the foundations necessary for the breakthrough work of Johann Semler.

Richard Simon and Textual Criticism. While textual criticism as a science has roots that go back at least to 1514 with the publication of the Polyglot edition of the Greek NT and 1516 with the publication of Erasmus' Greek NT, only subsequent developments gave impetus to the careful study of the production of the NT text. Erasmus' quickly and carelessly prepared Testament, from relatively poor manuscripts, was the only one widely distributed and repeatedly reprinted. This text was regarded by most Protestant theologians of the time as the inspired text, often held to be inviolate. While some editions presented variants from manuscripts discovered by chance, no one attempted to make the slightest change in this received text. [42]

It was from this setting that a theologian set himself to the task of investigating the question of the historical facts met in the NT text. Richard Simon, a younger contemporary of Spinoza born in 1638, was a French Roman Catholic priest (later expelled from his order) who had an original and influential theological mind (cf. chapter five). A notable Semitic scholar, Simon had a "Molinist" view of inspiration (reflected, e.g., in his *Critical History of the Old Testament*) that led to the condemnation of his works as soon as they appeared. Following Jacques Bonfrere, he held a theory of concomitant inspiration whereby the Holy Spirit left the writer inwardly free to write what he will, while managing on the whole, by divine foreknowledge, to secure a written product containing nothing actually or overtly contrary to the will of the Spirit. In Simon, this view in relation to Scripture's production led to much critical focus on what he took to be the great human frailty (corruption) of Scripture (cf. discussion on Richard Simon in chapter five).[43]

Developing Spinoza's thought, Simon's subsequent "critical histories" of the NT text, of translations of the NT, and of the chief interpreters of the NT, resulted in the conscious divorce of Scripture from the type of study carried on by ancient and medieval interpreters. Further, by critical analysis of the church fathers (and all manuscripts available to him), Simon became the first to carefully use modern critical methods in a historical study of the traditional form of the text of the NT and of the proper understanding of it. But it must be understood, too, that Simon's motives were much more than historical. While stating that he only wished to serve the truth, he desired, too, that his work be of polemical use to the Catholic Church. He hoped to demonstrate that the Protestant doctrine of Holy Scripture as the only source of revelation (*sola Scriptura*) was false by showing Scripture to be so unreliably transmitted, so incapable of being understood by itself, that Catholic Church tradition was necessary if Scripture was to yield reliable teaching for faith.[44] Yet, in fact, this view cut away at the bases and doctrine of Scripture in both Protestant and Roman Catholic churches and was therefore rejected by both. In spite of this, at the turn of the seventeenth and eighteenth centuries, Simon's views were to stimulate further development of such consideration of Scripture (especially the NT), leading toward a strictly human and historical view of Scripture. Others also laid the path leading to Johann Semler. Alongside Anglican theologian John Mill, it was especially the work of Johann Albrecht Bengel, a pietist whose confidence in the NT as the Word of God had been shaken by the abundance of variants found in Mill's edition of the NT text (1707–1710). By means of his own textual studies Bengel "sought to regain confidence."[45] His resulting NT edition (1734) contained many textual alterations of the received text, though most were not significant. These were arranged in five groups according to their importance. But it was Bengel especially who developed the careful critical principles by which to approach the NT text. These, including his critical question, "Which reading is more likely to have arisen out of the others?" have since become basic to the science of textual criticism. To these questions (which Bengel regarded as a prolegomena) he added a brief exposition of the NT. This work, too, proved influential as a result of its consistent use of historical, contextual and grammatical exegesis.[46] Yet the inevitable outcome was still greater emphasis on independent thinking and use of creative, historical principles by the interpreter. Hence, from Spinoza's politically strategic use of emphatic, historical reconstruction, through the work of Simon and Bengel the historicity of the text tradition of Scripture entered the Christian consciousness and especially into Protestant scholarly circles.

The English Deists. This was a "theological" movement which reflected something of the rationalistic historicism characteristic of both Spinoza and later text critics. Prominent among these was Johann Jakob Wettstein, who was born in England in the late seventeenth century. English Deism itself was an attitude toward the critical study of religion and the convergent results of developing humanistic thought, English latitudinarian antagonism to Anglican orthodoxy, and, it has been said, the greater freedom of theological formulation found in Dutch Arminianism.[47] Other formative elements include the English Revolution of 1688 and, very significantly, the Toleration Act of 1689, which attempted to unify all denominational and theological positions by a "return to natural religion" and a declaration of war on all supernaturalism—including consideration of the nature of Scripture, especially the NT.[48] The developing impulse and desire of many scholars toward a totally historical consideration of Scripture could only be realized when the "way of seeing" Scripture was finally loosed from all theological *a prioris*, and then recognized simply as a witness out of the past framed wholly within the process of historical development.[49]

Herein the thought of John Locke was to have profound effect. As a professedly orthodox Anglican, Locke was concerned to show that reason and revelation were not in opposition to each other. He initially developed this principle in his *Essay on the Human Understanding* (1690),[50] later unfolding his program of a fully rational Christianity in his work *The Reasonableness of Christianity, as delivered in the Scriptures* (1695). Locke attempted to uncover true Christianity, which he thought to lie behind the many Christian confessions, by examining the NT alone. Therein he concluded that the NT demands only faith in Jesus' messiahship and resurrection, and that this faith emphasis remained pure only in the Gospels and Acts. The Epistles, with their occasional, ad hoc doctrines, diluted the truth with alien ideas, thus perverting the gospel. Locke's quest for a "rational Christianity" led him to a division within the NT and to the requirement that the NT texts be understood within their own contexts and lines of argument, thereby maintaining the sense or understanding of the author (i.e., not as decontextualized sentences standing in isolation).[51]

While Locke's primary goals were not actually historical as such, elements of his thought and method inevitably demanded such an emphasis. His attitude toward the NT text and proper approach to it are reflected in his demand that exegesis consider the text alone and in his conclusion that the NT was far from unified. Later Deists, such as John Toland and Matthew Tindal, advanced this line of thought well beyond Locke. Both Toland and Tindal limited revelation to abstracted rational truths, while separating Jewish Christianity from Pauline Gentile Christianity, for which the Law had no place.[52] Tindal published his *Christianity as Old as Creation* (1730), which came to be known as the "Bible" of Deism. Herein he presented Christianity as a new form of natural religion and asserted that reason (rationalism) must be the final arbitor of truth and error in regard to Scripture. Such identification of "true" Christianity with natural religion, and the consequent abstracting of true principles from false claims in Scripture, became basic to English Deism.[53]

Johann Semler and the Division of Text and Word

Major Contributions. Johann Salomo Semler, born 1725, was for a long period professor of theology at the University of Halle and is considered the actual "father" of the new critical theology ("Neology"). Semler was much indebted to the thinking and historico-rationalistic methodologies of the textual critics and the English Deists, as well as to Spinoza. Semler became the first theologian to consciously apply a thoroughly historical approach to the text of Scripture (to the NT specifically) in order to make NT study truly "scientific." Early on he immersed himself in classical and Semitic languages and, after inner struggle, largely rejected the "pietistic sanctimoniousness" of his upbringing. His university studies led him to embrace a rationalism reflecting keen historical concern molded by the contemporary deistic stimuli. Wanting to be "bolder" and "freer" than his predecessors, Semler intended to "interrogate all religious tradition" from a "rigorously historical point of view."[54] While Semler's writing is very unsystematic and, as Emmanuel Hirsch put it, "is probably the worst

German that a German intellectual has ever written,"[55] his topics cover the whole realm of theology. But to pursue his historical, scientific investigations with proper rigor, boldness, and freedom, Semler believed that the way had to be cleared and certain theological and cultural obstacles to proper study removed from his path. This led to what are often considered to be Semler's two primary contributions to modern scientific historical-critical methodology in the investigation of Judeo-Christian Scripture. These are presented primarily in the first two volumes of his *Treatise on the Free Investigation of the Canon* (1771–75). Both of these, especially the second, have direct bearing upon the concern of this chapter.

Semler's Theses. Semler's first thesis is that the question of whether a book belongs to the canon of Scripture is purely historical. According to Semler, this is because the canon only represents the agreement of the regions of the church with regard to the proper books from which church lectionaries were to be taken. Thus, every Christian is called upon "to freely investigate the historical circumstances under which each canonical book was written, and so whether or not it has permanent usefulness for morality."[56] All such decisions rest upon *a priori* human understanding of what qualities an act, event, or writing must have, be, or express for it to be properly regarded as "divine." It is this claim to human pre-knowledge of the good, the true, and the highest that leads him to say, for example, that

> If a reader is already familiar with the moral truths and their inherent value . . . if he is already so humane that he is glad to help all men . . . if he finds the tone of the Apocalypse unpleasant and repulsive . . . how can such a one find in their book nothing but divine, all-inclusive love and charity for the restoration of all men, without which he cannot regard it in a special, peculiar way the work of God who is sheer love in all his relationships with men. It must remain open to many . . . who have begun to experience the solitary power of truth [in the Enlightenment sense], to pass judgment in light of their own knowledge both on individual books and on certain parts of the many books with reference to their moral and generally beneficial value.[57]

"No one needs the whole [Bible]"[58] is Semler's point. For, given proper sensibilities and capacity to increasingly experience and recognize the true and the good in all humans, one is "entitled" to judge what reflects moral worth, true principles, and so what is of God. The "so-called *whole* Bible" is not, and, indeed, properly ought not to be so regarded.[59]

Semler's second thesis, and for our purposes even more directly at issue and of central concern is, again, the emphatic declaration that "the Word of God" and Holy Scripture are not identical, not to be identified in any way.

The Dualistic Disjunction of the Word of God from Scripture. This thesis, the clear separation of the text of Scripture from the Word of God, is methodologically crucial for Semler because, as noted above, it is deemed necessary if he is to freely pursue a purely historical-rational course of investigation of the NT text. It is also regarded as necessary to protect the true Word of God, i.e., ahistorical, abstract, transcendent truths, eternal principles. Further, Scripture cannot be the written Word of God, because it contains much that is not even properly directed toward such eternal truths but (cf. his "canonical" principles above) is found by means of strict scientific, historical methods to be relevant only to ancient times and is of no effect in contributing to the "moral improvement" of contemporary persons. [60]

As Semler unfolds this second thesis, the issue is often interconnected with questions of "inspiration" and textual criticism as located within historical-canonical concerns. Thus, he urges, the "problem of inspiration" is not important, as orthodoxy claims it to be, for textural criticism shows parts of "so-called inspired" Scripture to be not properly of the text. An obvious example which he uses is the story of the woman taken in adultery in John 8. If this story "is lacking in many ancient copies . . . [then] a piece of so-called Holy Scripture would then be lacking, but the true Word of God would be lacking in nothing, for it is and remains unchangeable, despite all accidents."[61] The answer to Semler's criticism regarding the present copies and the original texts is obvious; but also to be noted is his rationalistic conception of "the Word of God" as emphatically not text but rather abstract, ahistorical, immutable, eternal ("platonic") Truths.

Again, such reductionist attempts to make Holy Scripture merely a historical human deposit is believed to be necessary if Semler is to maintain that "scientific, historical" investigation is the only way to approach that text. Yet, in a typically dualistic way, he goes on to claim that the only proper proof of the eternal truth, or "Word of God," which is said to confront one through Scripture, is "the inner conviction" engendered by such principles. But these abstract, divine truths only come through some parts of Scripture, not all. This claim is then used against "all alleged inspiration" of the whole of Scripture. Only portions through which the principles which one recognizes to be (*a priori*) "divine or worthy of the highest being" are actually useful for reading. The rest can be left unread without loss. [62]

In this way, Semler advanced yet further through the dualistic, rationalistic door opened earlier by Spinoza and by the influential new historical-critical assumptions of the English Deists. And so Semler became the first to clearly and completely separate the historical text of Scripture from an ideal "Word of God." He says:

> Holy Scripture and the Word of God are clearly to be distinguished, for we know the difference. If one has not previously been aware of this, this is no prohibition that keeps us from making the distinction. To Holy Scripture, using the particular historical expression that originated among the Jews, belong [such nonbeneficial books as] Ruth, Esther, the Song of Songs, etc., but not all these books that are called holy belong to the Word of God, which at all times makes all men wise unto salvation.[63]

This last statement ought not be understood as a claim that some parts of Holy Scripture are to be identified as "the Word of God." The context, his argument, and many particular contrary statements make his point clear that some texts of Scripture are more useful, more conducive to leading persons to know and experience the rational "Word" principles, the timelessly true abstractions which do not and cannot partake of the shifting, malleable, accidental nature of history and of some historical text.

From such assumptions and claims that the text of Scripture is only the result of historical, human processes, and so to be vigorously, "scientifically" approached as such, Semler is fully willing to draw the inevitable conclusion. He requires not only that Scripture be interpreted strictly in terms of its own grammatical structure (which, unfortunately, his own presuppositions do not allow him to do), but he also limits Scripture's usefulness only to its ancient setting; it is only a human witness to its own time and not strictly meant for subsequent readers. Thus, while piously speaking of "inner conviction" of the truth of the "Word" and while defending the inviolable character of that eternal, beneficial "Word of God" obtained through and beyond the text of Scripture, Semler is mostly consistent in asserting that the books of the Bible were of direct and real use only for the original recipients—*ad hoc* documents meant only for them. Any contemporary benefits or edification of readers/hearers by means of Scripture (by those parts of Scripture which can affect such) were not and are not of direct and primary concern. Correct historical understanding is the primary concern now, though that eternal, unchangeable "Word of God" can still potentially be discerned "by means of the biblical witness."[64]

Thus the politico-theological intention of Spinoza to initially disjoin a rational, ahistorical "Word of God" from the accidental, historical textuality of Holy Scripture has, through rapid steps, led to Johann Semler's own strategy to free exegetical research from the confining strictures of a "sacred text" so that such scholarship, having purely historical assumptions, may become truly "scientific." Such bifurcation of the Truth of God from history, while emphasizing the need for faith in an ideal, transcendentalized "Word"/Truth of God, was to become basic to most mainline biblical and theological scholarship in, to, and through the nineteenth century (via Schleiermacher, Strauss, and Baur et al.) and twentieth century and beyond. As we will note briefly, the subsequent influence of Johann Gabler was also instrumental as a programmatic link connecting this attitude regarding Scripture to the nineteenth century dogmatic theology. Such dualist, rationalistic tendencies to "think apart," to think in terms of disjunction, rather than to think together or to think unitarily regarding the Truth of God is at the heart of much of our modern and postmodern theological malaise, a malaise reflected throughout Western culture.

To Johann Gabler, the Nineteenth Century, and Beyond

History and Rationalism: Semler to Gabler

The dual tendency toward a strong rationalism and the often consequent desire to separate Divine Truth/"the Word of God" as such from all matters historical and textual, exemplified in Spinoza and Semler, developed more programmatically from the eighteenth and then through the nineteenth centuries and beyond, in large measure via the thought of Johann Philipp Gabler (1753–1826), a student of J. G. Eichhorn. While Gabler's view of Scripture is not precisely that of Spinoza or Semler [there being some remainder of the notion of "inspiration" attached to some parts of Scripture, and so some sense of "divine authority" therein as the result of "Providence"], yet given Gabler's Enlightenment-rationalist bases, this appears to be something of a anomaly.[65] His repeated use of such phrases as "sacred writings," "sacred books," "sacred writers" and "the writing of the Holy Apostles" is not in keeping with his minimalist view of inspiration and certainly not in keeping with his Semler-like rationalist, dualist disjunction between matters historical and the eternal.

To clarify this point and the way Gabler advanced the Spinoza-Semler division or dualism to a new level, we will briefly examine his highly influential inaugural lecture, given at the University of Altdorf, entitled "An Oration on the Proper Distinction between Biblical and Dogmatic Theology and the Specific Objectives of Each." It is this work which is said to constitute the beginning of "biblical theology" as a purely historical discipline wholly autonomous from dogmatics (clearly developing Semler's thought).[66] Like his contemporary G. E. Lessing, Gabler presents what he considers to be the necessary methodological and conceptual differences basic to these pursuits in a way which entrenched yet more fully the decisive split between the contingent historico-textual nature of Holy Scripture from matters divine, and thus certain, ahistorical, and transcendent. From Spinoza and Semler and then through Gabler (along with the subsequent epistemological effects of Kant's *Critiques*), the Newtonian disjunction of the historical from the eternal becomes programmatically and problematically basic to Western theological conceptualization, notably with regard to the "Word of God" (cf. chapter three).

Again, Gabler maintains a kind of providential "inspiration" so that divine authority does relate in some sense to certain parts of Scripture, "providing sure guidance to men."[67] But such authority is not only occasional for Gabler, it is authority linked to Gabler's rationalistic concern for the transhistorical "unchanging, universal ideas."[68] Just as for Spinoza and Semler, for Gabler divine authority rests only in necessary concepts. One of Gabler's basic assumptions is that what is historical is other than and secondary to that which is true.[69] So in spite of seeking to clearly distinguish biblical and dogmatic theology, the first concerned simply and purely with the biblical writings which reflect the "feelings of holy men about things divine," the second a "subtle, elegant," largely philosophical process meant to deal with "universal [or divine] ideas" which are certain, and so in full accord with human reason,[70] Gabler still desires that the fruit of "pure" biblical theology be useful to dogmatic theology. This can occur when, by careful historical, linguistic, exegetical methods, biblical theology uncovers in the biblical text that which, directly or indirectly, can be formed into timeless, universal, sacred ideas. Yet this means the forceful separation of the temporal, changeable and textual as such (matters of "religion") from the necessary, rational principles (matters of "theology"). Thus, for Gabler, the nature of each of these scholarly foci and procedures requires that human and historical contingency be separated from the Divine in order to arrive finally at the ordered "ideas" or "doctrines" that "are truly divine." [71]

Though not so overtly and expressly radical as Spinoza and Semler regarding the nonidentity of the historical text of Scripture and Word of God, Gabler's rationalism requires that he, too, focus attention on the oft found literary and historical obscurities, the contextual and cultural particularity, and so the emphatic humanness of the (somehow) "sacred books" in a way that allows him to argue increasingly for the rationalistic disjunction of the historical and textual from the universal, unchangeable, pure notions.[72] All too typical of this modern rationalist and dualist way of thinking is Gabler's denial of "*theopneustia*." Having afforded an earlier place for what he termed "inspiration," he subsequently regards "*theopneustia*" to be the result of a faulty inference from other statements in Scripture, especially from Paul, all of which overlooks the very historical conditioning of Scripture. It also arises from fear, he says.[73] Thus he claims that apparent references to "inspirations" (plural) are at best "very obscure and ambiguous," so one must be careful "not to press those meanings of the Apostles beyond their just limits, especially since only the effects of the inspirations, and not their causes, are perceived by the senses"—an odd statement apparently referring to "exegetical observation."[74] For all practical purposes "inspiration" must be left out of consideration.[75]

Beyond Spinoza, Semler, and Gabler

Yet it is not Gabler's calculated ambiguities and inconsistencies regarding the text of Scripture that had the lasting impact upon theological thinking and "the Word of God" in the two centuries that have followed. From the side of theology, Gabler developed Spinoza's and Semler's rationalistic, dualistic separation of the text of Holy Scripture from the Word of God into what came to be the entire program of Western theological scholarship. Given that the Scriptures are finally (and simply) human and so historical, one's approach to the text must be just and only that, i.e., historical. In this way, the study of Scripture and biblical theology in the strict sense (historical-descriptive) is set apart as fully independent from "dogmatic" theology. As we will see in the chapter to follow, this was combined with and accentuated by Isaac Newton's cosmological dualism and Immanuel Kant's formative noumenal-phenomenal split in terms of epistemology. All of this has left much of modern and postmodern theology generally, and the question of Holy Scripture and the Word of God specifically, in the throes of conceptual isolation and disastrous division (cf. the German term, *krisis*). From Spinoza through Semler and Gabler (with Descartes, Newton, and Kant), the "mainstream" of Western theology has been caught in an "upper story"/"lower story" mentality. From Friedrich Schleiermacher and Albrecht Ritschl through Rudolf Bultmann and Paul Tillich, even to theologically applied elements of contemporary deconstruction and the larger postmodernism, the same basic dualistic disjunction of a "transcendentalized," ahistorical, noncontentful Word of God—a Platonic ideal—from all participation in history and the particular "textuality of the text" of Holy Scripture (intended as emphatic, not redundant) has plagued modern theology with a core incoherence which, in principle, threatens not only the incarnation but all interactive God-world-human salvific relatedness (via creation and gracious redemption). All such incoherence leaves us a God who does not declare himself and his purposes, a divine blank, and an agnostic church. But is this the God of Abraham, Isaac, and Jacob? The discursive God of "Thus says the LORD"? The God self-revealed above all in Jesus Christ?

Appendix

In the course of his argumentation, Spinoza gives much attention to the distinction he makes between passages of Scripture which contextually claim to be revelation (e.g., "thus says Yahweh" or "the Word of Yahweh came to me saying") and portions dealing with matters of mere fact or with mundane issues (e.g., Philemon). This distinction is a significant issue and must not be waived off. A noted evangelical theologian, for whom Scripture is not the written Word of God but the primary "vehicle of the Word of God," made a similar point, i.e., not all Scripture directly claims to be the written Word of God/revelation, so how can we even claim that it is all the written Word of God?

While 2 Timothy 3:16 tells us that "all Scripture is inspired by God," and 2 Peter 1:20-21 explains that Scripture is prophetic ("prophecy of Scripture") as the result of holy men being "borne along by the Holy Spirit" whereby they "spoke from God," do such passages allow us to say that the whole of canonical Scripture is revelation or the written Word of God in the immediate or *direct* sense? Maybe. Maybe not. Or, maybe yes and no. First, it might be proper, at one level, to acknowledge the literary phenomena of the many scriptural contexts, including the genres, by concluding that not all of Holy Scripture is revelation in the *direct* sense. We must surely reckon with the fact that there are a number of portions of Scripture which, in their original contexts, are not said to be immediately revelatory or direct disclosures of God and/or content-ful truth of God, but which in fact are quoted elsewhere and referred to as the direct, revelatory Word of God. But does this necessitate the application or reckoning of this phenomenon as a principle to *all* scriptural contexts wherein there is no such contextual divine claim? Maybe. But any conclusion there must be recognized as at least somewhat conjectural. Would it not be more readily and biblically affirmable to say that not all of Holy Scripture is revelation as such, or in the *direct* sense (some *indirectly*), though in fact it may well be, yet it is *all* and in *every* part *derivative* Word of God as the result of the historical processes of revelation and "inspiration" (*theopneustos*). In this way, what Spinoza points out about Scripture can be readily acknowledged, yet his negative conclusion must be properly denied. The point is that the historical text of Holy Scripture, whatever else we may affirm about it, is itself the content-ful Word of God, even in the matter-of-fact and mundane, as the result of the work of the Holy Spirit ("God-breathed") with the writers of Scripture in the processes of guidance and superintendence leading to enscripturation. And even then, of course, it is not a simple matter. The phrase "Word of God" means different things within the different scriptural contexts.[76] But as we will observe in the next chapter, Kevin Vanhoozer's and Nicholas Wolterstorff's analogical and constructive uses of "Speech Act Theory" have effectively portrayed the "mechanism" whereby we can understand "how" all of Scripture, as God's use of human speech acts, word-events, is a result of revelation and is thus the written Word of God. God is a speech-agent.

Endnotes

[1] Jody Veenker, "Culture Clash," *Christianity Today* (July 10, 2000) 19.

[2] Ibid.

[3] R. H. M. Elwes, "Introduction," in Baruch Spinoza, *A Theologico-Political Treatise*, trans. R. H. M. Elwes (Mineola, N.Y.: Dover, 2004) x–xi.

[4] Frederick Copleston, *A History of Philosophy*, vol. 4, *Modern Philosophy: Descartes to Leibniz* (New York: Doubleday, 1963) 206.

[5] Elwes, "Introduction," xvi.

[6] Copleston, "History," 207–8, 234–35.

[7] Elwes, "Introduction," xxiii–xxv, and Copleston, "History," 214–19.

[8] Copleston, "History," 208.

[9] Ibid.

[10] Ibid., 211.

[11] Baruch Spinoza, *Ethics*, trans. R. H. M. Elwes (New York: Aladdin, 1901) pt. 2, prop. 40, n. 2; pt. 4, prop. 24.

[12] Ibid., Part 2, proposition 28.

[13] Copleston, *History* 4:244, cf. Spinoza pt. 4, props. 36 and 19.

[14] Baruch Spinoza, *A Theologico-Political Treatise*, trans. R. H. M. Elwes (New York: Dover, 1951) 3–6.

[15] Ibid., 183, 188,190–91.

[16] Ibid., 184–85

[17] Ibid., 9.

[18] Ibid., 83–84. Cf. 82–92 .

[19] Ibid., 19–20.

[20] Ibid., 24

[21] Ibid., 24–25.

[22] Ibid., 25.

[23] Ibid., 33.

[24] Ibid., 15–19.

[25] Ibid., 19.

[26] Ibid., 18–19.

[27] Ibid., 57–76.

[28] Ibid., 120–46.

[29] Ibid., 157–65.

[30] Ibid., 165–75.

[31] Ibid., 165.

[32] Ibid., 167. Cf. 168ff. In the *Treatise*, 169–70, Spinoza concludes: "There are, then, three causes for the Bible's being called the Word of God: because it teaches true reason, of which God is the eternal Founder; because it narrates predictions of future events as though they were decrees of God; because its actual authors generally perceived things not by their ordinary natural faculties, but by a power peculiar to themselves and introduced these things perceived, as (though) told them by God." Then shortly thereafter in the same context Spinoza adds that "We have now shown that Scripture can only be called the Word of God in so far as it (positively) affects religion, or the Divine Law; we must now point out that, in respect to these questions, it is neither faulty, tampered with or corrupt . . . (i.e.) written so (very) incorrectly that the meaning cannot be arrived at by a study of the language, nor from the authority of Scripture (an odd but politically useful statement for Spinoza)" Ibid.,1.171–72.

[33] Ibid., 166.

[34] Ibid., 168.

[35] Ibid., 166.

[36] Ibid., 169.

[37] Ibid., 170.

[38] Ibid., 165.

[39] Ibid., 115 ff. and 175 ff. Cf. Ibid., 176–77 and 182 ff. In his section on "Definitions of Faith," Spinoza claims that "it follows that faith does not demand that dogmas should be true as that they should be pious—that is, such as will stir up the heart to obey; though there be many such which contain not a shadow of truth, so long as they be held in good faith, otherwise their adherents are disobedient, for how can anyone, desirous of loving justice and obeying God, adore as Divine what he knows to be alien from the Divine nature? However, men may err from simplicity of mind, and Scripture, as we

have seen, does not condemn ignorance, but obstinacy. This is the necessary result of our definition of faith, and all its branches should spring from the universal role above given, and from the evident aim and object of the Bible, unless we choose to mix our own inventions therewith. Thus it is not true doctrines which are expressly required by the Bible, so much as doctrines necessary for obedience, and to confirm in our hearts the love of our neighbor, wherein (to adopt the words of John) we are in God, and God in us.

As, then, each man's faith must be judged pious only in respect of its producing obedience or obstinacy, and not in respect of its truth; and as no one will dispute that men's dispositions are exceedingly varied, that all do not acquiesce in the same things, but are ruled some by one opinion some by another, so that what moves one to devotion moves another to laughter and contempt, it follows that there can be no doctrines in the Catholic, or universal, religion, which cannot give rise to controversy among good men. Such doctrines might be pious to some and impious to others, whereas they should be judged solely by their fruits.

To the universal religion, then, belong only such dogmas as are absolutely required in order to attain obedience to God, and without which such obedience would be impossible; as for the rest, each man—seeing that he is the best judge of his own character—should adopt whatever he thinks best adopted to strengthen his love of justice. If this were so, I think there would be no further occasion for controversies in the Church."

[40] Ibid., 176 ff, 182 ff, 190ff. As an example of how Spinoza variously states the point: "I do not wish to affirm absolutely that Scripture contains no doctrines in the sphere of philosophy, for in the last chapter I pointed out some of the kind, as fundamental principles; but I go so far as to say that such nature and definition I will now set forth. The task will be easy, for we know that Scripture does not aim at imparting scientific knowledge, and therefore, it demands from men nothing but obedience, and censures obstinacy, but not ignorance. Furthermore, as obedience to God consists solely in love to our neighbor—for whosoever loveth his neighbor as a means of obeying God, hath, as St. Paul says (Rom. xiii. 8), fulfilled the law—it follows that no knowledge is commended in the Bible save that which is necessary for enabling all men to obey God, in the manner stated, and without which they would become rebellious, or without the discipline of obedience.

"Other speculative questions, which have no direct bearing on this object, or are concerned with the knowledge of natural events, do not affect Scripture, and should be entirely separated from religion. Now, though everyone, as we have said, is now quite able to see this truth for himself, I should nevertheless wish, considering that the whole of Religion depends thereon, to explain the entire question more accurately and clearly. To this end I must first prove that the intellectual or accurate knowledge of God is not a gift, bestowed upon all good men of like obedience; and further, that the knowledge of God, required by Him through His prophets from everyone without exception, as needful to be known, is simply a knowledge of His Divine justice and charity." Ibid., 176–77.

[41] Ibid., 181–82, 190–91, 200–201.

42 Werner Georg Kümmel, *The New Testament: The History of the Investigation of its Problems*, trans. S. McLean Gilmour and Howard C. Kee (Nashville: Abingdon, 1972) 40.

43 F. J. Crehan, "The Bible in the Roman Catholic Church from Trent to the Present Day," in *The West from the Reformation to the Present Day*, ed. S. L. Greenslade, Cambridge History of the Bible 3 (Cambridge: Cambridge University Press, 1963) 218ff.

44 Kümmel, *New Testament*, 41.

45 Ibid., 47.

46 Ibid., 48.

47 William Neil, "The Criticism and Theological Use of the Bible, 1700–1950," in *The West from the Reformation to the Present Day*, ed. S. L. Greenslade, Cambridge History of the Bible 3 (Cambridge: Cambridge University Press, 1963) 238—93.

48 Kümmel, 51.

49 Ibid.

50 Neil, "Criticism," 240–41.

51 John Locke, *The Reasonableness of Christianity as Delivered in the Scriptures*, 290–95, in ibid., 54.

52 Kümmel, 54.

53 Ibid., 54ff.

54 Ibid., 63.

55 Emmanuel Hirsch, *History of Christian Doctrine*, vol. IV, 50. In ibid., 63.

56 Ibid., 63.

57 Johann Salomo Semler, *Treatise on the Free Investigation of the Cannon*, vol. 1 translated from W. G. Kümmel's quotations by S. McLean Gilmour and Howard C. Kee, in ibid. The pagination of the Semler text will follow its location in the Kümmel work. 25–26, cf. 53–54, and vol. 2, preface A, 4, 39–40.

58 Ibid., vol. 2, Preface A, 63–64.

59 Note the pages referred to in the two previous endnotes for further emphasis and elaboration along these lines of argument.

60 Kümmel, 63 Note for example where Semler says, "Holy Scripture and the Word of God are clearly to be distinguished, for we know the difference. If one has not previously been aware of this, that is no prohibition that keeps us from making the distinction. To Holy Scripture (using the particular historical expression that originated among the Jews) belong Ruth, Esther, the Song of Songs, etc., but not all these books that are called holy belong to the Word of God, which at all times makes all men wise unto salvation. . . . "The problem of inspiration therefore, is not nearly so important as it is still the custom to regard it. Let us suppose, for instance, that the whole story of the woman taken in adultery in John 8 were lacking, as it is lacking in many ancient copies and translations of large parts of the Church: a piece of so-called Holy Scripture

would then be lacking but the Word of God would be lacking in nothing whatever for it is and remains unchangeable, despite all these accidental and continuous changes in a document whose copyists, it must be admitted, enjoyed no divine aid . . .

"The only proof that completely satisfies an upright reader is the inner conviction brought about by the truths that confront him in this Holy Scripture (but not all parts and individual books) . . . . I have acted so frankly in all this, however, that at the same time I have added to it the subsumption: books or parts of books, where this argument cannot possibly apply, but in which the final aim of all alleged inspiration still lingers on, whether in large or in small writings, can be left unread and unused without personal anxiety or concern for this final aim. . . .

"In particular, the entire common idea of the Canon and of the equally divine origin and value of all books and parts hitherto included in it is absolutely not an essential part of the Christian religion. One can be a righteous Christian without ascribing one and the same origin of divine inspiration to all books that are included in the Old and New Testament, or regarding them on the same level and therefore also without crediting them with the same general utility. And there can be no universal, unchangeable certainty and character of the Christian religion and of its actual basic rational doctrines and principles." Semler, vol. 1, 75, 177; vol. 2, 39–40, vol. 1, 19.

[61] Ibid., vol. 1, 117. cf. vol. 2, Preface A, 4; and vol. 1, 53–54.

[62] Ibid., vol. 2, Preface A, 4ff.

[63] Ibid., vol. 1, 75.

[64] Semler, *Introduction to Theological Hermeneutics*, 6ff., cf. also 149–50, 160–62, in Kümmel, 65–66.

[65] Johann P. Gabler, "An Oration," in *The Flowering of Old Testament Theology*. Sources for Biblical and Theological Study, ed. Ben Ollenburger, et al. (Winona Lake, Ind.: Eisenbrauns, 1992) 497–507.

[66] Gerhard F. Hasel, *Old Testament Theology: Basic Issues in the Current Debate*. Rev. ed. (Grand Rapids: Eerdmans, 1975) 21.

[67] Gabler, 497.

[68] Ibid., 494 ff.

[69] John Sandys-Wunsch and Laurence Eldredge, "J. P. Gabler and the Distinction between Biblical and Dogmatic Theology: Translation, Commentary and Discussion of His Originality." *Scottish Journal of Theology* 33 (1980) 133–58.

[70] Gabler, "An Oration," 495ff, 498ff.

[71] Ibid., 496–97, 500–501.

[72] Ibid., 497, 500. Note the point then, that from this view the divine authority of the writings of Scripture is to be understood as existing only to the extent that they can be understood to yield to ahistorical, rational principles.

[73] Ibid., 497, 500. While often creating some ambiguity of meaning or intent about such, Gabler says, "But let those things that have been said up to now be worth this

much: that we distinguish carefully the divine from the human, that we establish some distinction between biblical and dogmatic theology, and after we have seperated those things which in the sacred books refer most immediately to their own times and to the men of those times from those pure notions which divine providence wished to be characteristic of all times and places, let us then construct the foundation of our philosophy upon religion and let us designate with some care the objectives of divine and human wisdom. Exactly thus will our theology be made more certain and more firm, and there will be nothing further to be feaed for it from the most savage attack from its enemies."

And Gabler further concludes, "And so the sacred authors, however much we must cherish them with equal reverence because of the divine authority that has been imprinted on their writings, cannot all be considered in the same category if we are referring to their use in dogmatics. I would certainly not suggest that a holy man's own native intelligence and his natural way of knowing things are destroyed altogether by inspiration. Finally since especially in this context it is next asked what each of these men felt about divine things (this can be understood not from any traditional appeal to divine authority but from their books) I should judge it sufficient in any event that we do not appear to concede anything which lacks some proof. I should also judge that when it is a case of the use in dogmatics of biblical ideas, then it is of no consequence under what authority these men wrote, but what they perceived this occasion of divine inspiration clearly transmitted and what they perceived it finally meant." Ibid., 496, 497.

[74] Ibid., 500–501.

[75] Hasel, *Old Testament Theology*, 21.

[76] As William Lane Craig has stated, "Were the Scriptures not inspired by the Holy Spirit, they would be merely the words of human authors, having no more authority than other ancient religious texts (though it could be asked whether they would have been produced at all without the "movement"/*phenomenoi* of the Spirit in relation to the authors). Thus, Scripture's authority ultimately is derivative, i.e., it derives from God himself." William Lane Craig, "A Classical Apologist's Closing Remarks," in *Five Views on Apologetics*, ed. Steven B. Cowan (Grand Rapids: Zondervan, 2000) 314.

3
Has God Said?
Post-Kantian Models of Holy Scripture
in Relation to the Word of God

It has rightly and insightfully been said that there is an absolutely critical relationship that has directly affected our understanding of revelation and the canon of Holy Scripture:

> Is it merely a coincidence that biblical criticism arose and flourished when deism was increasingly in vogue? Or that classical views of revelation and inspiration presuppose theism? In our time theism appears to be giving way to various forms of panentheism (the idea that God is not "over" the world as Lord, but rather that the world is "in God" who serves as its inner ground).[1]

One's understanding of God, the God-world relation, and so God's providence, is highly influential upon how one will then understand and/or limit what can and should be reckoned as revelation, the possibility of content-ful divine discourse, and even divine, self-disclosure taking written form (text/canon of Scripture). While much has been made of the fact that the rise of various historical-critical methods of approaching the text of Scripture (cf. chapter four) has been a significant factor in the dismantling of "the Scripture Principle," little has been written to show how the real basis of the dispute about the historical "Scripture Principle" is essentially *theological*. For what is at stake in the movement of thought, scientific and philosophical-epistemological, from Newton and Spinoza through Kant, et al. in the debates about Scripture is, finally, one's doctrine of God. Beyond that, perhaps the most important element of the doctrine of God and the God-world relation, having much bearing on the doctrine of Scripture, is divine providence and vice versa. Therefore, to an extent, the foundational issue in the doctrine of Scripture concerns the manner of God's involvement and activity in and with the words of Scripture, and so the manner of God's personal activity in the universe.[2] One's view of Scripture is connected to and affected by one's view of God, i.e., there can be no affirmation of Scripture as written Word of God without a corresponding understanding of God's lordly and active providence in the world.

As we will see, the reentrenchment of cosmological and epistemological dualism(s) via Isaac Newton and Immanuel Kant ("Newton's philosopher") effected a "construal" of God and the God-world relation which led, in some cases "deistically" and in others more "panentheistically," to the rejection of the historical Christian affirmation of the "identity thesis," "the Scripture Principle," i.e., that the text of Holy Scripture *is* the written, and so authoritative, Word of God, a crucial participating element in and of God's larger redemptive self-disclosive processes in, under, of, and from Jesus Christ, *the* Word made flesh.

David Kelsey makes the strong, and it would seem essentially correct claim that, first, the nature of biblical authority is a function of one's "construal" of Scripture, i.e., doctrines have one kind of authority, history another, narrative another. But, second, one's construal of Scripture is not determined finally by the text as such, but rather by the intersection of two extra-textual factors, the way Scripture is seen to be used in the church community, and especially the way/manner God is understood to be present in and related to the church, and so in the world.[3]

The Modern Intrusion of Dualism and the "Separation" of God from the World

During the period in which the Enlightenment, and so modernity, arose, several scientists and philosophers exercised great influence in what has been termed "the reentrenchment of dualistic/disjunctive thinking" (thinking realities apart rather than in relation) in the modern Western world: Galileo, Descartes, Spinoza, Newton, and Kant. As we have observed in the previous chapter, upon the methodological and conceptual bases laid by Descartes, Spinoza acted directly to separate the text of Holy Scripture from all divine authority and so from the Word of God. [4] But it is with Descartes and, especially, Isaac Newton and Immanuel Kant and their massive, often destructive, influence upon "scientific thinking," and especially upon Western understanding of the possibility of God's self-revelation in the world, the Word having empirical coordinates if you will, that I now wish to deal as the basis of much modern and postmodern separation of Holy Scripture from the Word of God.

In large measure, the "modern" (pre-Einsteinian) approach to knowledge of the world arose within the cosmological dualism of Newton and the epistemological dualisms of Descartes and Kant. As a result, alien disjunctions were clamped down on modern thought resulting in the loss of true objectivity. This modern dualism received strong impetus from the Cartesian *cogito ergo sum* which, among other things, effected the epistemological separation of subject and object, locating truth in the subjective pole of the knowing relation. [5] Newton's rigid, mechanical, deterministic mathematical system of cause and effect brought about the separation of absolute mathematical space and time from the relative space and time of ordinary experience. In this way, Newton made God into the "containing mind" which statically impresses rationality on the mechanistic universe, while necessarily remaining deistically separate—only outside the universe. [6] Kant's unique synthesis of rationalism and empiricism effected the absolute disjunction between the "knowable" phenomenal world and the noumenal world, which is unknowable by "pure reason" (i.e., Newtonian "scientific" reason). Hence, objective knowledge of God, God's interactive relation to, in and for the world, God's salvific acts as spatial-historical, are ruled out, barred from possibility *a priori*. [7]

If God is separate from the world then he doesn't reveal himself.

It was crucial for Newton's portrayal of the universe and finite events therein that he build into his physics an absolute inertial system, absolute time and space, and the *divinum sensorium* as separated from relative time and space. Absolute time and space he equated with the mind of God, the postulated *divinum sensorium* is God who, as infinite external "container," forms and imposes rationality on the infinite universe—from the outside. As a result, Newton's physics and conceptualization of the universe is rightly described as necessitarian, positivistic, and abstractionist for having clamped down on the universe an *a priori* geometric framework separate from all motion, change and phenomenal realities/events of everyday experience. He did this to rein in all change, all contingency, and to bring about the uniformity he thought to be necessary for all scientific formalization. The wholly separated, all determining absolute (or "mind of God") had to be maintained inertially ("absolute rest") as independent of all empirical reality. Therein, the data of the world were reckoned as isolated facts. Constitutive relations, interactivity, real motion and contingency were lost to the independent mechanical whole of the universe and so to absolute time and space.[8]

But of special importance here is Newton's problematic separation of absolute time and space from all relative, empirical time and space, and so the deistic separation of God from the world, and thus the negation of all objective, self-disclosive relations of God to and in the world. This projection of an unbridgeable gulf or chasm separated the wholly other deity and all intelligible realities from all sensible realities, theoretical from empirical, absolute from relative, in the name of *a priori* uniformity. This meant the *a priori impossibility* of miracle, of content-ful revelation, of incarnation. Indeed, in response to the classical Christian affirmation of the historical incarnation of the Word in Jesus Christ, Newton said, "God could no more become incarnate than a bucket [notion of external divine receptacle] can contain itself."[9] At best, Newton was an Arian Christian, the result of his imposed absolute-relative, God-world dichotomy. While post-Newtonian scientists acknowledge that Newton's physics have a very limited usefulness within narrow contexts, on the whole his view of the universe had harmful effects upon the sciences, scientific methodology, and, in theology, upon all understanding of real relation to God and redemptive, recreative knowledge of God in the world. In a Newtonian universe where God has only external, deterministic relation to the universe, there can be no divine revelation in the classical Christian sense, no spatio-temporal-empirical coordinates of God's self-revelation in any form, not in Christ above all, nor in the text of Holy Scripture.

Immanuel Kant has rightly been called Newton's philosopher. In the rise of modern dualism, cosmological and epistemological, it has been the work of Kant that has taken Newton's disjunction of absolute and relative time and space and applied it directly to the human knowing processes. After David Hume's "skeptical" empiricism had "waked" Kant from his "dogmatic slumbers," Kant reworked his earlier rationalism and, with his first *Critique*, ushered in his "Copernican Revolution" in philosophy and theology—pointedly in terms of epistemology. British empiricism had essentially agreed that the mind functions in a passive role, having no innate ideas. The mind is an empty vessel receiving "impressions" from the external world which it somehow collects together. It was this element of empiricism, the passive-receptor mind, that Kant found inadequate. So to set "knowledge" and metaphysics on firmer ground, he postulated that the human mind is "active" and *gives* form to incoming sense data.

> Hitherto it has been assumed that all our knowledge must conform to objects. But all attempts to extend our knowledge of objects by establishing something in regard to them *a priori*, by means of concepts, have, on this assumption, ended in failure. We must therefore make trial whether we may not have more success in the tasks of metaphysics, if we suppose that objects must conform to our knowledge. This would agree better with what is desired, namely, that it should be possible to have knowledge of objects *a priori* determining something in regard to them prior to their being given.[10]

Instead of beginning with the object as something given to which the mind conforms, Kant reverses the relation and so conceives the object as to some degree constituted, "formed," by the *a priori* mental capacities of the knower. The mind imposes on the "incoming" sense material its own forms of cognition, determined by those very *a priori* structures of active human understanding. These cognitive capacities for experience determine the possibility of objects of knowledge (i.e., what can and cannot be "known"). Thus Kant distinguished objects physically present as the basis of human sense experience as knower ("phenomena") from realities or objects that are nonsensible, that lie beyond the human capacity for knowledge by empirical experience ("noumena"). A noumenon is something apart from any empirical or sense relation to a knowing subject, such as the realm of essences, e.g., the essential nature of a table (*Ding an sich*/thing-in-itself) or a reality for which the human knower lacks the mental "categories" or capacity (*a priori*) to detect (supersensible objects such as God, self, world).[11]

Thus Newton's separation of the external God and "mind of God" from relative, empirical time and space, the unbridgeable chasm, was applied by Kant to the human mind, resulting in the separation of the "knowable" phenomenal world of sense "intuitions" from the unknowable noumenal realm of essences, of the *Ding an sich* ("the thing in itself"), of God and spiritual realities. Such *noumena* cannot be known by "pure reason." In this way, Kant transferred the "inertial absolute" from the mind of God to the mind of the human subject.[12] Formative effect upon the world has moved from the divine impress, the *divinum sensorium*, to the active, formative agency of Kant's *a priori* categories of the human mind. Accordingly Kant's synthetic *a priori* reduces all claims to "knowledge" of the external world to the outcomes of the molding, shaping effects of those inertial, absolute categories of the mind. Appearance is but appearance to the subject without real penetration into the *Ding an sich*.

Kant's strong form of epistemological dualism resulted in vast implications and great limitations for philosophy and, notably, for theology. While it did accomplish Kant's desire to rehabilitate a modified empiricism and so the possibility of scientific knowledge of nature, it "cut off" all knowledge of the "supersensible" realm, notably God, by "pure (sense) reason" ("Transcendental Dialectic"). Kant's actual point was that any reality that lies beyond space and time (nonphysical object) cannot be known by means of (Newtonian) science because physical science is based on sense experience; though nothing known in the empirical world contradicts noumenal realities. While it was apparently not Kant's intention to ground religious skepticism and so the *a priori* negation of all human knowledge of God, the roots of such skepticism lay in both his *Critique of Pure Reason* and *Critique of Practical Reason* (approaching the question from the direction of moral conduct) and in his subsequent *Religion Within the Limits of Reason Alone*.

As a result of Newton's conceptual closing off of the universe to God and to objective relation to God, and the Kantian cutting off of the human knower to any objective, content-ful revelation from God, there has occurred what Jewish philosopher Martin Buber has rightly called an "eclipse." The dualistic separation of absolute and relative space and time, sensible and intelligible realities, phenomenal and noumenal realms, the world from God and knowledge of God as he is, reflects the "eclipse" of objectivity, the "eclipse" or "conceptual letting go of God."[13] Klaus Bockmühl interestingly but accurately described this situation when he concluded that:

> (Modern theology) sets out from the fact that the whole orientation of modern thought has been determined by the Enlightenment's epistemological critique. . . . In his *Critique of Pure Reason*, Kant . . . concluded that human understanding cannot say anything cogent and universally valid about that which is beyond the sense world. An impenetrable cover lies over the world. . . . One result of Kant's critique is a sharp division of the world into "this side" and "the beyond." On this side, in nature and history, specific laws hold. . . . About the beyond, nothing can be said for certain. The wall that separated this world and the beyond is impenetrable. No intervention of the beyond into this world, such as God's revelation of himself in history, can take place.[14]

Theologically, this "schizoid thinking" has resulted not only in the rejection of God's objective, lordly interrelation to and in the world and all objective, content-ful, self-disclosure, e.g., incarnation, revelation taking textual form as the canon of Holy Scripture, but has also been applied to the historical Jesus (phenomenal Jesus from essential Logos or the Christ of faith, etc.). This has led to much false theological thinking which has spawned broad skepticism about any realist knowledge of God, all salvific actions by God in space-time, and brought such to full form in the various trajectories of Neo-Protestantism from Schleiermacher to the postmodern present. Loss of proper theological objectivity has meant the inevitable turn to subjectivity, God "eclipsed" by our turn to ourselves, to the human subject as the center of theological inquiry, rather than to the content-ful revelation of God. Thus we will find that Schleiermacher's Kantian epistemology led him to his theological method whereby one starts from human piety or one's feeling of "absolute dependence" upon God/All. Bultmann, too, reflects the damaging effects of both Newton and Kant throughout his dualistic theological call for subjective "authenticity." Bultmann's obsolete Newtonian cosmology forced him to portray God outside the mechanistic universe wherein God cannot act objectively. At the same time his Kantian epistemology necessitates that the knowledge of God as he is, is barred from possibility. Indeed, such damaging cosmological and epistemological dualism has been incorporated into almost every prominent movement of theology, Protestant and Catholic, for two hundred years.[15] Again, these developments coincide and dovetail with what has been said previously about Spinoza and Semler. The result is inevitably either an overemphasis on God's otherness (deistic) or God as radically immanent (panentheism), both leading to a centering on the human subject and the loss of the truth of God. We will briefly examine this influence upon several prominent formulations of divine revelation as it relates to the text of canonical Scripture: Friedrich Schleiermacher, Rudolf Bultmann, Paul Tillich and, briefly, Wolfhart Pannenberg, Process thought and one form of "post-modern" (a)theology. Two recent evangelical responses will follow.

Friedrich D. E. Schleiermacher

After the thought of Newton, Hume and Kant, among others, within the larger current of Enlightenment modernity, the question became whether one could yet participate in the Christian faith and so do theology as truly, distinctively Christian, especially in any classical Christian sense. Can revealed truth and so knowledge of God, content-ful knowledge of God, be the basis of Christian theology? Friedrich Schleiermacher was the first significant theologian to constructively respond in the context of this assumed dualism. Schleiermacher was influenced by Romanticism, Spinoza, the pietism of his youth and especially Kant. His intent was, in a sense, to counter Kant's epistemology and dry moralism, but the result of his attempted "end run" around Kant via God-consciousness was the reaffirmation of Kant's noumenal-phenomenal split.

Having agreed with Kant that God cannot be known directly as he is in himself, Schleiermacher rejected both practical (moral) reason and speculative idealism (Hegel) as alternative methods to "knowledge of God" out of the other pole of the relation, i.e., the human being as central to the "truth" of God. Unlike these, Schleiermacher started with religious "feeling" (*Gefühl*), God-consciousness, the feeling of absolute dependence on God/the universe.

> The common element in all diverse expressions of piety, by which they are conjointly distinguished from all other feelings, or in other words, the self-identical essence of piety is this; the consciousness of absolute dependence, or, which is the same thing, of being in relation to God.[16]

This "Copernican revolution," which moves the immediate center of Christian faith from God as objectively self-revealed, above all in Christ, to the subjective piety of the Christian, meant that theology must focus its attention not on content-ful revelation sourced in God by the Holy Spirit, which, after Kant, is "not possible," but upon one's own empirical religious feelings or piety. "Dogmatics must relate itself to piety, the explanation of this is that while piety is the object of this (theological) knowledge, the knowledge can only be explicated in virtue of a certainty which inheres in the determination of (religious) self-consciousness."[17] The Christian faith is here regarded not as a "knowing" or a "doing" (ethics) but, again, feeling. And theology is contemplation of these feelings as they bespeak the "whence" of one's feeling of God-consciousness, i.e., God, the All, the Infinite. But this "connection" is at best indirect for Schleiermacher, who dualistically rejects the possibility of any and all supernatural interventions or causality by God in history.[18] What Christians have historically taken as, e.g., miracle, is said to be the outcome of how the religious self-consciousness "takes" or understands particular occurrences in the closed system of the universe.[19] Given this separation of all true, objective knowledge of God from the scope of human possibility, the only other apparent option for those claiming the centrality of "knowledge" for the Christian faith would be knowledge of doctrines or dogmas. Yet this too is rejected because such "knowledge" does not enhance the feeling of dependence on God.[20]

But if the doctrines of the Christian faith are to be the product of reflection on one's religious feelings and not "divinely revealed doctrines" or "timeless, divinely authoritative propositions" (given Schleiermacher's

Kantian bases he must, like those who follow, actively disparage the position of historical orthodoxy in order to make his innovations palatable), what role might Scripture have, if any? Given Schleiermacher's Kantian assumptions, God and God's self-disclosure, the Word of God, even if potentially having a kind of "truth" content, cannot, as *noumena*, partake of the phenomenal form of historical text, nor as incarnate in the phenomenal person of Jesus of Nazareth. Yet the interrelation between the two is significant. And while he does use the term "inspiration" one must recall that he denies all divine causality in the world. Thus speaking *broadly* of all "sacred books" (applied also to Scripture) he says:

> Every sacred writing is in itself a glorious production, a speaking monument from the heroic time of religion, but, through a servile reverence, it would become merely a mausoleum, a monument that a great spirit once was there. . . . Not every person has religion who believes in a sacred writing but only the one who has a lively and immediate understanding [feeling] of it, *and who, therefore, so far as he himself is concerned, could most easily do without it.*[21]

Rather, like "miracle," "inspiration" (and "prophecy") is understood to be an extension of human God-consciousness in the sense that "fulfillment" of what is said to be prophetic is in the eyes of the God-conscious beholder. Thus Scripture is "inspired" if one's religious experience has been enhanced by it and consequently regards it as divinely authoritative. On the one hand, Scripture is the record of human religious experience. Donald McKim refers to this as "construing Scripture as experience" and George Lindbeck as an "experiential expressive" relation of Scripture to doctrine.[22] This approach has been highly formative on liberal and neo-liberal theologies ever since. Hence, Scripture is significant but not central to Christian faith or to the doctrine arising from that faith experience. Scripture is not the primary source of doctrine, but it can have positive effects upon the religious consciousness, which is the basis of theology. Scripture is valuable, for it records the religious experience of the earliest Christian communities. Even more important, the NT is said to present for succeeding generations the pure model of Jesus Christ's perfect God-consciousness and the force of that upon the earliest Christians.[23] Hence, the authority of Scripture is not inherent, nor is it finally divine at all.

For Schleiermacher that is neither possible nor desirable. Scripture can be no more than a model for Christian piety, and so for all Christian attempts to interpret the significance of Jesus Christ and his exemplary God-consciousness for one's own historical circumstances: "we can only say that all that has approved itself in the way of . . . Christian piety in later ages of the church has kept within the lines of these [NT] original forms (of piety), or is attached to them as an explanatory accompaniment."[24] So while disagreeing with Kant about the focus and manner of "religion" (feeling versus morality), Schleiermacher agreed with Kant's turn to human subjectivity as the center of theology and the separation of God from any content-ful, faith-ful human knowledge. As a result, he necessarily rejects Scripture as a participative aspect of God's self-revelation, centered and fulfilled in the incarnate Word, Scripture as the content-ful, textual product of the "breath of God" through and with human authors. He found many passages and entire books of Scripture unacceptable because they did not contribute to or contradicted the true feeling of absolute dependence on God. Leading the way for so many cosmological and epistemological dualists to follow him in theological modernity and postmodernity, Schleiermacher turned to what seemed to be the only remaining source of "religious truth." He turned within, to subjective human piety as the source of the content-less "revelation" of the unknowable God.

Rudolf Bultmann

Known first as a NT scholar and early participant in the "dialectical" movement in theology after WW I, Rudolf Bultmann was also one of the last prominent NT scholars to be directly influential upon theology. One of his chief concerns was to make Christian faith understandable to modern, scientific, twentieth-century people. And while he, with Barth, was highly critical of the immanentism of nineteenth century (especially Ritschlian) liberal theology ("culture Christianity"), Bultmann retained much of his "Neo-Protestant" foundation and methodologies. As such, Bultmann's hermenentical program of demythologization and his understanding of the theological task is stamped with the impress of Newton's cosmological dualism, whereby God is "deistically" shut out of the world, unable to act or speak directly within the "closed" continuum of history and the universe, and with Kant's epistemological application of Newton's system to the human mind and the consequent noumenal-phenomenal split, making God unknowable as he is in himself. Does Bultmann then have any role for Scripture, any role for Scripture in relation to "the Word of God's personal address to me" in my existence? Yes and No.

Bultmann asserts that "the message" of the ancient NT documents is the potential occasion of God's "Word" addressed to the individual calling him/her to an existential faith response. Further, NT exegesis and theology explicate human existence in relation to God by listening to that "Word" that addresses one through the "kerygma" of the NT.[25] Indeed, Bultmann can say about Scripture and the Word of God:

> Is it enough to say that faith grows out of the encounter with Holy Scripture *as* the Word of God, that faith is nothing but simple hearing? The answer is yes . . . [T]o hear the Scriptures *as* the Word of God means to hear them *as* a word addressed to me, as kerygma, as a proclamation.[26]

> God's Word is a real word spoken to me in human language, whether in the preaching of the church or in the Bible, in the sense that the Bible . . . is transmitted through the church as a word addressing us.[27]

Does this not seem to reflect a relatively orthodox connection, even a proper identification of Scripture as, in some real sense, the written Word of God? No. To understand Bultmann's point, the implications of his dualism, as well as his mission, must be recognized.

First, one must be clear about Bultmann's emphasis on the "transcendence" and "hiddenness" of God. Following Luther's *Deus absconditus*, Bultmann gives strong place to God's hiddenness and transcendence, but as filtered through the God-world relation reckoned by Newton and Kant. In response to the immanentism of much nineteenth-century theology, Bultmann followed the early Barth in his neo-Kierkegaardian conceptualization of the "infinite qualitative distinction between God and the world." God is qualitatively different from the world, so philosophy cannot provide knowledge of God. But in Bultmann's "Newtonian" hands, transcendence becomes deism. On the one hand, God is "wholly other"; there are no points of contact or correspondence with human beings. Also, this universe is a closed system of cause and effect. There are no breaks in the "linkage," hence, no miracles, no incarnation, no direct content-ful Word to humanity sourced in and from God.[28] Yet, Bultmann's concept of transcendence was also consciously formed in contrast to what he took to be the mythological, "spatial" transcendence of the biblical documents, and the Greek conception of divine transcendence as timelessness. Both are at odds with our modern scientific worldview. Rather, his nonspatial view of divine transcendence is said to refer to the biblical outlook regarding God as over against the material world, to God's absolute authority. Existentially speaking, God stands before us in the moment of decision, addressing us with his "Word," confronting us with the "call" to "faith" or "authentic existence."[29]

But this "call," this "Word of address" to the existing individual is never objective. Bultmann is emphatic that, given God's "separation" from the world and from all human knowing, he cannot be known and referred to objectively. He is never a "mere object" in the world, a datum. He is unknown except in terms of what he does through the kerygma, the authenticity we experience in "faith" as God paradoxically, but indirectly, "breaks in" to meet us in the moment of decision.[30]

Important to understanding Bultmann's larger theology of the "Word" of God is his hermeneutical approach, especially to the Gospels and the question of Jesus. While he was convinced of some connection between the historical Jesus and kerygmatic Christ (of faith), this cannot be verified. Bultmann's radical "Form Criticism," combined with his historical skepticism, led him to conclude that the Jesus of the NT is largely a faith projection of the early Church. The NT does not present the Jesus of history but the Christ of faith. But for Bultmann this is not the problem it was for the nineteenth century "quest for the historical Jesus." Rather, it is the kerygma, the message about Jesus in the early church, that is decisive for faith. This lack of concern for the historical Jesus is said to be reflected in the NT itself, especially in Paul and John.[31]

But the NT is said to reflect a prescientific, primitive worldview. Modern persons have a scientific worldview. "Myth," for Bultmann, is not a negative term. It does not mean "false." Rather all NT reference to God acting in history and speaking directly, all miracle, any notion of a "divine Son who descends to earth" for humanity is, in light of

Newton and Kant, impossible *a priori*. Should such "myth" be cut out as Ritschlian liberalism had done? No. It must be transposed or translated into modern, existential, Heideggerian terms so that the true *skandalon* of the gospel call to "faith"/authenticity may be truly heard *now*, and not be encumbered by unscientific, nonessential mythological forms.[32] By such demythologization, the true message of Christ can be genuinely encountered. Bultmann believed his hermeneutic opens the way whereby the transcendent God meets and transforms existing persons now ("authenticity"/*eigentlichkeit* to use the Heideggerian term).[33] Thus, it is the transforming power of God *through* the NT message/kerygma that *is* the Word of God. The NT and its "word of Christ," as historical text, cannot be the Word of God any more than the historical Jesus of Nazareth can be the ontological Word, the divine Son, made flesh. God is closed off from such direct action to existing persons. Not even those given new self-understanding by the "Word-Act" of God in the moment of faith can have adequate, content-ful knowledge of the Wholly Other.[34]

Bultmann's cosmological, epistemological, and existential *a prioris* led him to emphasize God as radically, indeed deistically, transcendent, a God who can be "known" only as he acts in me, only as he meets me and effects authentic existence in me. Hence, theology becomes reflection on the experience of self-understanding in that encounter, an outcome all too similar to that of Schleiermacher, i.e., the turn to the subject as center. God cannot be "known" objectively but only subjectivistically in privatized existential "faith." The "event" character of God's non- or ahistorical revelation means that Scripture merely occasions faith's self-understanding and, by early church examples, expresses that self-understanding.[35] Only in this "adoptionist," instrumental, functional way, for my here and now authenticity, is Scripture said to be "authoritative." The Newtonian/Kantian denial of knowledge of God *as he is* in Christ and in Scripture by the Spirit has reversed the object of theological reflection from the incarnate and inscriptuated Word of God to "the feeling of absolute dependence" (Schleiermacher) or "new authentic self-understanding" (Bultmann).

Paul Tillich

Paul Tillich referred to himself as one who ever worked "on the boundary," i.e., on the boundary between the old world and new world, theology and philosophy, Christianity and humanism.[36] Influences on his wide ranging philosophical-theological pursuits were many, including the medieval mystics, Neoplatonism, the German idealist tradition, Nietzsche, Kant and Heidegger's existential ontology. Tillich said of himself that he always thought in terms of "systems," and his *Systematic Theology* is, with Barth's *Church Dogmatics*, one of the two most influential constructive theologies since Schleiermacher. His theological work was intended to reflect on the relation of the Depth Dimension/Ultimate/Ground of Being or, symbolically, "God" in and through all of culture (and religions).[37] But more to the point, given his existential analysis of the human and cultural condition of "estrangement" from its depth dimension or Ground ("fallenness"), and our awareness of this loss, he says: "My whole theological work has been directed to the interpretation of (revelatory) religious symbols in such a way that the secular man—and we are all secular—can understand and be moved by them."[38]

For a short period, both Tillich and Bultmann were colleagues of, and much influenced by, Heidegger at Marburg. For Bultmann, Heidegger clarified human existence, inauthenticity and the need to be "called out" to authenticity. Tillich was affected more by Heidegger's existential ontology and so the human predicament in relation to Being-as-such, the relation of the contingent, finite human being to the Infinite, which "answers" and "overcomes" the threat of nonbeing. Indeed, "religion" is the state of being "ultimately concerned," or "that which concerns us ultimately, our being or not being at all," the absolute abyss of negativity and nothingness. The human being, as finite ex-istence, is thus contingent and anxious, especially after being gripped by the "ontological shock" or awareness that we do not have to be and someday will not be. Our human ex-istence means that we are estranged from "Essence," from the Ground of our being. We are questions without answers in ourselves. This situation points beyond itself; we "quest" for the "answer" we lack, for meaning and the Ground of Being we have lost.[39] As an "apologetic" theologian, Tillich affirms that our basic existential questions are "answered." That despite our human inability to "save" (*salvus*, heal) ourselves, our quest for "new Being" in the midst of estrangement has been and is "answered" or "spoken to" from beyond itself by means of revelatory "religious symbols," through which "the power of Being"/ "God" breaks.[40]

Central to Tillich's "apologetic" or answering theology is not only revelatory Christian symbols, but his "method of correlation" whereby he must "fit" the revelatory "answers," via Christian religious symbols, to the real, contemporary existential questions which arise within culture. Question and Answer can be joined at the one point of the "ex-isting human being" and his/her *"ultimate"* concern, and so "Being Itself." But Tillich is adamant that the revelatory "answer," through Christian religious symbols, must "fit" and thus be given its expressed "form" by the human existential question. "Man cannot receive answers to questions he has never asked."[41]

Once the true, contemporary, existential questions have been carefully established and formulated, in the movement from existential to (Christian) ontological, the theologian must use the Christian revelatory symbols, which form the ontological, and so the saving, redemptive answers, and express them so as to fit the questions. According to Tillich, a "symbol" (as opposed to a "sign") *generally* can be *any* finite, historically and culturally conditioned thing that uses its "material" to point *beyond* itself to something different, though the referent has participative relation to the symbol (e.g., American flag and the nation). Symbols "open" dimensions of reality not available without the symbol. But true *"religious symbols"* are finite things which point to and, by the "breakthrough" of the Infinite into the finite by "revelation," participate in the Ground of / power of Being or "God." A true religious symbol, then, is a finite entity which has the dual capacity to be what it is (e.g., a word, the Cross) and to be the finite place of the "breakthrough" of the Infinite/Ground of Being into finite human existence. When this occurs, says Tillich, something happens to the finite object ("miracle") and to an existing human recipient ("ecstasy") whereby a person is grasped, revealed and transformed by the "revelation" of the power of being via the symbol.[42] Tillich's *Systematic Theology* is constructed around five central existential questions and five central revelatory, ontological Christian symbolic "answers" (three are the heart of the system), starting with the human quest of reason under the conditions of estrangement and the "answer" "Revelation" of the power of Being. It is here, as one understands the nature of this revelation and how it relates to Holy Scripture, that one clearly sees, as with Schleiermacher and Bultmann, the effects of Newtonian-Kantian dualism.

In uncovering Tillich's conception of "revelation," the first correlation, Reason-Revelation is paradigmatic for the rest. As estranged, human reason's quest for meaning and Being itself meets its limit, and so seeks "Revelation." Herein, reflecting Kant's noumenal-phenomenal split, Tillich makes strong differentiation between existence and essence, from which human existence is estranged / "fallen." In existence, reason faces conflicts or disrupted polarities which it cannot resolve.[43] In questing after "Revelation," reason seeks that which resolves the conflicts and distortions of human existence; it seeks completion, and so is "open" to "Revelation" of the Ground of Being ("essential reason"). Tillich defines "Revelation" here as "the manifestation of the Ground of Being for human knowledge."[44] It is the manifestation of the power that reunites what has been destructively separated, thereby saving, healing, bringing re-essentialization out of conflict or estrangement. It is the unveiling of the mystery of being, the infinite Ground of our finite existence, the "self-manifestation of the depth of being and meaning."[45]

Central to Tillich's entire "System" is the symbol "the biblical portrait of Jesus as the Christ" and what "God" is said to have effected by the historical manifestation of the Messiah. "Messiah" means that in one particular historical person "essence" has entered "existence." That one human being was so "transparent" to the Ground of his being that "essential manhood" and existence without estrangement from God, world or others has actually occurred where we humans exist.[46] Our situation, as one of finitude, distortion, conflict, self-contradiction, hopelessness and despair calls out for hope within hopelessness. The biblical symbol "Jesus as the Christ" has answered our question, for in him "New Being" has entered the world whereby the victory of God has become manifest where humanity is. Tillich says we "know" this because the symbol "Jesus as the Christ" has been the channel whereby many have experienced reintegration, however fragmentarily.[47]

But does such reference to reason, the revelatory completion of reason, "essence in existence" and "knowledge" of God via Christian symbols reflect a conceptual, content-ful, even discursive self-giving of God and "truth" of God which actually bridges the noumenal-phenomenal or (to use Tillich's terms) "existential-essential" separation of God/Being Itself from human existents? No. Can "Word of God," as Tillich uses the phrase, have cognitive content and, among varied forms, even be manifested textually as Holy Scripture? Again, no.

Like Kant's practical reason, Schleiermacher's feeling of dependence, and Bultmann's call to authenticity via the kerygma, for Tillich the experience of "ecstacy" via religious symbols allows for no knowledge of the noumenal realm, or of "God" as he is in himself, no objective disclosure of God's nature and purpose at any level. There is only our being grasped and transformed in participative awareness of the Infinite in sustaining relation to our contingency and disruption.

Therefore, like so many influenced by the Newtonian-Kantian separation of God from the world, and so from any adequate human knowing of God as he is, Tillich rejected the classical Judeo-Christian claim that God reveals himself personally, lovingly and truthfully, and so too cognitively, even verbally-textually. Given Tillich's definition of God's "Word" it is not surprising then that God cannot express himself in human words, i.e., content-ful assertions or "speech acts." "Revelation" cannot be objective, nor can it convey truth content or information disclosed by and about God.[48] It is simply transformative power. This parallels his denial of the actuality or historicity of the Incarnation. Tillich's Christology is adoptionist and docetic-gnostic.[49] Any direct, literal and historical revelation of God, as is claimed by classical Nicene and Chalcedonian Christology is deemed impossible. Any worship of "Jesus as the Christ" is, for Tillich, idolatry (see his "Protestant Principle").

Is there a significant, "authoritative" role for Scripture in Tillich's "System," if not as written Word of God? Yes. But like his Christology it is functional, symbolic and adoptionist. This was illustrated earlier in his "biblical portrait of Jesus as the Christ." While Tillich regards any identity between Word of God and Scripture to be a destructive misinterpretation, as one would expect, he affirms that Scripture has a "symbolic" role. As a whole or in terms of particular biblical "images," especially "the biblical portrait of Jesus as the Christ," Scripture can mediate the transforming power of Being Itself. As Tillich says, "the concrete biblical material is not guaranteed by faith, in respect to empirical factuality, but it is guaranteed as an adequate expression of the transforming power of New Being in Jesus as the Christ."[50] Scripture is said to be capable of mediating a functional authority at two levels. On the one hand, Scripture "expresses" the "original revelation," which lies as the experiential-transformative basis of the biblical and especially NT materials because of its effect *through* the man Jesus on the first disciples. On the other hand, Scripture "occasions" events of "dependent revelation" *now* as, through the symbolic biblical picture of New Being, disrupted human lives are reintegrated, and that in continuity with the "original revelation."[51] Such is Tillich's view of revelation as power of Being breaking *wordlessly*, through symbols, across the gulf that supposedly separates us from the Being and "Truth" of God.

Some Subsequent Developments

Much theological development after the "shattering" of the theological spectrum of the (still influential) giants: Barth, Bultmann, Tillich, et al., has been toward the "concretizing" and often "politicizing" of theology in light of humanity's contemporary needs, combined with "hope" for God's future in relation to the present. Theologies of Liberation, Process, Hope, Secularity, and A-theism, within a varied postmodernity, reflect concerns for concrete human/world situation(s). Yet the destructive dualistic inheritance from Newton and Kant, leading to the denial of any knowledge of God as he is, to denial of the possibility of God actually speaking, performing "speech acts," and so denial of real personal-cognitive-responsive relatedness to God's person and truth, remains firmly in place. For such recent theological and a-theological developments the tendency has usually been, like Schleiermacher and Tillich, some form of radical divine immanence, variously panentheistic, but with "movement," or divine dynamism, in and with the world, in keeping with contemporary concerns (especially since Hegel-Marx).

According to the "Process" tradition from Heraclitus through (among others) Hegel and Hegelian teleology, Bergson, Alexander and especially Whitehead and Hartshorne, everything, including God is in a constant state of "becoming." God and the world are eternally co-dependent, each necessary for the ongoing evolutionary development of the other. Given its understanding of the God-world relation, and so the effects of God on the world and the world on God, Process Theology has been properly and widely regarded as a "new natural theology."[52] All creaturely elements, but especially and uniquely humans as sentient beings, receive their "initial aim" from God and experience God's "lure" as they variously, dynamically, and in multileveled, complex interrelatedness, "prehend" good from all other previous and concurrent "occasions." Therein humans, as uniquely intelligent, free and responsible beings, can affirm or deny, accept or reject, their initial aim. What is often regarded as the most particular form of "revelation" in Process Theology, in light of this understanding of the God-world relation, occurs when a person is "open" to the aim of God, becomes "transparent" to God, and (in ways very similar to Tillich's view) not only fulfills God's aim but becomes to that extent a positive occasion to be prehended both by God and all other entities, as God ever seeks greater creativity, novelty and harmony in the world.[53] The preeminent example of such "revelatory" openness, as one might expect, given the desire of Process theology to be used as (at least) a Christian theology, is Jesus Christ. As developed variously by Lewis Ford, Norman Pittenger and David Griffin, Process Christology asserts that the man Jesus became *wholly* transparent to God and God's aim and thereby became a central redemptive occasion in history for all who follow to prehend.[54] But then what of revelation, especially "special revelation" in the classical sense? The following statement, while carefully nuanced for the sake of acceptability, is quite telling.

> [T]heologians have argued that the use of philosophy as a natural theology implies that the philosophy has a higher authority than Christian revelation. . . . In the language of general and special revelation: if one is using a philosophy . . . as the criterion for judging the historic faith, one is refusing the authority of special revelation. In response to this objection, process theology rejects the sharp contrast of general and special revelation.[55]

In other words, God does not and cannot disclose himself "specially," objectively, personally and content-fully, as is clear from the whole of the Whiteheadian metaphysic (e.g., rejection of actual incarnation of God, divine historical "speech acts"). Rather the notion of "special" revelation is erased by supposedly absorbing it into "general revelation," understood as the process of God's indirect effects via his directedness for the world.

Wolfhart Pannenberg and Jürgen Moltmann have, variously but under similar influences, given fresh emphasis to God and God's revelation as eschatological and political in terms of "Hope." While neither is a Hegelian as such, both have used and adopted forms of Hegel's teleology and view of universal history in order to give form and expression to their theological tasks, and to their views of revelation. Both fall within the broad category of "Revelation as History," or God's historical acts.[56] Both have been influenced by Ernst Bloch's *Principle of Hope*, though with distinctive outcomes. We will focus briefly on Pannenberg.

Pannenberg's use of Hegel's teleology and of Bloch's "hope" lead him to understand "revelation as history," i.e., revelation is not to be found in a special segment of history but in universal history, the history of the world/cosmos as all moves toward its appointed consummation, and so Yahweh's self-demonstration. This seems very Hegelian. Yet in all history, whereby God is showing himself to be the true God (e.g., the Exodus pattern and Yahweh's "battling" the "gods" of Egypt), there are indirect revelatory events which, according to Pannenberg, are self-interpreting.[57] The central historical event of revelation is the resurrection of Jesus Christ as the "proleptic" revelation of the eschaton of God's victorious consummation.[58] Here it is noteworthy that Pannenberg expresses his view of revelation, and the possibility of such as direct, cognitive, expressable, and even textual, as Holy Scripture. "The self-revelation of God in the biblical witnesses is not of a direct type in the sense of theophany, but is indirect and brought about by means of the historical acts of God."[59] And yet he also states: "The Word relates itself to revelation as foretelling, forthtelling, and report."[60] This sounds similar to the classical view. It seems that Pannenberg is willing to acknowledge, among the biblical images of revelation or the Word of God, that God, in some sense, is portrayed as disclosing truth about himself and the world. This is an "admission" missing in almost all theologians who follow within the Kantian line. Pannenberg also acknowledges that this conclusion about God's self-disclosure has been a prominent emphasis through the entire history of Christian theology until the Enlightenment and historical criticism. Yet he concludes that divine revelation cannot be direct in this way, nor can the Word of God take the historical form of God speaking, let alone as verbal and authoritative text. This view he interprets as mythical, anthropomorphic and even pagan. At most "the Word of God" can witness metaphorically to a kind of "telepathic" experience to which the prophet gives interpretation.[61] Indeed, for Pannenberg, as for Moltmann, the biblical texts are promissory anticipations, witnessing, pointing toward the final shape of history which shall reveal God's nature and eschatological purpose. Hence, Scripture points toward "the Word of God" which is God's ultimate eschatological revelation. So like other variant forms of "revelation as history" Pannenberg has not only separated God's truth and any divine "speaking" from our receiving and knowing that truth, but has dualistically separated "God saying" from "God doing." This view, while closer to classical Judeo-Christian views of revelation, still stands in principle within the broad dualistic, experiential paradigm advanced by Schleiermacher in response to Kant.

The concept of divine revelation would seem to be inimical to overtly "postmodern" theology and vice versa. Yet in one sense this is not so. The particular strain of "postmodern" theology represented by Thomas J. J. Altizer ("God is dead"/Atheistic Theology) and Mark C. Taylor ("Atheology") has been variously guided by a radical form of Hegelian thought, F. Nietzsche, J. Derrida, M. Foucault, as well as radical "extensions" of Bultmann and Tillich. We will focus on Altizer, who, despite his "God is Dead" and "Theology of Christian Atheism" reputation, is often misinterpreted as atheistic in the classical sense. Not so. He has rightly been described as "the most radical of the process theologians" and "God intoxicated." From his radical Hegelian and neo-Nietzschian bases, Altizer asserts that at the Cross of Christ the abstract God of transcendence "died," i.e., the transcendent God of "theism" became, in that event, wholly and totally immanent in the world and in history ("History as Apocalypse").[62] But despite this emphasis on the radical immanence of "God," and in a way paralleling Tillich's emphasis on God's/the Ground of Being's revelatory "breakthrough" into human culture for "judgment" and reorientation, Altizer affirms that God's radical processive relation in and as world and history manifests itself "apocalyptically." Yet unlike Tillich, Altizer asserts that apocalyptic history raises up "prophets," literary visionaries of this dynamic divine relation to history. Prominent among these are the "apocalyptic" visions of history found in the works of Dante, William Blake, and Nietzsche. But, like the others we have examined, it is obvious that no such radically immanent a-theistic "God" can or will declare itself in any content-ful, humanly communicable way, whether incarnational or as enscripturated. Such teaching, as reflective of the "classical" Christian tradition, is ridiculed out of hand.[63]

Therefore, again, we are left with the Newtonian-Kantian "gulf" or "chasm" firmly (though variously) in place, and so the phrase "Word of God" or "revelation of God," if used, is inevitably, and often radically, reconfigured to adjust it to modern and postmodern perceptions of the God-world-human relation, however deistic or pan(en)theistic, and subjectivist, such may be.

Examination of Recent Evangelical Responses to Modern and Postmodern Dualism and the Present "Crisis" of God's Word and Holy Scripture

The term "crisis" here is rooted in the Greek *krisis*, "to separate," and is thus appropriate as applied to the modern/postmodern dualism, "disjunctive" thinking, thinking apart what ought to be regarded as interrelated aspects of one larger whole—in this case, historical orthodoxy's assertion, rooted in the classical Judeo-Christian teaching of the relation of Holy Scripture and Word of God, i.e., that Scripture is the written Word of God, an aspect of and participant in God's larger self-revelatory processes to and in the world. Increasingly since the Enlightenment there have been constructive responses to this dualism as applied to the possibility of "divine discourse" and so realist, content-ful knowledge of God by space-time humans. But two very recent responses, two constructive "bibliologies," in the face of the contemporary situation, stand out as significant attempts to heal the chasm and are here assessed as to adequacy for evangelical, Protestant and even broader historical orthodoxy: the studies of Telford Work and Kevin Vanhoozer.

Telford Work: Scripture as Icon

Living and Active: Scripture in the Economy of Salvation is Telford Work's (Westmont College) endeavor to shed fresh light and take a new approach to the doctrine of Scripture. Work's concern for the doctrine of Scripture reflects his own Christian pilgrimage finally to "new paradigm" (nondenominational, evangelical ecumenism) and his response to attacks upon the nature and function of Scripture and Scripture's authority from

Western culture as a whole and from modern theology in particular, via historical-critical studies. These powerful attacks from outside and inside Christendom are together named "biblioclasm" by Work, a naming intended to parallel the "iconoclasm" in the eighth-century church. In light of what Work has found to be the "failures" of traditional views and approaches to the nature and function of Scripture, especially claims of "inerrancy," and the findings of modern biblical criticism, he "hungered . . . for a truly satisfying, truly theological, truly sophisticated doctrine of Scripture."[64]

Work's formative questions are not new. They are "What is the Bible?" and "What role does or should Scripture play in the life of Christian communities?" Yet it is of central concern here to understand the relation of God to Scripture (often herein called "God's inspired Word" and other near equivalents) *within* the divine economy of salvation. Thus Work intends to develop a model for understanding the nature of Scripture which reflects

> a fully Trinitarian account of Scripture, establishing and exploring its divine and human character and its salvific purpose in its Church setting and beyond. It claims that the Christian Bible, as divine message, historical phenomenon and physical object participates in the Trinitarian economy of salvation.[65]

To that end, Work makes "the Analogy of the Word," i.e., Jesus Christ the Word and Holy Scripture as the Word, formatively central to all that he does, even as it has been central to much church thinking about Scripture since its earliest years. Thus Christology is central to Work's argument, especially as developed by means of Athanasius' focus on the Word's self-involvement in the world, Augustine's divine ontology of biblical practice, Barth's development of the threefold God and threefold Word, and von Balthazar's pneumatological, sacramental argument for the Word of the Holy Spirit. These sources, especially Athanasius and Augustine, are integrated critically, constructively and often *very* imaginatively to open the way for Work's own central analogy with the "triumph of orthodoxy," the eighth century response to the Iconoclasts by the Iconodules of the church, and so the justification of Christian icons in worship as *mediums* of God's salvific presence to the faithful perceiver (Second Council of Nicaea). Thus

Work develops his notion of biblical Word/words as "icons" by applying the arguments of John of Damascus and Theodore of Studium *for icons* to *Holy Scripture*.[66] The outcome is intended to be a new approach to the nature and function of Scriptural Word which answers contemporary "biblioclastic" questions and reflects the trinitarian nature of the God of the Word and the trinitarian economy of salvation. Scripture, says Work, is then the result of the will of the Father, has the Son as its message, and all in the power of the Holy Spirit.[67]

What then does Work regard the nature of Holy Scripture to be if, in fact, it is to be regarded "iconically"? Throughout his developing argument, Work refers to Scripture as "the inspired Word of God," "the Word *ad extra* (to Christ/Son as Word *ad intra*)," "the Word of God's revelation" and other forms of expression which *seem* to reflect, and so affirm, the historical position of all sections of the church, i.e., that the *text* of Scripture as such is the written Word of God, in Christ and by the Spirit. The text then is divinely authoritative. Yet while Work repeatedly acknowledges that, with some variation, this has always been the Church's theological position on the nature of Scripture, called here the "old" view, that view and approach is said to be no longer tenable in the aftermath of historical criticism and other developments. At the same time, he criticizes "modern bibliologies" which inevitably approach Scripture "from below." Rather, bibliology must reflect the divine economy and so "move" as God does "from above"; for "divine descent precedes and empowers human ascent."[68] He means to uniquely bring together portions of the "Alexandrian" Christological perspective (Word-man), which, with the Antiochene approach to Christ (Word-Spirit), can open the way for a full orbed "divine ontology of Scripture."[69] But again, this approach commends itself to Work because it not only answers modern questions but also because it corrects "crude" verbal or verbal-docetic "bibliolators" (often "fundamentalists," a term he links to all who claim that revelation and inspiration were in some real sense "verbal"/text related).

As Work develops his argument, his early apparent linkage of Scripture with the "Word of God," "revelation," gives way to emphasis on Scripture in relation to "God's presence" or "God's saving presence," despite historical evidence that points to the "old" view. Soon it is clear that the amorphous language of "God's presence," despite lack of basis, has been slowly preparing the reader for Work's formative constructive analogy, ultimately his essential equation of Holy Scripture with icons, i.e., a man-made channel, conduit, medium of God's presence, even as icons were so described at the Second Council of Nicaea. Indeed, Scripture as "medium" of God's presence becomes Work's primary way of referring (iconically) to the "divine ontology of Scripture." Claiming the propriety of the Church's use of icons because of the incarnation, and thus "God's materiality," Work asserts that this applies to Scripture.

> The image (Scripture) *takes on* the qualities of its prototype and *communicates God's saving energy* to the perceiver, eliciting a response of faith and worship. Because the image shares (participates) in the prototype's grace, honor . . . the unity in veneration is not divided. . . . Yet since in Jesus' face and lips (material) the image and words of God are then revealed as truly personal and truly human . . . (then that) gives all *other words of Scripture* their sacramental power to mediate his personal presence and work.[70]

Thus iconology is said to provide a helpful guide in forming a trinitarian ontology of Scripture.

> God's Word *takes* human words. . . . God's words are *mediated pneumatically through the words* of his disciples who receive the Son's gift of the Spirit. All these words participate in each other through the Spirit's mediating work.[71]

As icons, by the Spirit, are said to be "signs" mediating materially "God's presence," so too the verbal "signs" of Scripture, by the Spirit, are "mediums" whereby God's salvific "presence " is made *manifest when* one responds in faithful worship.

As an evangelical/orthodox response to the modern and postmodern cosmological and epistemological dualism (biblioclasts), Telford Work's "new approach" suffers from old problems. First, against the vast, solid, biblical Judeo-Christian, prophetic, apostolic and patristic evidence of the Iconoclasts, Work must side with the Iconodules and argue that the incarnation has reversed OT commands against graven images (contra NT and the Fathers). While using elements of Athanasius' and Augustine's Christology for his bibliology, Work ignores their own exceedingly strong

Work: Bible is revelation but indirectly.

identification of Holy Scripture as God's Word and as revelation in a *direct* sense. Also, while the biblical truth of God for human salvation is not all God reveals, it is a crucial aspect of the unitary whole of God's self-disclosure centered in Jesus Christ by the Holy Spirit. But in Work's "iconic" construction of the "divine ontology of Scripture" as medium, the issue of *truth*, God's truth, the truth of God to us, vanishes. But even more central to our concern, Work's bibliology, for all of its "language of evangelical piety" and apparent affirmation of Scripture as "inspired Word of God," falls prey to the same dualism that has infected so many modern views of Scripture. His "divine ontology of Scripture" finally turns the text of Scripture into a verbal "icon," a verbal "sign," a purely *human* text, which, while it is said to be a result of the "Word" upon the human writers, is still the human text *through* which God "adoptionistically" (or ebionitically) manifests his "salvific presence"—no truth of God, no content-ful divine self-disclosure, no divine discourse, just divine "presence." This is disturbingly similar to Tillich's conception of divine revelatory symbols through which "God breaks and manifests his transforming presence in estranged human existence," or even Bultmann's understanding of the kerygma *through* which God "redeems" one unto new authentic life. It is ironic that Work refers in passing to a statement by Alastair MacIntyre to the effect that the "solution" to one crisis may well weaken a tradition's ability to respond to future crises. Work's own "solution" to the current crisis is a good "biblioclastic" example.

For an effective, constructive evangelical response to the modern and postmodern dualistic separation of God and humanity, and so Holy Scripture from Word of God, we must look elsewhere.

Kevin Vanhoozer: Scripture as Divine (Illocutionary) Speech Acts

In the aftermath of and in constructive response to the reinjection of cosmological and epistemological dualism into Western culture, forming the bases of modernity and the mutations within divergent strains of postmodernity, Kevin Vanhoozer has been at work on the issue of divine revelation and its relation to Holy Scripture as *a form* and *aspect* of the broader reality of divine revelation. Vanhoozer is rightly critical of both modernity's inordinate claims to truth and knowledge via human inquiry and of postmodernity's overreactive rejection of modernity's excesses leading to the rejection of all claims to truth, meaning, reason, external authority, and objectivity in favor of relativism, play and the constitutive dictatorship of the Subject /Reader.

But it is Vanhoozer's response to the particular "crisis" created by postmodernity's rejection of objective, external truth and meaning as "oppressive" to "the other," and its impact on contemporary understanding of divine revelation, with which we are most interested. For most "postmoderns," such as Derrida, the two are intertwined. Vanhoozer interprets Derrida's statement, "There is nothing outside the text,"[72] to mean that we have no nonlinguistic access to the way things really are. We must think and speak about the world with language, and that language is an arbitrary social convention. Human words/statements do not refer to the real world and acquire meaning not by way of reference but by difference (Derrida's notion of *différance*, i.e., *differ* + *defer*) from other words. Thus language is a system of differences that society imposes on human experience. Whatever we think is always/already shaped by our language, i.e., all we "know" is culturally/linguistically constructed.[73] Upon such bases "deconstruction" endeavors to dismantle or *un-do* distinctions basic to traditional philosophy and literary criticism, and so the "logocentrism" (e.g., Reason, Logos, Word of God) basic to any claim to speak from a privileged position (that something is true). This has resulted in the "death" of the author (authorial intent), the "death" of the text (as external, objective linguistic standard), and inevitably the "death" of the reader.[74] For our purposes the *un-doing* of the author and its effects on textual authority, specifically of Holy Scripture, is of central concern.

By means of "Speech Act Theory" and its emphasis on the author as "communicative agent," Vanhoozer wants to "resurrect" the author, especially the Author, and present meaning as "communicative action" (discourse). A number of prominent philosophers and literary critics have had influence on Vanhoozer's thought about the "covenantal" nature (and rehabilitation) of human discourse generally and of Holy Scripture in particular, e.g., George Steiner, Paul Ricoeur, Jürgen Habermas, Ludwig Wittgenstein, William Alston, J. L. Austin, Nicholas Wolterstorff, and John Searle. Their insights into the nature of human language/discourse are variously integrated into a comprehensive theory of literary meaning as "communicative action." (Of necessity we will focus on "Speech Act Theory.") In this way, Vanhoozer can bring to light his primary thesis that God's communicative action, which is the core concept for thinking about the God-world relation in biblical terms, is essentially a matter of "divine illocutions."

Like the later Wittgenstein, J. L. Austin believed that the analytical and skeptical philosophies of language were too focused on words rather than sentences. Ordinary language philosophy analyzes what persons say, and especially *do*, by their discourse, when circumstances and situations are as important as the statements themselves.[75] For Austin language is like a toolbox and his main point is that our saying is also a *doing*, a performative act (e.g., "I promise"). It is not that such words represent, much less picture, some act. Rather the utterance itself, properly performed, *is* the performance of the act. Further, our verbal "doing" has within itself three distinct kinds of linguistic acts. Briefly stated these are: (1) the locutionary act: uttering/expressing words; (2) the illocutionary act: *what we do in saying* something (e.g., commanding); (3) the perlocutionary act: what we effect by our saying something (e.g., persuading). Locution has to do with a sign system (*langue*), illocutions and perlocutions with sentences, language in action (*parole*).[76] But it is especially recognition of the illocutionary act that enables Austin to distinguish between the content (e.g., sense and reference) and its force (what our sentence *does*). Vanhoozer believes recognition of illocutionary acts is all-important for it requires that we give attention to the speaker's/author's role as intentional communicative agent as a *doer*. Discourse cannot be dissociated from the speaker/writer. It is precisely illocution, *what is done* in saying/writing something, that has been overlooked in much modern and postmodern literary criticism, and theologically in the modern and postmodern dualistic disjunction between the historical text of Scripture and an ahistorical, content-less "Word of God." As William Alston has said, "If this is the line along which meaning should be analyzed, then the concept of an illocutionary act is the most fundamental concept in semantics and, hence, in the philosophy of language."[77]

Vanhoozer likens John Searle to Melanchthon and Austin to Luther in the development of "speech act philosophy," i.e., Searle was a systematizer.[78] Both Searle and Austin agree that the sentence/speech act is the basic unit of meaning. We move from noises in the air or marks on paper to meaning only by assuming that these were produced by beings using language to relate to others. Using language requires observing socially agreed-upon rules. Hence, a theory of language is part of a theory of action. In contrast to Wittgenstein, who believed there were countless ways of using language, Searle presents a typology of five speech acts, five things we *do* with language: we tell people how things are, we try to get them to do things, we commit ourselves to doing things, we express our feelings/attitudes, and we bring about changes. Often more than one act is done in the same utterance.[79]

Like Nicholas Wolterstorff, Vanhoozer develops the remarkable parallels and the constructive fruitfulness that lie in the relation between "Speech Act Theory" and the Christian biblico-theological portrayal of God's gracious action in his self-revelation, especially in/as Scripture.

> The notion of a divine speech act addresses both the problem of the nature of God's activity and the problem of the nature of biblical language. Specifically, it explains how God is involved with the production of Scripture and so overcomes the ruinous dichotomy between historical-actualist and verbal-conceptualist models of revelation, that is the dualism between God saying and God doing. Scripture is neither simply recital of the acts of God nor merely a book of inert propositions. Scripture is rather composed of divine-human speech acts that, through what they say, accomplish several authoritative, cognitive, spiritual and social functions.[80]

As a result, Vanhoozer carefully develops such interrelated themes as "communication as inherently covenantal and missional," "God as communicative Agent," "a Trinitarian theology of holy Scripture," "the triune God in communicative action as paradigm for a Christian view of communication," and, as particularly significant to our purpose here, "Scripture as God's illocutionary Action." Communicative action is an interpersonal situation. Thus speech action, whether oral or written, is not only locutionary, illocutionary and perlocutionary but also interlocutionary. Both agent and receiver are "communicants" with rights and obligations—not in the Enlightenment individualistic sense—but, as in Scripture, in the context of covenants with others and "the other." These covenantal obligations assume a network of relationality—"our word is our bond." While Anthony Thiselton gives covenantal emphasis to the speech act of "promising," Vanhoozer, acknowledging the prominence of God's promise in scriptural communication, understands that *all* communicative action is inherently covenantal.[81] Therefore, within the broader covenant of discourse, speaker and hearer, writer and reader are, theologically speaking, called to be faithful communicants, as at the Lord's Table.

Vanhoozer, then, regards language as a divinely given human endowment which serves as a critical medium for "relating with God, oneself, others and the world."[82] Communicative action ultimately rests in the fact that God is a communicative agent. Scripture is a "rainbow of divine communicative acts" and it repeatedly portrays God as a speech agent, e.g., one whose word comes to Israel in the Law and Prophets, whose Word came to the world in the person of Jesus Christ and in his gospel. Unlike human words, God is a powerful communicative agent, for with his Word he sends his Spirit to accomplish the purposes for which it was sent (cf. Isa. 55:11—a promise that is formative for Vanhoozer's thinking about revelation and particularly Scripture as God's revelatory communicative act). Hence God not only communicates information about himself, but he commands, he promises, etc. What is more, God communicates Himself and so, ultimately, salvation, a share in the divine life itself.[83]

> God as communicative agent clarifies the role and enriches the authority of Scripture for theology. . . . I submit that the best way to view God and Scripture together is to acknowledge God as a communicative agent and Scripture as his communicative action. . . . For if the Bible is a species of divine communicative action, it follows that in using Scripture we are not dealing merely with information about God; we are rather dealing with God himself—with God in communicative action.[84]

By thus observing Vanhoozer's model of God as communicative agent and Scripture as divine speech act, one can readily see the lineaments of his "Trinitarian theology of holy Scripture." From the fact that the Bible *is* the "Word" of God because it is the *result* of God's self-communicative action, Vanhoozer develops his formulation of "God's Mighty Speech Acts" by showing *how* God's being in speech act is trinitarian. Barth came to the doctrine of the Trinity by analyzing God's self-revelation as revealer – revelation – revealedness. Similarly, Vanhoozer, via "Speech Act Theory," unpacks the notion of verbal revelation. Scripture, as a species of divine communication has three aspects. The Father's activity is "locution," God the Father is the utterer, begetter and upholder of words. The words are the authorized words of the Father/Author. As in Heb. 1:1-2, the Father is the agent who in past times spoke by the prophets but who now speaks in the Son. The Father's locution results from his involvement in the lives of the human authors of Scripture working through human intelligence and imagination "to produce a literary account that renders him a mighty speech agent."[85]

The Logos-Son corresponds to the speaker's act of *illocution*, i.e., to what a speaker/writer *does* in saying/writing something. The illocution has content, reference and predication with specific intention (force) that shows how the communicative act/proposition should be understood. The illocutionary force makes a speech act "count as," e.g., command, promise. Which illocutionary act is performed is the determination of the speaker/writer. Hence the meaning is objective.[86] The Holy Spirit corresponds to the third element of a speech act, perlocution. Perlocution is the *effect* of an illocutionary act on the actions or beliefs of the receiver/hearer/reader. For example, by arguing (illocution) one might persuade (perlocution) another. Vanhoozer finds here not only much correspondence, but much benefit as, in terms of perlocutions, it helps us to "relate the Spirit's relation to the Word." The Spirit illumines the reader and so enables the reader to grasp the illocutionary intent, what the Scriptures may be doing. Further, the Spirit convicts the reader that the illocutionary point of the text calls for appropriate response (e.g., John 20:31). The Spirit does not alter the semantics of the biblical text. Locution and illocution in Scripture remain unchanged. The Spirit's perlocutionary agency consists in "bringing the illocutionary point (intention) home to the reader" thereby accomplishing the corresponding perlocutionary effect, e.g., repentance. By the Spirit's action the biblical statements "deliver" or "convey" illocutionary force for redemptive liberation.[87] In this way, Vanhoozer can maintain Barth's insistence that the Spirit remain "Lord of the hearing," properly understood, while correcting Barth's overemphasis on divine freedom in relation to the biblical text, freedom that jeopardizes God's covenant faithfulness. Throughout his argument he has consciously "deepened" speech act theory and philosophy via Christian theology, e.g., covenant, promise, trinity. The results are most fruitful. So here, Vanhoozer, like the Fathers, points out that "sending"/mission is at the heart of Christian thinking about the triune God. Again, Isaiah 55:11, so formative upon Vanhoozer's use of speech act philosophy, models intentional Christian missional communication in locution, illocution and perlocution: God sends his Word to nourish life on earth—"So shall my word that goes forth from my mouth not return to me empty, but it shall accomplish that which I purpose and prosper in the thing for which I sent it."[88]

Vanhoozer's central emphasis in unpacking and theologically deepening speech act philosophy is to thereby display, as Scripture so often does, God as communicative agent (God's speech acts), and particularly to answer the question "how God *does* things *with* biblical *words*." In terms of speech act philosophy, he says, the

> application to theology should be obvious inasmuch as *sacra doctrina* is tied up with *sacra pagina*. Theologians must do justice to the diverse uses of language—that is, to the different kinds of "speech acts"—in the Bible. But this is not all. One must also construe the model of God's presence vis-à-vis the Bible. I submit that God is present in Scripture precisely as a communicative agent, its ultimate author. The agency behind the variety of communicative acts in the Bible then, must be ascribed not only to its human authors, but ultimately to God. Scripture contains a wide repertoire of what *God does with human words*.[89]

Vanhoozer gives clarity and depth to God's divine verbal communication *as text* by setting it, as Scripture itself does, in and of the economy of the triune Godhead. Historically "the Scripture Principle" has identified Scripture with the Word of God.[90] But especially since the Enlightenment, as a result of Newtonian and Kantian dualisms and resultant historical critical methods, this identification has increasingly eroded; many would say it is an outmoded view from the past. Yet Vanhoozer explains how the demise of the Scripture Principle is rooted finally in one's doctrine of God and God's providential relation to the world, i.e., God's involvement in the words of Scripture and hence the manner of God's activity in the world.[91] By reflection upon God as communicative agent, God in his self-disclosure, in light of God's lordly self-giving to be known as he is, from the Father (locution), through the Son/Word (illocution) and in the effective power of the Holy Spirit (perlocution), Vanhoozer reestablishes and reaffirms the "identity thesis" (Scripture is the written Word of God), the "royal metaphor" (God's lordly relation to the world and history), and overcomes the false personal-propositional dichotomy in debates about what revelation can and cannot be.[92]

Having earlier observed Vanhoozer's "Trinitarian theology of holy Scripture," we can now follow after his even greater specificity at this point. As with his Word-Son, God is portrayed in Scripture as *doing things with words*—warning, commanding, promising, informing—and, like Wolterstorff, et al., Vanhoozer asserts that there is no philosophical or theological reason not to take these Scriptural depictions of the speaking God seriously. Only false gods are dumb. The Bible, rather, is God's illocutionary text act. Hence Scripture is "best viewed as a set of divine-human communicative actions that do many different things." Scripture is God's "work," his "text act," and "what God *does* with human language reveals God's *identity* . . . as the One who keeps his words."[93] When God "does things with words" he does not contravene the intentions of the human authors; Scripture is God's illocutionary act as he "supervenes" on the communicative intentions of the human authors.[94] In simultaneous majesty and humility, God has accommodated himself to use human media, human language, in his mighty speech acts. But for what purpose? Vanhoozer suggests "embodiment." Jesus Christ is the singular, unique, definitive embodiment of God's Word; he is then the divine foundation and fulfillment of the covenant. The church is the secondary derivative embodiment, the human response to the covenant of grace. "The written Word, as a diverse set of divine speech acts, seeks, in the power of the Spirit, to be embodied in the life of the people of God."[95] Therefore, with modifications reflected in speech act philosophy, Vanhoozer reaffirms the "received view of Scripture," "the identity thesis," "the Scripture Principle," and so with Warfield he affirms that

> a doctrine of Scripture is therefore right to conceive of the Bible as God's mighty (illocutionary) speech acts; not merely the record of the redemptive acts by which God is saving the world, but *as itself one of these redemptive acts*, having its own part to play in the great work of establishing and building up the Kingdom of God.[96]

Hence, Kevin Vanhoozer delivers what Telford Work only promises but fails to produce, i.e., a truly trinitarian doctrine of Holy Scripture that faithfully demonstrates the covenant God, the God who acts and speaks content-fully, while answering and bringing healing to the modern and postmodern disjunctive thinking that has created the "crisis," the loss of the Word of God.

Endnotes

[1] Kevin Vanhoozer, *First Theology: God, Scripture and Hermeneutics* (Downers Grove, Ill.: InterVarsity, 2002) 128, n. 4.

[2] Ibid., 29

[3] David Kelsey, *Proving Doctrine: Uses of Scripture in Modern Theology* (Harrisburg: Trinity, 1999) 161–74. The earlier edition was published in 1974 by Fortress Press with the title *The Uses of Scripture in Recent Theology.*

[4] John D. Morrison, "Spinoza, Semler and Gabler: headwaters of the Modern Disjunction of Holy Scripture from the Word of God," *Trinity Journal,* forthcoming.

[5] See Rene Descartes, *Principles of Philosophy,* I, 7, 10; *Meditations,* 2; *Discourse on Method,* 4. See also the trenchant criticism by Ralph McInerny, *Characters in Search of Their Author* (Notre Dame: Notre Dame University Press, 2002). These were the Gifford Lectures for 2001.

[6] See Albert Einstein's discussion and criticism of Isaac Newton's problematic, mechanistic and dualistic view of the universe and its effects on Western thinking in his Ideas and Opinions (London: Souvenir, 1973), cf. especially his chapters on "Geometry and Experience," 232 ff., and "Physics and Reality," 290–323. Cf. also the further analysis and criticism of the effects of Newton and hence Kant, upon the epistemology and theology / Christology of the West by T. F. Torrance in *Space, Time, and Incarnation* (Oxford: Oxford University Press, 1969) and *Space, Time and Resurrection* (Grand Rapids: Eerdmans, 1971). Many of Torrance's constructive works on theology endeavor to work against the damaging dualisms of Newton and Kant.

[7] Immanuel Kant, *The Critique of Pure Reason,* trans. Norman Kemp Smith (New York: Macmillan, 1929, 2003) 27–29, 74, 87, 149. Cf. also 89–90, 117, 531, 559–60, 565ff.

[8] Albert Einstein, *Ideas and Opinions,* 232ff., 290–323.

[9] T. F. Torrance, *Space, Time and Incarnation* (Oxford: Oxford University Press, 1969) 37–51. Cf. also T. F. Torrance, *The Ground and Grammar of Theology* (Charlottesville: University Press of Virginia, 1980), chapter six.

[10] Immanuel Kant, *The Critique of Pure Reason,* 22, 27–29.

[11] Ibid., 22.

[12] Ibid., 29.

[13] Martin Buber, *The Eclipse of God* (New York: Harper, 1952, 1957) e.g., 82. Cf. George Steiner's similar point: "God the father of meaning, in His authorial guise, is gone from the game." *Real Presences* (Chicago: University of Chicago Press, 1989) 127.

[14] Klaus Bockmühl, *The Unreal God of Modern Theology: Bultmann, Barth, and the Theology of Atheism* (*A Call to Recovering the Truth of God's Reality*), trans. Geoffrey W. Bromiley (Colorado Springs: Helmers and Howard, 1988) 9–10.

[15] In Protestantism, e.g., Schleiermacher, Ritschl, Harnack, Kaehler, Herrmann, Brunner, as well as those analyzed in this chapter. In Roman Catholicism, e.g., Blondel, Rahner, Küng, Congar, Dulles. Exceptions *may likely* be found in Barth and Balthazar.

[16] Friedrich D. E. Schleiermacher, *The Christian Faith*, trans. H. R. Mackintosh and James S. Stewart (Edinburgh: T. and T. Clark, 1928, 1960) 12.

[17] Ibid., p. 10. Note how he expresses this point about Christian doctrines when he says that they are "the result of the contemplation of feeling . . . The conceptions that underlie these propositions are nothing but general expressions for definite feeling . . . . They are not necessary for religion itself, scarcely even for communicating religion . . . but when feeling is made the subject of reflection and comparison they are absolutely unavoidable." Ibid., 87–88.

[18] Vanhoozer, *First Theology*, 97–98.

[19] Schleiermacher, *The Christian Faith*, 70–76 (69).

[20] Ibid., 11.

[21] Ibid., 91.

[22] Donald McKim, *What Christians Believe About the Bible* (Nashville: Thomas Nelson, 1985) 91ff. and George Lindbeck, *The Nature of Doctrine* (Philadelphia: Westminster, 1984) 16–17, 61, 78–79, 91–93.

[23] Schleiermacher, *The Christian Faith*, 265. Note Schleiermacher's claims and implications of the perfect God-consciousness of Jesus, but as fully and wholly human, 385–93.

[24] Ibid., 594. Cf. section 129.

[25] Norman J. Young, *History and Existential Theology* (Philadelphia: Westminster, 1969) 39.

[26] Rudolf Bultmann, *Jesus Christ and Mythology* (New York: Scribner, 1958) 71.

[27] Ibid., 79. Cf. ibid., 49.

[28] Ibid., 61.

[29] Rudolf Bultmann, "New Testament and Mythology" in *Kerygma and Myth*, ed. Hans Werner Bartsch (New York: Harper, 1953) 1–8. Cf. also Rudolf Bultmann, *Jesus Christ and Mythology*, 11–32.

[30] Bultmann, *Jesus Christ and Mythology*, 71

[31] Ibid., 84.

[32] Bultmann, "New Testament and Mythology," 1–2, 10–11; and Bultmann, *Jesus Christ and Mythology*, especially chs. 2–3, pp. 15–16, 51–55, 61.

[33] Ibid., 22–33.

[34] See Rudolf Bultmann, "How Does God Speak Through the Bible," in *Existence and Faith*, ed. Schubert Ogden (New York: Meridian, 1960) 169 where he says: "God's word is not a general truth that can be stored in the treasure-house of human spiritual life. It remains his sovereign word, which we shall never master and which can be believed in only as an ever-living miracle, spoken by God and constantly renewed . . . Belief in this word is the surrender of one's whole existence to it; readiness to hear it is readiness to submit one's whole life to its judgment and its grace. . . .The test of whether we have heard it aright is whether we are prepared always to hear it anew, to ask for it in every decision in life."

[35] David Kelsey, *Proving Doctrine: The Uses of Scripture*, 74–83, especially 80–83. See Bultmann *Jesus Christ and Mythology*, 71. The following statement by Bultmann helps clarify his position on Scripture within his larger program: "Is it enough to say that faith grows out of the encounter with the Holy Scriptures as the Word of God, that faith is nothing but simple hearing? The answer is yes. But this answer is valid only if the Scriptures are understood neither as a manual of doctrine (i.e., no truth content from God) nor as a record of witnesses to a faith which I interpret by sympathy and empathy. On the contrary, to hear the Scriptures as the Word of God means to hear them as a word which is address to me, as *kerygma*. . . . it is an event which happens here and now." Ibid., 71.

[36] Paul Tillich, *On the Boundary: An Autobiographical Sketch* (New York: Scribner, 1966) 13ff. Note that the list of "poles" between which Tillich lived are listed as more than twelve, and these form the argument of the entire book.

[37] Cf. Paul Tillich's *Theology of Culture* and *Christianity and the Encounter with World Religions* are two of many examples among his works.

[38] Paul Tillich, *Ultimate Concern: Paul Tillich in Dialogue*, ed. D. Mackenzie Brown (SCM, 1965) 88–89.

[39] Paul Tillich, *Systematic Theology* (Chicago: University of Chicago Press, 1951) 1:12–14.

[40] Ibid., 23, 64–66.

[41] Ibid.

[42] Ibid., 108–26.

[43] Ibid., 80, 94

[44] Ibid., 94.

[45] Ibid., 124.

[46] Paul Tillich, *Systematic Theology*, 2:29–44, 120.

[47] Ibid., 97–99, 113–17, 118–24, 126, 130–36, 145–46.

[48] Tillich, *Systematic Theology*, 1:118–19, 157–59.

[49] Cf. The criticisms of Tillich's understanding of revelation, of Holy Scripture, and the relation of such to revelatory symbols in Leonard Wheat, *Paul Tillich's Dialectical Humanism*; Adrian Thatcher, *The Ontology of Paul Tillich*; David Kelsey, *The Fabric of Tillich's Theology*; George Tavard, *Paul Tillich and the Christian Message*, Kenneth Hamilton, *The System and the Gospel*.

[50] Tillich, *Systematic Theology*, 2:115.

[51] Ibid., 88–89, 95–96, 110–11, 116, 138. David Kelsey's vivid description of Tillich's method helps to clarify the point. "It is as though Tillich construed the New Testament material as a kind of verbal equivalent of a very complex Byzantine mosaic. The mosaic might consist of a number of separate, highly stylized—indeed, expressionist—images . . . set in a formal pattern such that together they constitute one composite icon. The pattern among the component images might be fully as important as the content of any one, so far as the force of the whole, taken as a single work is concerned. So too with the biblical picture of Jesus as the Christ taken as a single religious symbol."

[52] See John B. Cobb, *A Christian Natural Theology: Theology Based on the Thought of Alfred North Whitehead* (Philadelphia: Westminster, 1965), and John B. Cobb and David Griffin, *Process Theology: An Introduction* (Philadelphia: Westminster, 1978) 13ff.

[53] Ibid.

[54] Cobb and Griffin, *Process Theology*, 95ff. Cf. David Griffin, *A Process Christology* (Philadelphia: Westminster, 1973) and W. Norman Pittenger, *The Word Incarnate: A Study of the Doctrine of the Person of Christ*, Library of Constructive Theology (New York: Harper, 1959).

[55] Ibid., 159.

[56] Cf. e.g., G. Ernest Wright, *God Who Acts*, Oscar Cullman, *Christology of the New Testament*, et al.

[57] Wolfhart Pannenberg discusses this at length in his *Systematic Theology*, trans. Geoffrey Bromiley (Grand Rapids: Eerdmans, 1991) 1:119–88.

[58] Avery Dulles, *Models of Revelation* (New York: Doubleday, 1985), see footnote twenty-four, p. 59, and Wolfhart Pannenberg, *Jesus: God and Man* (Philadelphia: Westminster, 1968) 132ff. Jürgen Moltmann, *Theology of Hope* (London: SCM, 1967) 84. Moltmann's use of Hegelian teleology, hope, etc., directs him to emphasize "revelation as promise" rather than history as a whole, though that element is significant for him, too. This would seem to be potentially more verbal, content-ful. But, again, Moltmann denies this. Like Pannenberg, Moltmann claims that a conception of revelation that emphasizes disclosure of divine truth and purpose in human terms is not biblical and more akin to pagan epiphanies. Yet he affirms that revelation, while neither direct nor as expressable divine truth, is manifest where and as God reveals his faithfulness in the world, which is radically open to transformation by the God of promise.

[59] Wolfhart Pannenberg, *Revelation as History* (New York: MacMillan, 1968) 123–58.

[60] Ibid.

[61] Pannenberg, *Systematic Theology*, 1:198–257, cf. especially 201, 206, 230ff., 234–44.

[62] This is declared repeatedly, and often at length, in all of Thomas J. J. Altizer's works, early and late, *The Gospel of Christian Atheism*, *History as Apocalypse*, *Descent into Hell*, *The Self–Embodiment of God*. E.g. *Radical Theology and the Death of God* (Indianapolis: Bobbs-Merrill, 1966), especially Altizer's own chapter therein entitled "Word and History."

[63] For Altizer the God of classical Christian theism (the God who "died" at the cross) and the historical Christian view of revelation, incarnation and of Holy Scripture are of "a piece," aspects of one whole that must be overcome in the Nietzschian declaration of the "death of God."

[64] Telford Work, *Living and Active: Scripture in the Economy of Salvation* (Grand Rapids: Eerdmans, 2002) 2.

[65] Ibid.

[66] Ibid., 106–10ff. See Work's larger contextual discussion, 106–122.

[67] Work asserts numerous forms of this type of claim through his text, and, indeed, the relation between Trinity and trinitarian effecting of human salvation is central to Work's larger point. But it does not reflect a classical view of revelation and inspiration, despite his use of J. I. Packer, 24–25. Cf. ibid., 35–36.

[68] Ibid., 34ff.

[69] Ibid.

[70] Ibid., 108–9. With (and yet distinguished from) iconology, note Work's analogy of the inspiration of Scripture with Mary mother of Jesus: "Attending to Mariology saves bibliology from a host of errors. It respects the role of prophets and apostles as *logotokoi*, "Word bearers," whose human bodies introduce God's eternal Word into the world in human language. By highlighting this real unity of divine Word and human words in the prophets Spirit—conceived speech—acts, it explains how they can truly be prophets and apostles. Mariology's emphasis on God's prior initiative highlights God's sovereign election and sanctification of the speaker as well as the speech, accounting for the privilege of those who speak on God's behalf. The Bible is only God's true story if God is its ultimate author." Yet for all of this apparent affirmation of Scripture as written (written speech–acts) Word of God. Work finally denies this in anything akin to the position of historical orthodoxy. He even rejects any notion of verbal or "oracular" accounts of inspiration. Ibid., 114–15.

[71] Ibid., 110.

[72] Jacques Derrida, *Of Grammatology* (Baltimore: Johns Hopkins University Press, 1976) 158, cited in Kevin Vanhoozer, *First Theology: God, Scripture and Hermeneutics* (Downers Grove, Ill.: InterVarsity, 2002), 20.

[73] Vanhoozer, *First Theology*, 20, and as more fully developed in Kevin Vanhoozer, *Is There a Meaning in this Text? The Bible, the Reader and the Morality of Literary Knowledge* (Grand Rapids: Zondervan, 1998) 19–25

[74] Vanhoozer, *Is There a Meaning in this Text?* 22, 27–28, 53–54.

[75] Ibid., 43–148. Vanhoozer calls this the "death of God put to writing."

[76] Ibid., 209.

[77] J. L. Austin, *How to Do Things with Words*, (2nd ed., Cambridge: Harvard University Press, 1975) chapters 8,9,10, in Vanhoozer, *Is There A Meaning in This Text?* 209. Cf. William Alston, *The Philosophy of Language* (Englewood Cliffs, N.J.: Prentice Hall, 1964).

[78] Kevin Vanhoozer, "The Semantics of Biblical Literature," in *Hermeneutics, Authority and Canon*, ed. by D. A. Carson and John D. Woodbridge (Grand Rapids: Academie, 1986) 85–92.

[79] John Searle, *Expression and Meaning: Studies in the Theory of Speech-Acts* (Cambridge: Cambridge University Press, 1979) 29; cf. J. L. Austin, *How to Do Things With Words*, 151–64, in Vanhoozer, *Is There a Meaning in this Text*, 209.

[80] Vanhoozer, *First Theology*, 131.

[81] Ibid., 174–75. Cf. Anthony Thiselton, ed., *The Promise of Hermeneutics*, (Grand Rapids: Eerdmans, 1999) 217, and Austin, *How To Do Things*, 10.

[82] Ibid., 167.

[83] Ibid., 34–35.

[84] Ibid., 35, and Vanhoozer, *Is There a Meaning*, 91–92, 117, 148–54.

[85] Ibid., 154, 227.

[86] Ibid., 154–55.

[87] Ibid., 155.

[88] Ibid., 168ff., 172ff.

[89] Ibid., 34-5.

[90] Ibid., p. 127. For Vanhoozer the following statement by John Calvin, *Commentaries: Hebrews* trans. and ed. Joseph Haroutunian (Philadelphia: Westminster, 1958) 83, is reflective of the historical orthodox Christian understanding that Scripture is to be identified with the Word of God: "We have to do with the Word which came forth from God's mouth and was given to us. . . .God's will is to speak to us by the mouths of the apostles and prophets. . . .Their mouths are to us as the mouth of the only true God." Ibid., 127–28.

[91] Ibid., 128–29.

[92] Ibid., 148–49.

[93] Ibid., 153–57.

[94] See Vanhoozer's discussion of "Supervenience," ibid., 106–8, 115, 292. Cf. Nicholas Wolterstorff on Scripture as written Word of God, *Divine Discourse* (Cambridge: Cambridge University Press, 1996) 194.

[95] Ibid., 158, 188ff., 193ff.

[96] B. B. Warfield, *Inspiration and Authority* (Phillipsburg, N.J.: Presbyterian and Reformed, 1979) 161, in ibid., 158.

4

Biblical-Critical Methodology and the Text of Scripture as Written Word of God

A Call for Careful Balance

> If, then, the unity could not be brought about by an ascent, then it must be attempted by a descent. . . . In order for unity to be effected, the god must become like this one. He will appear, therefore, as the equal of the lowliest of persons . . . in the form of a servant. But this form of a servant is not something put on . . . but it is his true form . . . Look, there he stands—the god. Where? There. Can you not see him? He is the god, and yet he has no place where he can lay his head. . . . Thus does the god stand upon the earth like unto the lowliest through his omnipotent love . . . bearing the possibility of the offense of the human race when out of love one became our Savior. . . . Look, behold the man!
>
> —Søren Kierkegaard[1]

First then, whatever these men [Bultmann, et al.] may be as critics, I distrust them as critics. They seem to me to back literary judgment,

to be imperceptive about the very quality of the texts they are reading
. . . . If he tells me that something in a gospel is legend or romance, I
want to know how many legends and romances he has read, how well
his palate is trained in detecting them by the flavour; not how many
years he has spent on that gospel. . . . I find in these [biblical critics] a
constant use of the principle that the miraculous does not occur. . . .
This is very sensible if we start by knowing that inspired prediction can
never occur. . . . [T]he canon "If miraculous, unhistorical" is one they
bring to their study of the texts, not one they have learned from it . . .
[thus] they speak simply as men; men obviously influenced by, and
perhaps insufficiently critical of the spirit of the age they grew up in. . . .
These men ask me to believe they can read in between the lines of the
old (biblical) texts; the evidence is their obvious inability to read the
lines themselves. They claim to see fern seed and can't see an elephant
ten yards away in broad daylight.

—C. S. Lewis[2]

Today many Protestants refuse to identify the Bible as the Word of
God. The Bible may contain the Word of God, or be a vehicle for the
Word, it is said, but can no longer be equated with that Word itself. . . .
It would seem that the only healthy attitude for conservatives is to
welcome (biblical) criticism and be willing to join in it. The problem is
to define the nature of (verbal) inspiration in the light of the (literary,
human) phenomena contained therein.

—Everett F. Harrison[3]

Kierkegaard's point is that our minds are scandalized not by notions of the
"divine" but by God's particularity, the historical facticity of God's acts, the
that-ness and there-ness of God's activity in history. We are scandalized by
what Kierkegaard refers to as the "Absolute Paradox," "the god in time,"
by the datum that that man walking the dusty roads of Galilee is "the
god" revealed, given as human phenomena. We demand that the "divine"
be diffused, Platonically ahistorical, general. That the divine Word, God
himself, would become flesh, or that, *mutatis mutandus* by the power of
the Spirit, through derivative processes, a particular historical, humanly
written text could be the written Word of God, is regarded as impossible,
improper, wrong by definition. It is the second aspect of this scandal that

78

I wish to pursue here: can Holy Scripture be the written Word of God, given the historicity and humanness of its textuality as explained by biblical and literary criticism. Or are biblical and literary-critical approaches to Scripture inimical to the historical orthodox affirmation that Scripture is the written Word of God? Especially since the late seventeenth century, the human phenomena observable in the text of Scripture have been used to justify the separation of Scripture from "Word of God" (whatever that is understood to be).

Has the modern rise of biblical criticism effected a split (real or perceived) between the text of Holy Scripture and "the Word of God" for modern theology? Much of modern and postmodern theology has answered "Yes." John Baillie's summary is typical of what most mainstream modern and contemporary systematic theology has concluded. He points out that Spinoza's rationalistic severance of Scripture from an ahistorical, contentless "Word of God," as magnified through Immanuel Kant's epistemological dualism, effected a dominant view of Scripture as only human text, especially from Schleiermacher through the Ritschlians. For these revelation is noncognitive, inexpressible and necessarily nontextual.[4] Eventually Baillie's summary carries with it this perceived disjunction of Scripture from "Word of God," as rooted in biblical-critical assumptions about Scripture as simply a human text from engendered human literary processes, into the twentieth century, via Herrmann, Tillich, W. Temple and others, leading to his own conclusion that Scripture "is essentially the story about (i.e., points toward) the acts of God history."[5] Usually this modern tradition concludes and then assumes that biblical-critical methods have proven conclusively that Scripture is only the outcome of pious human literary creativity—pointing toward "God's Word." But it is not an aspect of God's Word. Emil Brunner, too, argued in like manner.

> It is clear why the [orthodox] Church reacted as violently against historical criticism, which undermined the position of the Bible as revelation. . . . So long as the ecclesiastical principle which governed the view of the Scriptures was understood in terms of the orthodox doctrine of verbal inspiration, even the smallest concession to biblical criticism . . . was a catastrophe for the whole fabric of this doctrine. . . . So we perceive that the labors of the historical critics are not . . . hostile to the Christian faith, but are a help for a right understanding of the Word of

God . . . .Historical Criticism certainly destroys a great deal [of Scripture's human elements], but it destroys nothing of the truth of God.[6]

Does this conclusion really follow?

So a "right" understanding of "the Word of God" must clearly distinguish it from the historical, human text of Scripture, which has at last been shown to be wholly human by biblical criticism. Rather "the Word of God" must be understood to transcend such historical, textual instantiation. It refers only to "the whole of divine activity for the salvation of the world . . . the 'acts of God' that reveal God's nature and His will, above all, Him in whom the preceding revelation gains its meaning . . . Jesus Christ. He Himself is *the* revelation. Divine revelation is not a book . . . [it] is God Himself in His self-manifestation in history."[7] Hendrikus Berkhof also takes the typical path arguing that, given the results of the "modern study of the Bible" (historical-critical methodologies) regarding the human origins of Scripture, "Scripture cannot be identified with revelation. It is the human reaction to it. Here we meet revelation indirectly, in the mirror of the human witness."[8] These are representative of much of the Enlightenment and post-Enlightenment shift from the affirmation of Holy Scripture as the written Word of God to revelation as essentially content-less, salvific divine encounter, largely as a result of what is taken to be the "assured" results of biblical criticism. Revelation or "Word of God" is thus redefined and so safeguarded, from the affects of biblical criticism.

That evangelical scholars differ on these historical-critical methodologies was instructively exemplified in successive presidential addresses to the Evangelical Theological Society (1997, 1998). In his address "Beware of Philosophy: A Warning to Biblical Scholars," Norman Geisler expressed his concern that, contra Paul's exhortation to "beware of philosophy" (Col. 2:8), many evangelical biblical scholars are naively practicing various biblical-critical methodologies as though they were neutral tools, not recognizing the philosophical assumptions that lie at the base of each. Geisler had often spoken of concern at the readiness among evangelicals to partake of Kittel's *Theological Dictionary of the New Testament* despite its naturalistic underpinnings.

Most of the address describes prominent philosophies and how they exert influence upon the assumptions and approaches of "negative" biblical-critical methods, and so their assessment of the nature of Holy Scripture. The philosophies Geisler examines are numerous, but three are prominent: naturalism, agnosticism and evolutionism. "Naturalism" is foundational to Geisler's larger argument, as directed toward negative "historical criticism." Naturalism is the "philosophy that denies that there are supernatural interventions in the world."[9] This "is at the root of modern negative biblical criticism." As was shown in chapters two and three, Geisler correctly asserts that this connection began, within the larger context of Newtonian scientific determinism, with Spinoza's *Theologico-Political Treatise* (1670). Therein Spinoza explained that nothing occurs in nature contrary to the universal laws—all must follow from these. Hence miracles are absurd. All events reported in Scripture necessarily occurred according to natural laws. By thus approaching Scripture via his naturalistic rationalism, Spinoza consistently concluded that the prophets did not speak and write from supernatural revelation, and the discourse used by the apostles in the New Testament shows clearly that they were not written by revelation but only "by the natural powers and judgment of the authors."[10] Spinoza's naturalism resulted in the first modern systematic, negative criticism of Scripture. His motivation for writing was largely personal and political. Yet, as Geisler notes, the *Treatise* had rapid, far-reaching effects upon the doctrine of Scripture. Among the many developments of Spinoza's naturalistic approach to Scripture and to the Christian faith was David Hume's own subtle but powerful attack on miracles and any activity of God in historical events.[11]

Geisler then points out how this naturalistic "way of seeing" the Judeo-Christian tradition and the text of Scripture, along with its offspring, Kantian agnosticism and Spencerian mechanistic evolution, has continued to have a very powerful effect on the rise of "negative historical criticism." David Strauss wrote the first "desupernaturalized version of the life of Christ" and, as Geisler puts it, "the rest is history. Or better, the rest is the destruction of—particularly miraculous-history recorded in Scripture."[12] The consequences of negative biblical criticism are well known, including the denial of predictive prophecy, two Isaiahs, the post-dating of Daniel, etc. But, as Geisler points out, these conclusions arose not from "facts," but from philosophical *a prioris* about what can and cannot occur in a naturalistic, deterministic closed continuum.[13]

For comparison, Geisler points out the differences resulting from willingness to give up such philosophical presuppositions, leading back toward historical orthodoxy, e.g., W. F. Albright, and Rudolf Bultmann, a prime exemplar of naturalistic bias, who turned Gospel history into religious mythology while paradoxically emphasizing a call to Heideggerian "authenticity" through the Gospel.[14] But it is especially evangelical exegetes who, like Bultmann, have uncritically accepted the *Zeitgeist* as applied to their approach to Scripture, that concern Geisler. He refers to those who accept the "Four-Source Hypothesis" for the Synoptic Gospels like other form critics; to those whose "criteria for authenticity" allow for "inauthentic" (unhistorical) elements in the Gospels, etc., but who still piously assert biblical authority; to those whose use of source, form, and redaction criticism casts serious doubt on many *logia Jesus*. Geisler's list goes on.[15] This shows, he says, lack of awareness of the presence of damaging philosophical assumptions basic to negative critical methodologies. Without such awareness one easily falls prey to subtle influences of such *Weltanschauungen* on one's view of Scripture.[16]

Moises Silva's address, "Can Two Walk Together Unless They Be Agreed: Evangelical Theology and Biblical Scholarship," takes much of its starting point from the venting of James Barr's *Fundamentalism*, especially Barr's criticisms of evangelical biblical scholarship, and from the late Ned Stonehouse's contribution to evangelical biblical criticism. First, Silva exposes Barr's numerous errors, misrepresentations, and biases leading to *ad hominem* conclusions and characterizations. But, as Silva states, Barr "has several insightful criticisms of evangelical scholarship that we need to take with utter seriousness."[17] In this way, Silva explores the problematic way evangelicals relate to mainstream critical biblical scholarship.

Barr complains that conservative literature often uses a double standard when assessing the validity of critical views and methods. Evangelicals often exploit the fact that critical reconstructions are not certain, while using the same probabilistic element to achieve the most conservative picture. Thus we disallow artificial judgments that cannot be demonstrated without coercive proofs while conservative judgments on the same issues cannot be disproved except by the most coercive proofs. Second, evangelical biblical scholarship tends to adopt the critical point of view only when it supports the evangelical agenda. Some evangelicals will read "liberal" works to look for arguments negating the conclusions of other "liberal" exegetes.

Third, evangelicals who engage directly in critical biblical scholarship often willingly explore text–critical problems, analyze linguistic data, pass historical judgments on the text, etc., but are unwilling to take the next theological step. Avoidance can occur simply by focusing on areas that do not seem to conflict with evangelical convictions. Barr notes that while evangelicals are proud of the fine scholars who defend orthodox ideas, yet these high reputations often result from the extent they are willing to betray orthodox convictions.[18] Barr is suggesting the well-known situation of scholars identifying themselves as evangelicals but abandoning distinctive evangelical principles. Secrecy or attempts to alter those principles are both dishonest. More alarming for Silva (like Geisler) is the number of evangelical scholars blissfully unaware of having adopted approaches/ positions that conflict with their convictions at a basic level.[19]

Silva wants to highlight the "tension" reflected in his subtitle "evangelical theology and biblical scholarship." Can they walk together? Can they agree on the doctrine of Scripture as the written Word of God? Silva's resolution is exemplified in Ned Stonehouse and his thoroughly evangelical biblical-critical approach to Scripture (as standing within the exegetical–theological line of Old Princeton-Westminster scholarship). In the first presidential address to the Evangelical Theological Society, Stonehouse stressed biblical infallibility as indispensable to evangelical progress. The more clearly and consistently evangelicals take their stand upon that position, the more assuredly they shall make genuine advance in biblical and theological studies.[20] But Stonehouse went on to issues that to some would appear at odds with his previous affirmation. He expressed concern about those who too readily reject the two-document theory of Gospel origins, who make Matthean authorship of the Gospel an article of the faith and who conceive of biblical inerrancy in an *a priori* abstract manner. But further Stonehouse addressed the centrality of the hermeneutical question and the useful role of conservative biblical criticism in relation to the doctrine of inspiration.

Was this advocacy of a proper, nonspeculative and conservative use of, e.g., redaction criticism, meant to dilute evangelical distinctives on the nature of Scripture as the truthful Word of God written? Hardly. As Silva says, "I want to argue for an intensification of our theological convictions by insisting on the inseparable tie between those commitments and biblical research."[21] There are complexities and tensions. All hermeneutical methods can be misused. But evangelical scholars must be committed to the integration of the whole theological agenda.

Norman Geisler has rightly expressed the dangers inherent in biblical-critical methods. These are not neutral tools. They are loaded with unexpressed conceptual assumptions that can skew outcomes. Moises Silva has followed the admonition of J. Gresham Machen who said "[we] do not hide ourselves from the real state of affairs in biblical study at the present day, and we make an honorable effort to come to an understanding with the ruling tendency."[22] There are benefits from circumspect usage of biblical-critical methods as they deal variously with historical, literary human processes which went into the writing of Scripture. (In this advocacy of the careful use of elements of biblical criticism Silva joins with many evangelicals: Leon Morris, Carl Henry, Simon Kistemaker, (the late) Kenneth Kantzer, I. Howard Marshall, Grant Osborne, et al.) All of this is neither contradiction nor paradox. But first, historical background and overview are needful for the upcoming major points in the developing argument.

The Rise of Modern Biblical Criticism

Within the context of dominant intellectual dualisms, anthropological, cosmological and epistemological (Descartes, Newton and later Kant among others), modern biblical criticism began in earnest with Spinoza's *Treatise* wherein he separated the text of Scripture from "Word of God" by focusing on various literary details of OT and NT books as evidence of their thorough humanness. Indication of human literary processes disqualifies Scripture from any designation as "Word of God." "Word of God" must be something else. No "Word of God" would be manifested in crude human literary forms.[23] Thus, for basically political reasons, Spinoza, within the emerging Enlightenment, initiated the modern rejection of the historic Judeo-Christian tradition, and the divine authority of the text of Holy Scripture, with the aid of rationalistic historical criticism. Spinoza's purpose was advanced by Roman Catholic scholar Richard Simon (*A Critical History of the Old Testament*, which was condemned by the Church, cf. chapter five) and especially Johann Semler (b. 1725) in his multivolume *Treatise on the Free Investigation of the Canon* (1771–75). Herein, Semler's "theses" advance a clear disjunction between the mere historical text of Scripture and "the Word of God," which cannot by definition be anything historical, but is rather understood to be ahistorical, immutable, eternal, and essentially "platonic" Principles/Truths. The effect of Deism on his thought is obvious.[24] Like Spinoza, much of Semler's motivation for this dualistic disjunction was that by thus emptying Scripture of divine authority he would be free to pursue "scientific" historical criticism of that merely historical human text. After Semler, J. G. Eichhorn and his student Johann Gabler were prominent in the further advancement of biblical-critical approaches to Scripture, as coupled with a dualistic separation from "the Word of God," and so from all abiding divine authority. This led to the so-called "Tübingen School" headed by Ferdinand Christian Baur (1792–1860).

According to W. Ward Gasque's cogent argument, the flowering and dominance of biblical criticism, especially NT criticism about the middle of the nineteenth century, took two directions, each of which became formative from that point to the present: the "Tübingen School" and the "Cambridge School." F. C. Baur, a theologian at Tübingen and not primarily an NT exegete, has been called "the father of historical criticism" and still exercises "an eerie influence" over a certain brand of "radical" biblical criticism, despite many changes since his time.[25] He wrote much that effected the reconstruction of what had been understood to be the nature of the early church, that being the environment of the NT. Armed with contemporary idealist philosophy, especially Hegel's dialectic, and Baur's own rejection of "supernaturalism," Baur claimed that contrary to the impression one receives from the NT documents of essential unity of doctrine among the churches, early Christianity was marked by severe conflict between two different conceptions of Christianity. Working from Paul's correction of Peter in Galatians (and the reference to "parties" in I Cor. 1:12), Baur asserted that conflict between a Petrine (Jewish) party and a Pauline (Gentile) party is crucial to understanding the NT.[26] In this way, Baur reflects his hermeneutical method known as *Tendenzkritik* ("tendency criticism"), i.e., the study of NT documents in terms of special, dialectically opposed theological points of view in the context of primitive Christianity. Baur's many fervent disciples did much to develop, apply, and disseminate his method. But it was especially David Strauss, Adolf Hilgenfeld and Albrecht Ritschl, through Rudolf Bultmann and the post-

Bultmannians, in a dominant theological position, who maintained the radical Tübingen tradition.[27]

By contrast, the "Cambridge school" of biblical criticism found its effective source in Baur's young English contemporary, J. B. Lightfoot. Lightfoot, with B. F. Westcott, and F. J. A. Hort, through Sir William Ramsay, and recently F. F. Bruce and I. Howard Marshall et al., reflects significant differences from the Tübingen school in his critical approach to the text of Scripture: first, the Cambridge school has rarely been antiorthodox theologically; second, it has been grounded in historical (rather than philosophico-theological) research. Contra Baur's naturalistic Hegelianism or Bultmann's naturalistic Heideggerianism, etc., the "Cambridge" line has emphasized philological and especially historical concerns. As A. C. Headlam has said, it brings the study of Christian antiquity back from speculation and fantasy to the sober realities of genuinely critical investigation.[28] Literary criticism is coupled with authentically historical research, historical exegesis rather than speculative reconstructions. There is caution in rejecting any traditional Christian views rather than negatively assuming their falsehood.

Does this mean these traditions are mutually exclusive? Hardly. The differences lie often more in the assumptions brought to the text of Scripture rather than in the use or nonuse of a specific biblical-critical methodology. What then are some of the prominent biblical-critical and literary-critical methodologies, and can they be, in terms of their *basic* procedural elements and goals, properly applied to Scripture as the written Word of God?

Biblical- and Literary-Critical Methodologies and the Doctrine of Scripture as the Word of God Written

Bibical-Critical Approaches

On occasion this writer has heard it said that biblical-critical methods are not properly applicable to Holy Scripture given the claims of Scripture about itself and thus the process, by the Holy Spirit, by which it came into being, e.g., "all Scripture is God-breathed," "no prophecy [of Scripture] was ever made by an act of human will, but men moved by the Holy

Spirit spoke from God" "[the Holy Spirit] will teach you all things, and bring to your remembrance all that I have said to you" and "[the Holy Spirit] will guide you into all the truth . . . and he will disclose to you what is to come."

Assuming all such passages variously apply to the divine-human processes whereby Holy Scripture was produced, do they necessarily contradict or conflict with the basic purposes and methods of the various branches of biblical criticism and the even more directly literary approaches to interpretation? We will examine some of the foundational foci of several of these critical methods, in light of Scriptural claims, to initially assess problems or potential usefulness, while being mindful of the philosophical underpinnings already mentioned. These biblical-critical methods for the study of the text of Scripture were intended to variously recover the history of the text's development.

Source Criticism. Having already mentioned Baur's *Tendenzkritik* we will start with source criticism. J. G. Eichhorn first referred to the help of "higher criticism" (a term with previous history) for examining the structure of a biblical book, including the sources upon which an author drew and the way in which he used or combined them in the historical development of the text (diachronic). Source criticism can be pursued confidently if the sources of a work have survived. The Chronicler used Samuel and Kings as main sources, thus we can make more definite statements about his use of them. To the extent that Mark is in fact a significant source for the other Synoptic Gospels, we can directly study their use of Mark. But often, sources are not extant, thus making source criticism much more speculative and uncertain.[29]

No one has properly doubted the use of sources by biblical writers. References in OT historical narratives to the Book of the Kings of Judah, or Israel, or Jasher, and Luke's reference to his use of sources (Lk 1:1-4) are clear. Concern arises with willingness of some exegetes to speculate and then make definitive statements about nonexistent sources. And what is the motivation behind a desire to "unearth" a hypothetical source behind the authoritative text? Is it not often the post-Enlightenment desire to negate "external" divine authority by the exposure of the human processes of its production? Will direct knowledge of the book of Jasher or of Luke's sources help us to understand those Scripture texts more fully? Possibly, though I doubt it. But does the fact of this or that human process whereby I

Kings or Matthew's Gospel was produced negate the text's divine authority as the written Word of God? No. How could it? Such a claim is a radical *non sequitur*, unless one presupposes that historical human processes are "not fit" to be united as one with God's historical revealing and inspiring acts and activities, which is obviously false. The only *final* concern and authority is the canonical text *as it stands* and not sources which might lie behind it. Anything "behind" the text can only be of real use if it sheds light on the canonical, authoritative text.

Form Criticism. *Formgeschichte* typically developed as a "reaction" to source criticism, though it does not conflict with it. As developed by Herman Gunkel and others, form criticism, like source criticism, is diachronic as it seeks to find the original form and setting of a passage. This approach especially emphasizes the *oral* prehistory of written documents or sources, with concern for classification of the biblical materials in terms of their various "forms" or categories, e.g., narrative, discourse, etc.[30] *Formgeschichte* assumes that the key to the meaning of a biblical passage is found in its original use and not in its final form (which is regarded as distorted). *Formgeschichte* also studies texts in light of other texts which are similar in structure, content and language (e.g., pentateuchal laws and other ancient Near Eastern law codes). Form criticism is strongly sociological in its approach to original forms and settings, and in the OT has shed light on, e.g., the principal types and settings of many psalms.[31] In relation to the NT, form criticism has been applied extensively to the Gospels, especially since Dibelius, Schmidt, and Bultmann. In pursuing form classification of the material of the synoptic evangelists (not necessarily Matthew, Mark, or Luke), form critics divide the material between narratives about Jesus and sayings of Jesus. These pericopes are further subdivided into, e.g., pronouncement stories, healing stories, parables.[32] Thus form critics see the Gospels as pericope collections wherein one seeks two *Sitze im Leben* (life settings) of/for the material: the original life setting or situation of Jesus and that of the early church community which, in light of its needs, included and created stories about Jesus.

But despite apparent usefulness as a tool for locating and classifying pericopes, *Formgeschichte* has often shown itself to be limited and problematic in the hands of negative practitioners like Dibelius and Bultmann and their disciples. Its claims to know the hypothetical life setting in the early church for a pericope and to know (using various "criteria") whether this or that saying of Jesus or event of Jesus' ministry from the Gospels is or is not "authentic" (usually not authentic, cf. Bultmann's *NT Theology*) arise often from arbitrary presuppositions and speculative projections far beyond the capacity of form-critical methodology.[33] Even the NT points out that the early church made a clear distinction between their own views on disputed issues and the teaching of Jesus (e.g. I Cor 7:10ff.). Further, focus on individual pericopes and blocks of material tended to piecemeal the gospels and to lose sight of the gospels as *whole* literary units. And they overlooked the constructive, even theological, role of the evangelists as authors and not just collectors.

But can form criticism have constructive usefulness? Beyond the radical use of form criticism by some in order to assess the authenticity and authority of this or that OT or NT passage, often coupled with highly speculative reconstructions which lack any factual basis (the Tübingen tradition), form-critical desires to go *behind* the canonical text for the purpose of discovering some more original oral form taken to be more authoritative is false and unjustifiable. For example, the entire "Ritschlian" desire to get back to the "real Jesus" behind the NT, as more authoritative and as something to strengthen faith, was shown to be an illusory quest (like Tillich's "god beyond god"). It is also unjustifiable in the face of the canonical text itself and so stands self-condemned. We cannot get to some authoritative event beyond the canonical text, but only in, with, and from it by the Spirit.

Yet does this totally negate the potential value of *Formgeschichte*? No. To the extent it is used with the constraints required by the limitations of the method it can be of real help, e.g., in classifying and clarifying "types" within the various genre, in locating individual pericopes, etc. As T. W. Manson has said,

> If *Form criticism* had stuck to its proper business it would not have made any real stir. We should have taken it as we take the forms of Hebrew poetry or the forms of musical composition. But Form criticism got mixed up with two other things. One was K. L. Schmidt's full-scale attack on the Marcan framework; the other was the doctrine of the *Sitz im Leben*.[34]

Redaction Criticism. *Redaktionsgeschichte*, too, is a response and corrective to flaws, one sidedness and elements of neglect in form criticism.

The sociological orientation of form criticism neglected the active role played by the evangelists in the manner in which they used the received gospel traditions. It became clearer that the Gospel writers were not mere collector-editors (*Sammler*) of the various pericopes, nor were the Gospels simply pericope collections. The Gospels themselves are literary units with special arguments and viewpoints, and they reflect some of the unique emphases, concerns and theology of the Gospel writers. Thus Dibelius was wrong when he claimed, "The composers are only to the smallest extent authors. They are essentially collectors, vehicles of the tradition, editors."[35] Redaction history recognizes the evangelists as true authors *and theologians.* In this way the individual gospel writer was recognized as a third distinct *Sitz im Leben*, alongside the two recognized by form criticism, i.e., the life and ministry of Jesus and the situation of the early church. And again, form criticism fragmented the text in its concern to isolate particular pericopes while largely ignoring, e.g., Matthew's special emphases and theological themes.[36]

The rapid rise of redaction criticism in the 1950s did not mean that earlier exegetical-critical studies had not noted the contribution of the Gospel writers. But it was with Hans Conzelmann's *The Theology of Luke* and W. Marxsen's *Mark the Evangelist* especially that the importance of this aspect of the formation of the Gospel texts became clear for interpretation.[37] While such concern to do justice to the contribution of the authors of the biblical books has been applied elsewhere, e.g., the Chronicler's use of material, it has been especially the NT Gospels that have been the focus of much often fruitful (and often unfruitful) study.

Yet the definition and the proper, *legitimate focus* of redaction criticism can be difficult to specify. The late Norman Perrin, of the University of Chicago, said that redaction criticism's goals are to understand why the items from the tradition were modified and connected as they were, to identify the theological motifs that were at work in composing a finished Gospel, and to elucidate the theological point of view which is expressed in and through the composition.[38] F. F. Bruce succinctly stated that redaction criticism has been particularly fruitful as it analyzes "the way the individual evangelists shaped and presented, in accordance with their distinctive perspectives, the 'tradition' which was delivered to them."[39] Grant Osborne distinguishes two types of redactional analysis. The first, more technical, requires composition analysis of the literary work (e.g.

Gospel) to find and to understand the ways the writer used his sources (received traditions/stories). Here word-for-word comparisons, word statistics, etc., help to clarify what vocabulary was distinctly Marcan or Matthean. There is obvious dependence here on a particular theory of Gospel origins, the role of Q, the assumptions being basically that of Marcan priority and that the collection of *logia Jesus* (Q) was used by Matthew and Luke. The second type of redactional analysis, rooted in the first, compares the Gospels to note differences between them, to identify additions, omissions and expansions in order to uncover the evangelists' major emphases.[40] Robert Stein, while contextually emphasizing the unique theological purposes of each Evangelist (and also the much they have in common), defines *Redaktionsgeschichte* as "the attempt to arrive at the third *Sitz im Leben* . . . [and so] to ascertain the unique theological purpose or purposes, views and emphases that the Evangelists have imposed on the materials available to them."[41]

Stein helpfully clarifies the proper relation of form criticism to the redactional method developed from it. Though there is difference of opinion, Stein appears to be correct in illustrating the relation as two persons walking along a garden path until a "fork" in the path leads along the way of the particular interests of each. Redaction criticism uses form-critical processes to first isolate elements of the text, and so the redaction of the Evangelist. After this, though, redaction concentrates on the Gospel as a whole and therein the unique contributions of the writer to the canonical text. This is done by investigating the Evangelist's "seams" connecting the stories, the insertions (comment or explanation), his summaries, any "modification" of traditional material (for emphasis not falsification), the selection and omission of material found in other canonical accounts, arrangement of pericopes for emphasis, introductory and conclusion material, vocabulary and chosen Christological titles.[42] Most evangelical practioners of redaction criticism point out the limitations of these procedures and that one must recognize the element of speculation from the data. For example, one cannot say with *certainty* why Matthew excluded this miracle story or his *theological* motive for including that one.

Evangelical redaction critics are usually quick to point out the limitations and potential dangers of even properly used redaction criticism—especially in light of unrestrained speculations and largely unverifiable conclusions about Scripture (especially the Gospels) and its meaning by "radical" redaction critics. These enumerate examples where philosophical assumptions and other unexpressed *a prioris* have skewed the results from the start. But even more to the point, there is also a strong inclination among radical redaction critics to speculate from the textual data to assumptions about the very nature of the text, the early Church and the person and work of Christ that, again, have no verifiability from what *is known*. There is, for example, the problematic conviction that, to the extent the four Evangelists reflect unique theological concerns, that the argument of the Gospels is therefore unhistorical, inauthentic. Importantly, redaction critics regularly claim that redaction-critical methodology provides sufficient "criteria" (inherited from form criticism) for assessing negatively the historicity of the Gospel events. Note Perrin's negative assumptions toward the question of the "authenticity" of the Gospels: "[C]learly, we have to ask ourselves the question as to whether this saying should now be attributed to the early Church or to the historical Jesus, and the nature of the synoptic tradition is such that the burden of proof will be upon the claim to authenticity."[43] Gospel events are presumed to be unhistorical. Both Osborne[44] and Donald Carson[45] have shown, I believe, that redaction-critical procedures do not have the capacity to establish or deny the authenticity of any Gospel passage. Carson rightly critiques at length some of the often "ridiculous" criteria used to assess authenticity.[46] It is clear that erroneous historiography arising from the requirement of certainty, naturalistic and historical skepticism, negative Christological presuppositions and the dualistic separation of sources (tradition, pericopes) from redactional emphases have falsely, but inevitably, led to the negative conclusions of many such critics.[47]

Carson rightly calls some evangelical redaction critics up short by pointing out that this literary tool cannot necessarily uncover elements of the Scripture text which are *basic* to redaction critical goals. For example, one cannot move with certainty from a particular traditional form used in the text to a creative *Sitz im Leben* in the early church. It is also clear that even careful evangelical redaction criticism sometimes "sees theology" and doctrinal development in alterations to the sources that could better be explained by other reasons.[48]

Given the problems ensuing when redaction criticism is used beyond its capacity to investigate questions of authenticity, at least two developments in the works of Robert Stein call for some comments. While agreeing with

Osborne contra Perrin that the burden of proof lies with those who would reject the authenticity of the Gospel materials, Stein argues that (at least in principle) nonauthentic sayings attributed to Jesus may well be found in the Gospels (he does not specify), but even so such sayings are authoritative. This is accomplished by splitting the "historical" question from the "theological" one of canonicity, i.e, an authoritative saying of Jesus is one that is canonical and so possesses divine authority as inspired by God.[49] While his defense of this literary situation, via a unique interpretation of John 16:12-15 emphasizing "authoritative interpretation" for the creation of *logia Jesus* may be feasible and the situation of *unhistorical authoritative* events may be (in principle) possible, the bases in a disjunction between history and theology is at minimum very dangerous and almost inevitably harmful.[50]

Yet none can come to Scripture as a blank state. All have and must come with presuppositions and questions. Text and reader do inevitably form "two horizons" in the interpretive relation.[51] The question is one of priority, one not only of final interpretive authority but of divine authority. As Osborne exhorts,

> From our vantage point we ask not whether we must employ presuppositions but rather how we may work with our *a prioris* and ask "which kinds of preunderstanding are valid and which are not." Above all, one must allow the text to dominate, challenge and determine one's presuppositions.[52]

While much redaction-critical study has been applied to Scripture, especially the Gospels, over the last several decades, it has often lacked the self-critical capacity to invalidate illegitimate presuppositions (especially about the God-world relation), to rein in speculative flights of unhistorical reconstruction, or to restrict the application of redactional investigation from issues beyond its ken. For many the "limited goals and aims of redaction criticism were not properly understood."[53] These and other concerns with redaction criticism reflect real dangers to which evangelical scholars must be sensitive and responsive. But if the central intent of redaction criticism is to seek after: (1) the unique emphases and theological views of the writer that are distinctive from his sources; (2) what unique emphases the writer places upon received sources; (3) what theological purpose(s) the writer has; and (4) what *Sitz im Leben* the writer formulates his book from—while *recognizing* that the last two are the most hypothetical—is there anything here that necessarily reflects a view of the origin and nature of Holy Scripture contrary to what Scripture says about itself? Is there anything that negates verbal inspiration or what Jesus, or later Peter, says about the active role of the Spirit in relation to the *active* role of the human writers in the text's historical, literary production, and hence as an aspect of God's self-disclosure, the written Word of God? Nothing that I can find. Those who assert that redaction criticism (or other forms of biblical criticism) ought not be used by evangelicals because of their development by radical critical scholars commit the genetic fallacy.

Within its properly limited scope, are there potential exegetical-theological benefits to be reaped from redaction criticism? Surely so. If we are really concerned with "authorial intent," as manifested in the historical text (we can go no further back than that) then understanding of, e.g., the primary emphases and theological concerns of Luke can enhance proclamation and theology.[54] But there is a sense in which this has always been true in responsible exegesis. Redaction criticism can potentially enlarge our knowledge of Scripture if it can avoid authentic/inauthentic claims, even implicitly, in relation to the text. History *and* theology, theology *and* history together as wholly (though not exhaustively) true in all that it affirms, as instantiated in the biblical text as the written Word of God, has always been and must remain basic to the Judeo-Christian tradition and to evangelical orthodoxy in particular.[55] By way of a note, it would seem that in principle redaction criticism's primary concern for the Scripture *text as it is* makes it, by comparison, even more useful and legitimate than those methods seeking that which is *behind* the text.

Recent Literary-Critical Approaches

While source, form and redaction criticism are literary tools for analyzing the very literary text of Scripture, the last thirty years have seen the rise to prominence of interdisciplinary literary critical approaches to biblical interpretation (i.e., in light of modern and post-modern theories of the nature of literature). Unfortunately, space will not allow more than brief description of this currently powerful influence in biblical studies (cf. the activity and production during the last decade in the "Bible as Literature" Study Group at annual Evangelical Theological Society meetings and in the journal of that society). Directly and indirectly the literary theories of Ferdinand de Saussure, Northrop Frye, J. L. Austin, E. D. Hirsch, Robert Alter and John Searle have influenced this writer in relation to the nature of Scripture and biblical interpretation. In sweeping terms we will attempt to reflect on the bases and primary foci of several prominent literary-critical methods in relation to Scripture, and especially potential benefits and/or dangers in light of the question of Scripture as the written Word of God.

Author-Centered Theories

Traditional Criticism. Traditional criticism has taken much interest in the author. It was thought that the key to interpretation lay in knowing the history and thought life of the writer, thereby finding the author's intentional meaning. Under the influence of Romanticism, it was believed that to know the psychological details of Isaiah, Paul or Milton was to know their mental intention as reflected in their texts. But is it possible to get back "into the head" of authors *behind* what they have written? Authors themselves have shown the difficulty of reconstructing previous intentions by often being their own worst interpreters. Too often traditional critics have so focused on authorial "biographies" that the actual text before them is lost.

E. D. Hirsch has given helpful balance and modification here. In the face of dominant contemporary approaches, which often lose the author and the text in favor of the reader (cf. below), Hirsch rightly asserts that to disregard an author's intention in writing a text means "death" to any established meaning of a text. Authorial intent gives a firm basis amidst otherwise interpretive subjectivity and relativity. But, aware of the problems, Hirsch seeks the author's intent by study of the *text itself* (especially genre) in relation to other texts, and recognizes the role of the reader in interpretation. In so doing, he helpfully distinguishes textual "meaning" from its "significance" to this or that reader.[56] Much of biblical criticism, as we observed earlier, gave primary focus to "authors" one way or another.

Text-Centered Theories

Traditional criticism's one-sided approaches, which studied everything but the literary text, brought needed response (from the 1940s to the present). Literary criticism shifted to the study of the *text* itself (object theory of interpretation).

New Criticism. "New Criticism" dominated literary criticism in the 1940s and 1950s. It emphasizes first that the literary work is self-sufficient. It is an "artifact" on its own. Thus authorial intent has no importance. These critics restrict themselves only to very careful analysis of the literary text. Thus, since meaning lies in the text, careful analysis of the complex internal relationships of the whole text is required, i.e., the emphasis is on close analysis for understanding literary works *holistically* (e.g., a poem). The influence of New Criticism on biblical studies has been varied. The "Sheffield School" in biblical studies has effectively used numerous insights from New Criticism in its exegesis. Some have noted that Brevard Childs' "canonical method," emphasizing the self-sufficiency of the biblical text as understood within a literary tradition (canon), is similar to these principles (though Childs denies the connection). New Criticism, while still having influence, lost dominance in the 1960s.[57]

Structuralism. In the 1960s literary critics began to give special attention to certain deep structures thought to lie behind all human life and thought. Structuralism has had greater influence on biblical studies than New Criticism. Indeed, structuralism's impact on literary analysis *and beyond* has been and continues to be immense (including the fields of linguistics, anthropology, law, philosophy, sociology). Structuralism as a highly varied interdisciplinary movement is a general theory of human culture. With Charles Peirce, the linguist Ferdinand de Saussure is regarded as the father of structuralism. He pointed out the *sign* nature of language. Briefly, he proposed a set of linguistic distinctions that set the stage for modern studies. His famous distinctions between *langue* (a system, set of rules, norms) and *parole* (actual sentences used), between "signifier" (a word or acoustical sound) and "signified" (the arbitrary concept evoked by the signifier) and between "syntagmatic analysis" (analysis of linguistic/literary interrelations) and "paradigmatic analysis" (analysis of isolated literary "parts") have been highly formative on not only linguistics but many fields, notably literary criticism, since the 1960s.[58]

Developing out of linguistics and desiring to be "scientific," early structuralist literary criticism (cf. Roland Barthes, et al.) sought for rigorous statement and an exacting analytical model. This concern lessened over time. But still stucturalist literary criticism sought to maintain its linguistic roots (Saussure on "sign") and to extend these linguistic bases to other "semiotic" systems (thus, the other name "semiotics"). Herein literature is a *second-order* semiotic system constructed from language. Hence, literary texts are capable of structuralist analysis. Emphasis was given to literary competence whereby one learns a literary tradition, its conventions, rules, its deep underlying structures which are found throughout literature as a whole (like the rules of a game for effective participation) and to the notion of literature as a system whereby, through the various literary conventions, *meaning* is communicated *within that* closed system.[59] Thus authors are simply users of previous literary devices and their work is thus a compilation of literary conventions found in previous works. Textual meaning resides in the literary conventions, the rules, which have public meaning, *not* in an author's intention. Structuralist critics then study the integrity of the text's literary conventions to explain the text's *form* and *structure—not* for any referential qualities (e.g. what the text is *about*).[60]

Refinements to the structuralist approach to narrative by A. J. Greimas have had great influence on structuralist studies of Scripture, especially his "actantial mode" as part of his larger analysis. Yet few agree on how best to apply this to texts, and great differences in conclusion result. Daniel Patte's application to "the parable of the Good Samaritan" is complex, but a few elements show something of the nature of structuralist literary criticism of Scripture. Accepting Greimas' three structural levels (deep, intermediate, surface) Patte deals with the intermediate only, which he then divides into semiotic and semantic. The semantic narrative structure of the parable is then divided into six hierarchically distinct elements: (e.g., sequence, actant, utterance, function, etc.). He begins by separating the sequences by analyzing the "disjunctional functions" (e.g. movements, encounters). He thus uncovers eight sequences in the parable. To these are applied his "actantial model," etc., and on and on. Regarding "functional relations," Patte concludes that the sender is unknown, the object is the injured man's "status as subject" (recovery), so the receiver is the injured man, the subject/hero is the Samaritan, the opponents are the robbers, and the helpers are the oil, wine, donkey, money and innkeeper. Thus the narrative is reduced to its basic elements.[61] In this way, real insight can be gained into the elemental "bones" and "organs" comprising a literary text. Yet, again, it is very complex and many structuralists reflect little concern for understanding the meaning of the text in a "classical" sense.

Reader-Centered Theories

Is the role of the reader in relation to meaning one of responsibility or creative "free play"? Here is the problem of the reader of literary texts and the ethics of meaning. In the 1970s, 1980s, and 1990s many literary critics rejected "textual positivism" (text as scientific object of study) and began to emphasize the active, even creative, role of the reader. This "Reader's revolt" stresses the incompleteness of the text until it is (de)constructed by the reader. Herein, among the more radical elements, the names Stanley Fish, Jacques Derrida, and Michael Foucault stand out, along with more moderate and constructive approaches and elements, e.g., Hans-Georg Gadamer and Paul Ricoeur.

General Reader-Response Theories. Anyone working with other people to interpret a text knows the diversity that can ensue. If, according to contemporary views, meaning is not inherent in the author nor in the objective text, how can one evaluate diverse interpretations? Can one or ought one to attempt it? One reader-response approach is to say all interpretations are equally valid. Meaning is found in the reader, not the text. The reader creates the meaning of the text. But many reader-response theories are not this radical. Rather meaning arises from the "meeting" of text and reader; the interaction produces the meaning. Readers are not free to do what they will with the text, which is in some sense a constraint on interpretation. Hans-Georg Gadamer and Paul Ricoeur have done much constructive work explaining "how interpretation is *possible*" after the metaphorical shift away from the author and after the epistemological shift away from Newtonian objectivity. Both agree at least in "privileging" the intention or "horizon" of the text as a source of possible meanings from which diverse readers draw varying interpretations. Thus, in Gadamer's terms the "hermeneutical circle" requires the meeting of the horizon of the active interpreter's preunderstanding and the horizon of the text creating interpretative fusion.[63]

Gadamer's "two horizons" have been effectively developed for biblical interpretation and within broadly evangelical concerns by Anthony Thiselton, whose philosophical analyses of and application to particular biblical books and texts has produced much that is useful (e.g. his commentary on 1 Corinthians). Others apply reader-response theories more ideologically and politically. Liberation and feminist theologians consciously approach the biblical text as readers with particular agendas or via modern political philosophy (e.g. Marx).

While a purely objective approach to Scripture is not humanly possible, and all interpreters come with personal and cultural baggage, still these more radical options, to the extent that they do not even attempt to hear the text itself, are problematic. In approaching Holy Scripture one must be ready and open to change in response to a content-ful text over against the self. Yet it is also true that ideological readings of Scripture have brought much clarity to elements too often passed over previously (concern for the poor, the role of women, etc.)

Deconstruction. Some would classify deconstruction as beyond even radical reader-centered theories. We disagree. Though emerging in the 1960s with the literary-philosophical work of Derrida and Foucault, et al., this neo-Heideggerian "new wave from France" came to the forefront in the 1980s and it too has brought *strong* reactions—both ways. Though deconstruction has "killed" both author and text as external (and therefore false and oppressive) authorities, it has gone far in "killing" the reader as well. This was inevitable.[64] Deconstruction seeks to demonstrate the great problems in *any* correspondent literary theory that defines literary meaning as univocal (fixed, correspondent truth) in terms of authorial intent, literary conventions or reader's experiences. Thus Derrida attacks the Western philosophical tradition (since Plato), which subordinates writing to speaking. This means speech has long been regarded as closer to pure thought than writing. Writing, it has been claimed, removes communication further from the "presence" of the author. On the contrary, says Derrida, this understanding reflects a false belief in *presence*, which is finally rooted in what he calls "the transcendental signified" or an absolute foundation outside "the play" of language, which effectively establishes the whole linguistic system (i.e, his antifoundationalism). This anchor is thought to fix particular meaning of spoken and written language.[65]

But writing shows more clearly the "slippage" in all language, the chasm between "sign" and "referent," "signifier" and "signified." This reflects Derrida's extreme language skepticism, which claims to negate meaning in all acts of literary communication (including his own, one assumes). To this end, Derrida's analytical attack on Western philosophy (via particular philosophers) delves into "systems" to discover their basic contradiction, as grounded in their problematic *logocentrism* (belief in an ultimate metaphysics of "presence"). His goal is demonstration that, against all philosophical "truth" claims, the texts of Western philosophy are no different from fiction. But again his point is (starting from Saussure) the *différance* (*differ* plus *defer*), the magnification of distance between signifier and signified, thus negating all literary communication. There is no meaningful "presence" but only "absence" in the infinite "play" of language.[66]

While experimental deconstructive "a-theology" continues to be produced (e.g., Mark Taylor, Charles Winguist, Robert Scharlemann), application to biblical interpretation has been slower to emerge, though some has been done (e.g. John Dominic Crossan). But its negation of literary meaning hardly makes it a natural choice.

Must these literary-critical approaches to the understanding of the textual, literary and historical reality of Holy Scripture assume (or do they show) that Scripture and the literary texts (genres) which comprise it are finally and only of human literary origin? Are these analytical techniques for understanding texts inappropriate for evangelical/Protestant orthodox use in exegesis? Are these "insights" into the nature of written language without benefit for the scholarly Christian analysis of Scripture as the written word of God? If Scripture can be understood in terms of human literary conventions (and it can), does this negate the possibility and actuality of its being the written Word of God? On all points the initial broad answer is No. But this must be explained and nuanced.

Traditional literary criticism's strong author-centered orientation, seeking as much authorial data as possible, often to the near "loss" of the text, is largely problematic. Given the "authorial-authority" connected to the prophetic-apostolic nature of Scripture, "authorial intent" cannot be cast away, but we cannot and will never get "into the head" of Isaiah or

Peter. We can go no further than the textual level. All claims to directly know what lies behind the text are subjective fabrications. That is why E. D. Hirsch's increasingly balanced (concern especially in his second volume) for *textual*-authorial intent with an eye to the role of the reader (significance) is a good corrective. This goes far toward reflecting God's historical self-disclosive processes whereby, through revelation and inspiration, he has revealed himself personally and content-fully, incorporating therein and thereby human beings and human literary processes unto historical, textual manifestation (Holy Scripture).

Among text-oriented literary approaches, New Criticism's emphases on the self-sufficiency of the text as it stands and the need to analyze a work holistically, properly understood and applied, creates no interpretive difficulty for the divine authority of Scripture. Pseudonymity of some OT and NT books is well known; and would one be stopped from interpreting Luke's Gospel if one did not conclude that it was written by Luke? Still, advantages do result from knowing something of the author. But holistic interpretation is more in keeping with the nature of the narrative, poetical, epistolary, apocalyptic, etc., nature of the biblical texts which, for the most part, have unitary argumentation appropriate to the first recipients, who would have first *heard* rather than read the texts. The piecemealing of the text without complementarity and unitariness within the interactive field of communicative relations inevitably means interpretive loss. Structuralism (semiotics) reflects this tension, at least potentially. Its belief in and desire to uncover the deep structures, the conventions of literature generally and in application to specific literary works, has often led to insights regarding both intratextual as well as intertextual relations and meaning, and also to overisolation of textual elements and the loss of the story's wholeness as an outcome of overzealous analysis. But does the fact that Scripture could be clarified, its meaning fruitfully uncovered, by processes that examine the deep structures and functions of this or that passage negate the possibility and the actuality of its being the written Word of God? Of course not. How could it? Only false, rather platonic presuppositions that God could not or would not use such mundane, human literary conventions, structures and signs would make such foolish claims. No. God has usually made himself known in terms of the relatively weak things of this world to confound the wise (the confluency of Scripture).

But what of "reader-centered" schools of literary criticism? Are not the presuppositions, the apparent subjectivism, the radical skepticism about meaning and so much more, necessarily problematic for evangelicals and to any claim that the text of Scripture, as it stands external to and over against the human subject as interpreter, *is* the written Word of God? Maybe. Or better, yes and no. First, any radical reader-response claim that meaning is wholly created by and is exclusive to the reader (or even a reading "community," e.g., Stanley Fish) is not useful here, having nothing external to itself to test conclusions. But such radicality is not that common among practioners of reader-response literary theories. Most give at least a formative, even corrective role (of sorts) to the text and not only to the reader. Gadamer's hermeneutical circle has been fruitfully developed, as noted, by Thiselton in a number of works, and in his hands recognition of "the two horizons" means seeking for what lies in the authoritative text of Scripture as (hopefully) fused to the reader's "horizon." It seems that, following Thiselton's usage, a Gadamerian reader-response approach could be used in a way reflective of and in keeping with the affirmation of Scripture as the written Word of God.

But the "deconstruction" of the French neo-Heideggerians poses grave concerns. First, Derrida's expressed motivation (rooted in the oppression of his Jewish childhood in German-occupied French Algeria) to negate external authority and all external truth claims as oppressive and evil, is itself an evil. His war on all truth as "totalization" (= totalitarianism) can lead only to the outcome he most fears. It is certainly contrary to biblical claims that the God self-revealed above all in Jesus Christ is the Lord, the God of all truth, the King (" the Truth shall make you free")—though *that* must radically relativize all purely human claims (e.g., Hitler). Also Derrida's radical skepticism about any meaning (and authority) that abides in a text would be in opposition to historical orthodox teaching on Scripture as the written Word of God. But! Yes, but, let me add that Derrida, as the end result of the tradition, from Kant, critiquing human reason, gives a philosophy of "limits" which, like postmodernity generally, correctly critiques the overly grand Enlightenment claims for human rationality.[67] We do not know and cannot know all that we thought we could know. At its best, deconstruction does show that. There is a break between words and their referents. But does that mean that we know nothing, and that all literary texts are nonnecessarily referential? That, too, is a *non sequitur*. Such a negative, reactionary conclusion is not borne out by the actual epistemological situation.[68] God does communicate himself and truths about himself in the context of gracious covenantal relation. God does *contentfully refer*—to himself, to his acts, to his love, his judgment, and centrally to and in his Son. As an essential and interrelated aspect therein, instantiated in space-time, revelatory meaning has and does occur by revelation and inspiration *textually* in and as Holy Scripture (as well as other forms in, under and from Christ the Word).

Conclusion and Methodological Admonition

By now it is hopefully clear that in a real sense I agree with both Geisler and especially Silva that biblical criticism specifically, and as an aspect of the larger realm of literary-critical approaches to written texts, does pose potential dangers and does offer many potential benefits. Indeed, is there anything beneficial found in this four-dimensional space-time creation that does not have potential dangers or side effects? Various biblical-critical practices were developed by those holding dualistic, disjunctive, skeptical, antisupernatural presuppositions which, as applied to the text of Scripture, were passed on in resulting exegetical conclusions.[69] Certainly elements of, say, the redaction-critical methodologies of Ernst Kasemann, Willi Marxsen, and Ernst Fuchs would thus manifest *a priori* elements inimical to the historical orthodox position on Scripture as the written Word of God. But does this of itself negate the potential exegetico-theological usefulness of careful, properly limited application of the *core foci* of these biblical-critical / literary-critical methods to the text of Holy Scripture as Word of God? If these methods *can* be applied carefully to the human literary elements of Scripture, the human processes involved, do they *ipso facto* negate the possibility and actuality of Scripture being the written Word of God? Again, no.

What of the tendency of many practitioners of biblical and literary criticism, as applied to Scripture, to move off subjectively, imaginatively and speculatively into unhistorical reconstructions of *Sitze im Leben* in the early church for which, e.g., the sayings of Jesus are said to be created *ex nihilo*. Are such tendencies inherent in the practice of these biblical and literary-critical methods (*much* more the first than the second)? No, not necessarily. As noted, such effects seem to be found much more readily in the presuppositions of the Tübingen approach for cultural, philosophical and theological reasons. These speculative leaps are not inherent to the methods as such, and ought to be avoided as manifestations of our openness toward temptation, the lure for the new and exciting rather than the proven, sure and effective. As D. A. Carson has said:

> Why have these and other [older exegetical] tools, for many scholars, become out of date? They are certainly no weaker than radical redaction criticism; indeed I would judge them much stronger; but to fail to use them and give them grades at least as high as redaction criticism betrays a sort of contemporaneity chauvinism. To use a multiplicity of methods, to adopt several competing literary tools, is a necessary safeguard.[70]

So, again, as literary tools related *specifically* and *only* to the human, historical, literary processes whereby the varied books comprising Holy Scripture came into being, do these tools as such negate Scripture as being also the written Word of God? Or, given Holy Scripture as the written Word of God, is the careful application of these critical methods to the biblical text therefore wrong? No to both. As each method is kept carefully to its own proper and limited literary–critical task, related to and only to the historical, human processes of literary production, the various biblical and literary–critical methods can uncover much. But they cannot legitimately, of themselves, make negative or positive conclusions regarding Scripture as the written Word of God. Any such claim can result only from faulty subjective human extrapolation that in no way follows from the data.

That brings me to my additional admonition, one which was not touched upon directly by either Geisler or Silva or any others of whom I am aware. I am referring to the possible "psychological" effects resulting from much use of biblical/historical and literary–critical approaches to Scripture. I am convinced by actual cases that *this*, more than any actual problematic "discoveries" or "conclusions" from historical–critical processes, can lead some scholars slowly, inexorably, but falsely toward the conclusion that Holy Scripture is not the written Word of God but only a human literary production. As with other potentially problematic elements in the various critical approaches wrongly used, and as "leading" some to this "conclusion," this too is a serious *non sequitur*. It is rather the slow, *careless* outcome of a psychological reductionism leading to this false conclusion, i.e., if one can regularly, over and over, apply these critical methods to Scripture, thereby gaining insights into the historical, *human* processes involved, then, in time one may unconsciously come to conclude that Scripture *is only* a human text. *That* is a *real danger* in any useful exegetical method, but especially in these we have examined, despite the fact that such an outcome *ought not* be so.

Endnotes

[1] Kierkegaard, Søren. *Philosophical Fragments, Johannes Climacus*, ed. and trans. Howard H. Hong and Edna V. Hong, Kierkegaard's Writings (Princeton, N.J.: Princeton University Press, 1985) 31–33.

[2] C. S. Lewis, "Fern Seed and Elephants," *"Fern Seed and Elephants" and Other Essays on Christianity*, ed. Walter Hooper (Glasgow: Wm. Collins Sons, 1975) 106–13.

[3] Everett F. Harrison, "The Phenomena of Scripture," in Carl F. H. Henry, *Revelation and the Bible* (Grand Rapids: Baker, 1958) 237–39.

[4] John Baillie, *The Idea of Revelation in Recent Thought* (New York: Columbia University Press, 1956) 3–18.

[5] Ibid., 41–61ff.

[6] Emil Brunner, *Reason and Revelation*, trans. Olive Wyon (Philadelphia: Westminster, 1946) 273ff., 292.

[7] Ibid., 8.

[8] Hendrickus Berkhof, *The Christian Faith: An Introduction to the Study of the Faith*, trans. Sierd Woudstra (Grand Rapids: Eerdmans, 1979) 79–87 (see especially 79ff., 87). As William J. Abraham also confirms, much of the basis for such conclusions about Scripture and revelation is rooted in the modern development of the historical and scientific disciplines, which lie behind biblical criticism.

"The settled conviction that traditional conceptions of revelation [and all 'supernaturalism'] are incompatible with modern developments in history and science. . . . [S]uch a conception of revelation is quite literally incredible given the canons of judgment that must be exercised today. These canons . . . are now regarded as indispensable for an adequate reading of the Bible." But in a response, Abraham correctly points out that these ". . . [modern and contemporary] theologians who [still] make claims about God's intentions or purposes without having within their theistic commitments a concept of direct divine speaking are without warrants for such claims. In so far as they continue to make such claims, they are trading on the resources of a theological tradition which they have rejected." William J. Abraham,

Divine Revelation and the Limits of Historical Criticism (Oxford: Oxford University Press, 1982) 1–2, 23–24.

[9] Norman Geisler, "Beware of Philosophy: A Warning to Biblical Scholars" *Journal of the Evangelical Theological Society* (Hereafter *JETS*) 42 (1999) 3–19.

[10] Benedict Spinoza in Geisler, Ibid., 4.

[11] Ibid., 5.

[12] Ibid.

[13] Ibid.

[14] Ibid.

[15] Ibid., 14.

[16] Ibid. Similar wholly antagonistic criticisms of biblical criticism and its methodologies in total can be found in, e.g., Harold Lindsell, John Warwick Montgomery.

[17] Moises Silva, "'Can Two Walk Together Unless they be Agreed?' Evangelical Theology and Biblical Scholarship," *JETS* 41 (1998) 3–16.

[18] Ibid., 9–10.

[19] Ibid. Note Silva's discussion on p. 11 where, like Geisler, Silva, too, is alarmed at the growing number of evangelical scholars who are "blissfully unaware of having adopted approaches on positions that conflict with their religious convictions at a fundamental level." Then in footnote twenty-six he enlarges on the failure of many to face the implications of their decisions, as when an evangelical scholar rejects inerrancy by saying we ought not get bogged down in details but then feels free to tell us Jesus was mistaken in thinking the end was near, right after Jesus says heaven and earth will pass away but *not his words*. If Jesus our Lord is so willing to stake his credibility on a statement we will not accept then what meaning is left to our theological claims.

[20] Ned Stonehouse, "The Infallibility of Scripture and Evangelical Progress" *Bulletin of the Evangelical Theological Society* (1958) 9, in Silva, 11.

[21] Silva, 16.

[22] J. Gresham Machen, in ibid., 15.

[23] See the discussion in chapter two. With Spinoza, a notable writer at the "headwaters" of biblical criticism and the separation of the text of Scripture from "the Word of God" is Jean Astruc.

[24] Johann Semler, *Treatise on the Free Investigation of the Canon*, 1:25–26, 53–54, 63–64; 2:4, 39–40.

[25] W. Ward Gasque, "Nineteenth-Century Roots of Contemporary New Testament Criticism," in *Scripture, Tradition and Interpretation*, ed. W. Ward Gasque and William S. LaSor (Grand Rapids: Eerdmans, 1978) 149.

[26] Ibid., 150.

[27] Ibid., 152. Cf. Gerald Bray's fine discussion of this topic in *Biblical Interpretation: Past & Present* (Downers Grove, Ill.: InterVarsity, 1996); and Horton Harris, *The Tübingen School* (Oxford: Clarendon, 1975).

[28] A. C. Headlam in ibid., 154.

[29] F. F. Bruce, "(Biblical) Criticism," in *International Standard Bible Encyclopedia*, vol. 1. 2d ed. (Grand Rapids: Eerdmans, 1979) 817–25, and Tremper Longman, *Literary Approaches to Biblical Interpretation* (Grand Rapids: Zondervan, 1987) 22. Probably the most well known application of source criticism is by J. Wellhausen's application to the Pentateuch and the four hypothetical sources (JEDP).

[30] Ibid., 822.

[31] Longman, 23. E.g., lament, thanksgiving, royal.

[32] Bruce, 823.

[33] Robert H. Stein, "Introduction" and "What is Redaction Criticism?" in *The Gospels and Tradition*, ed. Robert H. Stein (Grand Rapids: Eerdmans, 1991) 13–36.

[34] T. W. Manson, *The Teaching of Jesus* (Cambridge: Cambridge University Press, 1935) in Bruce, 823.

[35] Martin Dibelius, *From Tradition to Gospel*, 3, in Stein, 22, n. 2.

[36] Stein, 13–14, 21–22; and Longman, 23–24.

[37] Longman, 22–24. E.g., Matthew's emphasis on the life and teaching of Jesus as the fulfillment of the OT, and, at the turn of the century, much discussion arose with Wilhelm Wrede's monograph on the theme of the "Messianic Secret," and J. Weiss also contributed much at that same period on particular views of the Gospels.

[38] Norman Perrin, *What is Redaction Criticism?* (Philadelphia: Fortress, 1969) vi.

[39] Bruce, 824.

[40] Grant R. Osborne, *The Hermeneutical Spiral* (Downers Grove, Ill.: InterVarsity, 1991) 169–70. Note too, Grant R. Osborne, "The Evangelical and Redaction Criticism: Critique and Methodology" *JETS* 22 (1979) 305 ff. Cf. G. R. Osborne's recent article "Historical Criticism and the Evangelical" in *JETS* 42 (1999) 193–210.

[41] Stein, 30.

[42] Ibid., 51–67.

[43] Norman Perrin, *Rediscovering the Teaching of Jesus* (New York: Harper and Row, 1967) 39; and D. A. Carson, "Redaction Criticism: On the Legitimacy and Illegitimacy of a Literary Tool" in *Scripture and Truth*, ed. by D. A. Carson and John D. Woodbridge (Grand Rapids: Zondervan, 1983) 137–38.

[44] Osborne, 310–15.

[45] Carson, 123–28.

[46] Ibid.

[47] Osborne, 310–15.

48 Carson, 126–28.

49 Robert H. Stein, "Authentic or Authoritative Sayings: What is the Difference?" In R. Stein, *Gospels and Tradition*, 149. The issue of the "authenticity" of Jesus' sayings found in the Gospel materials relates directly to how the evangelists reported such, often seeking the essence or gist (*ippissima vox*) rather than necessarily the exact wording (*ippissima verba*). That this is appropriate in terms of historical reliability, note the excellent statement by Paul Feinberg. "*Inerrancy does not demand that the Logia Jesu* (the sayings of Jesus) *contain the ipsissima verba* (the exact words of Jesus), *only the ipsissima vox* (the exact voice). . . . When a New Testament writer cites the sayings of Jesus, it need not be the case that Jesus said those exact words. Undoubtedly, the exact words of Jesus are to be found in the NT, but they need not be in every instance. For one thing, many of the sayings were spoken by our Lord in Aramaic, and thus had to be translated into Greek . . . . Thus, it is impossible for us to know which are direct quotes, which are indirect discourses, and which are free renderings (italics in original). "The Meaning of Inerrancy," in *Inerrancy*, ed. Norman Geisler (Grand Rapids: Zondervan, 1979) 270. For further discussion of this issue see Grant Osborne, "Historical Criticism and the Evangelical," *JETS* (June 1999) 203ff. and Darrell Bock "The Words of Jesus in the Gospels: Live, Jive or Memorex," in *Jesus Under Fire*, ed. Michael J. Wilkins and J. P. Moreland (Grand Rapids: Zondervan, 1995) 73–99.

50 I have concerns about Stein's argument on ibid., 151–52, which parallel Carson's concerns, 138. But by way of further critical assessment of Stein's a defense, I would add that Stein's apologetic for the use of redaction criticism to establish the authenticity (or inauthenticity) of the Gospel materials and especially of the sayings of Jesus (despite his claims to their full authority) is questionable. His first answer, "because it's there," sounds more like the inability to resist temptation. His statement that the student of the Gospels cannot but have a *natural curiosity* is thus anything but strong. His second point is that such investigation, were it able to firmly establish a few authentic sayings of Jesus, would help establish bridges between the Christ of faith and the historical Jesus. After saying "thank you Martin Kaehler," the question is, establish bridges *for whom*? The radical critics are not listening, and few others are even aware of this false dichotomy. Finally, Stein says that being able to *know* we have *both* the authentic words of Jesus (in Greek translation?) *and* the authoritative interpretations/modifications is to be "doubly blessed." Can Stein be serious? Directly or indirectly, intentionally or not, this is the creation of a canon within the canon, a far more limited and *perpetually tentative* (given the shifts in *all* empirical historical assessment) "red letter edition." "Doubly blessed" is simply a pious cover for impious curiosity and need for certainty beyond what the authoritative text of Holy Scripture offers. To go behind, above, beside the text of Holy Scripture, whatever the "pious" claims, is to be on false ground. The canonical text is, under Christ and by the Spirit (then and now), *the present place* of authoritative "historical transcendence." Note the expansion of this notion made by Ray S. Anderson, *Historical Transcendence and the Reality of God: A Christological Critique* (Grand Rapids: Eerdmans, 1972) 212–14, 220–23.

51 Anthony C. Thiselton, *The Two Horizons: New Testament Hermeneutics and Philosophical Description* (Grand Rapids: Eerdmans, 1980), esp. chaps. 11, 12, and 14. Note herein the highly influential work of Hans-Georg Gadamer, *Truth and Method*, trans. Garret Broden and John Cummings (New York: Crossroad, 1982).

52 Osborne, 319, quoting G. N. Stanton "Presuppositions in NT Criticism" in *New Testament Interpretation*, ed. I. Howard Marshall (Grand Rapids: Eerdmans, 1978) 67.

53 Stein, 17–18.

54 Kevin J. Vanhoozer, among others, has explained very effectively how finally the interpretive process must rest not in any claim to knowledge of the mental state of the author (e.g., Paul) when writing a text, but in the text itself, understood in terms of contemporary "Speech Act Theory." Cf. Kevin J. Vanhoozer, *Is There a Meaning in This Text?* (Grand Rapids: Zondervan, 1998), esp. ch. 6 , and Kevin J. Vanhoozer, *First Theology: God, Scripture and Hermeneutics* (Downers Grove, Ill.: InterVarsity, 2002) 127–58 where Vanhoozer explains his understanding of Scripture in relation to and as an aspect of "God's Mighty Speech Acts" and so as the written Word of God. Note too similar development in Nicholas Wolterstorff, *Divine Discourse: Philosophical Reflections on the Claim that God Speaks* (Cambridge, England: Cambridge University Press, 1995). Note again discussion of Vanhoozer's views in the previous chapter.

55 Carson finds that redaction criticism's proper domain is quite focused when he says: "The one place where redaction criticism may offer considerably more help, and where it may function with some legitimacy, is in aiding us to discern more closely the Evangelists' individual concerns and emphases. In one sense, of course, interpreters have always been interested in such questions. In the broadest sense, therefore, redaction criticism is nothing new. But even here redaction criticism must tread softly. The distinction between what is traditional and what is redactional is not a happy one; it is too fraught with overtones of "authentic" and "inauthentic". And even when some snippet is demonstrably redactional, it does not follow that any particular alteration owes its existence to theological concerns. Moreover, if the method presupposes the entire package of radical form criticism and a simplistic adoption of the two-source hypothesis, then the results will inevitably prove not only slanted but ephemeral: a new scholarly fad is bound to shake one or both of these theories in years to come, jeopardizing a vast amount of current work. It seems best, then, if redaction criticism, as applied to discerning distinctive emphases, is to produce work of lasting importance, that it should not take its pedigree too seriously and it should not speak too dogmatically, for instance, of Matthew's change of Mark, but rather of the variations between the two.

56 Vanhoozer, 71ff.; Longman, 19ff.

57 Ibid., 26, 82, 157; Longman, 25ff.

58 Ibid., 26, 53, 61; Longman, 27ff. Cf. Moises Silva's excellent discussion of the history, nature and biblical application of the insights of modern linguistics from Saussure and post-Saussurian linguistics to biblical studies in *God, Language and Scripture* (Grand Rapids: Zondervan, 1990).

[59] Longman, 31–32.

[60] Vanhoozer, 26.

[61] Daniel Patte, in Longman, 36–37.

[62] Vanhoozer, 106; Longman, 38ff.

[63] Hans-Georg Gadamer, *Truth and Method*, trans. Garrett Groden and John Cummings (New York: Crossroad, 1982) 359. Cf. Thiselton, *The Two Horizons*, ch. 11.

[64] See Vanhoozer's excellent and insightful critical discussion of these developments in *Meaning*, especially ch. 3 and 4.

[65] Longman, 42.

[66] Ibid. Note, too, Vanhoozer's critical analysis (and acknowledgement of the insight) of Derrida at this point, p. 37.

[67] *Is There a Meaning?*, 80.

[68] Ibid., chapters 5–7, and especially 8.

[69] As Carl F. H. Henry has concluded, "What is objectionable is not the historical-critical method, but rather the alien presuppositions to which neo-Protestant scholars subject it . . . [When] it is freed from the arbitrary assumptions of critics . . . [it becomes] highly serviceable as a disciplined investigative approach to past historical events." *God, Revelation and Authority*, vol. 4 (Waco: Word, 1979) 393, 401.

[70] Carson, 139–40.

5

Developments Regarding the Nature of Holy Scripture in Modern Roman Catholic Thought

The nature and purpose of Holy Scripture are issues that have been considered vital in the church implicitly and explicitly since its early years. But through the centuries, with the development of doctrine and, therein, with regard to emergent conceptions of the centralized authority of the Church, the question of the nature and purpose of Holy Scripture became more complex. The Reformation, the Counter Reformation, and the Council of Trent all sought clarification of these issues, yet the problem of scriptural authority in Roman Catholicism has remained in the ensuing centuries to Vatican I, Vatican II, and beyond. The purpose here is to grasp prominent elements of the developing theological constructions of the nature of Holy Scripture in relation to the Word of God within modern Roman Catholic thought, with special focus on representative views developing from Vatican II.

The Tridentine Creed and Beyond

Holy Scripture in the Decrees of the Council of Trent

Martin Luther had appealed to a general council to bring about reformation of the Church, but soon was convinced that general councils had erred (e.g., the Council of Constance which condemned Hus) so that "he had to trust exclusively to the Word of God and the Spirit of God in history."[1] In response to the Reformation, a Council was opened by order of Pope Paul III at Trent, December 1545, lasting (because of interruptions) until December 1563. The Tridentine decisions related to both doctrine and discipline, the former being divided into positive decrees of dogma and condemning canons applying the *anathema sit* to dissenting views. Protestant views are exaggerated and often mixed with real heresies condemned by both sides. After the third *sessio* had accepted the Niceno-Constantinopolitan Creed as a basis for the decrees, then the next *sessio* focused on canonical Scripture (*Decretum de Canonicus Scripturis*).[2]

Given its larger purpose, a central task of the Council was to specify the spheres of Scripture and Tradition in the transmission of Catholic doctrine. Usually Tradition introduced persons to doctrines, while Scripture was used at a later stage to test and amplify these doctrines. Thus, Aquinas had said that only canonical Scripture—as distinct from apocryphal writings—is the rule of faith (*sola canonica scriptura est regula fidei*).[3] Yet there were doctrines accepted on the authority of Tradition alone, and these were objects of concern among the Reformers, e.g., purgatory, invocation of saints, transubstantiation, etc. What then is the nature and value of Tradition in relation to that of Scripture?

The issue here must be understood on at least two levels, leading to a third, as reflected in the summary of Trent. First, the Council concluded that it received and held in honor with *equal* devotion and veneration (*pari pietatis affectu ac reventia*) the books of Scripture and the apostolic traditions which concerned faith and morals. But does this decision intend to say that Tradition is inspired and/or revelatory in the same way that Scripture is, or that Scripture is reckoned to be merely another form of human, pious tradition? The answer is No to both.

While Trent's decision is bound up with regard for the "spiritual sense" and the types which God is said to have placed in Scripture, the "ontological" distinction between Scripture and tradition, as well as their necessary interrelation, is maintained.[4] Persons of faith are exhorted to accept from the Church an authoritative teaching on the question of how far God's written Word extends. The Word of God in the Bible is said to be of higher dignity than any tradition because it has come from God by direct inspiration. Apostolic traditions have come rather by a general assistance which the Spirit has given to the Church. Yet as interrelated, Scripture is said to depend on Tradition "not in itself but in so far as our knowledge of it is concerned."[5] In this way, the Council claimed that Scripture and Tradition must be received by believers with equal reverence (*pari affectu*). This is reflected in the "Summary of the Tridentine Creed" (1563):

> I also admit the holy Scriptures according to that sense [Tradition] which our holy Mother Church has held, and does hold, to which it belongs to judge of the true sense and interpretation of the Scriptures; neither will I ever take and interpret them otherwise than according to the unanimous consent of the Fathers (*juxta unanimem consensum Patrum*).[6]

Diversity Regarding Inspiration

During the sixteenth and seventeenth centuries Roman Catholic views on inspiration of Scripture became increasingly diverse. Verbal inspiration, which often had been understood in terms akin to dictation, was increasingly modified or rejected outright, despite the consensus and tradition of the view reaching back through the early Fathers. Following the lead of Jewish convert Sixtus of Siena Leonard Lessius asserted that "a book such as 2 Maccabees, written by human industry without the aid of the Holy Spirit, may afterwards, if the Holy Spirit give testimony that it contains nothing false, be ranked as Holy Scripture."[7] After criticism, Lessius revised the view somewhat, taking out the reference to Maccabees and calling his view simply a hypothesis about what God might do, not what he had done. But Jacques Bonfrére (1573–1642) returned to Lessius' original view related to books written by unaided human effort, pointing to the way in which citations are taken up into Scripture (e.g., that of Aratus in Acts 17:28) as models of the way in which whole books might be given recognition as Scripture by the Church under the guidance of the Spirit. (This lack of differentiation between the inspired writer/ writing and Church authority was later condemned at Vatican I). But Bonfrére became a forerunner in applying the Molinist theory of divine assistance to the production of Scripture. Thus his theory of concomitant inspiration portrayed the Holy Spirit as leaving the human writer free while managing to secure a faithful written product by the use of divine foreknowledge.[8] Yet this perceived freedom of wording meant an approach to the text and the signs of its humanity that had not been allowed in relation to the traditional views of inspiration. The problem of inspiration and divine grace became the source of many debates.

During this period, Roman Catholic thought, biblical, theological and philosophical, began to experience the effects of the intrusion of cosmological and epistemological dualism into Western culture, notably through Richard Simon. Richard Simon (1638–1712), a scholar considered by many to be far ahead of his time in his thinking on Scripture, moved Roman Catholic thinking about Scripture yet further. A notable Semiticist, logician, and a Molinist in his view of inspiration, Simon had his works condemned as soon as they appeared. This was considered to be a loss by many. Simon's concern for textual criticism, along with his Molinist view of scriptural production in his understanding of the nature of Scripture (and at a time when one *formula consensus* had declared that all biblical vowel points and accents were from the Spirit), led his English translator to pen the following poetic summary of his method:

> To vindicate the Sacred Books a new
> But only * certain method you pursue
> And showing th' are corrupted, prove'em true.[9]

His recognition of the effects of time and scribes on the text of Scripture did not negate his Molinist view of biblical inspiration, which included faithful scribes like Paul's amenuenses.

While Simon was accused by some of claiming that inspiration and the status "Word of God" only applied to doctrinal issues reflected in Scripture, he was in fact critical of this view. It was held by Paris theologian Henry Holden in his theory of *obiter dicta* (incidental comment). But Simon extended his own Molinist view of inspiration to the whole of Scripture, including changes which it may have undergone at the hands of such editors as Ezra (but not those resulting from negligence).[10]

Holden developed his above mentioned theory from the notorious work of Marcantonio de Dominis, whose subtle view on the relation of Scripture and Church meant that all parts of Scripture which contain revealed truths are divinely authored, but the inclusion of any particular book results from human testimony. Parts of Scripture not containing revealed truths but which only state mundane facts depend on human tradition. De Dominis' conclusion, "Scripture as such is not the Word of God, but contains and proposes to us the Word of God," was accepted by Holden without his being able to consistently say what criterion enabled him to distinguish where revelation began and ended.[11]

The First Vatican Council

In 1864, ten years after his proclamation of the sinlessness of the Virgin Mary, Pope Pius IX issued an encylical, *Quanta cura*, known as the "Syllabus," which catalogues eighty errors of the age which threatened the Church and society. The encylical was meant both to exhort and to prepare for a Church council, wherein the central concern would be papal infallibility. Under the first of the Syllabus' ten major headings were placed[12] the following errors: "Divine revelation is imperfect, and subject to indefinite progress" and "The prophecies and miracles of the Bible are poetic fictions, and Jesus himself is a myth."[13]

After the papal call for a Church council in 1868, Vatican I convened in December 1869, adjourning almost one year later in the face of a changed political climate in Europe. The "Dogmatic Constitution on the Catholic Faith" was reduced to four chapters followed by eighteen canons in which numerous errors taken from the "Syllabus" were again listed and condemned. In the chapter on revelation, the Council reaffirmed Trent and declared the books of Holy Scripture to be canonical because, under the inspiration of the Holy Spirit, they had God as their author and, as such, they had been committed to the Church. In this way the Council rejected theories which claimed that Scripture was only human in its production but then given authority by the Church ("subsequent inspiration"). The First Vatican Council, like Trent, also forbade all Scriptural interpretation which did not agree with Roman Catholic tradition, the Vulgate and "the unanimous consent of the Fathers."[14]

Newman and the Inspiration of Holy Scripture

Through this period, John Henry Newman, prominent convert from Anglo-Catholicism and eventually a cardinal of the Roman Catholic Church, worked with a view of inspiration much dependent on Holden. It was Holden's theory which gave Newman (and others) confidence in the noninterference of science and Scripture, a view which had much in common with the dualistic thinking later espoused by Rudolf Bultmann.[15] Biblical inspiration meant a guidance that kept the writer sound in faith and morals and left him to do his best with the history and science of his day. But Newman's theology was to lead to "the modernist crisis" at the turn of the twentieth century.

In a later article, Newman elaborated on Holden's theory. After receiving much criticism, he wrote "What is of Obligation for a Catholic to Believe Concerning the Inspiration of the Canonical Scriptures." Herein, Newman reflects some modification of his earlier theory. He now brought within the bounds of inerrancy those historical statements of inspired writers which were linked to dogmatic teaching. But he still classed statements such as Paul leaving his cloak at Troas among the *obiter dicta* which might be false with no harm to the inspiration of the text.[16] Yet, as before, Newman did not clarify how an *obiter dicta* would be recognized, and a user of this theory could pass off any claim of error by saying it was an *obiter dicta*.

Newman sought to defend Holden's theory of Scripture by claiming that both Trent and Vatican I had taught that "the divine inspiration of Scripture is to be assigned especially to matters of faith and morals." But, in fact, while Trent said that the Vulgate may be safely used in matters of faith and morals, the word "inspiration" is not mentioned in this connection. At Vatican I the Tridentine decree had been reiterated with the addition that the books of Scripture were not accepted as canonical by the Church because they had been produced by unaided human thought and then crowned/canonized by the Church, but because under the inspiration of the Spirit, they had God as their author and as such were committed to the Church. While those convened at the First Vatican Council meant specifically to exclude views of "subsequent inspiration" held by those influenced by Lessius and Bonfrère, yet this definition did not justify Newman's claim.[17]

In 1893, without referring to *obiter dicta* specifically, Pope Leo XIII published an encylical stating that limiting inspiration to faith and morals was an error. As a result, some claimed that Holden's and Newman's theory had not been condemned. But in 1943, Pope Pius XII stated that *obiter dicta* as a theory regarding Scripture was rejected.[18]

Roman Catholic Modernism

"Roman Catholic modernism" refers to a combination of factors which developed at a time when many Catholic scholars were abandoning historical church positions. It rose from Pope Leo XIII's encyclical on the correct attitude of a Catholic exegete toward physical scientific conclusions: "It will be advantageous to apply these ideas to cognate disciplines, especially to history." Many exegetes believed this to be a signal to diminish the historical value of the Old Testament.[19] Pére Lagrange's famous course "Historical Method in the Old Testament," given at the University of Toulouse in 1902, presented a detailed working out of an analogy which related to Old Testament statements about the physical world claiming to be historical. It was here that consideration of literary genre was first presented as a pertinent principle for possibly overcoming apparent discrepancies.[20]

In October 1902, Leo XIII set up the Biblical Commission. Its purpose was to encourage Catholic scholars in their study of Scripture, to be a clearing house for ideas and opinions, to utilize the most recent helps to exegesis available, and to guard against anything which might be contrary to the true sense of Scripture established by tradition. Its first decisions related to the historical character of Scripture; e.g., was it lawful to appeal to the implicit citation of sources in order to excuse the inspired writer from having fallen into historical error?[21] Subsequently, decisions about individual books came forth, responding to modernist publicity. Sounding somewhat like Henry Holden, the Commission concluded:

> In so far as there are proposed in the decrees of the Commission opinions which are not directly linked with the truths of faith and morals, the exegete has full liberty to prosecute his researches and to evaluate his

findings, though always with due regard to the teaching authority of the Church.[22]

When assertions of scriptural errors threatened Church doctrines, the papacy dealt directly with the matter by means of periodic encyclicals in the first half of the twentieth century.

Developments from Modernism to Vatican II

Roman Catholic Modernism soon vanished, but it left the Church in need of a solution for the question of how to understand the divine and human elements of Scripture. Modernism had made Scripture all too human, denying that it was substantially united to the nature and activity of God. Conservatives, reflecting an attitude long held in the Church, asserted strongly that *all* Scripture was divine. A middle way was proposed in the encyclical *Divino afflante* (1943), which included a comparison of the incarnate Word to the written Word.[23] While there was precedent for such it had been lost or rejected during the modernist controversies. It now became useful in reckoning the nature of Scripture, for it provided a way to group together

> the various "exemptions" allowed to the inspired author, mistakes in grammar, use of inaccurate citations, choice of strange metaphors, use of literary genre which depart from strict history, stylized grouping of facts in historical narrative, and so on.[24]

All these were seen to be signs of the writer's humanity, which had to be recognized, though God was understood to be guiding the writer throughout. Otherwise all of the books would be alike and perfect in style. Additionally, the incarnation analogy provided a useful way of saying where such condescension must stop. As in Christ there was humanity without sin, so also in Scripture there is the humanity of the writers without formal error (i.e., the writers do not assert as their own, ideas which are false).[25] Yet the incarnational principle was only slowly accepted among the Church's theologians at all levels, who admitted its usefulness to exegesis but rejected it as a proper defense of the inerrancy of Scripture.

As a result, Roman Catholic exegesis began to flower, as did debate which endeavored to further clarify the relation of Scripture and Tradition. But up to the call to convene Vatican II, the overall developments in Roman Catholic understanding of the nature of Holy Scripture had clearly undergone both crisis and significant development since the Council of Trent. Paralleling liberal Protestantism in ways reflective of its own perceptions of authority and Tradition, Roman Catholic understandings of the nature of Scripture began to shift from Scripture as the written Word of God, in an almost *wholly* divine sense and with little regard for the human elements, to a model analogous to the incarnation of Christ, giving full heed to both the deity and humanity of the written Word. But is this incarnational model a final answer to the question: In what sense is the written text of Scripture the written Word of God; or is it finally the word of man through which divine ideas/dogmas are "incarnationally" brought to human attention? The incarnational model of Scripture, the compromise result of modern discoveries and the modernist crisis, while useful to a point, and effective in setting some boundaries, gives very few real answers. The parameters allowable are still very wide. And if the humanity of Jesus can be distinguished (abstracted) from his deity, then, if one presses the model, the human text of Scripture can be distinguished and finally separated from revelatory action which lies somehow *only beyond it*—however necessary the human text of Scripture is regarded to be as a conduit for the process of divine disclosure. This "incarnational" latitude was to be reflected in developments in Roman Catholic bibliology in the documents of Vatican II.

Vatican II and Beyond

Holy Scripture in the Documents of Vatican II

Among the sixteen documents of Vatican II (1962–1965), "Dei Verbum," ("Dogmatic Constitution on Divine Revelation") makes a number of concise statements describing the nature of Holy Scripture. Yet much potential breadth of interpretation still exists. In an excellent statement in chapter two, reflecting both Christocentricity and the multiplicity of the modes of divine disclosure, "Dei Verbum" states:

> In His goodness and wisdom God chose to reveal Himself and to make known to us the hidden purpose of His will by which through Christ, the Word made flesh, man might in the Holy Spirit have access to the Father. . . . Through this revelation, therefore, the invisible God out of the abundance of his love speaks to men as friends. . . . This plan of revelation is realized by deeds and words having an inner unity: the deeds wrought by God in this history of salvation manifest and confirm the teaching and realities signified by the words, while the words proclaim the deeds and clarify the mystery contained in them. By this revelation then, the deepest truth about God and the salvation of man shines out for our sake in Christ, who is both the mediator and fullness of all revelation.[26]

Herein the interrelation of the divine acts in history with the necessity of the divine words of interpretation of those acts, represented as aspects in, from and under the Word made flesh, Jesus Christ, is well presented.

But soon further clarification is made. While the statement emphasizes that through revelation God communicated Himself and the decisions of His will for human salvation, the document asserts too that "those divinely revealed *realities* which are contained and presented in Sacred Scripture have been *committed to writing* under the inspiration of the Holy Spirit."[27] Recalling the earlier councils, the document adds that the books of the Old and New Testaments in their entirety, "with all their parts, are sacred and canonical because written under the inspiration of the Holy Spirit, they have God as their author and have been handed on as such to the Church itself."[28] Then, after acknowledging the debates which had occurred since Vatican I, it adds that, given the revelatory nature of Scripture, "everything actually asserted as true by the inspired authors must be held to be asserted by the Holy Spirit," so that it follows that "the books of Scripture must be acknowledged as teaching solidly, faithfully and without error that truth which God wanted to put into sacred writings for the sake of salvation."[29] Roman Catholic theologians have often taken this last soteriological phrase as formative of how Scripture can be construed as "the Word of God," i.e., *as used* redemptively by God.

But this statement which appears to affirm Scripture as the written Word of God is balanced by the recognition of the humanity of Scripture.

Because God speaks in Holy Scripture through human beings and in a human manner, one must "investigate what meaning the sacred writers really intended, and what God wanted to manifest by means of their words."[30] This human fashion in which God revealed Himself and His will is developed in the document, focusing especially on the various literary genres found in Scripture. So the focus is first upon proper hermeneutical method before mention is made of the "living tradition of the whole Church." Thus the point of "Dei Verbum" on the nature of Sacred Scripture understood incarnationally is apparently that it is simultaneously a divine and human Word.

> In Sacred Scripture . . . while the truth and holiness of God always remain intact, the marvelous condescension of eternal wisdom is clearly shown . . . how far He has gone in adapting His language with thoughtful concern for our weak human nature. For the words of God, expressed in human language, have been made like human discourse.[31]

But how was this statement about the nature of Holy Scripture and its participation in the revelation of God as "the written Word of God" developed after Vatican II?[32] The following analyses reflect the variety of interpretations of "Dei Verbum" by prominent moderate and progressive Roman Catholic scholars as they strive to express such for the contemporary situation. Each reflects the fact that despite seemingly strong statements on inspiration and Scripture as the written Word of God, "Dei Verbum" is actually a compromise document containing subtle elements reflecting the background council debates and, thus, broadly moderated conclusions.

Karl Rahner on Scripture and the Word of God

Karl Rahner, often regarded as the most significant Roman Catholic theologian of the twentieth century, exercised much influence at Vatican II, where he helped to form the documents on salvation and revelation ("Dei Verbum"). According to Rahner, the modern loss of the transcendence of God arose from modern thinking which affirmed radical immanence. Rahner spent much of his career working against such tides of modernity and the supposed conflict between divine immanence and divine transcendence, divine glory and human freedom, always holding the two together.[33] Central to his task and his understanding of the revelation of God was his "transcendental method." Since Immanuel Kant, the "transcendental method" has been used to uncover the necessary conditions for facts, "the condition of the possibility of . . .". Given something undeniable, what must be true for that fact to be true?

As influenced especially by Immanuel Kant, G. W. F. Hegel, Joseph Maréchal, and Martin Heidegger, Rahner's transcendental reflection is a philosophical means to show that human experience is not intelligible apart from the "holy mystery" we call "God." Holy, ineffable mystery is encountered and known unthematically and nonconceptually in the ordinariness of life.[34] By transcendental reflection, Rahner also wanted to show that the human being is "spirit," "transcendent," inclined to God, "open to receive revelation" of the infinite mysterious horizon of being, i.e., "God" in the Christian tradition.[35] Rahner finds that "transcendental experiences" in ordinary human experience show human beings to be naturally oriented to holy mystery, that God is not separated from human nature but rather is intrinsic to (and co-extensive with) human nature as the "necessary condition" of human subjectivity, freedom, and the capacity to "transcend."[36] Yet such immanent holy mystery remains transcendent and knowable only as it makes itself known—in "transcendental revelation" and "categorical revelation."

In affirming the inclination of human subjectivity to divine revelation, Rahner distinguishes the reality and potentiality of human nature for hearing and doing the Word of God. The "transcendental knowledge" (revelation) or experience of God results from the grounding of all human nature and history in the self-giving of God. That is the condition of "transcendental knowledge." So Rahner speaks of the "divinized transcendentalizing of man" who freely actualizes his essence in history.[37] But this actually occurs *a posteriori* as the transcendental experience of one's own free subjectivity by means of encounter with the world and other persons. We are oriented to God, and this experience, this "transcendental revelation," is *always* present as unthematic experience which, as "knowledge" of God, we have implicitly when we are thinking of and concerned with *anything*. This *unthematic*, nonconceptual knowledge or experience of God is foundational to all thought, and hence it is that from which *thematic* knowledge of God emerges (i.e., religion). Therefore, Rahner rejects the "purely extrinsic concept of revelation" which he portrays and defines as any notion of divine intervention in human history. Instead, revelation is "the transcendental experience of the absolute and merciful closeness of God, even if this cannot be conceptually expressed . . . by everyone."[38] But as experience *of God*, this revelation is not an encounter with a "particular object alongside others." Even as the condition of human transcendentality, God remains absolutely beyond.[39]

Still, human transcendentality is immanently borne and fulfilled by this divinizing "self-communication of God" in history as the history of salvation and revelation for every person. Divine revelation is always and everywhere present *as* the communication of holy mystery, *as* the innermost center of all existing persons and of all human history (the "supernatural existential"). This "history on God's part" and the "transcendental" structures of all persons are understood by Rahner as truly historical because they are

> grounded in God's free and personal self-communication. This history is also free on God's part...(reflecting) the basic relation between creator and creature, the beginning of this history . . . [is] an event of God's freedom (as well as the human being's) which can give itself or refuse to give itself. . . . [It is] a history which really is the one true history of God himself . . . [which] manifests his power to enter into time. . . . [The] history of salvation and revelation is always the already existing synthesis of God's historical activity and man's at the same time.[40]

Again, this universal, transcendental revelation, as the basis of human supernatural transcendentality and as co-extensive with (but not identical to) human history, can become explicit, thematic, and conceptual. Rahner is emphatic that this "categorical [or 'real'] revelation" is not to be narrowly identified only with "revelation in Old and New Testament history (i.e., sacred Scripture)," but is understood to be manifested in many religious contexts. The implicit knowledge is the condition of reflexive and thematic knowledge of God. Categorical revelation is revelation in history through events, symbols and words:

> [Categorical revelation] is not simply given with the spiritual being of man as transcendence, but rather has the character of an event. It

is dialogical, and in it God speaks to man, and makes known to him something which cannot be known always and everywhere in the world through the necessary relation of all reality in the world to God.[41]

By categorical revelation God communicates his inner reality, his personal character, his free relation to human subjectivity as spirit.[42] The history of God's transcendental revelation shows itself to be directed toward a "highest and comprehensive self-interpretation of man" and so to "ever more intensely and explicitly religious self-interpretation" of the experience of God.[43] Yet it must be remembered that, for Rahner, this explicit religious and categorical history of revelation is but a "species" or "segment" of the transcendental revelation. It is simply a "successful instance or full realization of the single history of revelation."[44] Clearly, if that is so then there must be categorical revelation "outside" of "Old and New Testament history." These are "brief and partial histories within this categorical history of revelation in which a part of this self-reflection and reflexive self-presence of universal revelation is found in its purity."[45] Like Paul Tillich, Rahner says that Jesus Christ is the criterion for distinguishing both misunderstandings of the transcendental experience of God and legitimate interpretations. Jesus Christ is "the full and unsurpassable event of the historical self-objectification of God's self-communication to the world."[46] It is significant that Rahner's formulation of "categorical revelation" is an outcome of his consistent concern to emphasize both divine and human freedom in revelation. There is a sense in which free human responsiveness to the unthematic revelation of ineffable mystery "*creates*" the "categorical" disclosure, *makes it* reflexive, successful, and thematic. It occurs *wherever* human beings, by God's grace, freely actualize their own transcendentality.[47] Thus categorical revelation "depends" on "graced" human activity. Still it is "only when God is the subjective principle of the speaking and of man's hearing in faith can God in his own self express himself."[48] The boundary between God and creatures is said to remain firm.

For Rahner, Holy Scripture arises within the context of categorical revelation as a *further* stage of the successful objectification of the original transcendental self-communication of God. This falls within the "special official history" of revelation—i.e., revelation in "the usual sense." It is "really identical with the Old and New Testament history . . . the valid self-interpretation of God's transcendental self-communication to man."[49] As the further thematization of the emergent universal categorical history, it *does not have to be* made *thematic* in a *religious* or sacral way.[50] Yet "prophets," persons who were "original bearers" of such (thematized) revealed "communication" from God "are to be understood as unique persons" in whom the self-interpretation of this original, transcendental experience and its history occurs "in word and in deed." In this way something comes to *particular* expression which is unthematically present *everywhere* and in *all* persons. While the "prophet" is regarded as free and creative in this objectification of the universal communication of holy mystery, Rahner's concern to integrate human and divine freedom requires that this self-interpretation and historical objectification of a supernatural transcendentality not be explained as only a human and natural process. The "prophet" is specially constituted by the personal self-communication of God. "If it interprets itself historically, then God (thereby) interprets himself in history, and the concrete human bearers of such self-interpretation are (thus) authorized by God in a real sense."[51]

But what distinguishes the "prophet" from all others who have precisely the same unthematic self-communication of absolute mystery constituting their historical being? Here Rahner reflects not only Hegel but also Heidegger, Tillich, and William James. The "light of faith" given to all persons is grasped and declared by the "prophet" out of the center of his or her human existence. This "light" is the divinized subjectivity of all humanity, but it is the "prophet" who correctly mediates this light. The prophet is the "believer who *can express* his transcendental experience of God correctly." It is the prophet who then "becomes *for others* the correct and pure objectification of their own transcendental experience of God." Such prophetic self-interpretation, which "really succeeds" and takes on a living form for the community and its multiple experiences of self-interpretation, becomes a "productive model, an animating power and a norm for others."[52]

What then is the specific relation of transcendental and categorical revelation of God to the text of Holy Scripture? As would be expected, Scripture is understood within the historical, categorical and mediational role of the Church. Again, Christ is the ultimate and final locus of divine revelation.[53] The OT gains significance only as proximate to and as the prehistory of Christ.[54] From the incarnation, that definitive, final divine revelation is passed on through the Church, especially the apostolic community. That apostolic community, as proximate to Christ, is the locus of normative teaching about the Christian faith.[55] Herein, Holy Scripture emerges as the "objectification" of the apostolic consciousness of faith:

> Everything which belongs to the original apostolic *kerygma* has been written down in Scripture. . . . For Catholic Christians too, tradition and the teaching office's understanding have their material source and *norma non normata* only in Holy Scripture.[56]

Rahner finds, then, that Scripture as canon is a "moment" within the formative early life of the Church *as* the normative bearer of revelation. More broadly it is a "successful" moment of the categorical objectification of the original transcendental self-communication of the divine that is present everywhere.

Can this objectifying "moment" be regarded as, in some real, participative sense, the written Word *of God*? Rahner first responds ironically to classical Protestant emphases (*sola gratia, sola fide, sola scriptura*) in order to enter constructive discussion of "Scripture as the Church's Book." Within divine grace and revelation, Scripture can only be reckoned as a product of the Church, which is itself a product of categorical revelation. The Reformation's emphasis on *sola scriptura* is dependent on the idea of *verbal* inspiration, whereby Scripture is regarded as the one and only product which comes immediately from God independently of. . . . the living testimony of the Church."[57] This "is untenable from a historical point of view. . . . Rather, scripture is a literary concretization of apostolic church's testimony, and *as such* it can be called "the written word of God" which remains the norm for the Church's understanding of the faith.[58]

Rahner's problem, given his understanding of revelation, is how to unify "transcendental" and "historical" (categorical) revelation. His answer is formulated in terms of the mediation of the original and primary form through the many emergent, historical vehicles of original, universal grace. The "history" *through* which grace is mediated, or through which "God's turning to man in revelation" is channeled, is not essentially *as* concept or word, let alone *as* Scripture, but as salvation history. But when this becomes thematic, explicitly when it takes religious form, it becomes revelatory. As a "moment" within this process, Scripture is understood as "the word of God" only as connected to grace, and so to God's transcendental (unthematic) self-communication.[59] As in Rahner's understanding of the role of the "prophets," revelation has become concrete in an authentic and pure way in the special *history of* the OT and NT. The new covenant especially is the objectification of the apostolic church which is always normative for the postapostolic Church. As the objectification of apostolic consciousness of faith, Scripture then has the character and characteristics belonging to *this* church, as proximate to Jesus.

But how does this make God, as the historic, authoritative documents of Roman Catholicism state repeatedly, "the *auctor* (author) of Holy Scripture"? In answering the question, in what sense God can be regarded as the "literary author" of Scripture, which is the historical position of the Church, Rahner distinguishes his formulation from the "psychological theories" of "school theology." So to unify transcendental revelation and the historical, apostolic objectification in writing, Rahner explains "inspiration" by denying that God is the "*literary* author" of Scripture, pointing rather to other options whereby the metaphor "author" may be approximated and scripture still be called "the word *of* God."[60] Scripture *can*, he says, be called "the word *of* God" because it is not merely caused by God but is the objectification of God's salvific self-expression, which is "effected by God and is borne by grace, and which comes to us without being reduced to our level." [61] In terms of "historical revelation," if God has founded the Church by his Spirit and in Jesus Christ, and if that apostolic Church as norm for the future Church is a special object of God's action in a qualitatively unique way, and if Scripture is a constitutive element (objectification) of the apostolic Church as an ongoing norm, then, in that very indirect sense "God is the author of Scripture and that he inspired it."[62] It is in this sense the "word of God."

In this creatively ambiguous way, Karl Rahner can "affirm" the documents of the Church, which speak of God as "author" of the text of Scripture, while portraying God's relation to the biblical writers and writings as essentially one of primordial "impulse" toward creative-responsive literary effluence, and while also affirming the results of radical historical criticism, i.e., the very human, culture bound nature of these "normative" writings.

Raymond Brown on Scripture and the Word of God

In an article entitled "'And the Lord said': Biblical Reflections on Scripture as the Word of God," prominent Roman Catholic New Testament scholar Raymond Brown examines what such a statement might mean in light of biblical criticism. He clarifies his approach and basic assumption when he says, first, that he is coming to the issue not as a philosopher nor as a historical or systematic theologian but as biblical critic, and second that he fully accepts "the Roman Catholic doctrine of the Bible as the Word of God."[63]

The phrase "the word of God" has a prominent place in all Judeo-Christian thought and is, in reference to Holy Scripture, found throughout Roman Catholic liturgy and theology. Thus Brown asks:

> Are the Scriptures themselves the word of God or do they contain the Word of God? In either case do we literally mean word of God? Does God speak? And if one smilingly replies, "Not in the physical sense of emitting sound waves," there is still the question of whether God internally supplies words to the recipient of revelation and/or inspiration.[64]

With such questions guiding his inquiry, Brown intends to bring increased clarity to a doctrine too often left vague, especially by modern theologians in their theories of inspiration, as if they were reflecting only "on books like Genesis, the Gospels and Romans," while in fact "they might do better by trying their theories out on the first nine chapters of I Chronicles . . . or Qoheleth."[65]

In Brown's biblical reflection on Scripture as the written word of God, two distinctions within the larger question are basic for Brown's analysis as a Roman Catholic exegete. First, he distances himself from "adoptionistic" approaches to the nature of Scripture, often linked to left wing Roman Catholic theologians.[66] Rather, with both the "centrist" and "right wing" Catholic theologians, he prefers an "incarnational" model. Second, as distinct from "right wing" positions, Brown intends to develop what he calls "the traditional Catholic distinction between revelation and inspiration."[67] He uses these terms to distinguish a fully proper Catholic approach to Scripture from that of some Protestants (e.g., Carl Henry) for whom he believes the distinction is almost lost, and who have significantly influenced many modern Roman Catholics. Such a distinction structures Brown's whole argument.

Brown's argument is cast within the theological context and climate of post-Vatican II Catholic–Protestant debates regarding biblical truthfulness. Reflecting the question of God speaking words and the strong revelation-inspiration distinction, Brown begins by examining various rabbinic interpretations of the biblical materials wherein God is said to speak. He initially affirms the view of G. Scholem who concludes that "every statement on which authority is grounded would become a human interpretation, however valid and exalted, of something that transcends it." This Brown applies, following Hebrews 1:1-2, to the words of Jesus recorded in the NT, concluding that "in the words of Jesus it is obvious that one encounters an unconditioned, timeless word spoken by God."[68] This is because the Jesus of the Synoptic Gospels spoke and thought as a Jew of the first third of the first century. Yet the Jesus of the Fourth Gospel is different in this respect. After having included the "words" of the risen Jesus, i.e., that in referring to such "words" in the category of "speaking" there is actually an "approximation of this revelation to ordinary experience," Brown then presents an initial thesis on the larger question: that human beings speak words, and revelation by the word of God really "only means divine revelation to which human beings have given expression in words."[69] If this is his conclusion, then it seems that Brown denies the historical claim that Holy Scripture is "the written word(s) of God."

Yet this is not so, though, as in the previous statements about the words of Jesus, Brown does find fault with *a priori* views of the nature of Scripture and biblical inerrancy which tend to claim the "unconditioned and timeless" quality of biblical statements. While perhaps emphasizing more than necessary the humanity and the culture-time-conditioned "incarnationality" of Scripture (e.g., claiming even "religious errors"), Brown proposes to put the affirmations of Vatican II regarding Scripture as the written word of God in true biblical context. Roman Catholic methodology, having moved from *a priori* to *a posteriori* approaches to the question of revelation and Scripture, allows one to recognize that

> Every clearly discernable action of (God) has been a surprise, how can we
> be so sure what He must do? This means that we shift to an *a posteriori*
> approach to inerrancy. Using the best biblical methods available, scholars

seek to determine what the human author meant ("literal meaning") with all his limitations. Combining this with a belief in inspiration, they recognize that there is a *kenosis* involved in God's committing His message to human words.[70]

The compromise nature of "Dei Verbum" focuses attention on the truth of Scripture as word of God, but primarily *as related* to the salvific purpose for which God intended the Scriptures.[71]

So what does this mean with regard to the propriety of any reference to Holy Scripture as directly the written word of God? Brown is as opposed to what he calls simplistic (docetic?) claims for such, even as he is opposed to liberal denials. He notes, returning to the Christological "incarnational" comparison, that Jesus as fully divine and fully human is rejected consciously by nonbelievers and unconsciously by believers, who often regard the *full* humanity of Jesus to be incompatible with the full divinity, balking at Jesus' ignorance, temptations, and limitations. In the same way believers in revelation and inspiration can problematically insist that the biblical word is not really human, has no time-conditioning or limitation, and such persons will accuse one who recognizes these qualities in Scripture of denying that it is the word of God.[72]

Rather, says Brown, like the historical limitations of the Word made flesh, the words of Scripture remain very much human words, reflecting both "partial" divine insight and time-conditioned vision. But, since only human beings use words (a highly questionable point, cf., chapter three), then whenever one has called divine communication "word(s) of God" one has in fact "indicated that the divine communication is *in human words*, and therefore that the communication (of God) is in a time-conditioned and limited form."[73] So, for Brown, the very human and limited words of Scripture are also, in some actual, even historical, sense, no less the expression or words of God. Such is said to be the extraordinary reality of God's "kenotic," historical and human communication to us for our salvation.[74]

Avery Dulles on Scripture and the Word of God

For many years Avery Dulles has been one of the most prominent and prolific Roman Catholic theologians in the English-speaking world.

He was recently named a cardinal by John Paul II. Both revelation and ecclesiology have been issues of central concern for Dulles. Two of his works on revelation of special significance for our question are *Models of Revelation* and "Faith and Revelation" within the larger work *Systematic Theology: Roman Catholic Perspectives.*

Dulles' interests in the nature of divine revelation are both constructive and ecumenical. It is his firm (and correct) belief that the early christological controversies, the split between Churches East and West, the Reformation struggles, and today's differences between orthodox, modern, and postmodern, experiential and evangelical, etc., are tied to the question of revelation. As he says, "The great theological disputes turn out, upon reflection, to rest on different understandings of revelation, often simply taken for granted."[75] How, then, does Dulles relate revelation and Holy Scripture?

In *Models of Revelation*, Dulles makes use of Michael Polanyi's distinction between tacit and explicit knowing by the use of "models" in order to examine and identify the basic questions and issues surrounding the doctrine of revelation in our time. To this end, he sets forth five broad models of revelation representing the most significant Christian approaches in the twentieth century. Then, gleaning what regards to be the truth of each, Dulles draws all of these together under his integrating theme of "symbolic mediation," a view intended to reflect the Catholic tradition of symbol in relation to revelation. Regarding the model "Revelation as History" (the "biblical theology movement"), he finds the emphasis to be not on divine words or statements but on decisive divine deeds, what God does.[76] The "Revelation as Inner Experience" model, represented by Schleiermacher, George Tyrrell, Wilhelm Herrmann, and Tillich, understands God's revelation to come through an experience of "God-consciousness" characterized as numinous, holy, ultimate concern, an experience reflected in all religions. Here the contribution is the recognition of the mystical and personal dimensions of revelation.[77] Interestingly, Barth and Bultmann are classified together under "Revelation as Dialectical Presence." This model emphasizes revelation as the Word of God which *confronts* us *through* Scripture, "an over-againstness" that overturns our agendas and expectations.[78] In "Revelation as New Awareness," a model found to include process theology, Gregory Baum, John Hick and Gabriel Moran, God is immanent in nature and history and therein is moving the world toward an intended goal. Revelation here is the sensitizing of persons to or toward the divine activity with the invitation to participate in that purposive world. The useful insight here is focus on the affective nature of revelation through performative symbols rather than *merely* cerebral and propositional.[79]

The fifth view, especially as compared and related to Dulles' "symbolic mediation," is of special significance. Dulles calls this "Revelation as Doctrine," a model he links to Roman Catholic neoscholasticism and to "conservative evangelicalism" represented by Carl Henry, J. I. Packer, and Gordon Clark. This view emphasizes God's disclosive work in providing "information" about God and God's purposes which is "cast in clear cut and abiding propositions," "timeless truths" found in Scripture and, for the Roman Catholic viewpoint, in the dogmatic formulas of the Church. On the "evangelical view" of revelation, Dulles claims to borrow from Benjamin Warfield in saying that

> For effective knowledge of the salvific truth, supernatural (or "special") revelation is necessary. This supernatural revelation was imparted in early biblical times by theophanic phenomena and prophetic visions, but as the revelation progressed it took on to an increasing degree the form of doctrine. In the final period, revelation characteristically occurred through a "concursive operation" whereby the Holy Spirit inspires and controls human powers as they are exercised in historical research, logical reasoning, and literary composition.[80]

The "evangelical" view of Scripture is said to be, first, one which distinguishes revelation from inspiration, while keeping them closely connected (i.e., initial communication of information and effective consignment of such to writing). Second, Scripture as a whole and all of its parts are regarded as so inspired that, in the original manuscripts, it is free from error and is God's written word, objectified revelation.[81]

Dulles assesses these models by seven criteria: faithfulness to the Bible and Christian tradition, internal coherence, plausibility, adequacy to experience, practical fruitfulness, theoretical fruitfulness, and value for dialogue. The "propositional model" is found to hold up well at several points. First, it has "a certain foundation in the Bible" *if* one takes references to God's communication as literal. "While there is no cogent proof that every passage from Scripture is regarded as God's word, many biblical passages are quoted as if God said what the Bible said."[82] He rightly acknowledges that most Church Fathers and doctors of the Church to the nineteenth century, Catholic, Orthodox and Protestant, tended "to treat individual biblical statements without reservation as the Word of God."[83] Also, the "propositional" model has strong internal coherence. If the premises are granted, the whole follows. This then engenders theoretical fruitfulness with a firm basis for doctrinal standards. Especially strong is its practical fruitfulness. It encourages faithfulness to the Church's foundational doctrines and a clear sense of identity for the maintenance of orthodoxy as well as a strong sense of mission and growth. These strengths of the propositional model of revelation Dulles wants to incorporate into his own model.

But based on his *a priori* criteria, reflecting his own broader agenda, Dulles sees problems. First, the propositional view is in decline in many circles. Second, the Bible does not seem to claim propositional infallibility for itself, nor was it so considered by all ancient or medieval exegetes. But this conclusion he tries to defend by equating "propositional" with literalistic, then by pointing to the patristic hermeneutical tendencies toward allegorical exegesis. Third, he says that the claim of revealed truth in every declarative sentence of Scripture is not plausible in an age of critical thinking, and the theory rests on an objectifying theory of knowledge now widely questioned. The propositional model is also inadequate to experience, i.e., it is authoritarian, requiring submission to concepts from very different, ancient situations from those now experienced, thus missing the evocative power of the biblical images and the immanent "signs of God's presence in one's own life and experience."[84] Finally, the propositional theory is not conducive to dialogue with other religions, another stipulative conclusion given this criterion.[85] Does Dulles mean then that God's revelation is devoid of cognitive value, or that the clear teachings of Scripture are without connection to revelation? Not so. There are elements here that Dulles intends to incorporate. But the adequacy of such and the ongoing problem of dualistic, disjunctive thinking will be questions we will need to pose.

In terms of Dulles' own "symbolic mediation" model of revelation, which attempts to incorporate the strengths while avoiding the weaknesses of the models analyzed, revelation is symbolic communication. This he sets within the context of what he terms "participatory indwelling," i.e., revelation as symbolic mediation occurs within the formative, directive, and interpretive parameters of the community of faith, and this "within the realities to which the symbols refer."[86] Therein one can "dwell" confidently "in the clues that *point to* Christian revelation."[87] Scripture, with Church tradition, revelatory events/encounters, etc., serves as a clue or "lens" by which God's revelation can be apprehended. The revealing God can disclose His reality *through* these kinds of created media.

But what is meant here by "symbol" and why is this approach regarded as both necessary and as a way to unify the five models? With guidance from Tillich, Mircea Eliade, H. Richard Niebuhr, Polanyi, and Norman Perrin, Dulles asserts that revelation never occurs as a purely interior experience or as an unmediated encounter with God. Revelation is always mediated through symbol, i.e., by an externally perceived sign which works mysteriously on human consciousness, suggesting more than it can clearly describe or define. "Revelatory symbols" express and mediate God's self-communication.[88] This reflects Dulles' emphasis on the inability of discursive language to disclose the transcendent mystery of God. But a symbol is a "sign pregnant with a plenitude of meaning." But this is understood to be evocative meaning which cannot be adequately stated, though it does create a "vast potential of semantic energy" in those affected. Language is but an indicative sign, a "clue" by which one integrates a wider range of feelings, impressions and affections. [89]

Thus, for Dulles, revelation is not contentful; it is not informative. Rather, divine revelation as mediated via symbols is evocative and its "truth" is simply its capacity to create "a new vision of the world and new possibilities." To justify this conclusion, attention is drawn to "revelatory symbolism in Scripture." There are revelations found in Scripture which are constituted by symbolic ingredients. These Dulles divides into events (e.g., miracles, theophanies, events in the life of Jesus), all possessing numinous phenomena and themes (e.g., Kingdom of God). In terms of genre, there is much metaphor in Scripture and prominent elements of symbol (e.g., ritual). But are these scriptural examples actually noninformative "disclosure situations" which create only an awareness of a nondiscursive, nameless Other? It is very significant that Dulles, wanting a biblical basis for his understanding of revelation as transformative, illuminative mystery, fails to mention Scripture's own perspective on God's self-revelation. To pick but one prominent omission, Dulles totally passes by the OT prophetic entré to disclosure, "Thus says Yahweh." He sunders the simultaneity of the transcendent glory and fearful mystery of the living God from God's loving condescension, from his coming to and for human redemption by means of content-ful self-disclosure.

How can Dulles recover the element of "truth" in the "propostional" theory while reckoning revelation to be only transcendent, evocative mystery and, too, his conclusions about the incapacity of human language to do justice to the unlimited, multidimensional, creative, transforming revelation of God? Dulles is sensitive to the charge that his rejection of any of direct divine speech and truth-content in favor of amorphous mystery leaves Christianity doctrinally void. By cunningly equivocating on the term "meaning," he says

> Symbol achieves the joint meaning of diverse and seemingly incompatible particulars *by an effort of imagination*, whereby our tacit powers of integration are aroused to an exceptional degree. By eliciting participation, a symbol can convey a richer and more personal apprehension of reality in its deeper dimensions than propostional language [which he also disparages as "mere measurements and numbers, statistics and bloodless abstractions"!] can do. Its distinctive mark is not the absence of meaning but the surplus of meaning. . . . [but] symbols frequently require explication so as to clear up their ambiguity. . . . Because of the *cognitive content implicit in* the originative *symbols*, revelatory symbolism is able to not only "*give rise* to thought" but also to *shape* the thought it arouses.[90]

In the faith community, by "vitally indwelling" the revelational reality to which the symbols refer, one is said to be opened to transformative mystery and thus enabled to give conceptual expression and interpretation to mediated revelation. This is the same faithful awareness and responsiveness to the divine which originally gave rise to the imaginative, integrating images of Scripture and Tradition. Yet somehow Dulles claims that creative response to such mystery is "not indefinitely pliable." Christian symbols create a network which forms a context. And, as interpreted within the living faith community, they give directives for thinking and conduct.[91]

Dulles' need for symbolic mediation; his rejection of content-ful, objective, as well as personal, divine self-disclosure; and his transcendentalizing of God and the "revelation" of God is rooted in the same disjunctive thinking grounded in Kant's noumenal-phenomenal split. As a result, Dulles cannot say what revelation is. The *Ding an sich* of God's self-revelation is unknowable. Yet he must try to fend off the agnostic implications of his vision of nameless, mute Otherness or amorphous divine mystery by enlisting culturally positive terms from popular, personalistic psycho babble, falsely claiming (a la Bultmann and Brunner) the relational-personalistic high ground for nondiscursive mystery, while falsely disparaging "propositionalism" as the reduction of divine richness to impersonal calculations.

Clearly Dulles will not allow any level of identity between Holy Scripture and divine revelation or "Word of God." Yet he must seek some significance for Scripture within God's revelatory processes and purposes. Revelation as it works affectively in human lives leads to *human* literary objectification. Very indirectly, divine causality is in view. God's people, by symbolically mediated revelation, are moved to bring written objectivity to their experience. God who first "authors" the faith community, is indirectly "author" of the responsive writings of that community.[92]

More recently, in his "Faith and Revelation" in *Systematic Theology: Roman Catholic Perspectives*, Dulles expresses himself in more classical Roman Catholic fashion saying that the Bible is called "the written word of God" because "God's grace impelled the human authors to write and directed them to give a pure and reliable expression of the faith of the people of God at their particular stage of salvation history."[93] The Roman Catholic view of inspiration is then said to be the whole complex of internal graces and external helps which "enabled the writers and editors of the biblical books to produce normative texts for the Church's guidance."[94] Being constrained by this more official setting, Dulles says that the Bible, as the basis of Church belief and teaching, is a "*reliable witness to* God's revelation as communicated in its formative period. The inspiration given . . . prevented (the sacred writers) from falsifying what God had revealed."[95] This rather Barthian (cf. chapter six) statement reflects a somewhat more traditional view than previously found in Dulles. Yet Scripture's dualistic distinction from the Word of God is still clear. One wonders how "falsification" can possibly occur in relation to a contentless revelation.

Richard Swinburne on Scripture and the Word of God

Richard Swinburne, until his recent retirement, was professor of Christian philosophy at Oxford University. He has long been engaged in giving philosophical expression and justification to classical Christian theological themes and questions from a Roman Catholic perspective. In his book *Revelation: From Metaphor to Analogy*, Swinburne gives a stimulating, exasperating and, occasionally, confusing reflection of yet another foundational Christian issue, the deeds and truth of God. His direction is clear. Some religions (e.g., Judaism, Christianity, Islam) claim that God has revealed truths which are crucial for persons to know or believe. What are the bases for believing that some act, book or creed conveys divinely revealed truth?

After examining linguistic elements related to the role of truth statements or propositions, analogy, metaphor and genre, and why we might properly expect revelation of divine truth, Swinburne unfolds his argument for the probability of the Christian revelation claim and its relation to the Church, Creeds and Scripture.[96] Contrary to many post-Kantian notions of "revelation," Swinburne asserts that revelation may be either *of* God (or God's acts), and so nonpropositional, or *by* God of propositional truth. His special focus is upon revelation in this second sense, i.e., revelation of propositional truth. But with his argument for "propositional" revelation, he argues more basically that there are good reasons for believing that there is a God from what is observed in nature, and that yet further reason for belief in divine revelation would be provided by the fact (if it is a fact) "that there are creeds and books of purported revelation of a kind which is to be expected if there is a God."[97] Given such a method of probabilist argumentation and affirmation, Swinburne's view of Holy Scripture as related to the Word of God would seem to be sure. This is not so.

While Swinburne rails against modern historical-critical views which assert that revelation, whatever that might be, cannot be propositional, cannot have truth content, pointing out how such denials diverge from historic Christian teaching, he then turns around and praises the historical-critical method for its capacity to get behind Scripture to the real event of revelation. How does Swinburne bring these elements together and how is this formative to his understanding of Holy Scripture and the Word of God? First, he differentiates what he terms "the original revelation" and any documents or institutions by which the truth or teaching of that revelation is conveyed. He states that

> The original propositional revelation was the teaching of God to the Israelites . . . about himself and his dealings with them and other nations, culminating in the teachings of Jesus Christ, including his teaching about the significance of his actions and the teaching of the first apostles about the significance of those actions.[98]

Again, this would certainly seem to refer, at some level, to Holy Scripture as a consequent aspect of this contentful revelatory process. Again, this is not so. For Swinburne, references to divinely revealed truth, teaching, message, etc., are *not textual*. Such "original revelation" is not, at any level, manifested as a written document, though he does say that it may somehow be found through and expressed in written language form.[99] In this way he can argue against Protestant reverence for Holy Scripture and its claim that Holy Scripture itself is to be understood as an aspect of "original revelation," that Scripture is a direct product of God's speech-action. This he claims, fits badly with the fact that there were Christians in the first four centuries AD without a complete canonical text of Scripture.[100] This point is of highly questionable significance.

Throughout his formulation of divine revelation, Swinburne reflects an antiverbal bias ("acts rather than *mere* words"). Interestingly, his understanding of propositional revelation is of that which is verbal and true (e.g., the oral teaching of Jesus) and yet nontextual. This means that he must argue along the following lines. First, God gave the original propositional revelation. Second, God intended that this revelation be available for ongoing generations of people, so he founded a Church to interpret that revelation correctly.[101] Thus, no matter what the gospels might assert about Jesus, in fact Jesus taught what the Church says he taught, including the fact that the New Testament is basically correct. While Swinburne believes that historical-critical methods can uncover much of the original teaching behind Scripture, and so even to the original act of God beyond the text of Scripture, still he has to acknowledge that such methods cannot grant certainty about such teaching.[102] Only the authorized Church interpretation can give such certainty. According to Swinburne, then, propositional revelation from God is indeed truth or teaching, but yet it is to be found beyond Holy Scripture.[103] Why, then, is there a Scripture at all? And what then of the creeds in relation to Scripture?

Swinburne responds to such issues. By means of a discussion of modern and contemporary hermeneutical issues, Swinburne's real purpose to give strong affirmation to the various historical-critical methods and presuppositions (e.g., source criticism and the documentary hypothesis) becomes clear. In this way, he can underscore the formative authority of the Roman Catholic Church while humanizing Scripture, but without impuning God. When Swinburne comes to the question of "inspiration" (a term he never examines), he begins by claiming a "strong sense" of God's authorship of the biblical text, even quoting Gregory the Great: "Holy Scripture is a letter of God almighty to his creature."[104] Despite this apparent connection between the Word of God and the text of Scripture, Swinburne is actually claiming here that God was the author of original insights and traditions which the human writers of Scripture often misunderstood or falsely expressed, and so these insights can only be understood by what comes later. His illustration from Joshua is instructive. God's revelatory insight to Israel was that it is not good to worship lesser gods and that such false worship deserves punishment. Swinburne says that the writer of Joshua *correctly* grasped these insights but *failed* to realize differences in regard to such punishment (e.g., ignorance, children with parents) and the role of divine mercy. Thus Swinburne says

> God is the author of the Bible only in the sense that he "inspired" the human authors to write and compilers to compile the books they did; yet not merely did those human authors have their own style and presuppositions and God sought only *to breathe his message through* those. . . . but also the human authors and compilers were less than fully pliable. They were not fully open to divine truth.[105]

How are we to discern the difference? We must be able to recognize the discrepancy of the writers of Scripture from God's main message. Swinburne says that we must accept nothing "at odds" with Scripture's central message, i.e., the Church's creeds ("and other known scientific and historical truth").[106] Thus the Old Testament is to be understood in the light of the New, and the New in the light of the Church's creeds. How the early church could have arrived at the truth contained in the great creeds as a result of their soteriological interpretation of Scripture, apart from the creeds, is never dealt with, though "tradition," like "insight," is apparently an *a priori* revelatory (nontextual, nonverbal) reality.

Thus, for Richard Swinburne, Holy Scripture is at best indirectly "inspired" and is "the paramount vehicle of revelation,"[107] but it is not the written Word of God, not itself a participatory aspect of God's self-revelation. The "propositional" truth of God, found *through* Scripture by the Church is embodied in the Church's creeds. In all, Swinburne has, in fact, made numerous, untraditional, un-Catholic claims regarding Holy Scripture and divine revelation in order to undergird his own (often circular) apologetic for supreme Church authority within the revelatory acts of God.[108]

The Nature of Holy Scripture in the New Catechism of the Catholic Church

In his opening statement for the new *Catechism of the Catholic Church*, John Paul II explained the connection of this new document to Vatican II. He had participated in drafting Vatican II, and now, seeking to "implement its (apostolic and pastoral) directives concretely and faithfully," he called an "extraordinary assembly" of the Synod of Bishops on the twentieth anniversary of its close (1985). One purpose was that "all the Christian faithful might better adhere to it and to promote knowledge and application of it."[109] There many bishops expressed the desire for a *new* "compendium of all catholic doctrine" regarding faith and morals. Such a biblical, liturgical document must become a reference for the whole Church and also as an aid for the formation of regional/cultural catechisms which represent local concerns.[110] John Paul II commissioned its preparation in 1986, under the leadership of then Cardinal Joseph Ratzinger (now pope Benedict XVI), seven diocesan Bishops and a group of "experts in theology and catechesis" who, assisting the commission, did the real work of drafting the new Catechism which . . . was officially given by John Paul II to the Church on the thirtieth anniversary of the opening of Vatican II (1992).[111]

The opening sections speak repeatedly of the *Catechism* as an "organic synthesis" of the essential and basic contents of Catholic doctrine, not only in *light* of Vatican II but "the *whole* of the Church's tradition." Thus, as our concern here in this chapter is with the document's understanding of the nature of sacred Scripture, it is important to note principal authoritative sources for the document: "the Sacred Scriptures, the Fathers of the Church, the liturgy and the Church's Magisterium."[112] Footnotes make clear the wide range of sources used beyond Vatican II, which does not provide even a majority of the references. In fact, it is Holy Scripture which often provides a majority of the references. The *Catechism*'s primary discussion of "Sacred Scripture" is set within the second chapter, "God Comes to Meet Man" and its three articles, "The Revelation of God," "The Transmission of Divine Revelation" and "Sacred Scripture." Yet this is to be reckoned in light of the prior section, "Man's Capacity for God." The fallen human being

> stands in need of being enlightened by God's revelation, not only about those things which exceed his understanding, but also about those religious and moral truths which of themselves are not beyond the grasp of human reason.[113]

Beyond "natural reason" and our "capacity" for God as "made to live in communion with God," there lies *another* order of knowledge which humans cannot arrive at by their own powers, "divine Revelation." God has freely chosen to reveal himself and to give himself to humanity. This he does by "revealing the mystery, his plan of loving goodness, formed from all eternity in Christ, for the benefit of all men." Central to the *Catechism*'s presentation of revelation is Jesus Christ. By sending God the Son at the incarnation God has fully revealed his plan.[114]

Yet contrary to many modern theologians for whom God has his one Word, Christ, but no words, the *Catechism* seems quite clear that by "stages" and "by deeds and words" God has been making known and realizing the mystery of his will through the whole history of his covenantal relationships, e.g., with fallen Adam and Eve, Noah, Abraham, and with Israel through his acts *and words* at the Exodus and in the giving of the law "*through* Moses."[115] But in Christ, "the Mediator and fullness of all revelation," the Father has given his "one, perfect and unsurpassable Word. In him he has said everything; there will be no other word than this one."[116] But what of Holy Scripture? Or the New Testament, given that "no other word than this one" and "no new public revelation is to be expected" because of the definitive coming of the incarnate Word? Is the OT passé? Is the NT just a human witness to Christ the Word but not itself an aspect of divine revelation, according to the *Catechism*?

The articles on the transmission of divine revelation and the relation of such to Sacred Scripture clarify the issue somewhat, but, like Vatican II ("Dei Verbum"), they do so dialectically. Given God's desire that "knowledge of the truth," as it is above all in Jesus Christ, should come to all persons, and so his revelation "to the ends of the earth," it is certain that the *Catechism* regards divine revelation as contentful, something which can be "handed on" to others. Quoting "Dei Verbum" it is stated that "God graciously arranged that the things he had once revealed for the salvation of all peoples should remain in their entirety, throughout the ages, and be *transmitted* to all generations."[117] This "transmission" of revelation through history, including the apostles, took multiple forms, including oral and *written*, e.g., "under the inspiration of the same Holy Spirit [the apostles] committed the message of salvation to writing."[118] Yet ambiguity, and so the possibility of final disjunction of Scripture from Word of God/divine revelation, remains in the article "Sacred Scripture." *Both* Christ *the* Word of God and sacred Scripture as Word of God are emphasized. On the one hand, it is asserted that God, purposing to reveal himself to persons, "speaks to them in human words . . . the words of God expressed in words of men." While one might wonder what "words of God" might be apart from human expressions, the point is that this use of human language is contextually presented as analogous to God's taking "the flesh of human weakness," and that *through* the words of Sacred Scripture, God speaks only one Word, "i.e., Jesus Christ, the center, focus and final content of all revelation."[119] While one would want to agree with this christocentric thrust regarding revelation, the connection or relation to Scripture could be taken here as similar to that of existentialist, dialectical or "Barthian" conceptions (cf. chapters two and six).

But this existentialist thrust alone does not seem to be the real intent of the *Catechism*. Indeed, there are repeated "classical" statements regarding the fact that "God is the author of Sacred Scripture," that Scripture simply *is* "the Word of God" and that Scripture reveals "the mystery of the divine will" and "divine realities" *because* of the action of God in the power of the Holy Spirit upon, in and through the writers of Scripture. For example,

> The divinely revealed realities which are contained and presented *in the text* of Sacred Scripture, have been written down under the inspiration of the Holy Spirit.[120]

> The Old and New Testaments, whole and entire, with all their parts, on the grounds that written under the inspiration of the Holy Spirit, they have God as their author. . . .[121]

> And throughout this article Scripture and Word of God are used interchangeably with clear intent.[122] It is noteworthy, too, that "Sacred Scripture" is repeatedly said to be truthful in all its affirmations, e.g.,

> The inspired books teach the truth "since therefore all that the inspired authors . . . affirm should be regarded as affirmed by the Holy Spirit, we must acknowledge that the books of Scripture firmly, faithfully and without error teach that truth which God, for the sake of our salvation, wished to see confided to the Sacred Scriptures."[123]

Therefore the *Catechism* affirms that sacred (sometimes "divine") Scripture *is* the written Word of God, *is* a crucial aspect of divine revelation which, like all divine revelation, is rooted, centered and focused on the Incarnate Word, Jesus Christ.

Yet, again, there are also elements which could be used to modify interpretation of these affirmations, as set within contemporary theological discussions. Church tradition is at least of equal authority and, with Scripture, makes up a "single deposit of the Word of God."[124] The inspired text of divine Scripture, said to be "the speech of God put down in writing under the breath of the Holy Spirit," here obviously includes the Apocrypha.[125] "Veneration" for Scripture is likened to veneration of the body of Jesus, a comparison which could be pushed to lend force to separating Scripture from the Word of God.[126] Also, occasional expressions describing Scripture's role in God's purposes, e.g., "The Word *through*

Scripture" and "Word of God *contained in* Scripture," which are used in modern and contemporary discussions in order to *deny* Scripture as the written Word of God or as a participative aspect and result of divine revelation, are used in this section of the document. Yet in the contexts such conclusions do not seem to be the intent.[127] Finally, on occasion when Scripture has just been strongly extolled as the written Word of God, there will follow disclaimers about Christianity *not* being a religion of *the book*, not written and mute, but "incarnate and living." Surely this reflects individual differences among the framers of the *Catechism*. Yes, the role of the Holy Spirit is obviously a crucial element, but such seeming reticence or reversal is used contextually to re-affirm Church Tradition and the Magisterium.[128] Still the affirmation of Scripture as the revealed, inspired Word of God, in and under Christ the Word, must be taken as the basic import of the *Catechism of the Catholic Church* regarding the nature of Sacred Scripture.

Conclusion

Since Trent, and especially since the Enlightenment, Roman Catholic views of authority, revelation/Word of God and the relation of Holy Scripture to divine revelation have been anything but stable, ebbing and flowing in ways that followed or paralleled trends in Protestantism and the larger culture. On the question of Holy Scripture, one theologian has rightly pointed out that "The traditional Roman Catholic position is that God is the primary author of Scripture and the human beings the secondary authors."[129] But after Trent, the increasingly diverse perspectives regarding inspiration in relation to and in the light of perceived phenomena in the text led to ever more creative and oblique ways to affirm the Church's historic dogma regarding Scripture as the Word of God. Many of the effects of Catholic liberalism were overcome, and the "incarnational model" of Scripture as Word of God became useful for a time, as reflected in Vatican II. But the "incarnational model" is quite ambiguous, and since Vatican II this has often been exploited by "progressives" in order to reflect divergent and radical views of Scripture and "Word of God."

The Vatican II document "Dei Verbum" owes much to the influence of Karl Rahner, and so contains built in ambiguities regarding the nature of sacred Scripture so that, while apparently reaffirming Scripture as the written Word of God, it creates great allowance for wide-ranging views on revelation/Word of God and, consequently, regarding the relation of the Word of God to Scripture. Earlier dogmatic statements of the Church, which affirmed Holy Scripture to be *directly* the inspired Word of God in a strong sense, are typically re-interpreted (usually anachronistically) and understood in light of the current situation. In this way progressives like Rahner, Dulles, and even Swinburne can creatively reformulate the nature of revelation and its relation to Holy Scripture. Moderate Raymond Brown is, to an extent, an exception. Clearly then the classical Roman Catholic recognition of Scripture as the written Word of God in a direct sense has often shifted to Scripture as an existential point or place of "revelatory" mediation, thereby following Protestant neoliberalism (e.g., Tillich, Bultmann) under the formative influence of Hegelian immanentism. This relativizes official Roman Catholic dogma as a whole and its specific statements regarding the nature of Scripture as the Word of God in order to conform to radical historical-critical conclusions of the total humanity and culture boundedness of Scripture. *Present context* becomes the formative content of dogma on the nature of Scripture, and Church dogma itself becomes a "wax nose" whose actual shape depends on the winds of contemporary theological creativity. It is, then, historically and theologically noteworthy that, under the firmer hand of John Paul II and then Cardinal Ratzinger, the recent *New Catechism of the Catholic Church* has taken steps to solidify the classic Roman Catholic affirmation of Scripture as the written Word of God while leaving some "room" for a "bounded" diversity.

Still the larger theological situation parallels the postmodern death of the author (intent) and of the external text in order to give preeminence, even dominance, to the horizon of present creative interpretation as brought to the text by the reader/subject. Yet the fact that such thinkers as Rahner, Dulles and Swinburne continue to respond to Roman Catholic dogma means that they each reflect the continuing need to somehow, however indirectly, "connect" revelation/Word of God and the text of Sacred Scripture. But to this writer it is Raymond Brown's work in relation to the textual phenomena of Scripture whose particular "incarnational" conclusions seem to have the most potential fruitfulness for understanding the relation of Holy Scripture *to and as* the written Word of God.

Endnotes

[1] Phillip Schaff, *The Creeds of Christendom* (Grand Rapids: Baker, 1977 Reprint) 92.

[2] Ibid., 94.

[3] Thomas Aquinas, lectio VI on John XXI, in F. J. Crehan, "The Bible in the Roman Catholic Church from Trent to the Present Day," *The Cambridge History of the Bible*, vol. III (Cambridge: Cambridge University Press, 1963) 199.

[4] Crehan points out that "It is time . . . that in drafting the decree the Council rejected a form of words that would have canonized the view that the doctrine of the church was transmitted partly in Scripture and partly in Tradition. It refrained for the moment from deciding the question whether there were doctrines that had come down through Tradition only, or through Scripture only, but this suspension of judgment did not prevent the Council at later sessions . . . from basing its teaching in practice on Tradition alone," 200.

[5] Ibid., 201.

[6] Schaff, 99.

[7] Crehan, 217.

[8] Ibid., 218.

[9] Ibid.

[10] Ibid., 221.

[11] Ibid., 222.

[12] Schaff, 130ff. E.g. headings from the "Syllabus" include: "The denial of (God's) revelation," "(that) Divine revelation is imperfect," "[that] the prophecies and miracles of the Bible are poetic fictions."

[13] Ibid.

[14] H. Denzinger, ed. E*nchiridon Symbolorium et definitionum*, 783–86, in Crehan, 229.

[15] J. Seynaeve, ed. *John Henry Cardinal Newman's Doctrine on Holy Scripture* (Louvain, Belgium: Publications Universitaires, 1953) 70. J. H. Newman, in a work he was preparing on "Inspiration," wrote: "I am not proposing to comment on Scripture, nor am I proposing to reconcile Scripture with the conclusions of human sciences; so far from it that I would rather contend that there is little to reconcile, because there is little possible common between them. I am to adjust rather than to reconcile; that is, I aim at showing how theology sits easy . . . *in its own domain*, without any fear, as time goes on, of any collision between itself and secular knowledge, as regards the statements of the written Word, provided each party will but consent to remain within its own boundaries. . . . nothing that science or inquiry can discover is able to reach, for confirmation or for damage, those sacred truths and facts which the voice of the church, or of her doctors and schoolmen, or of her Bishops and people *in orbe terrarum*, has recognized and declared to be dogma in the written Word." Crehan, 226–27.

[16] Newman defined an *obiter dictum* as "a phrase or sentence which, whether statement of literal fact or not, is not from the circumstances binding upon our faith." Crehan, 228.

[17] Crehan, 229.

[18] Crehan, 230. In the encylical *Divino afflante*, Pope Pius XII negated the theory of *obiter dicta* by stating that "Certain Catholic writers...dared to restrict the truth of sacred Scripture to matters of faith and morals only, and to consider the remainder, touching matters of the physical or historical order, as *obiter dicta*, and as having no connection whatever with faith. These errors found their merited condemnation in the encylical *Providentissimus* . . ."

[19] Ibid., 231.

[20] Ibid.

[21] Ibid.

[22] Ibid., 232.

[23] Ibid., 234.

[24] Ibid.

[25] Ibid.

[26] "Dei Verbum," chapter one, section 2, in *The Documents of Vatican II* (London: Sheed and Ward, 1965) 375–76. Cf. chapter one, section 4.

[27] Ibid., chapter one, section 6, 377.

[28] Ibid., chapter three, section 11, 381.

[29] Ibid., 381–82.

[30] Ibid., chapter three, section 12, 382.

[31] Ibid., chapter three, section 13, 383.

[32] Ibid.

[33] Karl Rahner, *Foundations of Christian Faith*, trans. William V. Dych (New York: Seabury, 1978) 87.

[34] Ibid., 51ff. Cf. Developments of such lines of thinking in contemporary Roman Catholic theologians and philosophers of religion, e.g., Nicholas Lash, *Easter in Ordinary* (Notre Dame, Ind.: Notre Dame University Press, 1990).

[35] Ibid.

[36] Ibid., 57ff.

[37] Ibid., 138.

[38] Karl Rahner, "Revelation," in *Encyclopedia of Theology: The Concise Sacramentum Mundi*, ed. Karl Rahner (New York: Seabury, 1975) 1461.

[39] Ibid., 53–54.

[40] Ibid., 142.

[41] Ibid., 171.

[42] Ibid.

[43] Ibid., 154.

[44] Ibid., 155.

[45] Ibid., 156.

[46] Ibid., 157ff.

[47] Ibid., 150.

[48] Ibid., 157ff.

[49] Ibid., 158.

[50] Ibid.

[51] Ibid.

[52] Ibid., 159–60.

[53] Ibid., 175.

[54] Ibid., 157.

[55] Ibid., 328–30. On 330 in *Foundations*, Rahner says of the apostolic community as connected to Jesus Christ and, thus, as the locus of normative teaching about the Christian faith, that "wherever ecclesial Christianity is found, it is convinced that it had its origins in Christ. . . . If continuity and identity are to be maintained within an entity which exists historically, then it is inevitable that in an earlier phase of this historical entity free decisions are made which form an irreversible norm for future epochs."

[56] Ibid., 364.

[57] Ibid., 362.

[58] Ibid., 363. Cf. clarifying discussion on 362–65.

[59] Ibid., 370. One ought to note the marked influence of Hegel's is thought here, as, of course, throughout Rahner's theology.

[60] Ibid., 374.

[61] Ibid.

[62] Ibid.

[63] Raymond E. Brown, "'And the Lord Said': Biblical Reflections on Scripture as the Word of God" in *Theological Studies* 42 (1981) 4.

[64] Ibid.

[65] Ibid., 8.

[66] Ibid., 5.

[67] Ibid., 7.

[68] Ibid., 11. One should note, in this context, the comments of Gershom Scholem regarding the view of Rabbi Mendel on the very mystical nature of revelation from

God and the role of human writing in relation to it. Cf. Gershom Scholem, *On the Kabbala and Its Symbolism* (London: Routledge, Kegan Paul, 1965) 29–31.

[69] Ibid., 13.

[70] Ibid., 15. Note Brown's point on the compromise nature of Vatican II's statement in "Dei Verbum" and how the final form of the statement sets side by side the older, stronger statements about Scripture as the written Word of God, and newer formulations. The resulting ambiguity leaves room for both "minimalist" and strong (maximalist) readings, p. 16 and footnote 41.

[71] Ibid., 16–17.

[72] Ibid., 19.

[73] Ibid., 18. Note that in regard to the question about the sense of the phrase "word of God" and the objection that "word of God" is also a title for the second person of the Trinity, Brown replies that it is a title given to that person alone who took to Himself the human, the time-conditioned, and the limited. Cf. Endnote 47.

[74] Ibid. Brown herein points to the comments of then cardinal Joseph Ratzinger on the document "Dei Verbum" 9 where he says that "It is important to note that only Scripture is defined in terms of what it *is*: it is stated that Scripture *is* the *word* of God consigned to writing. Tradition, however, is described only functionally, in terms of what it *does*: it hands on the Word of God, but *is not* the word of God." This point by Ratzinger clarifies the truly unique status of Scripture in relation to tradition when understanding the statement in "Dei Verbum" 10 which states that "the task of authentically interpreting the word of God, whether written or handed on, has been entrusted exclusively to the teaching office of the Church. . . . This teaching office is not above the word of God but serves it.

[75] Avery Dulles, M*odels of Revelation* (Mary Knoll, N.Y.: Orbis, 1983) xix.

[76] Ibid., chapter 4.

[77] Ibid., chapter 5.

[78] Ibid., chapter 6.

[79] Ibid., chapter 7.

[80] Ibid., 37–38. Cf. B. B. Warfield, *Revelation and Inspiration* (Phillipsburg, N.J.: Presbyterian and Reformed. 1948) 15–25.

[81] Ibid., 38. Cf. B. B. Warfield, *Inspiration and Authority of the Bible* (Phillipsburg, N.J.: Presybterian and Reformed, 1948) 442.

[82] Ibid., 46.

[83] Ibid.

[84] Ibid., 51.

[85] Ibid., 48–52.

[86] Ibid., 144.

87 Ibid., 128.

88 Ibid., 131.

89 Ibid., 132.

90 Ibid., 142–44.

91 Ibid., 144. In a context wherein Dulles is typically extolling the "richness" of meaning of symbolic mediation compared to the "propositional" view, which he disparages (no doubt for self-defensive purposes) as the reduction of divine qualities to abstractions, numbers and measurements (a false descriptive play used also by many Protestants who also want to make their own unbelieving denial of content-ful divine disclosure "spiritual"), he says: "Even more is this true if we would achieve awareness of the transcendent, which is the proper theme of revelation. God, though utterly beyond description and definition, is eminently real. Symbolic events and language can mediate, albeit deficiently something of God's reality." Ibid., 142.

92 Ibid., 201–92ff.

93 Avery Dulles, "Faith and Revelation" in *Systematic Theology: Roman Catholic Perspectives*, Vol. 1, ed. Francis Schüssler Fiorenza and John P. Galvin (Minneapolis: Fortress, 1991) 118–19.

94 Ibid., 119.

95 Ibid.

96 Richard Swinburne, *Revelation: From Metaphor to Analogy* (New York: Oxford University Press, 1992) 2. Swinburne refers to these as the documents and institutions of the purported revelation.

97 Ibid., 3.

98 Ibid., 101. Cf. 118.

99 Ibid., 96, 101ff.

100 Ibid., 103.

101 Cf. Swinburne's cruical discussion (for undergirding his own idiosyncratic formulation of the Roman Catholic view of the role of Church and tradition in relation to revelation) of the criteria for knowing/recognizing the true Church and the Church's true interpretation of Scripture. Ibid., 122ff., 130ff.

102 Ibid., 112–13.

103 Ibid., 103.

104 Ibid., 196.

105 Ibid., 198.

106 Ibid.

107 Ibid, 199–201.

108 That Swinburne's account of revelation and Scripture is indeed contrary to the Roman Catholic doctrines of such is excellently developed in an unpublished essay by Roman

Catholic philosopher Eleonore Stump, "Medieval Biblical Exegesis: Augustine, Aquinas, and Swinburne," in *Reason and the Christian Religion: Essays in Honor of Richard Swinburne*, ed. Alan G. Padgett (Oxford: Clarendon, 1994) 161–97. Further, Stump faults Swinburne for having a deistic view of revelation.

[109] *The Catechism of the Catholic Church*, English translation by the United States Catholic Conference (New York: Bantam Doubleday Dell, 1994) 2.

[110] Ibid., 3. It was the stated and repeated concern of John Paul II and of the commission he appointed for the task of this new *Catechism of the Catholic Church* (the first in about four centuries), that it be readily useable as a foundation and reference for the writing and rewriting of regional/ cultural catechisms which can emphasize those elements most needful for the particular place and time of the Church's ministry.

[111] Ibid., 15

[112] Ibid., 11

[113] Ibid., section 38, p. 21.

[114] Ibid., Introduction to chapter two, 23

[115] Ibid., sections 54–64, pp. 24–27.

[116] Ibid., section 65, p. 27.

[117] Ibid., section 74, p. 29.

[118] Ibid., section 76, p.30.

[119] Ibid., sections 105–6, p. 36.

[120] Ibid.

[121] Ibid., cf. section 85.

[122] Note examples from sections 136–40, pp. 43–44.

[123] Ibid., section 107, p. 37.

[124] Ibid., sections 80–85, 113, pp. 31–32, 38. Some statements by Karl Barth about the Roman Catholic view of tradition in Vatican II, even with the new weight it gave to Scripture, are noteworthy. In response, Barth still found it necessary to stress "the Scripture principle" in contrast to Roman Catholic teaching. In distinguishing "Evangelical" from "Roman Catholic" confessions, Barth emphasized that the first emphasizes the Bible as strictly the first word over against church tradition, while the second tends "to understand the Bible in the Light of tradition." In Karl Barth, *Karl Barth: Letters, 1961–1968*, trans. Geoffrey W. Bromiley (Grand Rapids: Eerdmans, 1981) 137.

[125] *Catechism*, section 120, p. 40.

[126] E.g., ibid., sections 103, 127, 138, 140, pp. 36, 41–42, 44.

[127] E.g., ibid., sections 79, 102, 135, 137, pp. 30, 35–36, 43–44.

[128] E.g., ibid., sections 82, 108, pp. 31, 37.

[129] Donald G. Bloesch, *Holy Scripture: Revelation, Inspiration and Interpretation* (Downer's Grove, Ill.: InterVarsity, 1994) 86.

6

Barth, Barthians, and Evangelicals:
Reassessing the Question of the Relation
of Holy Scripture to the Word of God

As we have previously observed, from the Enlightenment there has arisen the strong tendency in theological circles to bifurcate, to dualistically separate, the text of Holy Scripture from "the Word of God," which is something reckoned to be necessarily other than all discursive communication and all texts as such, whatever "the Word of God" is thereby understood to be. The chasm, especially between Scripture text and "Word," continued to grow through the nineteenth century as a result of philosophical developments and, notably, the further development of historical-critical approaches to the study of Holy Scripture. As a result of both reaction and appreciative response to such, many of the developments of twentieth century theology and its prominent schools of thought (especially in the first half of the century), followed by the "shattered spectrum" of multiplied theologies and the entrenchment of postmodernity, have variously affirmed, enforced and assumed the separation of the text of Scripture from some noncontentful, nondiscursive, nonhistorical "Word of God" which is regarded as the transcendent seat of divine truth and authority. Hence religious authority has been located anywhere but in the text of Scripture, which was regarded as simply another human religious product resulting from the effect of or "encounter" with "divine Truth/Word of God."

Into the midst of this theological fray came Karl Barth, who, because of his prolific, powerful and consistent Christocentric theological writing, came to be known as the greatest theologian of the twentieth century—perhaps the greatest since Calvin. Barth did much to turn European and American theology, for a time, back to serious theological and christological engagement, and to the serious use of Holy Scripture for the theological task.

Yet at the same time Barth's theology became a center around which diverse criticism swirled, as well as affirmation and appreciation. Classical liberals and later neoliberal and existentialist theologians criticized much, including Barth's apparent readiness to return to Reformation themes and doctrines. "Orthodox" Protestants were quite varied in the form and focus of their responses to Barth, and were at first mostly critical, though usually not without constructive interest and appreciation for the new direction in which Barth was taking Christian theology. Suspicion was coupled with regard for Barth's emphases on the Godness of God, the Trinity, the centrality of the incarnate Word, Jesus Christ, for all Christian thought and theology as truly Christian, and also emphases on human sinfulness and real redemption through the life, death and resurrection of Jesus Christ from among the dead. But among the most repeated points of concern, from several theological directions, was (and *is*) Karl Barth's understanding of the nature of revelation and so "the Word of God" and its relation to Holy Scripture.

In any case, "Barthianism" or more broadly "dialectical theology" ("neo-orthoxy" is not really an adequate designation) was a position understood to be something of a *tertium quid* between more "liberal" or even (after the rise of Bultmann) "existential" theologies and the loose elements of Protestant orthodoxy. As a result, the label "Barthian" was attached to many, including more and more "post-fundamentalist" or "post-conservative" evangelicals, who found a place to stand in what they perceived to be Barth's simultaneous confession of the classical doctrines of the Christian faith and his subscription to modern, scientific, historical-critical approaches to the very human words of Holy Scripture. Thus, through Barth, many were attracted to the possibility of a substantially "orthodox" faith commitment and confession but without the need to wholly follow what they regarded as the "premodern" Reformers and, even more, pre-modern Protestant Scholasticism's location of present historical authority in the actual concrete text of Holy Scripture as verbally inspired, the written Word of God, and so an *aspect* of God's self-revelation in Jesus Christ and by the Holy Spirit. As James Robinson put the matter, "Barthianism consists . . . of a meeting of the later Barth's move to the right with conservatism's opening itself to influence from the center."[1] Or as evangelical theologian Bernard Ramm put the matter, "At that moment the thought came to me: Barth's theology is a restatement of Reformed theology written in the aftermath of the Enlightenment, but not capitulating to it."[2]

In this way, Barth's theology was often regarded as an avenue whereby one could be both faithful to the historic Christian faith while avoiding the labels *premodern, unscientific, obscurantist, theological dinosaur*. It is especially Barth's "Doctrine of the Word of God" (with special focus on *CD* I/1, I/2) and, therein, the relation of Holy Scripture to "the Word of God" and God's (self-)revelation, *as it is* and as it has been *interpreted* by both "Barthians" and "evangelicals," and as it has and continues to exercise monumental influence on evangelicalism's estimation of the nature of Holy Scripture, that I wish to analyze in this chapter. To that end we will first briefly present Barth's own, often misunderstood, presentation of the "ontology" of Holy Scripture, i.e., that Scripture as the Word of God, like the triune God, has its "being in becoming." Second, we will cursorily examine representative "Barthian" misinterpretations of Barth's own doctrine of Holy Scripture and the Word of God, noting how Barth has been regularly mishandled even by those who claim to follow in his theological footsteps. As we will see, "Barthians" (with some reason) have usually understood Barth to assert that Scripture, as simply a human, written text, suddenly "becomes" what it is not, "the Word of God," when God sovereignly chooses to "speak" (noncontentfully) *through* the text, so as to thereby meet or encounter persons who respond to God's action in faith. Next we will examine representative evangelical criticisms of Barth's view of Scripture showing, again, theological misinterpretion of his multileveled revelational dynamism regarding "the Word of God". We will conclude with an example of a prominent evangelical theologian, who, under the influence of "Barthian" presuppositions, methods, and conclusions (contra Barth's own), was led to finally separate the historical text of Holy Scripture from "the Word of God," and so from any and all real participation in and as an aspect of the self-disclosure of the triune God as centered in Jesus Christ.

Karl Barth's Ontology of Holy Scripture

Karl Barth's christocentric argumentation, and so his theological intention, can sometimes be difficult to pinpoint because each element stands in lively and interactive relation to the massive whole of the *Church Dogmatics*. And so there is often a multileveled complexity that interpretation tends to "flatten out" within the overall "unity (Christ)-in-diversity (development)" of his thought. This is certainly true of Barth's understanding of the nature of Holy Scripture.

As mentioned, then, it is indeed understandable that both "Barthians" and evangelical critics (and admirers) should see in Barth's view of Scripture a situation of dualistic separation from "the Word of God" which seems to come to persons "through" the human text of Scripture, which is said to be the "primary witness to the Word of God." As a result of this apparent "channeling," Scripture is said to (adoptionistically) "become" the Word of God. Many of Barth's own statements in the *Dogmatics* appear to say just that. Given that for Barth, Jesus Christ, the Word made flesh, is the one Revelation of God, the one "revealed Word of God,"[3] then Scripture, "the prophets and apostles," as the primary witness to Jesus Christ,

> is God's Word in so far as God lets it be His Word, so far as God speaks through it. . . . The statement, "The Bible is God's Word," is a confession of faith, a statement made by faith that hears God Himself speak in the human word of the Bible....The Bible therefore *becomes* God's Word in this event, and it is to its *being* in *this becoming* that the tiny word "*is*" relates, in the statement the Bible is God's Word. It does not become God's Word because we accord it faith, but of course, because it *becomes* revelation for us . . .[4]

Given Barth's actualism, it seems as though God's Word as such always has the character of an *event*, and Scripture thus "becomes" in/as an event, e.g., "The Bible is God's Word to the extent that God causes it to be His

Word, to the extent that He speaks through it."[5] This is also repeatedly reflected in Barth's emphasis that this event of "becoming" is a "miracle," and this is related to his primary stress on the "inspiration" of Scripture as the *ever present* divine decision which is continually made in the life of the Church.[6] Thus in one sense Scripture "is the literary monument of an ancient racial religion and of a Hellenistic cultus religion of the Near East. A human document like any other."[7] But, it seems, it is a document which, paradoxically is "the Word of God" by the divine decision, as well as the word of man. Apparently for Barth the Word of God is not something tied or connected to the text of Scripture, for *the* Word is nothing other than the *free* divine disposing of God's grace, specifically the incarnation.[8]

Given that such statements are numerous in the *Dogmatics* and his many other works, it would appear that all that can be positively said about the relation of Holy Scripture to "the Word of God" is in terms of its "becoming" Word of God—a kind of divine alchemy, a turning of lead to gold, or perchance negatively, "bibliological adoptionism." But in fact this is not the whole picture. What Barth states regarding Scripture, as on any of his theological issues, is formed by the larger context of his theological ontology, "God's being is in becoming." For Barth, all that is has its being in becoming, but not everything becomes what it is under the same set of conditions. As applied to God, there is nothing here akin to process theology's notion of divine "becoming" or evolving. Rather the being *of God* is Self-determined being in an absolute sense. As Eberhard Jüngel points out, for Barth God's "being in becoming" reflects the fact that the living God can reveal himself, and that this is a capacity of pure grace and does not arise from necessity.[9] God's revelation is his Self-interpretation; in God's revelation "God's word is identical with God himself."[10] Revelation is that event in which the being of God comes to word, and Revelation is, too, God's free decision in eternity to be *our* God, and so to bring himself to speech for us. Thus the ontological interrelatedness of the triune God is irreversibly tied to the world, relations *ad extra* corresponding to relations *ad intra*, yet always lying in the ontological *difference* between God and the world. So while God's gracious covenantal being-for-us does *not define* God's being, God's being-for-us, pointedly in the event Jesus Christ, does *interpret* God's being (his self-relatedness) to us.[11] Jüngel concludes, regarding Barth's foundational theological ontology, by stating that

God's self-relatedness thus springs from the becoming in which God's being is. The becoming in which God's being is a becoming out of the word in which God says Yes to himself. But to God's affirmation of himself there corresponds the affirmation of the creature through God. In the affirmation of his creature, as this affirmation becomes event in the incarnation of God, God reiterates his self-relatedness in his relation to the creature, as revealer, as becoming revealed and as being revealed. This Christological relation to the creature is also a becoming in which God's being is. But in that God in Jesus Christ *became* man, he is as creature exposed to perishing. . . . There, where God's being-in-becoming was swallowed up in perishing, the perishing was swallowed up in the becoming (italics his).[12]

While this foundational theological ontology is not often grasped, its application in Barth's doctrine of Scripture within his larger doctrine of revelation is almost never recognized. But Geoffrey Bromiley, a primary translator of the *Dogmatics* and a noted Barth interpreter, moves in the right direction when, in analyzing and assessing Barth's doctrine of Scripture, he notes that while for Barth Holy Scripture is not itself directly revelation (Barth's point being to differentiate Word as Scripture from the incarnate Word), he maintains that Scripture was raised up *within the event of revelation* and is regarded as perichoretically part of it.[13] While Barth stresses Scripture's *function* as "witness to" the Word (Christ) and, as witness, its *present* inspiring, and so its present "becoming" as the Word of God now by the Spirit, he thereby only "mutes" his affirmation of the *past inspiration* of Scripture. For Barth, then, Scripture is authoritative because, in terms of what it *is*, God inspired it once and for all when he raised up the prophets and apostles to speak and write the primary words of testimony. Contrary to common opinion, Barth intended to present Scripture's authority as objective by the Spirit in Christ the Word, thereby negating the notion that present authority is locked up in human subjectivity.[14] Scripture's "becoming" the written Word of God to one now by the Spirit is grounded first in its "being" the past inspired Word of God. Thus Scripture's unique priority and authority beyond any and all other human writings, as the Word of God, is rooted in the Spirit's act which causes contextual human language to be God's own words to us.

Yet Bromiley's interpretation at least allows for the possibility that, in some sense, Barth's view of Holy Scripture as the written Word of God, as a participative aspect in the event of revelation which is Jesus Christ, arises from "bibliological adoptionism," that God's past act by the Spirit was to "*adopt*" *as his* written words prior human texts. Gregory Bolich, despite some questionable "axes" which he grinds, brings yet greater clarity to Barth's intention regarding Scripture. For Barth, Christianity is valid only when "it is not ashamed to be actually and seriously a book-religion." Under God, who raised it up, Scripture's authority rests *in itself*. As Barth put it, "Scripture is (now) recognized as the Word of God (by faith) by the fact that it *is* the Word of God." As a result it has, as the Reformers, noted, too, authority for, in, and *over* the Church.[15]

But it is only recently, within the larger breakthrough work on Barth's thought by Bruce McCormack, an evangelical who is Weyerhauser Professor of Theology at Princeton Theological Seminary, that Barth's ontology of Scripture, its being-in-becoming, has been given sufficient clarity and as a result, many concerns have perhaps been answered. McCormack rightly expresses what has often been the concern of many in evangelicalism regarding Barth's theology when he points out that, given Barth's principle whereby Scripture is *not* revelation *as such* but the "primary witness" to revelation (Jesus Christ), he seems to erode the needed distinction between what was written by the prophets and apostles and the witness to Christ borne by all Christians. Or more to the real point, paralleling the issues between the "Orthodox" and "Arian" parties at Nicaea, "on which side of the great divide which distinguishes God from all things human do the prophets and apostles stand?"[16] Does Holy Scripture stand on the "divine side" with and as the Word of God which founds the church, or is it merely the first in a historical series of later human witnesses? Herein McCormack has found that much misinterpretation of Barth's view of the nature of Scripture, including much evangelical criticism, results from failing to take Barth's more striking statements in their proper context. This proper context is immediately the ontology, or being-in-becoming of Holy Scripture, and more broadly Barth's theological ontology as a whole.[17]

Again, according to Barth, everything that is has its being in becoming. But not everything becomes what it is under the same conditions. God's being is Self-determined being in an *absolute* sense; the human being is self-determining subject in a *relative* sense. Thus God's being-in-becoming differs from human being-in-becoming and from all things creaturely. The ontological chasm is absolute.[18] But the conditions by which Holy Scripture "becomes" *what it is* are seen to differ again from those of God and the human. Scripture is not a person. It is a thing, an object. Yet it thereby stands between two competing but unequal wills. The will of God determines Scripture's true being as the written Word of God. The will of all fallen human interpreters purposes to hear in and through Scripture *everything but* the Word of God.[19] Barth's intent is first to emphasize that what Scripture *is* is defined by the will of God declared in his act of giving it to the church. This means that where and when Scripture "becomes" the Word of God, it is only "becoming" what it *already is*. But, second, where and when Scripture does not "become" the Word of God, there God had chosen provisionally not to bear witness to himself to this or that particular reader. But note that according to McCormack, this changes nothing as to the true nature of Scripture as defined by the divine will. Hence, the being-in-becoming of Holy Scripture as holy and as the Word of God takes place first in the relation of faith and obedience in which the reader/hearer stands to the God whose Word the Bible is, and second that God is willing to grant faith and obedience to the reader so that the first condition might be fulfilled.[20] When one "hears truly" Scripture in its authoritative, redemptive role by the Spirit, at that moment Scripture "becomes" for that person now what it already was, the Word of God.

According to McCormack, then, how did Barth understand the process by which Holy Scripture was produced, a process which would reflect this outcome? Briefly stated, revelation (Jesus Christ) engenders Scripture, which attests that revelation as the commission laid by God on the prophets and apostles. Revelation as such (Jesus) is then distinct from such divinely commissioned witnesses, while being both judge and guarantor of what they say. In this way, and by means of the event of "inspiration," these persons become the speakers and writers of the Word of God. Because the original revelation uniquely engenders Scripture, the written record which is Scripture could become the canon.[21] Regarding this divine calling and commission, McCormack adds:

> And so Barth can say that "What we have in the Bible are human attempts to repeat and reproduce this Word of God in human words and thought and in specific situations." But he does not mean to suggest

that what we have in the Bible are *only* human attempts of this kind. For the witness of the prophets and apostles takes place in the fulfillment of an office to which they were not only called but for which they were also *empowered* (italics his).[22]

The outcome, like Jesus Christ, is neither divine only nor human only nor a mixture (*tertium quid*), "But in its own way and degree it is very God and very man, i.e., a witness of revelation which itself belongs to revelation."[23] Therefore, that the Church is able to say anything at all about the event of the incarnation is "only because something unique has taken place between

> God and these specific men and because in what they wrote or what was written by them they confront us as living documents of that unique event. The existence of these specific (commissioned) men is the existence of Jesus Christ for us and for all.[24]

For Barth, then, the prophets and apostles are said to be the foundation on which the church is built *together with* Christ the cornerstone (cf. Eph. 2:20). All of this means that in answer to the earlier question, on which side of the "great ontological divide," which distinguishes God from all things creaturely, would Barth place the canonical writings of the apostles and prophets, Barth would assert that the Scriptures *precisely in their humanness* stand on the *divine side*. While Holy Scripture and church proclamation may be similar as human phenomena, they are *dissimilar* in Barth's understanding in that Scripture has "absolutely" constitutive significance for the latter. Scripture is canon and norm and as such continually imposes itself upon the church.[25] For Karl Barth, then, it seems that when his thought is grasped in its multileveled dynamic, Scripture's being-in-becoming means that when it "becomes" the Word of God for this or that reader this "becoming" now is grounded in and arises from the fact of *what it already is* essentially as a result of revelation (Jesus Christ) and the Holy Spirit of God, the Word *of God*. If what McCormack has said is true, it would seem to bring greater coherence to Barth's monumental theological project.

"Barthian" Misinterpretations of Karl Barth's Understanding Of the Nature of Holy Scripture

Previously Bruce McCormack pointed out that much evangelical criticism of Karl Barth's doctrine of Holy Scripture has failed to understand its theological-ontological context. But it is first noteworthy that Barth's position, Barth's "striking statements" about Scripture, have also been mishandled by recognized "Barthians." Indeed, the views reflected in this section represent what has come to be known as the "Barthian" view of Scripture, as it must be distinguished from that of Barth himself.

David Mueller

Mueller asserts that in light of Barth's comprehensive, christocentric definition of the Word of God as synonymous with God's self-revelation, Barth regards the written and preached Word of God as secondary forms pointing to the acts of God in covenant history culminating in Jesus Christ. These can "become the Word of God" by God's gracious action and presence in the Spirit. The writers of Scripture are said to have a special place of authority in the church because they are the "primary human witnesses" to those mighty acts of revelation. Scripture then is but the testimony of those primary witnesses *to* God's revelation.[26] Mueller finds, then, that Barth is always careful to firmly distinguish God in his revelation from all human testimony to that revelation. If so, then how can Barth speak of Scripture as in any way the Word of God? How can this fallible, human text of the prophets and apostles "become" what it is not, the Word of God? Barth, he says, is correct to regard Scripture as God's Word only if and when God speaks *through* it. Or, as Scripture has, does and will "become" to the church a witness to revelation it *then* "becomes" holy, the Word of God. "Thus, *when* God . . . makes himself present in their testimony through his Spirit once again, we can [then] confess that the Bible is the Word of God."[27]

Otto Weber

Otto Weber was for many years professor of theology at the University of Goettingen, the University of Barth's first theological appointment. He is noted as a prominent advocate and expositor of Barth's work, as well as a significant constructive theologian in his own right. Relatively early in his career, Weber wrote an "introductory report," an explanation of Barth's *Church Dogmatics* to that point (I/1-III/4). Therein his brief explanation of Barth's doctrine of Holy Scripture is representative (and confusing) as a "Barthian" interpretation of an aspect of Barth's theology.

Reflecting Barth's own language, Weber states that for Barth, "[the] Bible is the witness to revelation," for it has actually given an answer to our human question *about* God's revelation. But, again, the point is that the Bible is said to be only a witness to that which it is not, to that from which it is wholly differentiated, i.e., from God's Word. "[It] is only a human witness" in terms of what it says, yet it is "special" because in it is unique and contingent testimony to the "majesty" of God's Word.[28] But if, for Barth, Scripture is only a human witness, how does Weber explain Barth's giving to it a distinguished position in relation to other witnesses? Weber's answer is, first, in terms of the content. Scripture decisively attests the resurrection of Jesus Christ. Further, Scripture awakens faith and so proves to be God's self-witness. Yet this is hardly unique to Scripture. But additionally, Scripture's uniqueness is also said to be found in the contingent function of the "first witnesses." These saw and heard in a way that happens but once. Yet Weber, too, notes that Barth does occasionally say that, as original and legitimate witness to God's revelation, Scripture *is* God's Word. What can this mean? Weber describes this only in terms of "becoming," as divine decree, as act, as decision whereby such happens now as "event" for hearers of the Word. God's Spirit is *ever* "breathing" in and through Holy Scripture.[29]

This interpretation of Karl Barth's view of Holy Scripture is brought to greater clarity in Weber's later three volume *Foundations of Dogmatics* where he states that he is "following Karl Barth's doctrine of the threefold form of the Word of God."[30] With a strong current of existential personalism more reflective of Emil Brunner than the later Barth, Weber makes clear that the Word of God is "Event" wherein God is revealed as the One he is. When God discloses himself as Word it is also historical, concrete,

Has God Said?

The Evangelical Theological Society
Monograph Series

David W. Baker, Editor

VOLUME 5

Has God Said?
Scripture, the Word of God,
and the Crisis of Theological Authority

personal. The Word is the form of God's self-giving address to humanity. How does this occur? The Word of God is God's decision "made about me which demands my decision." As Word it "happens"; it is historical, temporal, not timeless. Thus, Scripture points us toward the One in whom God himself addresses us as person—*not in mere words* but in the form of the Word become flesh. "The speaking divine I is recognized in the Word become flesh."[31] How one is to recognize the personal speaking God as lordly Subject remains mystically vague. Yet Weber does say that the Word of God "takes the form" of the biblical witness, but then he is quick to disclaim any ascription of a "supernatural" character to the text of the scriptural witness. The Word of God truly refers *only* of "the original event of the Word which happened and is happening."[32] The biblical documents make the acts or events of God's past revelation present by the Spirit. The witness to the Word of God contained in Holy Scripture proclaims what has happened once for all so that it will be believed as the event which is once for all. In thus reformulating Barth's understanding of the Word of God, Weber concludes that Scripture's uniqueness occurs in the "process of revelation" "as witness to the Word and as a vehicle that makes the Word-event known to us as valid for today."[33]

Arnold Come

Arnold Come, for many years a professor of theology within the Graduate Theological Union, has stood squarely within the "Barthian" tradition and its interpretation of Barth's doctrine of Holy Scripture. His well known *An Introduction to Barth's Dogmatics for Preachers* contains a lengthy interpretive overview of Barth's theological arguments and emphases, including Barth's teaching on "the Word of God." Come explains that in beginning with the *actuality* rather than the *possibility* of revelation Barth's beginning point in all theology is the fact of the self-disclosure of the Triune God. God's Word is the "event" of God's free self-revelation as his personal address to persons. This Word became objectively and concretely present in Jesus Christ. As central to all of Barth's theology, Jesus Christ is the temporal, historical event who is the objective reality of revelation. "The Word became flesh." "Word" declares the historical person of Jesus as Subject to be the eternal God in free act. "Flesh" asserts that in this act "the Word assumes all the qualifications of real human existence."[34]

But the whole revelation of God which concretely and historically takes place in Jesus Christ "is set before us in the Bible." As the written Word of God? No. In typical "Barthian" explanation of Barth's thought on this question, Come explains that Scripture is rather a collection of witnesses to the event of the Word in the form of expectation and recollection. Scripture is not revelation, is not the written Word of God, in itself, but contains ordinary human words that point away from themselves. As a result, revelation occurs *through* Scripture. When this happens Scripture *becomes* God's Word to us by God's Holy Spirit. Scripture as witness is the human conduit, the only medium, of the immediate presence of Christ the Word. So Come, too, takes Barth "in the flat," i.e., he denies any ontological basis to the claim of Scripture as ("being") the written Word of God, but rather that only in the present event of God's adoptive use of these human witnesses does Scripture "*become* the Revealed Word when God freely chooses to be immediately present to men through them."[35]

T. F. Torrance

T. F. Torrance, long time professor of dogmatic theology at the University of Edinburgh (now retired), has been widely recognized as one of the most prominent constructive (neo-) Barthian theologians in the world. His role as a prominent "Barthian" led, at one point, to his being approached by Barth himself about taking over of the writing of the *Church Dogmatics* should anything happen to Barth (at close of World War II). On the question of divine revelation, the Word of God, and its relation to Holy Scripture, Torrance tends not (so much) to use the "becoming" language often found in Barth, and in most "Barthians," but rather he is even more inclined toward Barth's use of the word "through," i.e., the Word of God "through" Scripture. As a result, the relation Torrance often formulates represents Scripture as an *opaque* (though somehow "inspired") human medium which is dramatically made transparent by the "coming" of the Word "through" that medium by the Holy Spirit in order to redemptively "Encounter" the human hearer.

Within Torrance's larger ongoing struggle against modern epistemological and cosmological dualisms which he correctly finds to have distorted Western scientific and Christian theological, christological thinking, he claims to stand (with Barth) within the "Hebraic-Patristic-Reformational pattern" of critical realism—especially in terms of real knowledge of the Trinity in Christ and by the Spirit. By "Hebraic" Torrance means essentially "Scriptural" (contra Hellenic). This means that God, desiring to make himself known to humanity, chose one small group of people, Israel, and subjected this people "to intensive interaction and dialogue with himself" in order to mold and shape this people for the service of his self-revelation. Hence, as Torrance understands it, God founded this covenant kinship with Israel, thus imprinting himself upon the generations of the nation, his penetrating Word working its way, often "painfully," into and through the fabric of this people.[36] This historical process caused God's Word to penetrate ever more deeply, ultimately for all humanity, and culminated in the incarnation of that Word, God's actual, final, historical and ultimate revelation of himself. Israel was thus prepared by God as the "matrix" for the Word made flesh. Jesus is the one Word of God. From one perspective, Torrance regards Holy Scripture to be "the product of that process."[37] If so, does Torrance regard Scripture to be, in any real or actual sense, the written Word of God, an aspect of God's larger self-revelation, as centered in, under, of and from Christ the Word? No.

For Torrance, too, God's revelation, the Word of God *is* Jesus Christ alone. It is in, as and from the specific, historical person of the God-man that God has disclosed himself in order to be *known* by existing persons *as he is* in "cognitive" union with Christ by the Spirit. Everything redemptively, epistemologically, and so theologically, begins and works its way out from the "dictation" of the Word made flesh, the historical facticity of God's Word, Jesus Christ, the Mediator between God and humanity. The redemptive movement of God from the ontological (Trinity) to/through the economic-ontic (Trinity) culminating in the incarnation represents the "inner logic" of God for us and the way to true knowledge of and blessed communion with the triune God.[38] This gracious access one has to the Father, in Christ and by the Spirit, is not to be understood, says Torrance, in some "narrow biblicist way of thinking or speaking about God . . . (but) our thought (must) be determined by the Truth of God *to which* (the Scriptures) *direct us.*"[39] The point is that the Truth/Word of God in Christ, and so the inner logic of God's Word, has not been and cannot be manifested as human language and as human written text. God is not and cannot be a "speech agent." God cannot use human language to declare his covenant purposes. The Word of God is other than and beyond Holy Scripture. The Word "Encounters" one "through" the text of Scripture in a dynamic, transformative "Word-event." This is, says Torrance, real God-human meeting, but, in true "Barthian" form, it is the Coming of Christ the Word, e.g. "through the Spirit-inspired apostolic witness," "through" the diacoustic and diaphanous media (i.e., Scripture), and "enwrapped in the historical, biblical forms." The effective result of this Word-event, this God-human encounter as the coming of Christ through Scripture, is said to be realist knowledge of God as he is. Yet Torrance terms this knowledge as "mystical knowing," "intuitive knowledge."[40] In correspondence with this writer, Torrance presented the following illustration of the dynamic and almost conflictual relation of Christ the Word to the prophetic-apostolic witness to Christ—through which he comes to encounter the existing person here and now.

> Jesus, the Incarnate and crucified and risen Word who IS Jesus Christ comes to us through space and time and *through* the Holy Scriptures as *through closed doors*. He does not come in the kind of way one can specify with linguistic or logical tools . . . but in the power of the resurrection—really comes![41]

Daniel L. Migliore

Daniel Migliore, Professor of Theology at Princeton Theological Seminary, also sets forth an expressly "Barthian" approach to Holy Scripture which conveniently allows him to avoid alignment with, e.g., the "militaristic" and "patriarchal" elements of Scripture. In claiming to follow Barth's "threefold Word of God," Migliore claims that thereby we see how the Spirit of God works *through* particular human witnesses, "with all their limitations and flaws," to lead to right knowledge of God. Thus Scripture, and proclamation arising from it, cannot be ignored. But Christ is the center, the one revealed Word of God. Thus revelation, that which *is* God's

Word, Jesus Christ, must be clearly differentiated from "the concrete media that it employs."[42] Migliore admits that this threefold structure shows that God has chosen to give human beings an important role in the event of revelation. But, he says, this is singularly true of the incarnation of God in Jesus Christ. On the other hand, "The good news of God comes to us not directly but indirectly, *through* the fully (i.e., only) human witness, memory, hope and practice of a community of believers."[43]

So we have, says Migliore, the treasure of the gospel in the clay jars of Scripture, human language, which is a characteristic of all subsequent witnesses to Christ the Word. And, as noted, given that Scripture contains, e.g., "militaristic" and "patriarchal" ideas, then Scripture clearly stands, in many ways, in contrast to revelation (which revelation(s) is not specified). Thus, says Migliore, it is

> essential that a Christian doctrine of revelation distinguish clearly between Scripture's witness to the personal self-disclosure of God that culminates in Jesus Christ and the historical contingencies and ambiguities of this witness.[44]

The purpose of this section has been to show that Karl Barth's own dynamic, multileveled, interactive view of Holy Scripture, in relation to the Word of God, is grounded in his theological ontology whereby Scripture *is* the written Word of God so that it may "become" God's Word to this or that reader in the power of the Spirit. This position on Scripture is to be distinguished from the often truncated "Barthian" interpretation, and use of Barth's own view, whereby Scripture is regarded as only a human text, which by the Spirit of God can "become" that which it *is not*, Word of God, in the moment of "encounter" with the risen Christ. As Bromily has noted, Barth, having disowned much in his earlier dialectical, existential stage in his shift to theological objectivity, is clearly to be differentiated from what has commonly been called "Barthianism," or, more broadly, neo-orthodoxy, those whom Bromiley calls "his looser disciples." In fact, contra the faulty "Barthian" understanding and use of Barth's own theology, Bromily states that "[Barth's] discussion of the precise question of the authority of Scripture brings him very close to biblical and Reformed teaching."[45] But herein a further concern is to represent and assess evangelical criticisms of Barth's own and the "Barthian" view of Scripture and its formative influence upon much "evangelical" theology, one way or another.

"Evangelical" Misinterpretations of Karl Barth's Understanding of the Nature of Holy Scripture

Bruce McCormack has explained that many orthodox Protestant criticisms of Karl Barth's formulation of the relation divine revelation/the Word of God and Holy Scripture have foundered on the failure to interpret Barth in light of his overall theological ontology. They have worked primarily from his apparently more radical statements of separation between the two. But we found that many claiming to be Barth's disciples have made much the same interpretive mistake in their affirmations. Yet an examination of a few prominent evangelical analyses of Barth's view of Scripture is in order. We will begin with the most severe, Cornelius Van Til, moving to the more mixed and moderated responses of Gordon Clark and Carl F. H. Henry.

Cornelius Van Til

Cornelius Van Til, for many years professor of apologetics at Westminster Theological Seminary, was one of the first evangelical thinkers to critically engage Karl Barth's theology. But none can rival the length of critical engagement Van Til had with Barth's work, spanning some three decades. His first major work analyzing Barth (and Brunner), *The New Modernism*, was largely a polemical criticism of the bases and doctrines of "Neo-orthodoxy" coupled with a strong warning to evangelicals not to be enamored by it. Interpreting the later *Church Dogmatics* in terms of Barth's earlier work, Van Til concluded that despite deceptive use of orthodox language and concepts, Barth did not answer Feuerbach and theological liberalism (modernism), and, despite appearances to the contrary, he still stands within its line.[46]

With regard to revelation and the Word of God and the relation of such to Holy Scripture, Van Til begins by explaining Barth's "activistic" view of revelation. He says that in Barth's view, revalation comes from God as *actus purus.* Revelation is the realm of "primal history" (*Urgeschichte*), the dialectical union between God and man. Barth relates this to Jesus of Nazareth, but only *indirectly*, for the realm of "primal history" is not to be identified with human history or anything in history. "Revelation is super-history in the sense that there is eternal happening in God himself."[47] Yet this "revelation" somehow meets human beings in history, and it is the *tension between* the two realms (super-history and ordinary history) that constitutes "primal history," "God's time for us." It is there that God meets one and thereby gives meaning to ordinary history. Primal history is the realm of the Logos.[48]

But what role can Holy Scripture possibly play in such an understanding of God's "primal historical" meeting with persons in the incarnate Christ? Van Til approaches Barth through negation, i.e., he tells us that Barth rejects the doctrine of Scripture as taught in Roman Catholicism, in mysticism and in traditional Protestantism. Barth, he says, rejects historical orthodoxy's belief in "verbal inspiration," for it destroys the idea of revelation that Barth has already defined as nonhistorical, "primal history." Still, says Van Til, like orthodoxy, Barth yet claims that Scripture is the Word of God. What can this mean? First, that revelation occurs in Scripture and not behind or beyond it. Second, it means that one is not to distinguish this or that portion of Scripture as "the Word of God" while other portions are "the word of man." But while Van Til did find that Barth claimed the inescapability of the biblical texts for theology, and that he taught verbal inspiration in some sense, Van Til also found that Barth criticized orthodoxy for having absolutized this doctrine by making verbal inspiration "the symbol and climax of the idea of *direct* revelation of God."[49] For Barth, this can only mean the death of revelation, for the identification of Scripture with *direct* revelation denies the dialectical character of faith. Such identification wrongly makes God's revelation readily and historically accessible to humanity. *Direct* revelation for Barth, says Van Til, means no revelation. There can be no direct revelation, no direct Word of God, *in history*. Rather the "echo" of God's encounter with persons, the primal history of the Logos, is what is found in Scripture. Revelation is always contemporaneous act in speaking to the prophets and apostles, and *through* their witness. The text of Scripture as it "echoes" the voice of God witnesses to revelation, to the Word of God.[50] The freedom of God cannot be limited by a finished, direct revelation. Therefore Scripture, for Barth, in claiming no authority for itself, bears witness to the Word, and thereby *becomes indirect* revelation, even "double" indirect revelation. Van Til concluded that what Barth meant in saying that Scripture *is* the Word of God is that it is such so far as God *lets* it be when he speaks *through* it. Reversing McCormack's point, Van Til found that for Barth Scripture *becomes* the Word of God in the "event" of revelation and thereby *is* God's Word,[51] i.e., "becoming" as the basis for "being" rather than "being" God's Word as the basis for Scripture's "becoming" for one hearing in faith.

Gordon H. Clark

Gordon Clark was, until his death in 1985, possibly the leading evangelical Reformed philosopher in the United States. His career included tenures at Wheaton College (where he trained, e.g., Carl Henry, Edward J. Carnell, Paul Jewett) and Butler University. His presuppositional epistemology would seem to place him close to Van Til, but in fact they differed at several levels, and differed somewhat about Karl Barth. Before his prominent *Karl Barth's Theological Method* (1963), Clark had written "Barth's Critique of Modernism" and a mock dialogue with Barth, both of which reflected appreciation for several elements of Barth's thought. But it was above all Barth's "shattering attack" upon modernism, and so his rejection of modernism's anthropological orientation, his exaltation of God as *the* proper concern of theology and his personalistic conception of God that most appealed to Clark.[52] "Barth's God is the God who creates, who loves, who reveals himself, who is therefore a Person."[53] On these issues, then, Gordon Clark found Barth's analysis "accurate" and "devastating."

But, like Van Til, Clark found much that concerned him, notably Barth's "irrationalism" and with it his conception of revelation. Regarding the first, Clark rightly distinguished Barth's earlier more dialectical work from his mature theological work. But he was still disturbed by what he found to be Barth's inconsistency, with traces of irrationalism remaining in his theological method, while in other contexts Barth could be the great enemy of irrationalistic religion. Clark is well known for his respect for reason in theology, and its necessity if theology is to say anything worthwhile to the world.[54]

But it was in Barth's doctrine of revelation that Clark found the real theological-epistemological problem. Having noted that "theology of the Word" is probably the best descriptive phrase for Barth's system of thought, Clark explains:

> Barth stresses the Word of God. In the Word, in revelation, and not in any independent anthropology or the like, Barth locates the source of religious authority. The Word, then is the substantial core of Barth's theological method; it is the Logos or logic which governs his thought.[55]

In that context, Clark explains that Barth begins by referring to a "recollection" of revelation, but that this recollection is not a capacity of persons or of the Church as such, but is found in Christ's rule over the Church concretely expressed in that temporal but superior entity, Holy Scripture. "Simply by being there and telling us what God's past revelation actually is, Holy Scripture is the canon."[56] But despite Barth's strong and exalted claims regarding the nature of Scripture, thereby apparently pointing to Scripture as written divine revelation, to its verbal inspiration and its complete truthfulness, in fact, says Clark, he does not draw these implications. Indeed, Clark concludes that Barth's concept of revelation "fails of intelligible definition," and a crucial element of this failure is Barth's unwillingness to equate Scripture with revelation and so to affirm that revelation has been given in propositional or textual form.[57] Thus Clark is critical of Barth's initial doxological portrayals of Scripture which are then immediately negated or seemingly retracted, thereby both giving to Scripture and then robbing Scripture of its proper authority. After an extensive quotation from *CD* I/1 (123–24), wherein he finds some clarification of Barth's position on Scripture, including the oft-repeated statement "The Bible is God's Word so far as God lets it be his Word, so far as God speaks through it," Clark interprets:

> These latter statements of objectivity are to be accorded full force, and the shift from objectivity to subjectivity may be explained by the fact that the objectivity, real though it may be, is only momentary rather than permanent. The Bible *is* the Word of God, but only at certain instants; the Bible *becomes* the Word of God from time to time. Yet if these times

are those when God lets the Bible speak to us . . . it is difficult to see how "the Bible *is* God's Word" can be true quite independently of (our) experiences . . . Therefore [for Barth] it *is not* the Word of God.[58]

Carl F. H. Henry

Through much of the second half of the twentieth century Carl Henry has been widely regarded as the "dean" of American evangelical theologians. As a central figure and (with Bernard Ramm) a preeminent theologian in the postfundamentalist-modernist emergence of a distinct evangelicalism more directly engaged socially and intellectually with culture, Henry's theological and philosophical concern to "define" evangelicalism (vis-à-vis liberalism and fundamentalism) brought him into long term interaction with "neo-orthodoxy" and especially Karl Barth. In many ways, the fact that Barth's theology is sometimes considered a legitimate and scholarly alternative for "evangelical" thinkers regularly spurred Henry into *ongoing* "fruitful (and critical) interchange" with Barth and prominent "Barthians" (especially T. F. Torrance).[59] Henry is sharply critical of Barth's epistemological and theological positions while also defending him from zealous attackers who have clearly misunderstood or overlooked numerous commendable elements or who have been unwilling to reckon with real development that occurred in Barth's maturing thought. Along with concerns about his understanding of the Trinity, his apparent universalism and his interpretation and use of Reformation theology (notably Calvin), Henry has been especially critical of Barth's view of God's self-disclosure, of Holy Scripture in relation to that divine self-disclosure, and Barth's problematic, often "irrational," epistemology.

Henry sought to develop his own theology, and his conclusions on divine revelation and the knowledge of God, from an "Augustinian" perspective, i.e., *between* Tertullian (fideism) and Aquinas (empirical evidentialism/rationalism). In this way, Henry sought to unite presuppositionalism with rational inquiry while avoiding the excesses of both.[60] For Henry it is crucial that one recognize the essentially rational nature of revelation and that the revelatory process includes the conceptual and verbal/language elements. From these bases, Henry's many theological writings usually include at least some analysis of Barth's errors and inconsistencies, especially regarding revelation and Scripture.

While very appreciative of Barth's strong and insightful attacks on theological liberalism and his truly positive theological developments and correctives, Henry still concluded *early* on that Barth's view of revelation was on the one hand reductionistic, equating the Word of God wholly and only with Jesus,[61] and on the other hand Schleiermacherian, *refusing* to *identify* Scripture directly as an aspect of the revealed Word of God. Behind Barth's "halting return" to Scripture, Henry found a dialectical prejudice which imparts anti-intellectualism, a partial and distorted view of revelation and a failure to "acknowledge the inspiration or inspiredness which the New Testament ascribes to Scripture (2 Tim. 3:16)." At the same time, Henry notes that "even with respect to Scripture as the norm of Christian doctrine Barth has given us many statements which, as far as they go, have an evangelical ring and vigor."[62] Yet problems are said to remain and, at the root, Henry finds that the errors of "neo-orthodoxy" generally and of Barth in particular (while recognizing Barth's clear advance and superiority over, e.g., Brunner), lay in a combination of Kantian internal moral response and "existential faith in God's self-revelatory confrontation."[63]

It is in Henry's six-volume *God, Revelation and Authority* that one finds the fruition of Henry's theological thinking on central issues of evangelical orthodoxy and, too, his dialogical engagement with Karl Barth. While some of his earlier criticisms have been dropped as not applicable, Henry's central criticisms of Barth regarding revelation and Scripture remain and are clarified. Given that Barth not only seems to locate special revelation, even in Jesus the Word, beyond historical inquiry, but also that Barth rejects the necessity of rational revelation, asserts the impossibility of adequately speaking of God and *disparages human language*, Barth has doomed his own theology to an irrational ambiguity. Despite Barth's desire that theology and the truth of revelation remain independent of the dominating effects of particular philosophical schools, Kantian skepticism and Kierkegaardian "irrationalism" in his theology have made him "more than any other theologian responsible for encouraging the notion of irrational revelation in Euro-American thought."[64] Henry recognizes that Barth's mature thinking regarding human concepts of God makes significant advances from his early denials in *Römerbrief*; yet the advance is found to be partial, for he still asserts that human concepts of God gain adequacy only by a "divine miracle of grace." He continues to emphasize the cognitive gulf between the "known" God and the knowing human, in spite of confession of special revelation in Christ. But then Barth still denies significant validity to statements ("propositions") about God. By placing a gulf between the truth of statements about God and the truth of revelation, Barth "makes cognitive skepticism inevitable."[65] While clear that propositions/statements of fact are certainly not exhaustive of the truth, Henry is firm that all truth must be expressible in order to be intelligible and communicative for human beings. As a result, the effect of Barth's understanding of the nature of Scripture is clear and problematic. First, Henry notes how and why Barth's rejection of the truth of statements about God is contrary to the view directly and indirectly taught in Scripture itself—a basis of authority Barth consistently uses and maintains throughout the *Dogmatics*. Second, Barth, contrary to his own claims, has not in fact returned to the understanding of truth and revelation set forth by the Reformers.[66] Third, while Henry acknowledges that, contra theological liberalism, Barth often grants to Scripture a strong and seemingly exalted authority, especially over the church, yet he then strips all such authority away by denying Scripture any direct role in and as revelation, as the written Word of God. By definition, then, divine self-disclosure cannot *be directly* identified with any human words or concepts, and historical orthodox claims to the contrary are strangely said to reflect the influences of natural theology and secularization.[67] Henry points out that Barth will occasionally state that "God's revelation . . . gives . . . information," that it "informs man about God and about himself . . . by telling him that God is free for us," that "God's revelation is authentic information about God."[68] These claims seem to set him, at least on these occasions, against other existentialist-dialectical theologians who emphasize the totally noncognitive nature of revelation. Yet when relating these statements to Scripture, Barth reflects great inconsistency by concluding that "it is impossible that there should be a direct identity between the human word of Holy Scripture and the Word of God."[69]

> In his denying the objectivity of the Scriptures as God's written word [Barth] robs Scripture of any revelatory-epistemic significance as a carrier of valid information about God.[70]

The enigma of Barth's theory is: Why should revelation—which according to Barth is not to be hardened into concepts and words—ever have become so entangled in concepts and words that it requires the disentangling he proposes.[71]

Thus Carl Henry affirms much of what Barth has said theologically, applauds his insightful criticisms of theological liberalism, and could stand with Barth in much that Barth apparently *intended*. But because Henry finds Barth's epistemological bases to lead to denials of crucial elements of historical orthodoxy's understanding of divine revelation, of the adequate knowability and expressibility of God and the truth of God in human concepts, language and particularly in the text of Holy Scripture, he cannot describe Barth as an evangelical. Were Henry to recognize what McCormack may well have found to be the christological nature of many of Barth's apparent denials regarding Scripture in its "being and becoming" what it is, might Henry have reconsidered his conclusion? Perhaps. But he would have continued concern about Barth's formulation of inspiration as preeminently *present* inspiring, which is coupled with a *strongly* subordinated, modified notion of *past* inspiredness, and this would still be considered a problem—which it is.

Formative "Barthian" Influence on Evangelical Views of Scripture: The Case of Bernard Ramm

The "Barthian" understanding of Scripture (in contrast to Barth's own) as finally separated from the Word of God, as finally but the word of man adoptionistically used by God's Spirit, so "becoming"(in *this* sense) God's Word, has been very and variously influential upon numerous evangelical scholars. Among these are G. C. Berkouwer, Donald Bloesch, Clark Pinnock, James William McClendon, and even Alister McGrath. We will examine the instructive case of Bernard Ramm and his developing relation to the "Barthian" understanding of divine self-disclosure and Holy Scripture. This last section will thus be complicated by reflecting on how *not* Karl Barth's own doctrine but the "Barthian" interpretation and use of Barth's doctrine of Scripture has influenced this particular prominent evangelical theologian of the twentieth century. Given Bruce McCormack's uncovering of Karl Barth's theological ontology in relation to Scripture, we will examine both Ramm's developing interaction with Barth's theology and how the "Barthian" view led him increasingly to separate Scripture from "the Word of God."

Bernard Ramm's lifelong interest in the physical sciences directed him to study in the field at the University of Washington until his conversion to Christianity redirected him to philosophy and speech. After his divinity degree at Eastern Baptist Seminary, and while earning two graduate degrees (M.A., Ph.D. focusing especially on philosophy of science) at the University of Southern California, Ramm began his teaching career "within fundamentalism" at Biola. Growing discomfort led him into the wider "evangelical" circles at Bethel College and Seminary, Baylor University, Eastern Baptist Seminary and finally American Baptist Seminary of the West (GTU). During these years Ramm wrote much, especially in apologetics and the relation between contemporary sciences and the Christian faith. In the latter half of his career he moved toward directly theological/dogmatic issues. Early in his teaching career he began to hear criticisms of Barth's theology, but wanting to assess Barth for himself he began a program of study of the *Dogmatics*. Later he took a sabbatical year with Barth. But throughout the 1950s, 60s and 70s his works included discussion of Barth's theology, and often of Barth's view of Scripture, with critical assessment. At the same time, Ramm was grappling with the relation of evangelical orthodoxy to the revolutionary reality of the Enlightenment and, therein, the problem of evangelical definition/identity and methodology (like Carl Henry). As a theological leader among the new "evangelicals," Ramm experienced a "continuous upward spiral" toward an "open" evangelical Christianity—and Karl Barth continued to have a prominent place in that process.[72]

In his widely used *Protestant Biblical Hermeneutics*, Ramm defends "a full-fledged intelligent Biblicism" and so Holy Scripture as verbally and plenarily inspired and as the written result of the "revelational" process.[73] Thus he "severs company" with Karl Barth and "neo-orthodox" theology. Ramm acknowledges Barth's separation from liberalism, his concern for Reformation thought and "neo-supernaturalism," but is concerned about his denials of orthodox views of revelation, inspiration and infallibility. While Barth affirms that God speaks, that God reveals himself, says

Ramm, yet it is Barth's conclusion that since only God speaks for God, and revelation is only his presence, above all Jesus Christ, then God's speaking *cannot be in words*. Therefore, for Barth Scripture *is not* revelation, *is not* the word of God in any direct way. When the Word behind the words addresses me, *then* revelation occurs.[74]

In *Special Revelation and the Word of God*, Ramm represents Holy Scripture as a "product of Special Revelation" (revelation in the form of language, and so knowledge of God). Having explained the nature and indispensability of language and God's historical use of it, Ramm asserts, explains and defends the classical Christian view that special revelation has appeared in the form of written language: "Special revelation . . . appears in written form. The product of special revelation as speaking is thereby carried over *as writing*. . . . In the providence of God there is no better means of preserving the special revelation of God than by casting it *into* writing."[75] In all of this, Ramm rightly points to the incarnation of the Word as central and supreme as a "modality of revelation," but after this is the divine speaking, and "the creation of a Scripture is but the extension of the modality of the divine speaking."[76] To verify this scripturally, Ramm first provides a "provisional summary" of NT "revelational" contexts, thereby showing that Scripture's portrayal of God's revelatory processes (focusing on the Greek verbs and nouns) expresses the revealing action of God, a *deposit created* by the *revealing action* of God and the *identification* of Scripture with this deposit. Contrary to many modern theological trends which have disparaged written communication, Ramm argues carefully that Scripture's own attitude is that writing is as much a form of the mediation of the word of God as is speaking, and that the divinely given product/deposit of special revelation has been substantially cast into written form—the Christian *graphē* and canon. Indeed, it is noteworthy that it was (apparently) Bernard Ramm who coined the phrase "inscripturated Word of God."[77] By thus emphasizing the reality of God-given truth content, the truth *of God*, and the actual role of Holy Scripture as the inspired textual form (*graphē*) of that "deposit," Ramm was simply seeking for biblical balance. While appreciating Barth's emphasis on revelation as Event, Encounter and Personal, Ramm found such to be biblically inadequate. Rather, as including the biblical text and by the Holy Spirit, the whole revelatory reality is comprised of event *and interpretation*, encounter *and truth*, personal relation *and knowledge*.[78] Barth is right as far as he goes, reflecting the dynamism of the Word of God by the Spirit. But he tends to dualistically separate Scripture and revelation. Unlike his theological contemporaries, Barth discusses inspiration, as well as revelation, but the resulting relation of revelation to Scripture is merely functional.[79] Still Ramm's appreciation of "Barthian" theology was clearly growing.

Through the 1960s and into the 1970s Ramm was turning from apologetics toward the pursuit of a clearer definition of evangelicalism via positive constructive theological expression and historical theological analysis—the significance of which he found in Barth's *Church Dogmatics*. Emblematic of this multileveled development in Ramm's thought was his insightful, seminal monograph *The Evangelical Heritage*. Herein he defines "evangelical" to cover a broad stream of conservative Protestantism from fundamentalism, reformational confessionalism, Pentecostalism, etc., and those who bear "such a vague title as evangelical neo-orthodox."[80] Well and good, but how then is one to regard Barth's theology and particularly Barth's (or the "Barthian") view of Scripture? First, Ramm finds that, while Barth must neither be cast off as a modernist nor wholly appropriated, yet one can profitably respond to Barth's theology dialectically, assessing, evaluating, weighing, criticizing *and* approving.[81] Herein Ramm rejoiced in Barth's destruction of theological liberalism, his erudition and centrally his reaffirmation of the necessity of objective divine revelation. This is necessary, for "the evangelical believes that theology will have genuine dignity only if it retains (the) nonnegotiable element of the objective in its doctrine of revelation."[82] Ramm finds that "neo-orthodox" theology often tends to see revelation as internal decision or as the pure confrontation of God, thus evaporating any substantial knowledge of God. Fortunately, he says, Barth is "inconsistent," admitting "a disguised objective form" into his theology.

> If Barth wishes to call Scripture the witness to revelation, and not the revelation or a revelation, he has nevertheless tied Scripture into the concept in such a way that Scripture is certainly revelational. . . . The evangelical believes this is a certain amount of theological double-talk. He would prefer [Barth] come out and affirm that *revelation is polydimensional*, and that *one of these dimensions is Holy Scripture*.[83]

Clearly, Ramm still interprets Barth in "Barthian" terms, as separating Scripture from the Word of God, but not without the recognition that a "revelational" Scripture is, in fact, authoritatively central to Barth's own theological program. At this juncture, too, Ramm's relation to Barth is, indeed, dialectical—and yet critical of Barth's unwillingness to follow through and so recognize Holy Scripture as (being) the written Word of God.

But in Ramm's *After Fundamentalism* his "upward spiral" continued, and his radical concern that evangelical theology respond effectively to the Enlightenment led him to dissolve the dialectic and to call evangelicalism to its true future, Barth's theological methodology. As a result of the Enlightenment revolution, evangelicalism was faced with a crisis and so must move toward a new paradigm. Barth's Christian response must become, in principle, its own. Where the Enlightenment represented true knowledge and real advance, Barth was ready to incorporate such legitimate insights. Where it oversteps its bounds, e.g., rejecting the idea of biblical authority and questioning all revelation, Barth was its most severe critic. Finding the Enlightenment to be the great tide of modern thought, Ramm says that evangelicals, too, must accept what is valid in modernity without capitulating to its errors. Ramm did not intend by this to call for adopting the whole of Barth's theology but, more heuristically, to call for Barth's method of response for writing theology in the modern context. In light of his stated purpose, Ramm's review of several of Barth's major theological issues is significant. With each he presents Barth's careful grounding in the great tradition of the church coupled with his openness to valid elements of modernity.[84]

Ramm is most appreciative of Barth's subtle distinctions such as his balance between the humanity and divinity of Scripture. As he explains his understanding of Barth's doctrine of Scripture, Ramm develops, contra McCormack, what he takes to be the notion of the divine Word (*Bild, Sache, Wort*) in the words/text of Scripture, i.e., a divine Word *behind* the words of Scripture to which good exegesis of Scripture can reach by going *through* the biblical words.[85] While often describing this Word–words relation in Barth's theology in ways akin to McCormack's presentation of Barth ontology of Scripture—that Scripture truly *is* the Word of God for Barth[86]—Ramm clarifies the issue. For Barth, he says, the doctrine of verbal inspiration and inerrancy represents a *materialization* of the doctrine of inspiration. By "materialization" is meant that the Word of God is reduced literally to a book that one can carry around in one's pocket. . . . The wicked in the book of Jeremiah could cut up the words of Jeremiah and burn them in the fire (Jer. 36), but only because they were Jeremiah's witness to the Word of God and not the Word of God itself.[87]

Thus, Ramm's "Barthian" interpretation of Barth's doctrine of Scripture, as the transcendentalizing and platonizing of "the Word of God," is essentially affirmed when he portrays with approval what he takes to be Barth's teaching about Scripture as only "becoming" the Word of God when one believes, thus emphasizing the central role of the Spirit and Word.[88] We find in Bernard Ramm, then, not only the same "flattening" of Barth's position (Holy Scripture dualistically separated from the Word of God, the "Barthian" conception), but also a clear shift toward that position, in part as a result of the "pressure" of modernity.

Conclusion

Our ongoing concern regarding the destructive effects of the modern, and now postmodern, theological tendency to dualistically separate the Word or Self-disclosure of God from the historical text of Holy Scripture has been directed in this chapter through the massive, powerful, influential work of Karl Barth, especially as related to "evangelical" and/or contemporary "Protestant orthodox" theology. In recent evangelical analyses, both Karl Barth's own theology and "Barthian" theology have been understood to demand this separation of the Word of God from the text of Scripture, and to be influentially reshaping or inclining much contemporary evangelical understanding of the nature of Scripture toward such bifurcation, especially in the face of historical criticism. Is this true? Not totally. We have found that Barth did clearly and rightly distinguish (but not separate) the incarnate Word from the textual Word, but unlike the "Barthians," he did not finally separate "Word of God" from Scripture. Holy Scripture *is* the written Word of God and, hence, can "become" the Word of God for one hearing that Word in faith. Yes, I believe Barth has significant problems. His emphasis on present "inspiring" over "*inspiredness*" (which he also affirms) and his odd caricature, or strawman portrayal, of the historical orthodox view of inspiration, are certainly weak points. His strong assertion of "divine freedom" seems to allow God both to give and to retract his promise for the sake of that freedom. But almost all "Barthian" disciples and evangelical critics of Barth's doctrine of Scripture have basically focused only on his "radical" statements that Scripture is only prophetic-apostolic witness to the Word of God, and as such can, when the Word "breaks through" the human word, "become" the Word of God. For many, given the Enlightenment revolution, scientific methodology and historical criticism, Barth's apparent simultaneous affirmation of the divine Word, the transcendent triune God, the incarnate Son, an "authoritative" text, and also the radical historicity and total humanness of that text, seemed to allow the freedom and luxury of "having their cake and eating it too," of being in some measure orthodox in their Christian faith and yet thoroughly modern (Enlightenment) or postmodern people. Bernard Ramm, as a leading evangelical theologian, traveled far along that road, and many other evangelicals are succumbing to the same "Barthian" road in these days. But while Barth did find much in the Enlightenment that he could affirm as a Christian, yet as a Christian man and in light of the Word of God, he could and did become one of modernity's severest critics. Indeed, despite all philosophical, philological, epistemological and cultural-theological pressures to reject so-called pre-modern, historical "orthodox" conclusions, Karl Barth still finally asserted that Holy Scripture *is* the written Word of God which, by the Spirit, can "become" the Word of God, the Word of God's redemptive truth, and grace in Jesus Christ, to the one who hears in faith.

Endnotes

[1] James M. Robinson, editor, *The Beginnings of Dialectical Theology*, 2 vols. (Richmond: John Knox, 1968) 28.

[2] Bernard L. Ramm, *After Fundamentalism: The Future of Evangelical Theology* (San Francisco: Harper and Row, 1983) 14.

[3] Karl Barth, *Church Dogmatics*, I/1, trans. G. Thomson (Edinburgh: T. & T. Clark, 1936) 124–35. Hereafter *CD*.

[4] Ibid., 123–24.

[5] Ibid., 107.

[6] Ibid., I/2, 534–35.

[7] Karl Barth, *The Word of God and the Word of Man*, trans. Douglas Horton (New York: Harper and Brothers, 1928) 60.

[8] E.g., Barth *CD* I/2, p. 172; IV/1, p. 152, etc.

[9] Eberhard Jüngel, *The Doctrine of the Trinity: God's Being is in Becoming* (Grand Rapids: Eerdmans, 1976) 42ff., 89ff. Cf. also Jüngel's further massive development of this theme, especially in relation to the trinity of the God who is love in *God as the Mystery of the World*, trans. Darrell Guder (Grand Rapids: Eerdmans, 1984).

[10] Barth, *CD* I/1, 304.

[11] Jüngel, *Trinity*, 104–6, cf. 15–25.

[12] Ibid., 107.

[13] Geoffrey W. Bromiley, "The Authority of Scripture in Karl Barth," in *Hermeneutics, Authority and Canon*, ed. D. A. Carson and John D. Woodbridge (Grand Rapids: Zondervan, 1986) 290.

[14] Ibid., 291. Note Bromiley's introductory article, "The Authority of Scripture," on the doctrine of revelation and contextual discussion of Barth and (and distinct from) "neo-orthodoxy" on the relation of the Word of God to Scripture in *The New Bible Commentary*, 2nd edition, ed. D. Guthrie and J. Motyer (Downers Grove, Ill.: InterVarsity, 1970) 10–11.

[15] Gregory G. Bolich, *Karl Barth and Evangelicalism* (Downers Grove, Ill.: InterVarsity, 1980) 196–97ff.

[16] Bruce L. McCormack, "The Being of Holy Scripture is in Becoming: Karl Barth in Conversation with American Evangelical Criticism" (unpublished paper presented at Wheaton College, April 2001), p. 2. This paper was subsequently published in *Evangelicals and Scripture*, ed. by Vincent Bacote, Laura Miguelez, and Dennis Okholm (Downers Grove, Ill.: InterVarsity, 2004).

[17] Ibid., 2–3.

[18] Cf. Barth, *CD* IV/2.

[19] McCormack, 13.

[20] Ibid., 13–14.

[21] Ibid., 14.

[22] Ibid., citing Barth, *CD* I/2, 491.

[23] Barth, *CD* I/2, 501, cited in McCormack, 15.

[24] Ibid., 486. Cited in McCormack, 16.

[25] Barth, *CD* I/1, 102, 107. Cited in McCormack, 16

[26] David Mueller, *Karl Barth* (Waco, Tex.: Word, 1972) 56.

27 Ibid., 57.

28 Otto Weber, *Karl Barth's Church Dogmatics: An Introductory Report*, trans. Arthur C. Cochrane, (Philadelphia: Westminster, 1953) 57–58.

29 Ibid., 59.

30 Otto Weber, *Foundations of Dogmatics*, vol. 1, trans. Darrell L. Guder, (Grand Rapids: Eerdmans, 1981).

31 Ibid., 178–80.

32 Ibid., 182.

33 Ibid., 186, 188.

34 Arnold B. Come, *An Introduction to Barth's Dogmatics for Preachers* (Philadelphia: Westminster, 1963) 89, 90, 92.

35 Ibid, 93, 94, 89.

36 T. F. Torrance, *The Mediation of Christ* (Grand Rapids: Eerdmans, 1975) 16–17.

37 Ibid., 18–19.

38 See T. F. Torrance, *God and Rationality* (Oxford: Oxford University Press, 1971) 145, 158–59; and also Torrance, *Theology in Reconciliation* (Grand Rapids: Eerdmans, 1975) 80, 210, 226; *Space, Time and Incarnation* (Grand Rapids: Eerdmans, 1969) 75; and "The Doctrine of the Holy Trinity according to St. Athanasius," *Anglican Theological Review* 71 (1991) 395–405.

39 T. F. Torrance, *The Trinitarian Faith* (Edinburgh: T. & T. Clark, 1988) 57.

40 Torrance, *God and Rationality*, 45, 99, 137f., 155–56, 185; and Torrance, *Theological Science* (Oxford: Oxford University Press, 1969) 52, 87, 100.

41 Personal Correspondence by the author with Thomas Torrance.

42 Daniel L. Migliore, *Faith Seeking Understanding* (Grand Rapids: Eerdmans, 1991) 34.

43 Ibid., 35.

44 Ibid.

45 Geoffrey Bromiley, "The Authority of Scripture," in *The New Bible Commentary* (Grand Rapids: Eerdmans, 1970) 10. Note, too, Bromiley's clear concern regarding Barth's strong emphasis (but not total) on *present* inspiration of Scripture, in ibid., 9–11.

46 Cornelius Van Til, *The New Modernism: An Appraisal of the Theology of Barth and Brunner* (Philadelphia: Presbyterian and Reformed, 1946) x.

47 Ibid., 154.

48 Ibid.

49 Ibid., 138.

50 Ibid., 139–40.

51 Ibid., 394. Van Til's later work *Christianity and Barthianism*, consciously paralleling J. Gresham Machen's *Christianity and Liberalism*, essentially reiterates his earlier view of Barth's doctrine of revelation and Scripture, with special critical emphasis on Barth's treatment of revelation as *Geschichte*. He found that this "activism" undermines the incarnation and all revelation, for all is reduced to nonhistorical Act.

52 Gordon H. Clark, *Karl Barth's Theological Method* (Philadelphia: Presbyterian and Reformed, 1963) 48.

53 Ibid., 32.

54 Ibid., 59.

55 Ibid., 13.

56 Ibid., 160–65, 188ff.

57 Ibid., 184.

58 Ibid., 163–64.

59 Bolich correctly describes Henry as here reflecting Bernard Ramm's earlier recommendation that evangelicals engage in a "dialectical reading" of Barth with the goal of fruitful interchange. Bolich sees Henry as fulfilling that calling. Bolich, 94.

60 Carl F. H. Henry, *God, Revelation and Authority*, vol. 1 (Waco, Tex.: Word, 1979) 182.

61 Carl F. H. Henry, *The Protestant Dilemma* (Grand Rapids: Eerdmans, 1948) 89, 149.

62 Henry, *God, Revelation and Authority*, vol. 1, 62.

63 Ibid., 187.

64 Ibid., 276–77; and vol. 3, 290, 364–65.

65 Ibid., vol. 3, 224–27.

66 Ibid., 466–68.

67 Note Barth's explanation: "The gradually extending new understanding of biblical inspiration was simply one way, and in view of its highly supernaturalistic character, perhaps the most important way, in which the great process of secularization, on which post-Reformation Protestantism entered, was carried through." *CD*, I/2, 522. Henry, *God, Revelation and Authority*, vol. 4, 199–200.

68 Barth, *CD*, I/2, 29 30; and II/1, 210, in Henry, *GRA*, vol. 3, 466.

69 Barth, *CD* I/2, 499.

70 Henry, *GRA*, vol. 4, 267.

71 Ibid, 200. Note the important statement by Donald M. MacKinnon, late professor of divinity at Cambridge, who said (contra those who claim that the Christian faith has moved away from propositional truth to personalist I-Thou imperatives), "We cannot allow any seriousness to Christianity's claim to truth unless we can also claim factual truth in a simple, ordinary sense, for propositions (at the heart of the biblical faith)

. . . . If this foundation is ignored, or is treated as of little import, we shall surely find that we have lost precisely that which distinguishes Christianity from every other faith, namely its claiming, among its fundamental truth-conditions, the truth of propositions that might have been otherwise—and this as an aspect of its central affirmation that in human flesh and blood the ultimate secrets of God were disclosed, and…the ultimate contradictions of human existence resolved." This quotation comes from *Borderlands of Theology*, 83, and is cited in Henry, vol. 3, 456.

[72] Alan Day, "Bernard L. Ramm," in *Baptist Theologians*, ed. D. Dockery and T. George (Nashville: Broadman, 1990).

[73] Bernard Ramm, *Protestant Biblical Interpretation*, third revised ed. (Grand Rapids: Baker, 1970) 93–95, 126.

[74] Ibid., 69–73.

[75] Bernard Ramm, *Special Revelation and the Word of God* (Grand Rapids: Eerdmanns, 1961) 125–38.

[76] Ibid., 159–60 ff. Cf. the three sections from 161–67.

[77] Ibid., 160–69.

[78] Ibid., 159–60. Cf. 170, 174, 176 n., 180 n.

[79] Ibid., 174, 176, 178–79.

[80] Bernard Ramm, *The Evangelical Heritage* (Waco, Tex.: Word, 1973) 14.

[81] Ibid., 103–10.

[82] Ibid., 146.

[83] Ibid.

[84] Bernard Ramm, *After Fundamentalism*, 24–28.

[85] Ibid., 93–94.

[86] Ibid., 94–95, 117.

[87] Ibid., 118.

[88] Ibid., 124.

7

Scripture as the
Written Word of God:
Evangelical Assumption or
Evangelical Dilemma?

Within historical and modern Protestant orthodox Christian contexts it has been all but assumed that when reference is made to "the Word of God" it is Holy Scripture that is intended—that in spite of Protestant orthodox and/or evangelical christocentricity and thus the fact of "the Word made flesh." Modern evangelicalism, across its various denominational traditions, has consistently maintained the propriety of the claim that Holy Scripture *is* the written or, more recently, "inscripturated" Word of God, whatever else may rightly and more directly be identified as the Word of God. Indeed, much of evangelical theological identity, and its Christocentricity, is grounded in the confessional linkage whereby Scripture *is* the written Word of God.

Yet this contention cannot be regarded as confined only to modern evangelicalism. Historians of Christian theology have repeatedly pointed out, often in ways mixed with scorn, that this textual identification or connection of Word or revelation of God with Holy Scripture is the almost universal position of the Church Fathers and pre-Christian Judaism.[1] Historically, post-Nicene, medieval (East and West), Reformation and post-Reformation Catholic and Protestant Christianity has held firmly to the same position, despite historical, ecclesiological, conceptual and methodological shifts and developments. In fact, the often predominant position of the Church Fathers and Doctors, and on occasion of the Reformers, was not simply that Scripture is or can be rightly identified as the written Word of God, but that this very process even meant something near to the divine dictation of the books of Scripture. While such an extreme "docetic" view has rightly been disavowed almost unanimously in modern evangelicalism, the central contention about the revelatory character of Holy Scripture has continued to be basic. But it is this very point of identification, the "identity thesis," which has in recent years been increasingly yet carefully and subtly denied by Christian theologians who have claimed the label "evangelical."

In order to bring preliminary clarity to these claims, issues, questions and criticisms, as well as to constructive reformulation, several points regarding evangelical assessment of the nature of Holy Scripture and contemporary developments ought to be made. By thus identifying Holy Scripture as the written Word of God, the claim is then that God has revealed himself historically in acts, centrally and supremely in Jesus Christ. It also means that God has revealed himself personally to persons in order to redeem them; that God has revealed himself "content-fully," i.e., that God's self-disclosure is not fully given in a bare act or acts of power (e.g., the exodus) or in dramatic but conceptually empty, "will-o'-the-wisp" personal encounters, but "content-fully" in ways effectually expressible *in* and *as* human language, even *written* language. The theological result is not merely a Scripture which points to the Word of God (Christ), like John the Baptist in the Grunewald altarpiece,[2] nor a Scripture which "becomes" the Word of God and through which the Word of God "breaks" in order to meet us as "I to Thou,"[3] nor a Scripture which "brings" or "conveys" the Word of God to us—thus a Word of God that is other than Scripture, nor even a Scripture "in which" the Word of God can be found somewhere. Rather, like the historical position of the church generally, the evangelical position on revelation includes an understanding of Holy Scripture as the inscripturated Word of God, whatever may be its other Spirit-effected roles in relation to the larger redemptive self-disclosure of God as centered in and from Jesus Christ (cf. below). However we reckon Scripture's unitary connectedness to, in, under and from Christ *the* Word, by the Spirit, the historic evangelical position emphasizes the reality, the factuality, of the participation of Scripture within the economy of and as an aspect of God's gracious, condescending self-giving to be known objectively and redemptively as he is in himself by persons in the world. The point is that at some level Scripture-as-Scripture *is* (ontologically) the written Word of God. The historical evangelical position, like the historical position of the church, is not fearful of or repulsed by any and all historical connectedness and in any particular participation of the divine in the human, the material, and even in the linguistic at the level of real textuality.

But within evangelicalism there has recently been a subtle and nuanced move away from this identification of the Word of God and Holy Scripture at any level, except perhaps in a very formal, "adoptionist" or "Arian" sense. Whether finally correct or incorrect, these recent attempts to cut the divine Word of God away from the written text of Scripture is conceptually and methodologically reflective of the modern re-entrenchment of disjunctive or dualistic thinking which, in theology, inevitably bifurcates the unitariness of God's redemptive-kingdom purposes by cutting off the objective knowledge of God in the world. It is our purpose in this chapter to present, analyze and critique several recent evangelical discussions of Holy Scripture in relation to revelation/the Word of God, some separating the two and others emphasizing their unitariness or identity, and thereby to preliminarily present a christocentric revelational model wherein real participative place is found for written human language *in* and *as* the Word of God in the form of Holy Scripture.

Three Recent Evangelical Formulations of the Scripture - Word of God Relationship

Donald Bloesch

Donald Bloesch has long been an insightful, intelligent and effective evangelical theological light in the midst of late twentieth- and early twenty-first-century mainline Protestant theology. The balance of his great theological acumen and his humble, faithful, Reformed piety and devotion is to be found throughout his works.[4] In recent years, Bloesch has embarked upon the extensive theological project entitled *Christian Foundations*, already well known and much used in evangelical seminaries and colleges. In the second volume, *Holy Scripture: Revelation, Inspiration and Interpretation*, Bloesch endeavors to walk the *via media* between what he sees as the two theological pitfalls of (inerrantist) fundamentalism and liberalism on the question of Holy Scripture. This "Niebuhrian" dialectical structuring of what he perceives to be extreme against extreme is found on nearly every page of the work.

But the concern here is Bloesch's understanding of the relation of Holy Scripture to the Word of God, and thus the question of biblical authority in a primary sense. Again, one cannot really trace out Bloesch's position without seeing those ever present dialectical relations within which he sets up his view. Yet even here the point is not immediately clear. In addition to following James Barr's heavy-handed critique of a largely imaginary "fundamentalism" and so lumping, e.g., Carl Henry, Millard Erickson, and J. I. Packer into a "rationalistic neo-fundamentalism,"[5] he also chides neo-orthodoxy and liberalism in order to very questionably claim for his own position the high ground of the title "evangelical." How then is this evangelicalism reflected in his assessment of the character and authority of Scripture?

Against what he esteems to be the "frozen truth" of orthodoxy and its "docetic" view of Scripture, Bloesch sees the need to recover the "paradoxical unity of Word and Spirit" and a highly dynamic conception of the self-disclosure of God in Christ. To this end, he says, we must *distinguish* between the "transcendent content" of divine revelation and its historical form (Jesus) on the one hand, and any sense of Scripture as "written Word of God" on the other. That is, one must reckon Scripture only as a witness to the truth revealed in Christ, and as the "living Word" which Scripture "becomes" when it actually communicates the truth and power of Christ to us by the Spirit, rather than as the Word of God as such.[6] Indeed, these could be quite useful points of distinction in seeking to understand the various aspects of God's self-disclosure. But what Bloesch intends in terms of Scripture's relation to "the Word of God" is largely fashioned in the dialogical relation he maintains throughout his argumentation with the "dialectical theology movement" or "neo-orthodoxy" and with Karl Barth and Emil Brunner in particular. In terms of Bloesch's criticism of "neo-orthodoxy" the following statement is both telling and exceedingly ironic.

> Neo-orthodoxy . . . while calling for a recovery of biblical authority, was unable to hold together the divine and the human sides of Scripture. It can be faulted for fostering a Nestorian approach to the Bible in which the divine word and human word are only loosely associated and never function in indissoluble unity.[7]

Elsewhere Bloesch says that

> For Barth the Bible is the Word of God because. . . . [the] work of God is done *through* this text. . . . [E]very word or proposition in the Bible when taken in and of itself and when divorced from God's truth is open to error. At the same time, when united to the divine Word [Christ], the living, transcendent center of the Bible, it is then a *bearer* of the transcendent . . . the [Bible has the] potential of being a vehicle of divine grace.[8]

It is here, says Bloesch, that neo-orthodoxy advanced beyond "fundamentalism," i.e., by its "sharp distinction between Scripture as a historical and literary document and divine revelation."[9]

Bloesch, following what he understands to be Barth's position (cf. chapter six), understands God's revelation to be objective truth and event referring primarily and centrally to God's self-disclosure in Jesus Christ. But he says that it refers also to the dynamic and effectual meaning and significance of Christ.[10] Does this latter element refer to Scripture via the process of "inspiration"? No. Bloesch all but passes by any examination of classical passages on inspiration such as 2 Timothy 3:16 or 2 Peter 1:20-21, while defining "inspiration" dynamically after Barth's own pattern, which primarily emphasizes the ever present-ness of inspiration by the enactment of the Holy Spirit. To this definition of "inspiration" are joined other elements reflecting both Bloesch's strong concern for existential encounter with God's transcendent Word and his antipathy to any "static" identification between the transcendent Word/Truth of God and the historical, cultural, human witness to such, i.e., Holy Scripture.[11]

Yet Bloesch does not take a straightforward "Barthian" position. Contra the clear "Barthian" distinction, indeed dualistic separation, between Scripture text and the Word of God, Bloesch's position is more nuanced. Thus he says,

> The *content* of the Bible is indeed God's self-revelation in Jesus Christ, but this content comes to us in the form of a historical witness to this event or constellation of events. To know this content we need to get beyond "the right human thoughts about God (i.e., Scripture)" to "the right divine thoughts about men [i.e., "the Word," a quote from Barth]". . . . [the Scriptures] now function as the vehicle of the Holy Spirit. . . . [by whom we become] contemporaneous with the moment of revelation . . . through the word that we hear. The Bible is not in and of itself the revelation of God but the divinely appointed means and channel of this revelation."[12]

Since for Bloesch, the "Word of God transcends the human witness," transcends the "human word," it is not surprising that he must caricature what has been understood as the "evangelical" or "historical orthodox" position, which, according to Bloesch, regards the scriptural writings as the "stenographic notes of God's audible voice."[13] This is why Bloesch anachronistically and falsely claims that the "magisterial Reformers (especially Calvin)," along with the Puritans, including Jonathan Edwards, etc., also held to his own "neo-Barthian" emphasis on the "qualitative transcendence of divine truth over the earthen vessels." Thus, to defend his position that the Word of God "does not consist in revealed truths that are objectively 'there' in the Bible," he must simultaneously agree and disagree with Carl Henry, saying that "God reveals himself not only in acts but also in words." But does God reveal words and statements; is God a speech agent, and, if so, are these words identical with the biblical words? "Is there not a qualitative distance between the speech of God and the writing of humans?"[15]

An initial response to Bloesch ought to be to ask *why* there must be and *how* there can be this "qualitative distance" between God's Word and some transcendent "divine speech/words" (whatever that might be as an abstraction) and all human language *unless* there is an inherent limitation to the gracious condescension of God and his desire to make himself redemptively and objectively known as he is for us *in history*.

It must be acknowledged that the phrase "the Word of God" is used with contextual variety in Scripture. Holy Scripture is *not* "the Word of God" in the same sense, or better, as I will argue, at the same "level" as Christ the Word, for as the Word incarnate Christ is by nature the eternal, self-disclosure of God (John 1). And yes, Scripture is the God-given witness to Christ (John 5:39). Scripture, by means of the process of *theopneustos*, in, of, under and from Christ, is *derivatively* the Word of God. But by God's grace, it *is* the written Word of God, a conclusion affirmed by scriptural usage of the concept "the Word of God." It is here that Bloesch, like Brunner and "Barthians" in various ways, falls into disjunctive or dichotomous (dualist) means of conceptualizing the Word of God out of a Neoplatonic fear that an affirmation of such a historical, linguistic, textured Word of God would tarnish *the* Word of God. What then of the incarnation?[16]

This "transcendentalizing" tendency causes Bloesch (like the "Barthians") to back away from all such radical divine condescension and from all truly asymmetrical, interactive, unitary God-world-human (historical) redemptive relatedness. While wrongly chiding Barth for his revelational "Nestorianism," Bloesch is, from one perspective, almost as "Nestorian" as the Barthians and other dualists at this point. But from another side, Bloesch, with his desire to somehow lift up the "divine" authority of the finally human word of Scripture, is probably best characterized as an "Arian" regarding his understanding of the relation of Scripture to the Word of God.

Gabriel Fackre

For many years Gabriel Fackre has labored for what he has called a properly "evangelical" theology within the mainline streams of Reformed thought in the United Church of Christ, the Andover-Newton Theological School (where he was until his retirement Abbot Professor of Theology) and the Boston Consortium of theological schools. His writings have contributed much to recent thought on worship, evangelical ecumenism, and especially toward renewed thinking about the contemporary effects of the Noachic covenant and narrative theology. The last two issues especially play crucial roles within Fackre's argument in his new work, *The Doctrine of Revelation: A Narrative Interpretation.*

Much of Fackre's reformulation of the doctrine of revelation is formed under the broad influence of Avery Dulles' *Models of Revelation*, especially Dulles' emphasis on the centrality of revelation, i.e., that "[T]he great theological disputes turn out, upon reflection, to rest on different understandings of revelation, often simply taken for granted."[17] Also crucial for Fackre are Dulles' primary "models" or "intellectual constructs that express major tendencies," here for the field of "revelation."

Fackre draws on Dulles' five phenomenological models of revelation and transposes them into his own four "phases of revelation," which he sets forth in terms of his narrative theological approach and then exemplifies in terms of prominent twentieth-century Christian theological expressions or understandings of divine revelation. In terms of narrative, or the central "disclosive moments" within "the comprehensive story of reconciliation," Fackre's reconfiguration emphasizes first "preservation" or revelation vis-à-vis universal human experience; second, "action" or revelation in definitive acts of God, especially the election of Israel and then centrally the incarnation; third, and quite significantly for our purposes, "inspiration" or the "privileged" accounts and interpretations of the deeds of God in Scripture (a position Dulles terms "revelation as Doctrine"); and fourth, "illumination" or the role given to the light of God provided in all previous acts of divine disclosure. Within twentieth-century discussions of divine revelation, Fackre dialogically examines a series of "interlocutors" who variously typify each of the four particular aspects of the "Grand Narrative" of revelation, especially Paul Tillich ("preservation"), Karl Barth ("incarnate action"), Carl Henry ("inspiration") and Karl Rahner ("ecclesial illumination"). The intended final result is meant to be Fackre's evangelical concern that all such elements of revelation be holistically and properly seen together within the broad purposes of God's reconciling divine disclosure. But in the course of his discussion it becomes clear also that among these representative positions or aspects of revelation, Fackre too is essentially committed to the Barthian, christocentric position, not only as it *rightly* grounds all revelation in Jesus Christ, but also as it finally cuts off "inspired" Scripture from any and all direct participation *in* and *as* "the Word of God" in the strict sense. The relation of his chapters on "incarnate action" and "inspiration" are then clearly crucial in presenting Fackre's narrative case at this particular point of his concern.

All this is not to say that Fackre denies all cognitive revelation in order to reduce the heart of what may be called divine revelation to the content-less "encounter" of "dialectical presence" (e.g., so-called neo-orthodoxy or existential theology). In criticizing Paul Tillich's "ontological reason" and the role of religious symbols in revelation, Fackre implies such concern:

> While the symbols of myth and cult are said to give "knowledge" of ultimate reality, the word in that context means access to the *mystery* of being itself . Their purpose is expressive and evocative, not cognitive in its usual meaning.[18]

And in criticizing Barth's epistemology, Fackre somewhat obscurely points in this same direction when he states that

> The problems with Barth's epistemology arise when he departs from his own biblical standard for understanding the freedom of God for and among us. This might be described as the influence of an "actualism" with philosophical roots in existentialist philosophy. . . . The entrance of [divine sovereignty and the internal testimony of the Holy Spirit] into the doctrine of revelation is related to Barth's determination to protect the decisiveness of the ("incarnate action") chapter of the Story. Only here in Jesus Christ is God free *for* us . . . the actual address happens only when and where He wills it to be so . . . [thus] no assurance can be given that the media (e.g., the Bible) are always and everywhere bearers of the knowledge of God.[19]

Yet here, too, as in his critique of Tillich; the real nature of "the knowledge of God" and "cognitive" revelation is not at all clear. Given what we will see regarding Fackre's concerns about "propositional" (content-ful) revelation, and so of any identification of Holy Scripture with the divine Word of God in more than an indirect sense, one is left with as much doubt about Fackre and the cognitive element in revelation as Fackre had about Tillich.[20]

While critical of Karl Barth's view of revelation at points, and, as we will note, while bringing some proper initial corrective to the particular form

of Barth's (or the Barthian") christocentric concept of revelation, Fackre
often falls in step with that very same form of christocentricity as the core
of his understanding of that "Grand Narrative." For Fackre, "All that is said
in this [Fackre's] work on revelation is finally traceable to the Word that
God spoke to us in the historical event of Jesus Christ."[21] This means that
Christ is rightly regarded as *the* defining action of God, God's ultimate
revealing-redemptive deed and disclosure, and the "central chapter of the
story" which then determines what we see in all other aspects of the story.
This is true. But it also means that, for Fackre, Jesus Christ is finally the
one and only true Word of God. While emphasizing, much like the later
Barth, the freedom of God in promising a trustworthy Presence in and for
all of his reconciling work (and so the narrative), Fackre is also clear that
Christ is "the one Word" and Scripture, as "witness to that Word," stands
at last *outside* of what can be truly regarded as divine disclosure or the
Word of God. So Fackre's own strong christocentricity, no less than Barth's,
reflects again a fear that any historical claim to continuity (identity) with
the revelatory divine Presence, other than the incarnate Word, imperils
that centrality of Christ.[22] Thus Fackre expresses a significant point for his
larger and narrower purposes when he asks

> In what authority do we say that Jesus Christ is the centre of the narrative
> of . . . revelation? In the thought of Karl Barth, and throughout this work,
> we have turned to the "Bible" definitively and the "Church" derivatively
> as witness to the Word come among us.[23]

But why is this so? Why are Scripture and tradition, Bible and Church,
said to be "definitively" and "derivatively" *related to* the revelation and so
to authority? Our concern, again, is Holy Scripture, and Fackre's point is
directed to the inspiration of Scripture and to dialogue with the work of
Carl Henry. Herein Fackre confirms his chastened Barthian understanding
of Scripture and the Word of God.

Fackre's concern with what he calls "the much-neglected theme of the
inspiration of scripture," occurs via analysis of Carl Henry's work in order
to uncover why the Bible is an authoritative source of the narrative, "a
phase of revelation."[24] Such references to "authority" and "revelation" would
appear to mean *prima facie* that Scripture is itself as aspect of revelation.
Not so. Fackre emphasizes the crucial nature of the "inspiration" of the
text of Scripture but he formulates such in dialogical contrast to historical

evangelicalism's assertion of a divinely content-ful (i.e., propositional) text of Scripture as an aspect and product of revelation in and under Jesus Christ by the Spirit. Wanting to correct this formulation in a "properly evangelical" way, Fackre critically analyzes Henry's position along lines that are useful and often insightful (and unfortunately pejorative on several occasions), as well as formative for his own disjunctive, dualist understanding of the Word-Scripture relation.

It is in large measure true that Carl Henry's role in relation to twentieth-century theology has been to call theologians back to "inspiration" and so to the authoritative importance of the text of Scripture and the place of human language in the inspiration of Scripture. The acts of God are vacuous without verbal-cognitive interpretation. Fackre does acknowledge then that Henry's view of verbal inspiration arises from a legitimate concern for the place of propositions in the inspiration of Scripture. Put in narrative terms, Fackre asks whether biblical images and Scripture's "overarching story" correspond to actual human and divine states of affairs. And does Scripture make cognitive truth claims along these lines? Henry is clear that divine revelation cannot be reduced to only the (personal or) social power, whether that of personal divine "Encounter," metaphor or community story. While Scripture, understood as a participative aspect of revelation, *does* meet us personally and on the affective level and *does* constitute the unique language world of the Christian community, yet "its meaning is not exhausted by its evocative and expressive power." Paraphrasing what he takes to be one of Henry's central contributions, in terms of the "symbolic truth" of language philosophy, Fackre says that

> Biblical symbol . . . depicts Reality as well as drawing us into relationship with it. It discloses states of affairs, the way things are with both God and the world. However expressed . . . fundamental assertions about reality—propositions—are made that invite the response of Yes or No.[25]

All such is well and good as far as it goes.

Yet it is at this very juncture, wherein actual content-ful divine disclosure draws nigh to the Scripture text, that Fackre suddenly calls John Baillie and Karl Barth to his constructive aid lest any possible conceptual and expressible divine content be related too closely to a historical text.

Using Baillie's parallel critique of Austin Farrer's view of revelation and Scripture, Fackre says

> John Baillie is right in his concern that Farrer's images not be too simply juxtaposed to propositions for "images and propositional truths are inextricably intermingled." On the other hand, Karl Barth is right in contrasting the speaking of the Word in the person of Jesus Christ (i.e., incarnation) as "*Deus dixit*" with the "*Paulus dixit*" of the biblical words, thereby challenging theories of inspiration which identify one with the other.[26]

But while influenced partially by the "Barthian" dichotomy, Fackre finds Henry too to be correct in his defense of "propositional content," thus narrowing the "chasm" and allowing some kind of connection between *Deus dixit* and *Paulus dixit*. But again, this means simply a chastened, and so "narrowed," Barthian disjunction between the Word of God and the text of Scripture. While affirming in principle a content-ful revelation, Fackre, then, like Bloesch, retranscendentalizes such "content," a la "the Barthians" and then eschatologizes it, a la Jürgen Moltmann:

> The evangelical experience tempts closure of the distance between the Now and the Not Yet . . . . [epistemologically it is] to overlook the mirror dimmed and the glass darkened. Scripture is held [by Henry] to shine now with a light reserved only for a day yet to be . . . . The eschatological nature of verbal inspiration appears in Henry's construal of biblical propositions . . . . His understanding of (the propositions) as sentences . . . affiliates the human words themselves with the clarity of Light reserved alone for the End.[27]

Thus applying eschatologically, revelatorily and so epistemologically Martin Luther's *simul justus et peccator* to Scripture and to Henry-type evangelical views of Scripture, Fackre's central criticisms emphasize what he believes to be the problem of identifying or unitarily linking together the Word of God and Holy Scripture and so the failure to honor the temporal distinction between the eschatologically ultimate revelation and the penultimate medium, Scripture. Any collapse of eschatological truth into the verbal or textual, or the incarnate Word (the Centre) into the historical, epistemic text, is said to miss Barth's needed point in the *Barmen Confession*: the "one Word of God" is not replicated by, but "attested by" Holy Scripture.[28]

But, again, the problem is that Fackre's dualist or disjunctive thinking leads him to conclude that only such clear differentiations will suffice to set forth properly the "Centre" of the "Grand Narrative" of revelation, Jesus Christ, *the* Word of God. But this is not a necessary or even a useful principle—certainly not with regard to the Scripture-Word of God relation. A statement Fackre makes near the end of his discussion of "Scripture: Inspiration" is in many ways quite good, but not for Fackre's own reasons: "inspiration, while *part* of the revelation story, is neither the whole nor the heart of it, and must find its *derivative* place under the Word enfleshed and its *relative* place before the Word *eschatological*."[29] That is correct. Properly understood, this is a position with which Henry and, even better, Kevin Vanhoozer would agree. But the nature of "inspiration" (the force of which in both 2 Timothy 3 and 2 Peter 1 Fackre unfortunately seeks to blunt) of the historical text of Scripture is not intended to displace the centrality of Jesus Christ, the ontological and eternal Word made flesh, in the whole of God's redemptive self-disclosure. Holy Scripture *is* the inspired *witness* to Christ; it is such by the Holy Spirit under Christ the Word. But this subordinate servant's role is clear in Scripture itself and is affirmed historically by the church. Scripture is, to use Fackre's own term, the "derivative" Word of God, unitarily (and economically) grounded in Christ the Word, higher "level" to lower and historical "level," by the Spirit of God. This is a position taken in Scripture when Scripture reflexively refers to itself.

Therefore Fackre's narrative, broad-ranging willingness to speak *formally* of Holy Scripture as a "part" of revelation, as the "in-Spirited" media *integral* to "the Tale" told, by which Christ and (nontextual and apparently nonhistorical) content related to Christ (whatever that might be) come to us, reflects a desire to affirm an authoritative Scripture text that can in some sense be called "divine" as well as human, a result of the action of the Spirit. Yet it is a scriptural text which cannot be directly continuous or identified unitarily, even at a lower derivative level, to Christ the Word of God. His affirmation that God speaks, even "words," but words which are necessarily nonlinguistic, nonhistorical, and nontextual, reflects again the effects of underlying Platonic perspectives. As with Bloesch, using the early heretical christological positions analogously, we find in Fackre an "Arian" position on Scripture, a position resulting, like Arius' own, from an inherent dualism.

Clark Pinnock

Until his recent retirement, Clark Pinnock was professor of theology at McMaster Divinity School, and he continues to be engaged in issues of concern not only to evangelicals but also to many across the contemporary North-American religious scene. Scripture and biblical authority are among the issues with which he is most often identified. His thinking in *Biblical Revelation* (1971) was developed and altered eventually into his notable work *The Scripture Principle* (1984), with which we will now interact.

While this is the oldest of the three works examined here, it is in many respects the best. Herein Pinnock is forthright, honest and willing to openly grapple with issues in ways which others, perhaps concerned that they might be too clearly understood, would avoid. The problem is, of course, Pinnock's book reflects his thinking over twenty years ago and surely his views on a number of these issues have changed. But a clear statement of his current understanding of the nature of Scripture would be difficult to obtain from his recent more polemical writings.

Pinnock means by "The Scripture Principle," first, that there is a place where the Word of God is accessible in human form, that the creaturely text of Holy Scripture be seen as God's written Word and thus is the place where he reveals his mind, so that therein God has communicated authoritatively on subjects which call for our submission. Thus Scripture is an informative Word of God to the church, given as divinely authoritative and in contentful language.[30] Second, Pinnock intends to speak in defense of Scriptural authority and trustworthiness in the face of the contemporary crisis regarding "the Scripture Principle." Third, he wants "classical Christians," who maintain Scriptural authority, to "move ahead" in their understanding of such authority against the current crisis, at the heart of which is the "liberal denial" of the ancient, ecumenical, classical conviction that the text of Scripture is the written, authoritative Word of God. This crisis has arisen from the cultural shift to secular and rationalist modernity, and hence there is antipathy to any book speaking of God and humanity in premodern categories and to any orthodoxy which would rigidly lock God in a book.[31]

Like Bloesch and Fackre, Clark Pinnock rightly emphasizes the *christocentric* pattern and the *soteric* purpose of all self-disclosure of God. Yet contra the "Barthian" approach, and more clearly than Bloesch or Fackre, Pinnock is adamant that the biblical presentation of "revelation" is "not a single activity or a simple entity but that the 'pattern of revelation' within which Scripture fits is a complex web and set of actions designed to complementarily disclose the divine message of salvation" ("many and various ways God spoke"). Revelation is multifaceted and "bipolar" in structure, both objective and subjective; content is revealed, received and confirmed.[32] But "Jesus Christ is and must be the centerpiece of the Christian revelation, because in him God entered the parameters of a human life . . . the revelation of God without peer. Of all the forms of revelation, this is the best."[33] Thus Scripture exists to bear witness of him (John 5:39). The Christ Principle of the incarnation of the Word is at the core of all consideration of the richly variegated pattern of divine revelation.

In this way, Pinnock corrects not only the Barthian approach to revelation but most theological streams since Friedrich Schleiermacher by stressing the "content," the "objective truths of revelation," i.e., it is no mere existential address or content-less encounter. In this he advances beyond the similar correctives of modern views as found in Bloesch and Fackre, and stands against these tendencies which refuse to affirm

> a message full of content and truth given in intelligible speech and language-as if there were some kind of opposition between personal revelation and verbal communication. The New Testament knows no such dichotomy; it stems from modern philosophical objections to cognitive revelation and an objective knowledge of God.[34]

This is right to the point. Pinnock's analysis and criticism of the modern shift from objective, contentful revelation is exacting and correct. Whether in the context of Israel's covenantal anticipation or in the new covenant fulfillment in Jesus Christ, the incarnate Word, revelation according to Scripture itself is content-ful, intelligible, and speaks to persons on subjects they are able to understand.[35]

Does this correct affirmation truly give proper place to the text of Holy Scripture in Pinnock's "pattern of revelation" in such a way that at some level Scripture *is* ontologically the written Word of God? It appears so. Two points seem constructively significant here, particularly in contrast to Fackre. First, in a note, Pinnock points out that Klaas Runia has rightly criticized and corrected Barth's exclusion of the scriptural text from the revelation it attests,[36] and second, Pinnock clearly distinguishes "revelation" from the church tradition which it engenders.[37] While occasionally referring to Scripture as a "medium" or "vehicle" of revelation, Pinnock's early argumentation almost always relates "Scripture" and "Word of God/revelation" in a way fully in keeping with the historical position of the Church, i.e., "Scripture is the written Word of God" or "written revelation of God." Referring to the typical Old Testament portrayals, Pinnock points out that

> In the prophets . . . [we find] people who see themselves, in the tradition of Moses, able to mediate God's Word to the people. . . . [They] spoke out boldly the words he gave them. They were servants to whom the Lord had revealed his secrets (Amos 3:7). They believed that God had put his words in their mouths. . . . They spoke the very word of God to Israel.[38]

Pinnock finds the New Testament to be no different, especially as it both endorses and quotes from the Old Testament "as the Word of God,"[39] and then claims for itself the same status.[40] While he periodically expresses an occasionalistic view of Scripture as Word of God, i.e., that a portion of Scripture had been the Word of God but is no longer the Word of God *for us* (probably referring to applicability),[41] he does not press this idea. Essentially his position early in *The Scripture Principle* is that Scripture objectively presents us, informationally or content-fully, with the "plans and purposes of God." While pointing out that Scripture is unsystematic and fragmentary, Pinnock seems clear that its testimony suggests that it was God's will that "written revelation in the form of Scripture" should come forth out of the tradition of Israel and the church to "preserve the substance of the faith for posterity." At this point, then, Pinnock seems to affirm that "Holy Scripture is the inspired Word of God," a divine gift, as "classical Christians" have always believed.[42]

But the manifestation of what was only occasional early on in Pinnock's argument, i.e., Scripture as mere "medium," "vehicle" or "conveyor" of the revelation of God, revelation then being something different, other or beyond the text, and having only a formal and functional connection to the biblical text, becomes increasingly dominant and finally determinant for his point. This point is sometimes made, initially, in the "practical" sense whereby a knowledge of the Scripture text as such apart from faith is not knowledge of "the Word of God," lacking "the eyes of faith," a sense which most would agree with.[43] But the intent of the argument is more transitional toward something of a "sacramental" role for Scripture akin to Fackre's. All agree that Holy Scripture presents its truths in human language, and most hold to some form of accommodation. But does the humanity of the language of the biblical text require disjunction, separation from the self-disclosure of God in terms of any and all participation and identity? Or can such human language be both witness and conveyer of God's truth, and also a direct product of revelation, the inscripturated Word of God by the Spirit? By using a number of metaphors, the most noteworthy being John Calvin's picture of Scripture as "eyeglasses" and also an image of Scripture as a "freight train." Pinnock thereby builds his point that as the glasses help one to see reality "out there" and as the train carries freight that is not itself the train, so Scripture too is the divinely given medium *through* which the transcendent Word of God comes from beyond.

Yet here it must be noted that for Clark Pinnock, in contrast to Bloesch and Fackre, the interactive relation and inseparability of Word and text remain very strong. This seems to result from the conceptual implications of Pinnock's acknowledgment of the legitimacy of the incarnation analogy for our understanding of Scripture.

> Christian theology . . . [presupposing God] is not beyond its epistemic rights in claiming that God has reliably revealed himself and his will in a set of creaturely modalities . . . . So long as the God of the gospel is believed in, the Bible itself is no conundrum. It can be God's infallible Word in exactly the way that it claims to be his Word and the product of God's revelational activity. If Jesus Christ was raised from the dead . . . then the process of revelation and its products that center upon Christ are vindicated along with him.[44]

Yet despite such apparent affirmation, Pinnock's final dualistic disjunction of the Scripture text from the Word of God becomes quite plain. Affirming again that God ultimately gave Scripture to be that "literary vehicle of his Word," Pinnock further concludes that "Barth was right to speak about a distance between the Word of God and the text of the Bible." While the written medium is very limited, these restrictions are overcome by the divine message given *through* it.[45]

In one way, then, Pinnock takes a relatively strong view of the inspiration of Holy Scripture, affirming the dynamic work of the Holy Spirit as yet interfacing with culture-bound and limited human beings but as one who is still active in Scripture's production. So in some real sense, Pinnock considers the Bible to be a divine product, a divine and human writing, and as such a functional "Word of God," almost the *sine qua non* of our "hearing of the Word of God" which is conveyed *through* the text for us to hear and heed. In this way, Pinnock recognizes the divine nature of the text of Scripture, but it is said to be a text brought into existence to mediate the transcendent Word of God in Christ. Thus Scripture is, for Pinnock, not really so much a product *of* revelation as it is a product *for* revelation. It *is* the "switch track" by which the transcendent Word can be mediated redemptively into the space–time domain of human life. This disjunctive and "sacramental" conception of the relation of the Scripture text to the Word of God, reflected less adequately in Bloesch and Fackre, operates in ways significantly parallel to Emil Brunner, most "Barthians" and also analogically to Tillich's use of revelatory symbols. And the perceived need for such sharp differentiation arises again out of the injurious dualist impulse, and thus from the unwillingness to conceive the various aspects of God's self-revelation in terms of unitary, interactive "levels"—in this case "levels" of the one Word of God, whether ontological or derivative (cf. chapter eight below). There is no need to divide Scripture from the Word of God by reducing the former to a "functional" Word, contrary to scriptural usage and reference to itself. Rather, true scriptural differentiation within the multileveled, interactive and relational singularity of divine revelation allows one to reflect all aspects of the Word of God in their proper relations one to another within the unitary whole and ultimately under Christ, the Word made flesh.

My concern in the previous analyses of Bloesch, Fackre and Pinnock has not been to attempt to ascertain any movement into heterodoxy. All three seem to stand within the broader parameters of orthodoxy, and, when "push comes to shove," Pinnock especially stands very close to the historical orthodox position. But the concerns are, first, the entrance and disjunctive effects of modern and postmodern cosmological, ontological and epistemological dualism into the doctrine of revelation, a dualism which may, if pressed consistently, lead also to adoptionism or to an Arian Christology; and, second, the resulting dichotomous severing of the historical text of Holy Scripture from revelation as such, the Word *of God*, thus reducing any relation to the arbitrary and the merely functional.

Reformulation and Reaffirmation of Holy Scripture as the Written Word of God: Written Language - Word of God?

Is such a disjunctive severance of Holy Scripture from the Word of God (in terms of any actual ontological and historical participation and economic/ "leveled" identity) a much needed modern and postmodern corrective to the historical position of the church? In other words, reckoning the dualistic presuppositions involved, ought we to finally recognize the ideal-historical differences inherent in the issue of revelation, and so forgo any linkage, continuity or identity that might somehow jeopardize that transcendentalized, ideal Word of God which would result from actual historical connection? Must the Kantian noumenal-phenomenal split and the consequent positivistic skepticism about any real referentiality of human language to anything beyond the empirical be taken to heart and accepted by contemporary Christian orthodoxy? Or should such alien Neoplatonic, dualistic incursions be resisted and the reaffirmation of the revelatory nature of the divine-human text of Holy Scripture, as derivative Word of God (by the Holy Spirit), be given and re-stated? It is this second option which the argument here will now pursue.

Can *human* linguistic forms, human language, and specifically written human language ever be legitimately reckoned as the Word *of God*, indeed, ultimately God's own verbal expression? Can God thereby give objective, content-ful, as well as personal, disclosure of himself and his purposes for, to and in space-time? Is God a speech agent? Is there divine discourse?

204

Again, historically the answer has been "Yes." The writers of Scripture themselves clearly believed that Yahweh, the covenant God, the triune God self-revealed in Jesus of Nazareth, is the speaking God who declares himself and his ways to his prophets and apostles, who thus makes himself known personally, redemptively and also informationally to his people. God is a language (and genre) user. Old Testament prophets, Jesus, and the apostles were of one mind on this, regardless of contemporary views about such verbal-textual communicability within the God-world-human relation. Phrases such as "thus says the Lord" and "God/the Holy Spirit spoke through the prophets"[46] permeate both testaments and are clearly to be taken as in some sense literally true. If Jesus is recognized as God incarnate, then his speaking, teaching and *witness* to the Father, as the Father's own Word, further confirms God's own contentful use of human language (any claim for disjunctive difference between spoken disclosure and written communication is evasive, obscurantist nonsense). And again, as the Scripture writers did, the early church reaffirmed this categorically in the Nicene-Constantinopolitan Creed, echoing the scriptural language: "The Holy Spirit . . . who spoke through the prophets . . . ."

The Adequacy of Human Language: J. I. Packer

J. I. Packer finds that the modern theological aberration which rejects the possibility of God declaring himself to humanity objectively, content-fully (including informatively, factually) and in human linguistic forms, has multiple roots, two of which are especially pertinent to the formulations of Bloesch, Fackre, and, to a lesser extent, Pinnock. First, pervasively skeptical Western culture has accepted the unproven assumption that all language is inadequate as a means of personal communication. If such inadequacy and isolationism occurs at the common human level, the problem is surely much more true of God who is so different from our humanity.[47] Second, modern doubt regarding the possibility of content-ful divine communication has been much influenced by so-called "Eastern" religious notions, as well as by parallel emphases in resurgent Neoplatonism, both of which stress the ineffability and inexpressibility of the remote or undifferentiated "divine."[48] Third, and more directly applicable, Packer rightly points out the prominent contemporary doubt that human language can communicate transcendent realities at all.[49] Semantics and linguistic analysis, long under the dualistic sway of defunct logical positivism, have arbitrarily concluded that language cannot connote, denote, inform or point legitimately beyond the world of the senses. Finally, skepticism about the possibility of God's expressing himself in human linguistic forms arises from the widespread modern unwillingness of theologians to allow that in, as and through Scripture, God is actually discoursing, and informing human beings about himself and his relations with us.[50] Whatever may be acknowledged about Scripture somehow "mediating" contact with God/ the divine (why Scripture?), even so, many are yet more certain that Holy Scripture is not God's Word in any way, resembling Augustine's "what thy Scripture says, thou dost say." As alluded to previously, Immanuel Kant's Newtonian, deistic epistemological dualism led him to deny both the need and the very possibility of verbal revelation from God. Theological liberalism and neoliberalism, from Schleiermacher and Ritschl to the present, has remained faithful to Kant, despite variations in emphasis. Yet it has been the breakaway movement of "dialectical theology" or "theology of the Word" (or "neo-orthodoxy") which has been much more directly influential on contemporary evangelical thought at this point, and it too has maintained much of Kant's noumenal-phenomenal split and the consequent rejection of Holy Scripture as the written Word of God, except in some occasionalist, adoptionist and functional way.

Within contemporary evangelical discussion on the nature of Scripture, pointedly in the work of Bloesch, Fackre, and Pinnock, the third form of skepticism referred to by Packer (the inability of human language to adequately refer to the "transcendent") is both implicitly and explicitly formative in the argumentation—even reflected at times in unsubstantiated ad hominem statements meant to embarrass: e.g., God's Word certainly cannot be identified with ink on paper (why not?). Even more explicit is a Kantian dualism which, when combined with Buberian "personalism," ends in "transcendentalizing" and dehistoricizing both God and his Word, while yet declaring that very Word to be personal rather than propositional. Kant's deistic agnosticism left God both remote and unintelligible, and then dialectical theology (and even the mature Barth at times) concluded, as John Frame rightly points out, that

> God's transcendence [so understood] implies that he *cannot* be clearly revealed to men, clearly represented by human words and concepts. . . . (But) Scripture never deduces from God's transcendence the inadequacy and fallibility (let alone the impossibility) of all verbal revelation. Quite the contrary . . . verbal revelation is to be obeyed without question *because* of the divine transcendence.[51]

"Barthian" unwillingness to allow for any real, "substantial" continuity, connection, identity or ontological participation of the content-ful (and propositional) scriptural wording as being properly within the larger category "the Word of God" arises directly from such Kantian, dualistic, transcendentalist thinking evident especially in Bloesch and Fackre. There is no need to first deceptively extol Scripture's mediated glory and then to conclude that Scripture is finally the word of man after all rather than the Word of God, except in some sacramental sense. Such simultaneous bibliological Arianism-Adoptionism is only necessitated by these false and destructive dualist presuppositions.

This is not to say that Bloesch's, Fackre's and Pinnock's concerns with the idea of the real identity of Scripture and the Word of God are insubstantial, especially in light of issues understood to arise from the apparently "weak" elements of the text as related to human culture or to perspectives and to elements bound to a particular history and place. Nor are the linguistic-analytical questions empty as they give critical attention to the very human semantic forms of discourse such as analogy, parable, model, etc (cf. chapter four). Rather, the point is that, given the God-world-human interactive relatedness, established in creation, sustained in providence, and completed redemptively in the incarnate life, death, and resurrection of Jesus Christ (the Word made flesh in the power of the Holy Spirit), such concerns are answered. Calvin was right in emphasizing that God's gracious condescension, the "humility" of God whereby he lovingly identifies with that which is beneath him, means that in terms of revelation, inspiration, and Scripture God was willing to become "undignified" for human redemption.[52]

Affirming Scripture as the Word of God: Paul Helm

British philosopher Paul Helm takes much time to carefully discuss the question of the relation of Holy Scripture and the Word of God, in his work *Divine Revelation*. Crucial to his argument are the foundations for his commitment to the classical Christian affirmation, i.e., that special revelation (or simply "revelation" in the strict sense) is a cognitive concept in that it has to do with *knowledge*, an actual or possible mode of knowledge of that which cannot otherwise be known.[53] Thus, in keeping with our emphases above, Helm, too, acknowledges the need for divinely given content, indeed even information or truth about God and his purposes (the "propositional" element in revelation), in contrast to notions of contentless "personal encounter" or bare "Act," etc.[54] Thus he says that

> It is curious . . . that while the idea that the Bible is God's special propositional revelation has been charged with replacing God himself by propositions about God, examination of . . . periods when such a view was dominant suggests the exact reverse . . . [There] is no antithesis between believing a proposition and believing a person if the proposition is understood as the assertion of a person. . . . So the claim that the idea of propositional special revelation is essentially impersonal appears to rest on a misunderstanding.[55]

The modem theological claim that there is an antithesis between "propositions" (or more broadly content-ful, meaningful expressions or statements) and persons is surely false, given that propositions are only the utterance of some person. To deny this to God, in the interactive God-world-human relation, reflects an arbitrary assumption grounded in both metaphysical and epistemological dualism.

Helm's primary dialogue partner is Karl Barth (or more accurately the Barthian-Brunnerian viewpoint), and then those variously influenced by the primary "Barthian" reasons for denying that Scripture can *be* the Word of God. According to Helm, Barth's understanding of revelation (God-in-Christ as independent of the knower) is both ontologically objective and epistemologically subjective with respect to revelation (human knowledge of God). What are the results? Put briefly, Barth contends that the sovereign God is free in his revelation. Revelation cannot be "static." Yet the very notion of covenant and God's covenant faithfulness show that God is willing to limit himself. Second, and consequently, Barth says that any revelation of the sovereignly free God must be a personal act or event. But given the biblical pattern, special revelation cannot be bare Act or event of God, but rather must be acts or events of God *and* (their) *interpretation*. Third, modernity as a whole and "Barthian" formulations of revelation in particular have been extremely hesitant to allow for divine self-disclosure to be truly historical, an actual datum of history. In terms of the Word of God and Scripture, Helm explains that Barth emphasizes the fact that Scripture is a "worldly [historical] document" which then rules out *a priori* any possibility of the Bible being itself and as such God's written Word. Yet, says Helm, Barth's act/event formulation of revelation, as related to (yet different from) Scripture as the primary "witness" to revelation, means that the "words" of the text are altered in the moment they became the Word of God for an individual. In point of fact, most texts or passages of Scripture are not plausible as candidates for such an occasionalism of the Word. Also, Barth's emphasis on the scriptural witness *becoming* (the) Word of God "for me" leads to the "private language" problem and essential incommuniability.[56] But of special importance is Helm's analysis of the influential Barthian contention that Holy Scripture is only the "witness" to the Word of God, an analysis which, in effect, turns the Barthian contention on its head. If, as the Barthian presents the matter, the relation between Scripture and the Word of God is a noncontingent one

> then it must be one of *meaning*; there must be a connection of meaning between the two. And if there is a connection of meaning between the two then God's Word must be propositional, since the Bible is propositional and there is a logical relationship between the two. But if God's Word, special revelation, is propositional, then for Barth this must mean that it is "static" and manipulable. Once again, the relationship between the Bible and the Word of God, in the Barthian scheme of things, is seen to be wholly problematic.[57]

While Helm's subsequent argumentation about how one ought and ought not to present a positive case for the text of Holy Scripture as the written Word of God as an aspect of special revelation is very useful, his role here in this chapter has been primarily to respond to dualistic, transcendentalist presuppositions which have been basic to modern and contemporary denials of Holy Scripture as Word of God, i.e., show that such denials are rooted in serious misunderstandings at various levels. But before leaving this issue, the case here can be further developed by means of a very recent work uniquely aimed at these concerns for historical and textual revelation.

Affirming "Divine Discourse" in History: Nicholas Wolterstorff

In his influential Wilde Lectures at Oxford University, subsequently published as *Divine Discourse: Philosophical Reflections on the Claim that God Speaks*, philosopher Nicholas Wolterstorff has sought to examine the "strange but riveting" declaration introduced to humanity by Judaism that "God speaks to us on our way, and that our calling as human beings is to listen to that speech from beyond and hear."[58] The notion of God's speaking—divine discourse—if true, both an unsettling and a consoling assertion-has faced much modern hostility. But it is this hostility which Wolterstorff addresses as "ill-advised" and "self-defeating."

But what does Wolterstorff mean by God's "discourse" or speaking? Schleiermacher, Ritschl, Bultmann, Tillich, and, more recently, David Tracy and Gordon Kaufman have referred to "God's speaking," but for these the intention is at best metaphorical, symbolic, noninformative and noncontentful. For these, God does not speak *about* anything. Brunner discussed "God's speaking" at great length, but for him and like-minded theologians God's "discourse" or self-disclosure is his act or encounter without revelatory, interpretive, historical content. While variously influenced by these modern trends yet consciously endeavoring to likewise stand within Christian orthodoxy, Bloesch, Fackre and Pinnock are also very serious about "God's speaking." They do not want God's self-revelation to be totally reduced to merely wordless "events" or I-Thou existential "encounters." Yet these theologians, too, finally balk at the radical historicity required by any Christian orthodox claim of ontological connection or identity between Holy Scripture and the Word of God. What of Wolterstorff? Does an underlying dualistic assumption and scheme finally force him likewise to transcendentalize "divine speaking," *deus loquens*, to the transhistorical, beyond anything divinely auditory or written? Or does he attempt to correct such modern tendencies? Is God a speech agent?

While Wolterstorff is concerned primarily with the question of divine discourse/speaking rather than with divine revelation specifically, a fine distinction he makes and for which he labors effectively, the question of divine speaking as revelatory (as, e.g., with the written Word of God) is very significant to him. Moving illustratively from the words of the child, "*Tolle lege, tolle lege*," which Augustine took to be God speaking to him, Wolterstorff purposes to counteract modern philosophico-theologico-epistemological unwillingness to allow for historical, informative divine speaking, while at the same time strongly affirming, somehow, real divine revelation. The outcome of Wolterstorff's multileveled analysis of language theory, especially "speech-act" theory, is that, contrary to much modern and postmodern agnosticism, God need not remain incommunicative beyond bare act or meeting ("manifestational revelation"), but rather that God can make and has made historical "assertions," "propositions" ("non-manifestational revelation"), and that this speaking can result and has resulted "*in a text* which, when properly interpreted, transmits knowledge from God to us."[59]

As a consciously philosophical work which deals with theological questions, *Divine Discourse* develops its critical and constructive argument without much direct reference to Scripture texts as such. But when Wolterstorff does refer to Scripture, he is emphatic that the near consensus opinion among modern (post-Kantian) theologians (e.g., Barth, John Baillie, Bultmann, et al.) that revelation can only be nonlinguistic act, stands in conflict with the text of Scripture itself. Therein God is understood to be engaged in speaking or in giving propositional revelation related to himself and his purpose (e.g., in the exodus).[60]

But for our purposes, it is most instructive to note Wolterstorff's responses to Karl Barth and John Baillie, influential twentieth-century representatives of thinking resistant to the identification of the text of Scripture with the Word of God, responses clearing the way for his own primary constructive formulations. After effectively analyzing the Barthian emphasis on the need for christocentric understanding of "the Word of God," Jesus Christ, as the *one* speech-act of God (John 1), Wolterstorff capably points out that, for all of his emphasis on the Word of God, even

Barth largely avoids discussion of God's "speaking," of contractual usage in the text of Holy Scripture. The Barthian point is clear, that apart from God's revelation in the event of Jesus Christ there is no other Word of God, no human speaking or writing that is also truly a speaking in God's name by God. All acts of "witnessing" to God's one speech-act, though under the guidance of the Spirit, remain necessarily and only human speech. But Wolterstorff comments:

> What God does in addition [to the incarnation] is *bring it about* that what God said in Jesus Christ is both presented to us and, by some of us, acknowledged. But that "bringing about" is something different from speaking. Barth's thought is that the very being who is the content of Scripture and proclamation, Jesus Christ, the Word, the speech of God, so acts on us that we acknowledge that content. True enough. But is that action *more speaking*?[61]

While Barthians (such as Bloesch, Fackre) come very close to acknowledging this, in the final analysis they consistently avoid such a conclusion. Why?

Wolterstorff answers by rightly noting, first, such emphatic differentiation of Scripture from Word of God, from God's speaking, is regarded as the only way of honoring the results of biblical criticism while yet affirming Scriptural authority as the medium God uses *through* which to "speak" to us. This same concern is reflected in each of our three evangelical writers discussed above. Second, like Paul Helm, Wolterstorff reiterates Barth's fear that the assertion of God's authoring of Scripture in any direct sense compromises God's freedom. Responding at two levels, Wolterstorff points out that if such authoring and commissioning of human authors of a text is limiting, then perhaps we ought to take seriously the possibility that God is willing to limit his freedom in this way. But beyond Helm, Wolterstorff additionally finds that Barth may be working with an alien concept of "freedom." He finds it hard to see how God's decision to "appropriate" human speech compromises his freedom in any way. "Probably Barth never even considered the appropriation model as a way of thinking of God as author."[62]

While necessarily moving past Wolterstorff's insightful, careful argumentation, it is also needful that we briefly present the bottom line of Wolterstorff's own positive, constructive emphases on divine speaking as these relates to our question of Holy Scripture and Word of God. He asks why, if Scripture were a mere instrument or mere medium of "revelation" in the modern sense (as bare divine event or encounter), would one continually return and return . . . to Scripture's text? Mere mediation is used but once. When its work is done, one moves on. Wolterstorff's answer arises from his understanding of the relation of Scripture as textual, human written discourse to divine discourse, and how Scripture can be both simultaneously. Herein he works with four assumptions about the text of the Bible. First, the books of Scripture did not come into being by God directly producing inscriptions on parchments but by human beings doing so. Second, those human beings were themselves performing acts of discourse; they were not just writing words down. Third, God's discourse is a function not just of those human acts of inscription but "of those human acts of discourse generated by those human acts of inscription," i.e., one must know more than just the original text as such, including "what was being said with those texts" by whatever human beings authorized them as *their own* discourse.[63] Finally, in the fact that one person's discourse can count as another person's discourse, so here Wolterstorff finds a model for the text of Holy Scripture. By "deputation" (e.g., the prophets and apostles) and by "appropriation" as "supplemented" by inspiration, Christian Scripture as a whole and its various books is to be understood as God's discourse as well as human discourse.[64] Thus Nicholas Wolterstorff (like Kevin Vanhoozer, cf. chapter three) has clarified and demonstrated the "mechanism" whereby we can effect the transition from seeing Scripture as only a collection of human speech acts to seeing it properly in its canonical unity as a work of divine communicative action with God as a user of human language. Indeed, understanding human language in terms of speech acts closely approximates the manner in which Scripture itself treats language, human and divine. And it is Wolterstorff who has shown how speech act categories have the potential to enable one to understand, in terms of inspiration and simultaneous divine "appropriation," what it means to rightly apprehend Holy Scripture as "dual-author discourse" and so as God's own Word to humanity. While new questions may potentially arise from the form of this model, it does effectively allow Wolterstorff to give strong emphasis to authorial intention in hermeneutics in order to establish the meaning of that which is also God's own discourse.

Restatement: Word of God and Scripture

First, the claim here is that the "Barthian" (as largely distinct from Karl Barth's) understanding of the Word of God and the nature of Holy Scripture, as variously influential on sectors of evangelicalism and on our three evangelical theologians in particular, is both right and wrong at different levels. Barth's christocentricity, his point that *the* Word of God as such and ultimately, is Jesus Christ, is simply correct. John 1 and Hebrews 1, with other related texts of Scripture (Colossians) make clear enough that the logos who is God and who became flesh, Jesus of Nazareth, *is* the self-disclosure of God in an eternally unique, absolute and pre-eminent way. He is *the ontological* Word of God. But does this fact inevitably or necessarily negate any legitimacy in conceiving of Holy Scripture too as the written Word of God? Certainly not. Barth is again being very biblical in calling Scripture the primary "witness to the Word/Christ" for Jesus says the same in John 5:39. But, again, does this distinction (not separation) of Christ the Word from Scripture's testimony to Jesus Christ necessarily alleviate its continuity and nuanced identity with the Word as the written Word of God? No. Indeed, the Holy Spirit, too, bears witness to Christ. How then might these interrelated elements be conceptually and preliminarily brought together or modeled in a way that is in keeping with Scripture's own testimony to itself? As we will observe more fully in chapter eight, given the fact that Jesus Christ, incarnate, eternal Word of God, is said to be the utterly unique, supreme, objective self-giving of God to be known as he is; that the scriptural data of the OT and NT also speak often of their own proper status as an aspect of revelation or the written Word of God; that Scripture is distinguished from Christ as primary "witness" to Christ; and finally that God's revelation is one because God is one, then we must avoid a flat, blank, undifferentiated identity between Jesus Christ and Holy Scripture as being the Word of God in the same sense. But we must also strenuously avoid dualistic, disjunctive thinking which finally separates Christ the Word and the inscripturated Word, as though the latter were actually the mere word of man and at best functionally and adoptionistically Word of God if and when "used" by God. The need here is for unitary, interactive thinking, as reflected in twentieth and twenty-first century physics, thinking which endeavors to think after the identity-in-difference inherent in our question.

As we will develop in chapter eight, in *Physics and Reality*, Albert Einstein accounts for different "levels" or "strata" of knowledge in a scientific system, knowlege arising from natural cognition of ordinary experience. Scientific theory (e.g., "Relativity") must be brought to "logical" unity, and finally to a strict "higher level" of logical unity, as each level of knowledge is related to and grounded in the "higher" level. In this way, thinking penetrates more and more toward the interior connections of reality. Each level is "open" up to the next higher level and also "disclosive" down to lower levels. No level below the highest has its truth in itself, but is true as it is interactively related to and "open up" to the greater refinement at the next higher level, etc. All is interactively and interrelatedly grounded finally beyond the contingent in that sufficient reason for the lower contingent order of rationality and intelligibility.[65]

Even as this has been effectively related to the Nicene *homoousion*, reflecting unitary, interactive relatedness, identity-in-difference, so too is such a stratified model reflective of the incarnate Word—inscripturated Word relationship. At the "lower level," historical Scripture is the written, preserved record of divine revelation; it is the "derivative" Word of God by means of God's gracious self-disclosure and inspiration. As such, Scripture stands in, under, of and from Jesus Christ. Its truth is not simply *in itself* but, as "open up" unitarily in and under Christ by the Spirit, its truth is grounded in Christ the ontological Word, i.e., in the logos, and so finally in the perichoretic relations of the triune Godhead. Therein and therefrom, the inscripturated Word is "disclosive down" and within the present historical space-time situation of humanity. To lose this aspect or "pole" of the unitary Word of God is to disengage God's truth from history, to "transcendentalize" the Word. Content-ful (including propositional) revelation is thereby negated. God becomes mute actor. We become pious agnostics. This is the inevitable outcome of such disjunctive, separationist thinking. As Ray Anderson has rightly said,

> What is at stake in giving up that which a concept of propositional revelation seeks to preserve is the pole of transcendence which we have said lies in history and thus can serve to inform the act of faith "in the Spirit" of its transcendent grounds in the person of Christ . . . if the cognitive link with the content of God's transcendence as historical act

is broken, the act of faith must supply its own content to the divine Word.[66]

It is this very historical, content-ful revelation, grounded by the Holy Spirit in Jesus Christ, which is cut away by those dualistic forms of theological thinking analyzed earlier.

Significantly, something akin to this very "stratification" of the written Word of God in, under and from Christ is reflected in John Calvin's own understanding of the Word of God. Therein, historically, according to Calvin, the written Word of God stands "over" the church, i.e., the written Word of God is, in Einsteinian terms, "disclosive down" as the derivative/inspired Word of God to be heard and known here and now.[67] It is in the next chapter that we will seek to more fully develop these points in our reaffirmation of Holy Scripture as the written and authoritative Word of God, and so as an aspect of God's larger multileveled, interrelated, unitary Word of God as centered in, under, of and from Jesus Christ, *the* Word made flesh.

Endnotes

[1] Cf. J. N. D. Kelly, *Early Christian Doctrines* (New York: Harper and Row, 1960), ch.2,3; Bruce Shelley, *By What Authority?* (Grand Rapids: Wm. B. Eerdmans, 1965); Geoffrey W. Bromiley, "The Church Fathers and Holy Scripture" in *Scripture and Truth*, ed. by D. A. Carson and John Woodbridge (Grand Rapids: Zondervan, 1983)., John D. Woodbridge, *Biblical Authority: A Critique of the Rogers/McKim Proposal* (Grand Rapids: Zondervan, 1982). This is a position acknowledged by Pinnock but skirted by Bloesch and Fackre.

[2] This was a favorite illustration of Barth's for the role of Scripture in relation to Christ. The picture has John pointing to the crucified Christ, thus bearing "witness to him. A copy of the Gruenewald alterpiece hung just above Barth's desk at his home in Basel.

[3] Such "personalistic" emphasis, via the influence of Jewish existentialist Martin Buber, has played a prominent role in concepts of divine revelation in the past century, especially, e.g., in the thought of Emil Brunner, John Baillie, and to a lesser extent in Barth and Thomas Torrance.

[4] E.g. *The Struggle of Prayer, Wellsprings of Renewal, The Crisis of Piety*, and others, along with works directly related to "doctrinal" theology.

[5] Donald G. Bloesch, *Holy Scripture: Revelation, Inspiration and Interpretation* (Downer's Grove, Ill.: InterVarsity, 1994) 65–67, 94–101.

[6] Ibid., 24–25.

7 Ibid., 33.

8 Ibid., 101–2.

9 Ibid.

10 Ibid., 49ff.

11 Ibid., 117f, 126f.

12 Ibid., 56–57. Herein Donald Bloesch is much indebted to Søren Kierkegaard and his concept of "contemporaneity" as developed to relate Christ the Word to later believers in *Philosophical Fragments*. It is in regard to this very concern that this writer recently discovered a pertinent point made by Millard Erickson about Bloesh's view of Scripture, a point with which I am essentially in agreement. He says that "Bloesch chooses to identify with the 'sacramental' approach [to understanding the nature of Scripture] . . . this is not to say that the words of Scripture are directly revealed (as in the Scholastic approach) but that Scripture embodies the truth that God wants us to hear." "It is the Word of God in human clothing, the revelation of God transmitted *through* human concepts and imagery." Erickson says that it appears that we have here a view of revelation and the Bible that is basically the orthodox view, but influenced by elements of the Barthian view. Cf. Millard Erickson, *The Evangelical Left* (Grand Rapids: Baker, 1997).

13 Ibid., 58.

14 Ibid., 60.

15 Ibid., 67.

16 This is a concern and relation which Bloesch comes very close to acknowledging on 69–70.

17 Avery Dulles, *Models of Revelation* (Maryknoll, N.Y.: Orbis, 1992) xix.

18 Gabriel Fackre, *The Doctrine of Revelation: A Narrative Interpretation* (Grand Rapids: Eerdmans, 1997) 85.

19 Ibid., 137f.

20 In relation to such emphases one ought to note what Fackre is affirming via the thought of Donald Baillie; from 31–32 in ibid.

21 Ibid., 147.

22 It is noteworthy that in reference to *Holy Scripture*, Fackre acknowledges that Barth was correct in teaching a generation to be wary of theologies that "take deity capture in forms of human manufacture. The point is that like the Barthians, Fackre understands God's sovereignty, and thus God's freedom, to mean that the one place that God has chosen to be revelatorily free for us and among us is Jesus Christ. Thus it is to this one place that Scripture bears witness, Fackre, 137f.

23 Ibid.

24 It is in this context where Fackre responds to Carl Henry's contributions to the "narrative of revelation" in terms of the "inspiration" of the text of Scripture. Fackre says that "As all loyalties are rooted in a 'leap of faith,' so the doctrine of inspiration presupposes a primal decision: the Yes to the living Word by the inner testimony of the

Holy Spirit. The believer brought to Jesus Christ by that Word spoken and received through the power of the Spirit is led into the Great Narrative found only in this Book. To be drawn to Christ is to be drawn into the Story, into its 'source' text . . . The authenticity of the encounter with the Word, Jesus Christ, is inseparable, therefore, from the trustworthiness of Scripture." Such points reflect somewhat how Fackre juxtaposes the Word, Christ and the Scripture text, but this also leaves a question as to how and why Carl Henry was used at all—except to broach the topic or the category of "inspiration," 162.

[25] Fackre, *Doctrine of Revelation*, 167–68. Note that while Fackre can speak of "propositional truths," e.g., God created the world, Israel is called into special covenant, God comes among us in Jesus Christ to reconcile the world, etc. Fackre speaks of these as "truths of the symbol" and as "embedded in" each chapter of the Grand Narrative. Thus, he significantly states as a definition of "proposition," "that which is expressed in a statement as *opposed* to the *way it is expressed*." Cf. Fackre's illuminating endnote thirty-five to which one could wish that Fackre paid more careful attention., 176–77.

[26] Ibid., 168.

[27] Ibid., 170.

[28] Ibid., 172.

[29] Ibid., 175.

[30] Clark H. Pinnock, *The Scripture Principle* (San Francisco: Harper and Row, 1984) 62. Cf. xiii. Pinnock does appear to maintain the same dualistic separation of Scripture from the Word of God in the work he later co-authored with process (liberal) theologian Delwin Brown: Clark H. Pinnock and Delwin Brown, *Theological Crossfire: An Evangelical–Liberal Dialogue* (Grand Rapids: Zondervan, 1990) section 1, part 2.

[31] Ibid., vii, xiii, xiv.

[32] Ibid., 4, 5, 8.

[33] Ibid., 10.

[34] Ibid., 14.

[35] Note Pinnock's excellent list of modern factors which have led to the dualist, disjunctive tendency to negate contentful divine revelation. At this early point in his book he contends that "One could explain the dramatic shift away from [revelatory] content by listing a series of factors that incline modern minds to resistance: the theistic model presupposed by taking the Bible as written revelation, the miracles accompanying the story of divine redemption, Kant's dogma that one can have no knowledge of the transcendent such as the Bible claims to deliver, numerous objections to one or another of the biblical concepts, the belief in the fallibility of the Bible as propounded by liberal criticism, and the imperialism of any claim that makes Jesus the only way of salvation. But when it comes right down to it there is only one reason for the rejection of content in revelation: a lot of moderns are not willing to have dictated to them how they must think and how they must act. The idea that human beings must approach God on his terms, implied by the second commandment, not in ways they themselves define, is simply unacceptable to the autonomous people of today. We face such a resistance to

what the Bible teaches today that the battle necessarily takes place around the issue of revelation and inspiration." Then, even more to the core of the problem and its implications, Pinnock says, "By shifting away from the objective content of revelation, liberal theology has given the church a migraine headache. The truth foundations of the gospel are swept away and the validity of the gospel cast in doubt. We face a dilemma not unlike the one Luther faced: is the gospel and salvation based upon the Word and work of God, or is it founded upon human wisdom and achievement? Is Christian theology a clear rendition of the Word of God given in the Scriptures, or is it the highest and best human option? Emphasizing the objective side of revelation and the authority of the Bible has nothing to do with bibliolatry or rationalism. It has to do with keeping the church securely founded upon the apostolic scriptural witness, which is essential to its life and work." Ibid., 24, 27.

[36] Runia Klaas, *Karl Barth's Doctrine of Holy Scripture* (Grand Rapids: Eerdmans, 1962) 230, footnote thirty-four.

[37] Pinnock, 15.

[38] Ibid., 32.

[39] Ibid., 39–40.

[40] Ibid., 45–54. Cf. especially 43, 46, 54.

[41] E.g., ibid., 41.

[42] Ibid., 54. Note also 55–57, 62. On 62, Pinnock explains what a (not "the") Scripture principle means. "It means that there is a locus of the Word of God in a humanly accessible form available to us. It means that the Bible is regarded as a creaturely text that is at the same time God's own written Word, and that we can consult his Word, which reveals his mind, and seek to know his will in it. It means that God has communicated authoritatively to us on those subjects about which Scripture teaches, whether doctrinal, ethical, or scriptural, and that we believers willingly subject ourselves to this rule of faith. More than merely human tradition and merely existential address, the Bible is the informative Word of God to the church. The text is not reduced to an expression of human experience and tradition as in liberalism, but is a contentful language deposit that addresses, as it decides, with the authority of God."

[43] Ibid., 56.

[44] Ibid., 95. Note also 96–97ff. Therein Pinnock further negates, or at least strongly alters or transforms earlier statements affirming that Scripture is the written Word of God. This outcome reflects something of a bibliological "adoptionism" in some contexts and an "Arianism" in other contexts with regard to the status of Scripture and its relation to the Word of God.

[45] Ibid., 100–101, where, remarkably and surprisingly, Pinnock approves of Hans Kung's understanding of Scripture, i.e., that "*Through* all human fragility and the whole historical relativity and limitation of the biblical authors, who are often able to speak only stammeringly and with inadequate conceptual means, it *happens* that God's call as it finally sounded out in Jesus is truthfully heard, believed and realized." It is also here that Pinnock begins to voice the many levels of his quarrel with Calvinist orthodoxy

and what he sees to be the problematic effects of Calvinism's deterministic views on the modern formulations of biblical inerrancy, etc. Cf. also Ibid., 188, 191.

[46] E.g., Acts 28:25; Heb. 1:1, 3, 7.

[47] J. I. Packer, "The Adequacy of Human Language," in *Inerrancy*, ed. Norman L. Geisler (Grand Rapids: Zondervan, 1980) 202.

[48] Ibid., 205–6.

[49] Ibid., 203–4.

[50] Ibid., 204–5.

[51] John Frame, "God and Biblical Language" from *God's Inerrant Word*, ed. J. W. Montgomery, quoted in Packer, "Adequacy," 215. Note the effective and insightful critique of the separation of personal from propositional truth in twentieth-century theology, e.g. E. Brunner, in Paul Helm's *Divine Revelation*, 26–27. Cf. below.

[52] Cf. John Calvin, *Institutes of the Christian Religion* (Philadelphia: Westminster) I, viii, 1; also Calvin's comments on I John 3:12 in his commentary.

[53] Paul Helm, *Divine Revelation: The Basic Issues* (Westchester, Ill.: Crossway, 1982) 32ff.

[54] Ibid., ch. 2.

[55] Ibid., 26–27.

[56] Ibid., 40–44.

[57] Ibid., 46.

[58] Nicholas Wolterstorff, *Divine Discourse: Philosophical Reflections on the Claim that God Speaks* (Cambridge: Cambridge University Press, 1995) ix.

[59] Ibid., 27–28.

[60] Ibid., 30. Woltertorff's responses to both Karl Barth (and "Barthians" especially) and John Baillie are quite illuminating in clarifying his intentions and points. Cf. 298–99 on John Baillie's representative views.

[61] Ibid., 70, 73.

[62] Ibid., 74.

[63] Ibid., 186.

[64] Ibid.

[65] See the discussion on these issues in three works by T. F. Torrance, *Christian Theology and Scientific Culture* (New York: Oxford University Press, 1981), e.g., 12; *Ground and Grammar of Theology* (Charlottesville: University Press of Virginia, 1980) 11, 105; and *Divine and Contingent Order* (Oxford: Oxford University Press, 1981).

[66] Ray S. Anderson, *Historical Transcendence and the Reality of God: A Christological Critique* (Grand Rapids: Eerdmans, 1975) 213.

[67] See this writer's article, "John Calvin's Christological Assertion of Word Authority in the Context of Sixteenth Century Ecclesiological Polemics," *The Scottish Journal of Theology*, vol. 45, Number 4, 1992. Again, note Packer's critique previously in endnote 49.

8

Einstein, Torrance, and Calvin

A Christocentric, Multileveled, Interactive Model of Scripture as the Written Word of God

That [the Bible] has divine authority, that it is God's own Word, this I cannot prove. I simply confess it; I confess it because I am forced to do so, forced by the Bible itself. It has imposed its authority upon my mind and conscience by virtue of its contents, and I know that now I cannot refuse to acknowledge its authority as the authority of God's own Word without trampling on what personal, moral and intellectual integrity I possess.

—C. E. B. Cranfield[1]

Belief in Holy Scripture as the written Word of God has become problematic, as we have found, not only in "neo-Protestant" circles (to use Barth's term), where such affirmation has been rejected for over two centuries, but even in avowedly "evangelical" circles. The notion of the living God actively making Himself and, therefore, his truth known, objectively and content-fully, to us, *in*, as and so in *the form* of Holy Scripture,[2] seems somehow inappropriate and uncomfortably deniable for a number of reasons—many of which often remain unconscious or at

221

least "unofficial" in considerations of the matter. Despite the revisionist historical efforts of some to deny the church's consensus of belief in Holy Scripture as the written Word of God, the all but universal position of the church, including of its exegetical, theological, and philosophical leaders from subapostolic times on into the eighteenth century is that Scripture is surely the written Word of God.[3]

What has happened to so alter the viewpoint of so many on so crucial an issue as the nature, possibility, authority and especially the content-fullness and radical historicity—even textuality—of the Word or self-disclosure of God? From what we observed in earlier chapters, let me mention a few reasons (of many), all of them well-known, that have variously contributed to the current situation, though these are not, in fact, the real root of the issue. With the rise of modernity came attitudes, methodologies, and epistemologies which, in various combinations, have left many skeptical, even agnostic, with regard to the possibility, let alone the actuality, the reality, of a content-ful, historical revelation of God directly, dare I say, tangibly apprehensible by space-time humans. Of special noteworthiness, of course, is Immanuel Kant's noumenal-phenomenal split and, with such, the rise of "critique." So, too, did the development of the historical-critical approach to the text of Scripture and its coordinate attitude (from Spinoza through Semler, Gabler, and beyond to the present), the separation of Holy Scripture from the Word of God/divine revelation, contribute mightily to the continuity of modernity's and (in a different way) postmodernity's dualistic detachment of Scripture from the Word of God.[4] But along with such prominent developments there must be added a third element which, in a real sense, is to be found in the previous two. Often lurking with, in or behind the disclaimer or rejection of the possibility of divine disclosure, of the Word of God, taking radical historical, particular, and even textual form, is a squeamish, fastidious, often amorphous but all too pervasive Platonism, which feels that "the divine" will be sullied, contaminated by any empirical participation in history, by any participation in, with and as the human—and by the written forms of communication, the speech acts, produced by them.[5]

To be emphatic, the problem here is a false disjunctive-dualistic way of thinking, a thinking that overly compartmentalizes, separates what ought to be thought together. It is a new archaic way of thinking which epistemologically embodies outmoded "Newtonian" mechanics and inevitably disjoins what ought to be thought together, especially in light of the Lordly, asymmetrical, interactive God-world-human, God-human-world relatedness, i.e., pointedly and especially, God's transcendent, redemptive, objective, self-disclosure, as the present, historical, content-ful self-giving of God to be known as he really is, ontologically in Jesus Christ and derivatively in, as and so in the form of the text Holy Scripture, by the power of the Holy Spirit.[6] The need then is for faith-ful thinking, thinking unitarily in terms of "fields" or onto-relations, for thinking which "thinks after" the way taken by its own proper object, the triune God, who, as transcendent Lord, has given himself to be known as he is, apprehensively not comprehensively, in and as actual instantiated historical forms and by the power of the Holy Spirit.[7]

What then of the development of modern methodologies? What of the pursuit of legitimate, constructive historical-critical methods in relation to the text of Holy Scripture? Briefly put, we need first to be aware of the post-Newtonian recognition that there is not one "scientific method" but as many properly scientific "methods" as there are proper objective pursuits of knowledge, each in accord with the way in which the particular proper object discloses itself for investigation. But, second, we must not, like Spinoza or especially Semler, feel the need to "Platonize," to transcendentalize or rationalistically to "de-historicize" the "Word of God" and so to separate the gracious divine self-giving from the taint of history, and specifically from the historical text of Holy Scripture, in order to "clear the way" for a truly "scientific" approach to the text of Scripture. If one can in these ways change the perception of Holy Scripture, make people think of it as only a human religious production, then one is free to critique it at will.[8] But is this necessary? On the one hand, the historical-critical method can *unnecessarily* foster a false, reductionist attitude, i.e., the historical approach to the text therefore means that it is merely a historical human text. But, again, this is an unnecessary attitudinal by-product in the mind of the exegetical practitioner who is not careful, resulting from what ought to be a profitable and constructive process (cf. chapter four). But on the other hand, the very historicity of the text, like the historicity of the Word incarnate as Jesus Christ the God-man, ought to be faithfully relished and "followed after" as the way the transcendent, triune God has actively, economically and directionally taken to make himself redemptively known to space-time existing persons.

What this chapter will endeavor to accomplish is to briefly sketch a nondualistic, multileveled, unitary, relational, interactive and very christocentric (trinitarian) model of revelation, with the conceptual help of Albert Einstein (scientific and epistemological developments) and T. F. Torrance (his modified applications of such developments to theology), that will (I hope) allow freedom for fresh affirmation of Holy Scripture as, under Christ, the written Word of God. John Calvin's understanding of the nature and role of Scripture by the Spirit will help illustratively by means of reflection on his "multileveled" understanding of the Word of God and, therein, of Holy Scripture is participating in and as and for the disclosive relation(s) of God in a way that remarkably anticipates later post-Newtonian developments (cf. the Addendix).

Jesus the Word—Holy Scripture the Word: Contradiction or Theo-logical Relation?

The issue of constructive concern here regards "the Word of God," i.e., what or where or how is "the Word of God"? First of all, the contention here is that, biblically speaking, Karl Barth was surely correct in asserting in strong terms that Jesus the Christ was and is *the* Word of God, absolutely and preeminently. As self-disclosure of the triune God, Jesus stands alone as full, final, distinct and unique (John 1, Hebrews 1). Indeed, Barth's potent and consistent emphasis on the completeness and finality of divine revelation in Christ often *appears* to lead Barth to deny the designation "Word of God" to anything other than Christ. In Barth's "three-fold Word of God" (*CD* I,1), Scripture, "the prophetic, apostolic witness," *seems* to be regarded as capable of "becoming" what it *is not*, "Word of God," if and when in the existential moment of "inspiration" it is "adoptionistically" used as a vehicle of *the Word* of God to me in the power of the Spirit (though this is probably a misinterpretation of the multileveled dynamic of the Word of God in Barth's *own* thinking, in contradistinction from most "Barthians," as well as dialectical and existential theologians generally, cf. chapter six).[9] Yet primarily Scripture is, from John 5:39, *the* redemptive witness to Christ. This, too, is true. Scripture functions to bear witness not finally to itself but to the ultimate self-disclosure of God in Christ. But is it, then, the necessary correlate of the fact that Holy Scripture is the primary, "authoritative" witness to Jesus Christ that Scripture cannot also truly be the written Word of God, a participative, God-breathed aspect of God's whole self-giving to be redemptively known as he is? Must Scripture be only, finally, "the word of man" if Christ is truly *the* Word of God? Surely not. Indeed, the truly biblical affirmation of Jesus Christ *the* Word is always juxtaposed relatedly to the equally strong biblical affirmation of the historicity, the disclosive content-fulness (divinely informative) and often the textuality (as well as the variety) of the graciously given Word of God.[10] That divine revelation was given as radically historical, content-ful, and often written (with multiple genres) was basic to the faith, worship and self-understanding of the OT covenant people, to Judaism and to and from the early church (though many of the Church Fathers had a rather "docetic," somewhat dictational view).

But if the incarnate Word is *the* Word of God, how can Holy Scripture be Word of God? Or if Holy Scripture is, as a result of revelation and inspiration, the Word of God, does this not diminish the centrality, uniqueness and preeminence of the Word made flesh? The problem behind such questions is that they are fired by false presuppositions. They are rooted in outmoded disjunctive thinking, destructive dualism, which, again, "thinks apart" that which ought to be "thought together" relationally, interactively, unitarily—in this case Jesus Christ the incarnate, *ontological* Word of God, and Holy Scripture as (by the processes related to revelation and inspiration) the *derivative* Word of God.[11]

Albert Einstein's Emphasis on the Unitary, Interactive "Levels" of Objective Truth Disclosure

By his own admission, Albert Einstein stood scientifically and conceptually upon the Scottish realist shoulders of scientists Michael Faraday and J. Clerk Maxwell. Like Faraday, Maxwell worked to throw off the necessitarianism and dualism of Newtonian science while working from basic beliefs in the contingent rationality and intelligibility of the universe. And it was especially Maxwell's ability to grasp things in their wholeness, in their dynamic connections, rather than as mere isolated particulars, that led to his development of "field theory." It was this relational interpretation of the universe which prepared the way for Einstein's relativity theory, and thus the understanding of universe as open-structured, i.e., as finite, though unbounded, and so "open up" to yet higher "levels of rationality." This led Einstein toward the recognition of the "religious dimension" which contributes to a "religious spiritualization of our understanding of life" through the "humble attitude of mind toward the grandeur of reason incarnated in existence."[12]

Regarding knowledge of the world, Einstein spoke of the "miraculous" fact that the universe is intelligible and comprehensible to the human mind, i.e., he found that there is a preestablished harmony of correlation between human thought and the independent empirical world. The human mind *can* grasp the relational structures embedded in nature. In this way, Einstein sought after the natural unity of knowing and being in the more subtle structures of reality, thereby overturning the dualistic split between thought and experience or subject and object, especially that massive dualism erected in the sciences from Galileo to Newton.[13] To counteract such cosmological dualism (and its outworking or application in the epistemological dualism of, e.g., Immanuel Kant), Einstein found that he had to assent to, to submit to, and to obediently follow after the disclosure of ontological reality at the immediate level, the theoretical level, and finally back into the internal relations of objective reality itself. Indeed, the dynamic intelligibility of the universe, which Einstein found to be so wonderful, especially in its contingency and unity (and thus not self-explanatory), points beyond itself and demands a sufficient reason, what Einstein called a "higher level" of intelligibility.[14]

This kind of relational ("field"/unitary) thinking, for which Clerk Maxwell opened the way necessarily negates any mere "horizonality," any inadequate thinking in the "flat," in favor of (metaphorically speaking) "vertical" thinking which faithfully follows after and finds the "ultimate" basis of intelligibility. In his essay "Physics and Reality," Einstein presents an account of the different "strata" or "levels" of knowledge of the world in a scientific system. The "aim of science," as he sees it, is "a comprehension as *complete* as possible, of the connection between the sense experiences in their totality, and . . . the accomplishment of this aim *by the use of a minimum of primary concepts and relations* [italics his]."[15] In this way, Einstein sought ever greater unity in his picture of the world, which necessitates ever fewer logical elements. In physics, the first level is ordinary experience, "our everyday thinking," with its loosely organized natural cognition. But the "spirit which is scientifically minded" cannot stop here. The many concepts and relations are "lacking in logical unity." This leads to the second level, the level of scientific theory and its pursuit of that logical unity retaining fewer primary concepts and relations. Yet further penetration of the inner, intelligible relations of the world brings one to the "tertiary" or highest level with a minimum of concepts and relations. While Einstein notes that theoretically this process of faithful assent to the objective intelligibility of the world can have "multitudinous" levels going on until the level of ultimate concepts and relations is reached (as few concepts as possible and with the greatest conceivable unity) in actual practice the three levels are usually sufficient to enable thought to rise to a unified conceptual grasp of reality with the "field" relations of investigation. Herein each level of knowledge is *related to* and *grounded in* the *higher* level, and ultimately in the "highest" level of unity. In this way, thinking penetrates more and more toward the ultimate, interior connections of reality, which are themselves the ultimate basis of "everyday" cognition. Therefore the levels must not be thought of as separate but as unitary, ever interactive, interpenetrating (perichoretic) and interrelated in terms of refinement and extension as each level is "open up" finally to the ultimate refinement and consistency at the highest level.[16] All of this reflects the unfolding of one of Einstein's several well-known aphorisms: "God is sophisticated but not malicious"; i.e., the universe is incredibly complex and subtle on the one hand, yet reflects at the highest level ultimate simplicity and reliability.

Taking this further, Einstein's "levels" of thought and truth refer then to an interpenetrating "hierarchy" of knowledge and being: that the truth of the "lower" levels of reality is not something wholly possessed therein in isolation but rather in relation and in correlation to and in openness "up" to the deeper, more profound levels of intelligible reality "above," while the ultimate (highest) level of Truth/ intelligibility is said to be "disclosive downward," level by level, to the "lowest level." This is a result of post-Newtonian science's recognition and deeper understanding of the inherent but contingent intelligibility and order in the world, i.e., science's following the disclosure of nature's own intrinsic relations and unity. Because of this kinship of thought and reality, true science faithfully "follows," "assents" to, thinks after and "up" through the "levels" of truth of the contingent world finally to the sufficient Truth which is the basis of the truth at the "lower" levels. Objective reality reveals or discloses itself as it is, and true, faith-ful, scientific knowing results from the epistemic correlation which Einstein found to occur between the human mind and that which it seeks to know, and thereby a structural kinship takes place between the "stratification" of scientific knowledge and the actual, interactive "stratification" of the universe. The outcome is a theory or "disclosure model" (e.g., the Theory of Relativity) which, in natural science, is a conceptual construct "forced upon" the true scientist by the intrinsic intelligibility of some field of inquiry. Theory, then, is developed as "that through which the scientist then seeks to let the structures of that field disclose themselves yet more fully."[17] This "stratification" of truth can, analogically, be applied to understanding of God's self-disclosure and the nature and divinely established role of Holy Scripture therein as, under Christ and by the Holy Spirit, the written Word of God.

T. F. Torrance's Application of Einstein's "Levels" of Truth to Theological Science and the Word of God

Theologian T. F. Torrance's long and sustained interest in and dialogue with post-Newtonian physics arose from the changed relation between Christian theology and physics and the alteration of the nature of scientific methodology. The revolution in thinking regarding the world, resulting from Einstein, Planck and others, has restored true objectivity and critical realism, and so the proper way for theology as a science to faithfully pursue or "follow after" its own proper Object, God as Lordly Subject in his redemptive, personal self-disclosure to be known as he is above all in Christ— theological science. The relation between natural and theological science ought also to be one of reciprocity, complementarity, a position that Einstein appears to reflect in his modification of Kant's statement, "science without religion is lame; religion without science is blind."

As Einstein's physics (or the fields of biology or geology) must "follow after" its own proper, impersonal object according to the manner in which it discloses itself, so too must theological science faithfully follow after its own proper, Personal Object, God as the "person constituting Person." God establishes profound personal reciprocity with persons through his Word, and theological science is the personal, knowing, faith-ful response to the objective Word of God.[18] In such developments, Torrance sees the restoration not only of true objectivity but also of the proper *theo-logical* thinking which characterized the Nicene fathers. Just as Einstein had to use integrative, relational, unitary ways of thinking to overcome the effects of Newton's dualistic separation of matter from its field of relations, the Nicene Fathers (and the Reformers) were characterized by the same willingness to "think together," resulting in the *homoousion*, which Torrance repeatedly characterizes as the E=MC² of Christian theology.[19] The Nicene Fathers and Reformers (especially Calvin) allowed their relation to God's objective self-disclosure (the proper Object), the inner logic of the redemptive movement of God in Christ by the Spirit, to dictate the mode of rationality appropriate to it within a reciprocal, dialogical connection. So theology, after the dualisms of Descartes, Kant, et al., must again repent of false, disjunctive thinking and become truly scientific by assenting to the compelling Truth/Word of God, and so to faith-fully penetrate and express that inner logic of the triune God in Christ, the objective Word of God.[20]

It is the pursuit of that *theo-logical* goal, the *faith-ful*, scientific expression of the self-revelation of the triune God, from the Father, through in the Son and in the power of the Holy Spirit, that has engaged much of Torrance's energy and *theo-logical* concern. It is also that calling to such scientific, *theo-logical* "thinking after" (*Nachdenken*) its proper Object, the Word of God, that leads Torrance to make constructive, analogical use (*mutatis mutandis*) of Einstein's unitary, interactive, multileveled "disclosure model" in ways appropriate to the personal nature of God and to the personal, reciprocal, person-constituting nature of the multileveled, objective self-giving of God to be known as he is in Christ and by the Spirit.

It is here that Torrance develops and advances the theological method he finds in his mentor, Karl Barth. It is Barth, says Torrance, who, above all other modern theologians, has sought to *faith-fully* "think after" the way God has actually taken to reveal himself in Christ and by the Spirit, and so to restore *theo-logical* thinking as truly objective and scientific. Of special significance for Torrance's own onto-relational disclosure model of God's self-revelation (Word) is Barth's emphasis on God's Lordly, interactive relation with creation as Creator-Redeemer, which Torrance characterizes as God's "Being-in-His-Act" and his "Act-in-His-Being" in balance.[21] It is this redemptive disclosure movement of the triune God, in and from the ontological to the economic, which the scientific theologian must faith-fully "follow after" from the economic and reciprocal back "up" level by level (in Christ and in the power of the Spirit to the Father) to the ontological (the onto-relational, perichoretic, trinitarian realities within the Being of God). Such is the openness and self-giving of God to be known redemptively as he is, and such is the great responsibility of theological science to follow after God.[22] In the process, Torrance emphasizes that, in scientifically thinking after the "Being and Act" and "Act and Being" of God in a balanced way, "up" through the "levels" of God's economic self-revelation, one thinks or follows after according to the coordination of whole levels of conceptual relations with one another, and through finally to the ultimate coordination of the basic concepts with and in accordance with the actual, intelligible, triune relations of the eternal God.[23]

As this is actually worked out, Torrance, like Barth, correctly emphasizes the objective and christocentric nature of the divine revelation. The Word became flesh that human beings would have real, direct knowledge of God, which is life eternal. This is the way God has actually taken in history in order to be adequately and redemptively known as he is in the world. Thus the incarnation is epistemologically, cosmologically and, so, theologically and methodologically central. Realist knowledge of God occurs, then, only in the way specified by the actual disclosure of the Logos of God and in the power of the Spirit. Hence, true scientific theology thinks faith-fully after this revelation of the "inner logic" of God in the incarnation (*fides quaerens intellectum*). As a result, the faith-knowing relation and theo-logy can be true only if thinking moves in submission and assent (i.e., by faith) to the actual nature of the objective disclosure of God in Christ, the way whereby God has objectively revealed himself in the world with actual space-time coordinates to existing humanity. So, too, is this the way God continues to reveal himself. Torrance emphasizes that it is only through one's actual "sharing in the knowledge" of the Son by the Father and that of the Father by the Son, that God in Christ and by the Spirit can be known "as He has given Himself to us in Jesus Christ." Thus as Torrance's modified Barthian theo-logical thinking is thoroughly Christo-logical or Christocentric, then such scientific theology must think together relationally the interactive levels of God's revelation, and so move faith-fully back "up" the way God has actually taken "down" to us by the epistemological enablement of the

Spirit to and in Christ to the Father and, hence, to the inner, unitary, perichoretic relations in the Trinity. These "levels" of scientific theological thinking are, first, the basic evangelical and doxological level of experience and worship; second, the theological level, whereby inquiry is made after and into the economic trinitarian movement of God to and in the world; finally, scientific theological thinking moves to the deeper penetration, to the highest theological and scientific level, where thought is lifted to the level of the Ontological Trinity.[24]

This knowledge of God in Christ by the Spirit is described by Torrance variously as, e.g. "unknowing" (related to "repentant thinking") and often as "faith-knowing" (faith being the proper means for knowing the objective revelation of God) and as "intuitive knowledge." As such this knowledge is said to be direct, immediate, rational, cognitive. Borrowing partially from Kierkegaard's notion of "contemporaneity," Buber's existential personalism, Brunner's "encounter" language, as well as from Barth, Torrance also speaks of this true knowing of God in terms of event, meeting, and even "mystical" knowing.[25]

How then is the Word of God in Christ related by Torrance to the text of Scripture? As one would expect, given his "Barthian" bases (not necessarily true of Barth himself, cf. endnote eight as well as chapter six), God has his Word, Jesus Christ, but God has no words. God's self-revelation is not content-ful, but rather is given to be "known" as nonexpressible, as meaningful nonmeaning.[26] Herein lies the central difficulty in that like his fellow "Barthians," and for most of the same reasons, Torrance tends to *transcendentalize* the revelation of God at the very point where it must be most emphatically historical, and even textual. At bottom, his particular application of Barth's "Being in Act" and "Act in Being" to Einstein's multileveled, interactive disclosure model falls one step short. While helpful in reflecting something of the interactive, self-disclosive movement of God to us, such a bi-level model of revelation lacks the needed concrete, historical pole for God's redemptive relatedness to humanity whereby such objective knowledge and faith-ful thinking can occur in and from our space-time existence.

Indeed, Torrance's formulation bears a remarkable resemblance to the closing portions of books five and six of Plato's *Republic* where Socrates unfolds his definition of the philosopher, the "two worlds," and the four stages of cognition whereby the genuine philosopher is to "see the truth" or to "know the Forms" as they are. But like such formulations and those influenced by them, directly or indirectly (for Torrance, Kierkegaard, Brunner and most Barthians), there is difficulty in and even strong resistance to directly relating the Word of God to history and to the actualization and identification of such *in*, *with* and *as* historical, even *textual*, forms. As Ray S. Anderson has noted regarding Torrance's ardent desire to avoid content-ful, expressible, textual revelation,

> [Torrance attempts to state the case for the place of Scripture in a double sense, both above the church . . . [and yet] subject to all human finitude [as only, finally, the human witness to Christ the Word] . . . One can appreciate the efforts of Professor Torrance to maintain both the authority and the humanity of Scripture; but I am not sure it can be done . . . [by] separating its transcendence from its historicity. [27]

Anderson goes on to explain that, just as Dietrich Bonhoeffer noted regarding some aspects of Barth's concept of divine revelation, Torrance finally "transcendentalizes" the Word of God, makes the final movement of the Word *ahistorical*, by strenuously avoiding any notion of content-ful, expressible, even textual revelation. This final needed movement or level, which Anderson terms "historical transcendence," is transcendence as an actual historical experience in the world. And Holy Scripture, as the historical pole of transcendence, is the cognitive link with the content of God's transcendence as historical. If such is dualistically broken off then "the act of faith must supply it's own content to the divine Word."[28] At the critical point of actual historical relation by the self-disclosure of God in Christ, and in the space-time specificity of actual human existence, there thus occurs a problematic need in the "moment" to negate human historical actuality; there is a detemporization as a result of the transcendentalized "coming" of the Word and there is the timeless meeting of the human in the "Word-event," which becomes, in the words of Anthony Thiselton, an all too vacuous "Christ-mysticism."[29] Barth (especially the early Barth) strengthened and developed elements of Kierkegaard's thought, and Torrance has subsequently advanced, clarified and developed significant aspects of Barth's thought. But Torrance (at least partially out of antipathy to what he considers to be "rationalism") has fallen into the same "Barthian" difficulty whereby, in the "moment" of the divine Act of disclosure, the person is brought to mystical, noncognitive, nondiscursive "encounter" with the transcendentalized Word. This occurs because the divine Word is understood to jump the gulf between the divine and the historical human being, thereby negating all historical distinction in the "contemporaneity" of that coming of the Word and the "lifting up" of the Spirit. As a result the historical, revelational "link," the crucial pole of "historical transcendence," which traditionally has been understood in terms of the historical textuality of the Word of God as Holy Scripture, is lost. Scripture becomes, *adoptionistically*, the finally disposable historical, human conduit through which the in-breaking Word comes to meet one in the moment of confrontation. Thereby revelation is cut adrift as noncontentful event, empty otherness. Rather than a claim to a wordless Word, to a content-less "Christ-mysticism," to a God who has his Word but no words, should we not acknowledge afresh the historicity and often even the textuality of the Word of God, i.e., that "Scripture constitutes the Word of God in its capacity to communicate as well as to command" content-fully, as historical statements, in the form of various genre, the truth of God to humanity, the speech acts of God.[30] How might Torrance's disclosure model of divine self-revelation be corrected while remaining true to his own fruitful intention to reflect (*mutatis mutandis*) Einstein's insight into the interactive, multileveled way to objective, unitary, truly scientific knowing, but in a form which overcomes the dualistic subject-object "gap" that results from the problematic detemporization of Word of God? Again, this is a result of Torrance's neo-Barthian portrayal of God's self-disclosure as only God's "Being-in-his-Act" and his "Act-in-his-Being" in balance. Can the historical, textual pole of transcendence be established?

A Christocentric, Multileveled, Interactive Model of Scripture as Word of God

It appears that Torrance has left himself in something of a revelational "no-man's-land," even to the extent of *at least* endangering the possibility of the incarnation of the Word of God (which he does not want to do). Given his intentions, it seems that Torrance has two basic choices: the way represented by Paul Tillich or the avenue which can be represented by John Calvin. Tillich's understanding of the revelatory role of historical religious symbols could be most effective for crossing the ("Kantian") gap, for religious symbols do not merely mediate the wholly separate Divine ("the ground of being," etc.) but, in a sense, actually and rightly participate in Being Itself, while not being confused with it. Tillich could thus provide not only a way to model real divine-human-world differentiation, but also, importantly, divine-human-world unitary interrelatedness. But while Torrance (rarely) admits to affinities with Idealism, Tillich is too Hegelian, too necessitarian, for his theo-logical purposes. Torrance's own emphases on Nicene trinitarianism and Reformed thought point, rather, to John Calvin's theological and historical "textuality" as a way (broadly speaking) whereby one may find a more historical-human anchorage for the divine-human communicative reciprocity in true redemptive, historical and theological connection (cf. the "Appendix" on Calvin below), and in this way complete Torrance's disclosure model, linking the Word of God firmly to, in and *as* historical.[31] In other words, we hope to give Torrance's Barthian "Being of God in His Act and Act of God in His Being," with the claim of simultaneous authority and humanity of Scripture, another needed and completionary dimension or level. As a result, Scripture can be faith-fully understood as the historical "pole" of transcendence which, in and from the Father, through and under the Son/Word/Christ and by the Spirit, confronts the existing person as that which participates in, of and *as* the revelation (Word) of God in history, yet with all of the limitations and conditions which history also imposed upon the Word becoming flesh.

At the outset of the attempt here to sketch out what is hoped will be a more effective and complete "disclosure model" of God's self-revelation, which includes Holy Scripture in and *as* an aspect of that larger redemptive disclosure movement to and for humanity, several affirmations need to be made. First, Einstein's advance of and reorientation of physics, epistemology and true science and scientific method, as properly objective, relational and multileveled is of great illustrative, analogical usefulness for all sciences in relation to the disclosure of their own proper objects, including theology. Second, Barth has truly and with effectiveness called much of theology back to its own proper object, above all God's self-revelation in Jesus Christ, and Torrance, too, has advanced and scientifically clarified faith-ful theological thinking as "theological science," and so as relational, unitary, multileveled and interactive. Third, as noted above, Jesus Christ is *the* Word of God in a way that is utterly unique; he is *the* eternal, ontological Word of God.[32] As such and to that extent, Torrance and most Barthians are surely correct. Also, again, as Jesus himself stated, referring to Scripture, "it is these that bear witness of me" (John 5:39). Thus Scripture's role is as God-given witness to Christ the Word. But, finally, does this role as God-given witness negate the possibility of Scripture being, too, the written (inscripturated) Word of God? Hardly. That would be a *non sequitur.* This does not follow. Christ's own testimony to the nature of Scripture, Scripture's testimony to itself, and the all but universal position of the church until quite recent times is that, in some real, participative way or sense, Holy Scripture *is* the written Word of God. How might we bring these affirmations unitarily together?

To give historical completion to the bi-level Barthian-Torrancian "Being-Act, Act-Being" disclosure model, the proposal here is to follow Einstein more completely by means of a "Hebraic Three-fold Being-Act-Interpretation and Interpretation-Act-Being" disclosure model as a possible way to effect and reflect more satisfactorily the relation of revelatory historicity and humanity. This use of Einstein's portrayal of "stratified" truth is not to be understood as the intrusion of some new "natural theology" but is, again, being used analogically to illustrate a more helpful, biblical approach to God's revelation to humanity. John Calvin embodied this approach. For Calvin (see below), Holy Scripture is understood to actually be the Word of God in and as an aspect of the larger action of God in revelation as "inspired" interaction, response, witness and *interpretation.* Notable Semitic scholars such as G. Ernest Wright and William Foxwell Albright have shown that the Hebraic perspective, reflected throughout Scripture itself, stresses the revelation of God in real human history *as interpreted* theologically by the prophets and apostles. Knowledge of God is therefore "historical knowledge," which is best expressed in the dialogue of events together with the revealed understanding of the meaning of those events within the human struggle, in the otherwise meaningless stream and chaos of human experience. This realization of "revelation in history" led Israel to preserve these meaningful, interpretive historical traditions. Israel's historical knowledge of God, reflected in its concern for the direction of history, is said to have arisen from Yahweh's having actively chosen the contingent forms of history as the way and the place and the form in which he has revealed himself meaningfully, content-fully within the covenantal relation. By these divine actions *and* the God-given theological interpretation of the meaning of these acts, a new people were created.[33]

Jewish philosopher Abraham Heschel has noted that the Scriptures deal with universals through narration and recitation of everyday particulars of history. The God of Scripture is, in this way, dynamic; therefore one is able to know the living God, actually and in realist terms, in history. God is self-disclosed not only in bare transcendental Act, but also in narrative and in the cultural/linguistic/theological interpretation by the prophets of the meaning of such divine Acts in real redemptive relation to human history.[34] God does things with human words.

For Torrance to accomplish what he intends by his Barthian bi-level disclosure model, he needs to give the historical "prophetic and apostolic witness" to Christ, i.e., Holy Scripture, a significant place of actual participation *in*, and *as* an aspect of the movement of the historical disclosure of God in Christ by the Spirit, both in the world and in human existence. Otherwise, Torrance falls under Paul Ricoeur's criticism of the one-sidedness of any "idealism of the word event," despite Torrance's desire to "reaffirm the realism of the events of (real) history." Rather than being forced, by his two-level model, into a dualistic disjunction in the subject- (divine) Object relation, thus necessitating a "lightning" Word-event akin to that of Gerhard Ebeling or Ernst Fuchs, Torrance's theo-logical purpose can be better realized by what Abraham Heschel calls the Hebraic three-fold disclosive movement, which works out (as parallel) to "Being-Act-(prophetic-apostolic) Interpretation, (prophetic-apostolic) Interpretation-Act-Being." God's Acts, above all the Act whereby the Word became flesh, cannot be severed from the events and the Spirit-led (inspired) written interpretative accounts which both precede and follow it, whereby it is concluded that, e.g., the Jesus of the gospel accounts is the Son of the God of Abraham, Isaac, and Jacob. This *third* interactive "level," this realization of particular and historical divine prophetic-apostolic interpretation as text/Holy Scripture, and, as such, integral to and *as* an aspect of the larger economy of the self-giving of the triune God to be known as he is, means, that at this historical, textual "pole" of the redemptive processes of God, the focus is shown to be cultural, thus reflecting God's active and linguistic relation to and in human culture as this is expressed in Scripture in the various genres, in the histories, stories, prophecies and teachings of Israel, of fulfillment in the life, death and resurrection of Jesus Christ and the apostolic interpretation of God's accomplishment in Christ the early church. This God-human communicative interrelatedness in space-time and in the real relation of divine Act *and* Spirit-led interpretation is what Torrance, given his intentions, requires to complete his theo-logical disclosure model.[35] Scripture, within the revelatory movement of God in real salvation history and by the Holy Spirit, must constitute the real written/textual Word of God *in*, *under*, *of* and *from* the Word-Act of God at the higher level, Jesus Christ. As such, Holy Scripture would and does provide the needed "transcendent historical" linkage or relation, the needed revelatory "pole" lying in history, to "communicate" as well as command the truth of God to humanity, working to "inform the act of faith by the Spirit" of faith's transcendent, objective basis in Jesus Christ, and so, ultimately, the triune Godhead.[36] Without this content-ful, intelligible, cognitive link, faith must then, to use Torrance's own phrase, "fall back upon itself" and so provide its own subjectivistic content.

In a very real sense, the transcendence of God was most fully revealed when the incarnate Word was under the judgment of the cross. In Jesus Christ the word of man was the Word of God. If (*mutatis mutandis*) this is analogically applied to Scripture, then Scripture as "servant" must be reckoned as having this same "kenotic" function, but at the next "lower" interactive level, and within the unitary "logic" of God's gracious movement to us in historical transcendence. In this corrective completion of Torrance's own theo-logical model out of and "under" Christ and by the Spirit, Holy Scripture, as revealed and inspired interpretation of God's historical Acts, and so as the "derivative" Word of God, has this quality of historical transcendence (immanent disclosive relation) primarily with regard to its cognitive connection with the ontic reality of the triune God's economic, historical transcendence by the Spirit, as ever epistemologically "relevant." In this way, too, Torrance's Nicene reflection of the divine economy "from the Father by the Son and in the Spirit" can be unitarily related theo-logically from the Acts of God in the Son to, with and as the pneumatological-interpretive response. As a result the Holy Spirit can finally be given real, full economic function within Torrance's theology and disclosure model, as emphatically trinitarian.

Note. The model we have presented here is wholly complementary to the previously discussed insights of Kevin Vanhoozer and his covenantal-theological deepening of J. L. Austin's and John Searle's "Speech-Act Theory" for understanding what Holy Scripture says about God speaking-God as speech agent. As presented in chapter two of this book, Vanhoozer unfolds the remarkable parallels between "Speech-Act Theory" and the way Scripture portrays God "doing things with human words" and pointedly "with biblical words." In constructive response to modern and postmodern dualisms which reject the capacity of human language to speak referentially of divine realities or to be used by God in his revelation, thus separating Scripture from an ahistorical, content-less "Word of God," Vanhoozer (like Nicholas Wolterstorff) restores the intentional role of the author, especially the Author (God) in literary meaning, and shows how God is directly involved in the production of Holy Scripture. Within Vanhoozer's "Trinitarian theology of Holy Scripture," the Bible *is* the Word of God because it is the result of God's self-communicative action from the Father, in the Son and by the Holy Spirit. By showing how God "*does* things with words," with "biblical words," Vanhoozer clarifies and deepens the church's historical "Scripture Principle" or "identity thesis," i.e., that in, under, of and from Christ the Word, and by the Spirit, Scripture is itself a "species" of divine revelation, being composed of divine-human speech acts that, through what they say, "accomplish several authoritative, cognitive, spiritual and social functions." Vanhoozer's constructive and dynamic reaffirmation of Holy Scripture as the written and authoritative Word of God is, again, fully in keeping with, complementary to, and supportive of the christocentric, multileveled, interactive model of Holy Scripture as the written, authoritative Word of God which has been presented in this chapter. To be specific, Vanhoozer clarifies the "mechanism"; he shows "how" the words of Scripture are finally God's own words, that God as "speech agent" has, in the words of Scripture, done things with human words.

John Calvin's Word-Centeredness: An Illustrative Analysis of Calvin's Multileveled Approach to Scriptural Authority

In setting himself against many elements of the recognized ecclesiastical authority of the time, John Calvin felt impelled to point out that the true divine authority immanent in and for the Church was to be found in God's inscripturated Word. By means of this historical Word of God, the Holy Spirit of the exalted Christ could lead the Church effectively in truth and in life. All human authority was derived from or related to this Word of God by the Spirit of God. It will be necessary to take brief note of this side of Calvin's positive argumentation as he interacts with each realm of claimed Church authority in his *Institutes of the Christian Religion*.

The Scriptural Word and the "Level" of Doctrinal Authority

Prior to his explicit response to the Roman Catholic Church's claims of "immanent" divine authority for the establishment of dogma (whether by council, pronouncement, etc.), Calvin looked to scriptural examples of "ecclesiological" authority. In the Old Testament, Calvin saw the manifestation and exercise of authority, as given by the Holy Spirit, as most clearly reflected in Moses, the Levitical priesthood, and the prophets. The central principle is that divine authority "is wholly given not to men personally, but to the ministry to which they have been appointed; or (to speak more briefly) to the Word, whose ministry is entrusted to them." No one has authority to teach "except in the name and Word of the Lord." Crucial to Calvin's basic postulation of this Word-authority is the "witness of the Spirit" to the Scripture as the Word of God. This comes immediately from God. Since only God is a "suitable witness for his own Word. . . . It is necessary that the same Spirit who spoke . . . should penetrate our hearts in order to convince us . . ." that the message of the writers of Scripture is of God and therefore faithful.[37]

In thus stating his case, Calvin is laying the groundwork for continuity and discontinuity in the nature and character of Church authority and leadership. He distinguishes between the apostles and their successors, "the former were sure and genuine scribes of the Holy Spirit, and their writings are therefore to be considered oracles of God." Of those who follow, their "sole office . . . is to teach what is provided and sealed in the Holy Scriptures." To be faithful to God *now* is therefore, by definition, to avoid the formulation of new dogmas. Calvin is consciously cutting off all notions of ecclesiastical infallibility in the realm of doctrine if it is claimed apart from whole submission to the rule of Scripture and thereby to the rule of Christ at the highest level. Any such claim, whether for tradition, council or pronouncement, is "contemptuous of God's Word."[38]

The Scriptural Word and the "Level" of Legislative Authority

For Calvin, the authority of Holy Scripture is not only prior to and supreme in matters of doctrine, but it also rules at the level of the life of the church. Through the written Word of God, taught and proclaimed, Christ as Head rules his body. Calvin emphasized that the scriptural Word is truly over his church, both in the exercise of present authority and as divine truth, and must be allowed to freely rule therein. Thus, "this is the perpetual mark by which our Lord has characterized his people: Everyone that is of the truth hears my voice." This is held to be proper because the Church is Christ's Kingdom and "he reigns by his Word alone." Therefore, the acceptance of the present divine authority of Scripture means that the Church is "allowing Christ to rule within its life and to be the sole inspiration of its life."[39]

The Scriptural Word and the "Level" of Eccesiastical Jurisdiction

Calvin's own volatile situation at Geneva clarified for him the crucial nature of church jurisdiction. Though often accused of excessive "exercise" of what he perceived to be proper discipline, he held with relative consistency the principle that "the whole jurisdiction of the church pertains to the discipline of morals . . . [to] spiritual polity." The Church's power of jurisdiction will, as an "order framed for the preservation of the spiritual polity," scripturally establish "courts of judgement . . . to deal with the censure of morals, to investigate vices, and to be charged with the exercise of the office of the keys." Like many fellow Reformers, Calvin associated the power of the keys with the authority of the inscripturated Word of God.

Calvin's strong sense of order and disorder in an age of uncommon flux left him often in a strait between two equally felt needs: the coherent peace and order of human life, if it is to be truly human, and freedom in Christ. Clear for him, though, was the recognition that the overthrow of order was in fact contempt for "the sacred name of God."[40] Yet it is noteworthy that in actual pastoral practice Calvin was often exceedingly patient and went out of his way to make things right and to allow for human frailties.

But at the level of church jurisdiction, nothing is binding on consciences except for that which is specified in Scripture. Therefore the "command concerning forgiving and retaining sins, and that promise made to Peter concerning binding and loosing ought to be referred solely to the ministry of the Word." Regarding the doctrine of the keys which Christ has given and confirmed, it is not a merely human word, not of the apostles or their successors, but a word of God himself. Consequently, "the forgiveness of sins, the promise of eternal life, the good news of salvation" from God cannot be understood as mingled with the human and located in the hands of men by some reckoning of inherent divine authority. The power of Christ's minister is not, then, worldly power, but is directly under the lordly level of Christ and thus is directly subjected to the level of scriptural authority, direction and principles, by the Spirit. The church, as truly and faithfully Christ's, manifests his Kingdom only to the extent that it is thus obedient to his written Word.[41] In rejecting the "Romanist" legal system as being humanly devised, Calvin proposed instead that the church's authority rested only on Scripture. For Calvin, the authority of Scripture is not primarily to be found only in its acknowledged inspiration ("the very Word of God"), but rather,

> [Calvin's] argument is Christological. Christ is the wisdom and revelation of God, who alone has entered into the secrets of the Father. He is the source from whom the Old Testament writers drew their knowledge of God and when he became man he was the final witness to the Father. Hence his is the perfection of teaching. It would be impossible to surpass it, criminal to invent new. Let Christ speak and all be silent![42]

Thus, the Spirit of the church, which is the Spirit of Christ, is the Spirit of Christ's inscripturated Word, who, level by interrelated level, leads the church into the knowledge of the will of Christ by directing such into the knowledge of Scripture, the Word of Christ.[43]

Christ and the Church's Focus on Christ: the Christological Level of Calvin's Emphasis on Scriptual Authority

John Calvin's strong response to what he believed to be the problematic medieval mixture of the divine and the human, the holy will of God with sinful human inventions, arose in the light of what he saw to be the eradication of the gospel of Christ, "like pouring sour wine into good." The very worship services and ministries, which the medieval Church proposed to promote Christ's redemption in the people under its watch and care, only multiplied Calvin's concern to challenge its claim to authority.[44]

Throughout the *Institutes*, Calvin attempts to set forth Christ as the central focus and witness of the Scriptures. While there are several prominent subthemes in Calvin's active and often vociferous response to what he understood to be the late medieval teachings that blended an immanent divine authority within the official hierarchy of the Church, Calvin's emphatic point in asserting scriptural authority is again, as throughout, christological. To put the point differently, redemptive authority in the church is to be found simply and singularly, at the highest level, in and from the Person of the ascended, transcendent and ruling Christ as ever mediated in and within the temporal levels/dimensions of the church by the Holy Spirit in the divine Word of Scripture, as set historically over, within and before the church. Thus, all knowledge of God is mediated through Christ, the one mediator: all divinely uttered revelations are correctly designated by the term "Word of God," so this substantial Word is properly placed at the highest level as the wellspring of all oracles.[45]

In questions of authority, at that level of the church and in relation to doctrine, Calvin's limitation of the church's teaching to that which is disclosed by the Spirit in Holy Scripture is so that, in their calling "to build up the Church," the ministers must seek only "to preserve Christ's authority for himself; this can only be secured if what he has received from his Father be left to him, namely that he alone is the schoolmaster of the Church. For it is written . . . 'Hear him' . . .[46]

At the level of legislative matters, Calvin's assertion is, again, that the souls of people are called to deliverance and submission to Scripture for ultimately the same christocentric reason. To compound things divine and human, and thereby to govern by any law except the Law of Christian freedom in the Holy Word of the gospel, is not just an example of great impiety, he says, but it is to disdain the grace of Christ and to inflict consciences with human enslavement, consciences Christ came to set free. True polity in the church is governance in responsive *a posteriori* submission to that *a priori* ultimate disclosure of God whereby Christ the Word, truly and transcendently reigns over the Church. By Christ and from Christ only, as Head and Lord, the Church is built up by the Spirit of Christ in real relation in and through the written Word of God.[47]

Finally, at the level of ecclesiastical jurisdiction, Calvin's view that the power of the keys is the authority of the written Word of God is, again, preeminently christological. The authority inherent in the capacity for binding and loosing is immediately the redemptive authority of the gospel of Christ, for "Christ has not given this power actually to man, but to his Word." As "Christ cannot be properly known in any other way than from the Scriptures" it necessarily follows for Calvin that at the level of Christ's proper, abiding and transcendent lordship over and in the church, "Christ is rejected when we do not embrace the pure doctrine of the Gospel.[48]

The point at issue in this section has been the hierarchical interrelatedness of Christ the Word, Christ's written Word (Holy Scripture) and Christ's church. Or to put Calvin's contention a bit differently, it is the question of the place or relationship of the written Word of God, the text of Scripture, and of Christ in relation to Christ's own ministry to and in the church by the Holy Spirit. Given Calvin's great stress on God's transcendence and difference from the world and from human sinfulness, the Holy Scriptures, as God's own "accommodation" to our frailty in his address to us, are an absolutely critical historical and authoritative level of God's redemptive disclosure in his theology. Indeed, for Calvin the Scriptures are God's Word derivatively, functionally and mediately, but, under Christ and by the Spirit, they are the written Word of God.

Calvin's understanding of the disclosive role of Scripture within the divine economy by the Holy Spirit was set and expressed in the face of much controversy. It is Calvin's proper textuality, or his scripture-principle, as is also central to T. F. Torrance's own Reformed theology, that is being correctly emphasized here. This Reformed tradition of the historical and theo-logical "textuality" of God's revelation is appropriate to and for Torrance's own theo-logical purposes in order to bring a more complete unitariness to his christocentric-trinitarian theology, to his understanding of the real historical divine-human relation in Christ and by the Holy Spirit, wherein God is truly known redemptively as he is in himself.

It is at John Calvin's very christocentric-theologial point in the economy of God's trinitarian self-disclosure that Torrance's own disclosure model, if he would similarly maintain God's revelatory openness in the world in ongoing, truly historical interactive relatedness, could maintain a more fully "Reformed" position and would bring about the interactive connection needed. Thus, the example of Calvin's christocentric-trinitarian emphasis in relation to Holy Scripture as the written Word of God reflects, to a surprising extent, the type of hierarchical interactive disclosure model we are attempting here.[49]

Endnotes

1 C. E. B. Cranfield, *The Bible and Christian Life: A Collection of Essays* (Edinburgh: T. & T. Clark, 1985) 2–3.

2 It must be explained that such wording, "God actively making himself . . . known . . . in and as Holy Scripture" is *not* to be understood to be saying that Scripture is to be identified *as God*, but is an emphatic way of saying that God actually expresses himself in space-time contentfully and that this has sometimes taken written/textual form, i.e., Holy Scripture.

3 Cf. J. N. D. Kelly, *Early Christian Doctrines*; Adolf Harnack, *History of Dogma*; Bertrold Altanor, *Patrology*, Geoffrey Bromiley, *Historical Theology* and "The Church Fathers and Holy Scripture," Bruce Shelley, *By What Authority?*

4 Cf. Baruch Spinoza, Theological-Political Treaties, translated by R.S.H.M. Elwes (New York: Investigation Dover Publications, 1951); Johann Salomo Semler, Treatise on the Free Inveatigation of the Canon, in W. G. Kümmel, The New Testament: The History of the Investigation of its Problems, translated by S. McLean Gilmour and Howard C. Kee (Nashville: Abingdon Press, 1972). Also see chapter two above.

5 Cf. John D. Morrison, "Scripture as Word of God: Evangelical Assumption or Evangelical Question?" *Trinity Journal* 20 (1999) 165–90.

6 See the discussion relating to such in John D. Morrison, Knowledge of the Self-Revealing God in the Thought of Thomas Forsyth Torrance (Geneva: Peter Lang, 1997).

7 Ibid., especially chapter seven.

8 Albert Einstein, "Physics and Reality," in *Ideas and Opinions*, ed. Carl Seelig, et al. Trans. and rev. Sonja Bargmann (New York: Crown, 1954) 290–323. Cf. Discussion of T. F. Torrance's understanding and use of these matters in relation to "restored"

epistemology, truth, objectivity and scientific method in John D. Morrison, Knowledge of the Self-Revealing God referred to in footnote five above.

[9] In point of fact this description may not be true of Barth, though few of Barth's disciples, let alone his critics seem to have grasped Barth's redemptive, theological dynamism at this point. Certainly Torrance does not. According to Bruce McCormack's careful researches, Holy Scripture is, for Barth in some real sense, the written Word of God. But an unredeemed, unregenerate person regards Scripture as only "the Word of man" until, by the Spirit, he/she is redeemed, regenerated, whereupon Holy Scripture "becomes" for him/her at that point what it already was, the Word of God. See Bruce L. McCormack, "The Being of Holy Scripture is in Becoming: Karl Barth in Conversation with American Evangelical Criticism," in *Evangelicals and Scripture: Tradition, Authority and Hermeneutics*, edited by Vincent E. Bacote, et al. (Downers Grove, Ill.: InterVarsity, 2004) 55–75.

[10] In recent years, many exegetes have shown that the notion of *logos*, especially as used in John's Gospel and in reference to Jesus, has much mishandled throughout much of modern and contemporary theology. As Robert Gundry, among others, explains, the term *logos* in John's Gospel, as elsewhere, does not have the idea of a single word, but rather refers to a discourse, as in "the word of the LORD came to me saying . . . ." In the Gospel of John, "Jesus the Word gives voice to the words that the Father gave him to speak." See Robert H. Gundry, *Jesus the Word According to John the Sectarian* (Grand Rapids: Eerdmans, 2002) 1–50, and especially 1–12 and 37–50.

[11] Cf. Note the following from my earlier chapter on "Spinoza, Semler and Gabler": In the appendix I discuss the issue as follows: In the course of his argumentation, Spinoza gives much attention to the distinction he makes between passages of Scripture which contextually claim to be revelation (e.g., "thus says Yahweh" or "the Word of Yahweh came to me saying") and portions dealing with matter-of-fact or mundane issues (e.g., Philemon). This is a significant issue and must not be waived off. A noted evangelical theologian for whom Scripture is not the written Word of God but the primary "vehicle of the Word of God" made a similar point to this writer in correspondence, i.e., not all of Scripture even claims to be the Word of God/revelation, so how can we even claim that it is all the Word of God?

While, e.g., 2 Tim. 3:16 tells us that all Scripture is inspired by God" and 2 Pet. 1:20-21 explains that Scripture is prophetic ("prophecy of Scripture") as the result of holy men being "borne along by the Holy Spirit" whereby they "spoke from God," do such passages allow us to say that the whole of Scripture *is* revelation or Word of God in the *direct* sense? Maybe, maybe not. Or, maybe yes and no. First, it might be proper, at one level, to acknowledge the phenomena of the many scriptural contexts and genres by concluding that not all of Holy Scripture is revelation in the direct sense. We must surely reckon with the fact that there are a number of portions of Scripture which, in their original contexts, are not said to be revelatory or direct disclosures of God and/or content-ful truth of God, but which are quoted elsewhere and referred to as the direct, revelatory Word of God. But does this necessitate the application or reckoning of this phenomenon as a principle to all of Scripture wherein there is no such contextual divine claim? Maybe. But any conclusion there must be recognized as at least somewhat conjectural. Would it not be more readily and biblically affirmable to say that not all of Holy Scripture is revelation as such, or in the *direct* sense, though in fact it may be, yet it is all and in every part the derivative Word of God as the result of "inspiration" (*theopneustos*). In this way, what Spinoza (et al.) points out about Scripture can be readily acknowledged, yet the negative conclusion properly denied. The point is that the historical text of Holy Scripture, whatever else we may affirm about it, is the content-ful written Word of God, even its matter-of-fact, mundane elements, as the result of the work of the Spirit with the writers of Scripture in the process of inspiration unto enscripturation. And even then, of course, it is not a simple matter. The phrase "Word of God" means different things in the different scriptural contexts.

[12] Albert Einstein, "Physics and Reality," 296 ff.

[13] Ibid., 228 ff.

[14] Ibid., 286 ff.

[15] Ibid.

[16] Ibid.

[17] T. F. Torrance, *The Ground and Grammar of Theology* (Charlottesville: The University Press of Virginia, 1981) 125. Hereafter referred to as *GG*.

[18] T. F. Torrance, *Christian Theology and Scientific Culture* (New York: Oxford University Press, 1980) 7–8, 58, 75–76. Hereafter referred to as *CTSC*.

[19] T. F. Torrance, *GG*, 162. Cf. T. F. Torrance, *God and Rationality* (London: Oxford University Press, 1971) 100, and T. F. Torrance, *Theological Science* (London: Oxford University Press, 1969) 110–11. Hereafter referred to as *GR* and *TS*.

[20] Torrance, *GR*, 100; *GG*, 31–35.

[21] Torrance, *Reality and Evangelical Theology* (Philadelphia: Westminster, 1982) 42–51, 71, 139. Hereafter referred to as RET. Cf. Torrance, *GR*, 131–32; *GG*, 173; *CTSC*, 50–51.

[22] T. F. Torrance, *Reality and Scientific Theology* (Edinburgh: Scottish Academic Press, 1981) 138–39. Cf. *GG*, 168–72.

[23] Torrance, *GR*, 25.

[24] E.g., Torrance, *TS*, 138; *GG*, 156 ff., 160 ff., 168ff.; *RST*, 182–85; *RET*, 171–74.

[25] E. g., T. F. Torrance, *Transformation and Convergence in the Frame of Knowledge* (Grand Rapids: Eerdmans,1984) 195–203. Cf. *CTSC*, 69–70.

[26] Ray S. Anderson, *Historical Transcendence and the Reality of God: A Christological Critique* (Grand Rapids: Eerdmans, 1975) 212–13.

[27] Ibid., 213–14.

[28] Anthony C. Thiselton, *The Two Horizons* (Grand Rapids: Eerdmans, 1980) 337, 354, 385, 443.

[29] Anderson, 212–13. Cf. Morrison, *Knowledge*, 365–71.

[30] Ibid., 212f., and Morrison, *Knowledge*, 370–418.

[31] Cf. John 1, Colossians 1, Hebrews 1.

[32] Cf. John 1, Colossians 1, Hebrews 1.

[33] G. Ernest Wright, *The Old Testament and Theology* (New York: Harper and Row, 1969) 19, 21 ff., 49 and "Archaeology, History and Theology," *Harvard Divinity Bulletin* 28 (April, 1964) 88–89f.

[34] Abraham Heschel, *God in Search of Man* (London: Jason Aronson, 1987) 200, 204, 239. Cf. John Goldingay, *Approaches to Old Testament Interpretation* (Downers Grove, Ill.: InterVarsity, 1981) 74–77.

[35] Cf. The useful discussion of George Lindbeck, *The Nature of Doctrine* (Philadelphia: Westminster, 1984) and Hans Frei, *The Eclipse of Biblical Narrative: A Study in Eighteenth- and Nineteenth-Century Hermeneutics* (New Haven: Yale University Press, 1974).

[36] Anderson, 212–13.

[37] John Calvin, *Institutes of the Christian Religion*, 2 vols., ed. John T. McNeil, trans. Ford Lewis Battles (Philadelphia: Westminister, 1960) IV, vii, 2; IV, viii, 2–3; I, viii, 4.

[38] Ibid., IV, viii, 6, 9, 10.

[39] Ibid., IV, ii, 4; and Ronald S. Wallace, *Calvin's Doctrine of the Word and Sacrament* (Grand Rapids: Eerdmans, 1957) 100.

[40] Ibid., IV, xi, 1; and John Calvin, *Commentaries on the Prophet Ezekiel*, 2 vols. Ed. and trans. Thomas Meyers (Grand Rapids: Eerdmans, 1948).

[41] *Institutes*, IV, xi, 2; and Ibid. IV, xi, 8. See also T. H. L. Parker, *John Calvin: A Biography* (Philadelphia: Westminster, 1975) 58.

[42] Parker, *Calvin*, 58. Cf. *Opera Selecta*, 1:235ff.

[43] Ibid., 59.

[44] William Bouwsma, *John Calvin: A Sixteenth Century Portrait* (New York: Oxford University Press, 1988) 44.

[45] Calvin, *Institutes*, I, xiii, 7.

[46] Calvin, *Institutes*, IV, viii, 1.

[47] Note here Calvin's Christological and cosmological discussion relating to this larger issue in his commentary on Ephesians 1:20-1:23. Cf. Calvin, *Institutes*, IV, x, 14; IV, X, 7; IV, X, 2.

[48] John Calvin, *The Gospel of St. John 11–21 and the First Epistle of John*, trans. and ed. T. H. L. Parker (Grand Rapids: Eerdmans, 1961) 53. Cf. *Institutes* IV, xi, 5, 8 and 14; also cf. John Calvin, *Commentary on the Gospel of St. John 1–10*, trans. and ed. T. H. L. Parker (Edinburgh: Oliver and Boyd, 1959) 139.

[49] For a more complete discussion of this aspect of Calvin's thought see, John D. Morrision, "John Calvin's Christological Assertion of Word Authority in the Context of Sixteenth Century Ecclesiological Polemics," *The Scottish Journal of Theology*. 1991.

Appendix

The Authority of Holy Scripture and the Need for Hermeneutical Authority in the Theology of the Early Church Fathers:
A Paradigm for Contemporary Evangelicalism?

One of the emphases of the magisterial Reformers was *sola scriptura*, "the Scriptures alone!" In the ensuing centuries, orthodox Protestantism has continued to give emphasis to this profound "slogan" and to the implications for theological authority. Since the Enlightenment, with its epistemological dualism, subjectivism and anthropological isolationism, *sola scriptura*, especially as coupled with the "priesthood of all believers," has effected some questionable results. The situation of the Christians' relation to Scripture is now one which can be described as "individualistic," "subjectivistic," "ego-centric," destructive of Christian community and the authority of "the faith once for all delivered to the saints" (Jude 3). Is the Reformation claim for *sola scriptura* to blame? Perhaps.

In November 2004, the Evangelical Theological Society, whose core classical affirmation has always been: "The Bible alone, and the Bible in its entirety, is the Word of God written and is therefore inerrant in the autographs," passed a proposal to allow Society leadership to use the "Chicago Statement on Biblical Inerrancy" as an authoritative hermeneutical guide by which to assess potentially problematic theological positions within the Society. Fourteen years earlier the Society included in its statement the core trinitarian elements of the Nicene Creed. Do these developments compromise the Society's Reformational roots, a shift toward "Roman Catholic" views of authority, a dual authority base—Holy Scripture and church Tradition? Perhaps.

In the second century, Celsus recognized and attacked Christianity's "authoritative" character.[1] The writings of the early Church Fathers abound with references to authoritative bases for their teachings. Early on, these are usually implicit, assumed, and occur through allusion, echo and use, as well as explicit reference to a source's authority. But through developing circumstances, it was soon urgent that early Christians reflect on the foundations of their faith. The Fathers needed to understand these bases and to clarify, justify, and utilize them before others (pagan attacks and heresies). Reflection on the nature of divinely authoritative foundations, their revelation, involved theology, which is as old as Christianity itself.

Yet only with time and opposition could the *question* of authority, as we think of it today, arise. The problem initially was the separation that existed between the period of Christ, the apostles, and the immediately following generations. Only very slowly did the second-century church become conscious of the growing gap between the new covenant revelation, the apostolic era and its own situation. Under changing conditions, the church was often unclear about the parameters of its standards of doctrinal truth. At first, again, the sources were assumed. The church had normative authority for its teaching, the apostolic writings having survived the first century. But the church was not yet reflective about its standards of divine truth until forced by developments both within Roman culture and within the church. Only then was clarity required and increasingly achieved.

The earliest Christian writings were for believers only, which is readily observed in the Apostolic Fathers, e.g., the exhortation of Clement to the Corinthians, the *Didache*, and the letters of Ignatius of Antioch written to various churches. But as Christianity spread, it met hostility from outside and division within. External attacks called for a new form of Christian literature, so "the Apologists" endeavored to answer pagan accusations against this new religion and to "introduce" Christian faith and life. In the process, these advanced the church's consciousness of its "pattern of authority." But it was especially the threat of the heresies of Marcionism, Gnosticism, and Montanism which called forth extensive clarification of "the faith," and so the church's "pattern of authority," especially via the extensive writings of Irenaeus and Tertullian in the West, and Clement of Alexandria and Origen in the East, despite distinctive emphases among them.

What source or sources of doctrinal authority did the church look to? More specifically, how did the Fathers regard Scripture? What did they understand Scripture to be? If divinely authoritative, was Scripture the *only* source of authority for the Fathers? How did Scripture relate to the whole authoritative legacy "passed on" from the apostles, and so from Jesus Christ, the Word of God? If plural, how were these sources of authority related? Not only did the received OT continue to be regarded as the Word of God, but early on such recognition was accorded to the apostolic writings. But in addition, the church's "rule of faith (truth)" came to be regarded as, with Scripture, authoritative for proper understanding of the faith. Can the early church's "pattern of authority" be a pattern for the church, specifically the evangelical church of the twenty-first century?

The Issue: The Nature and Authority of "Tradition" in the Early Church

The attitude of the Apostolic Fathers to the nature of the Christian faith and its sources of authority can be stated roughly by saying that "Christianity came into the world as a religion of revelation."[2] The church claimed a supernatural origin for its gospel message. The early church clearly recognized the ultimate source of that revelation: the Person, words and works of Jesus Christ. He was the climax and fulfillment of divine revelation.

But a careful look reveals that the issue of divine authority in the church in the first generations to follow the apostles is complex. Of course, "Christian doctrine" is the teaching of the Catholic Church from the close of the first century. But this raises the question of "media" by which the original revelation in Jesus Christ was preserved and "handed down" (*paradosis*, *tradere*, i.e., "Tradition") in the church. A further issue regards the principles by which these revelatory media were to be interpreted by the church ("the rule of faith"). Differing interpretations necessitated criteria by which the church could judge teachings to be orthodox or heretical.

In a sense, our concern stands within the broad problem of "Tradition" (as it is now called, in distinction from usage in the early Fathers) and Scripture, i.e., their relation. The Fathers affirmed that God was the ultimate source of the revelation. But he had committed that revelation to inspired prophets, lawgivers, and the apostles, the eyewitnesses of the incarnate Word. The apostles "passed on" their authoritative teaching to the church.[3] Thus, contrary to common Protestant perceptions of the second-century church, early Christians understood the authentic faith to be located generally in the church's continuous "tradition" of teaching from the apostles. But prior to external and internal challenges, "tradition" here, in contrast to later understandings of "tradition," *included* Scripture and basic doctrinal teachings (often related to catechesis and baptism), all of which could also be found in Scripture. Indeed, Scripture was seen as the concrete manifestation of the divinely authoritative apostolic tradition. Even a much later statement by Athanasius illustrates the ancient meaning of "tradition" as "authoritative delivery" of doctrine, "the actual original tradition, teaching and faith of the Catholic church, which the Lord bestowed, the apostles proclaimed (as oral and written) and the fathers safeguarded."[4] This included unwritten doctrine related to and yet distinct from Scripture. In early Christian contexts, the primary sense of "tradition," broadly understood, was authoritative initial delivery. In relation to Christian doctrine (the church's teaching), tradition is teaching initially delivered by Jesus Christ and the apostles.[5] In this sense, at the beginning tradition must have been entirely oral. After some years it was written down. But the Gospels and Epistles did not force oral tradition from church usage. For some time the two remained as complementary authoritative sources of the one divine message.

Given these developments, Christians from the apostolic age to the middle of the second century are of great importance for understanding the bases from which the Apologists, and then Irenaeus and Tertullian in the West and Clement of Alexandria and Origen in the East sought to bring clarity to the "pattern of Christian authority."

Herein, not only did authoritative tradition from the apostles reach beyond Scripture, but the "NT" was not yet officially ratified (as canonical)—though the writings of the apostles were immediately "used" in an "authoritative" manner. For the early Fathers, Christianity meant a complex of beliefs and practices which Clement of Rome termed "the rule of our tradition," which went back to Christ himself. But in terms of immediately accessible divine authorities about Christ, this meant "the prophets" (OT) who, *properly interpreted*, foretold every detail of Christ's ministry, and the apostles, whether in oral or written form.[6] Here contentions over the Christian authority of the OT and the church's typological/christological exegesis must be dealt with.

Heresy and the Urgent Need to Clarify the Sources of Christian Doctrinal Authority

For a time, the primitive church allowed its bases of authority to remain somewhat ambiguous, limits unclear, the nature of such assumed and without development. "Heresy" always forces the church to bring clarification to its teaching, its doctrine, and to what orthodoxy is and is not. As a result of crises related to the very sources of church doctrine, created by the Marcionites, Gnosticism and Montanism, the church Fathers clarified and reaffirmed the divine authority of the OT for the church, established the canon as a whole, with the NT, and then set the nature of true, open, apostolic, tradition against Gnostic claims to esoteric "secret" tradition.

Christianity inherited from Judaism, and so from the OT, its understanding of the divine inspiration of Holy Scripture. Whenever Jesus and the apostles quoted the OT, they clearly regarded it as the written Word of God. The authoritative significance of the OT as a divine norm for doctrine in the early church cannot be overstated. The church received as its own the established OT canon. The doctrinal authority of the OT was grounded in the belief that, if correctly interpreted, it was a *Christian* book. Justin Martyr's claim that the Jewish Scriptures did not belong to the Jews, who misinterpreted them, but rather to Christians, had been basic in the church's thought.[7] Yet this conviction was facilitated by the church's christological (typological) exegesis, i.e., exegesis by "eyes enlightened" from the fulfillment of Christian revelation in Christ. Pseudo-Barnabas calls such exegesis *gnosis*, a claim later developed in the Alexandrian church.[8] But such a hermeneutic was no second-century church invention. It was used in the apostolic writings (later NT canon) and was reflected in Jesus' own teaching (e.g., Luke 24).

Until the second half of the second century, "Scripture" in the *official* sense referred to the OT, with rare exceptions. Judaism had its official collection of sacred books which "defile the hands" long before Christianity. Again, following Jesus and the apostles, the church appropriated the OT as its own, as the true heirs of the revelation fulfilled in Christ. As exegeted typologically, it was a book which declared the Savior "on every page." When the apostolic writings were officially recognized as Scripture (a process all but complete in the late second century), consistent ongoing use of the OT made it clear it had not diminished in status.

Yet the OT of the early church was the larger LXX translation, which was much less rigorous regarding authoritative books than was the text of Palestinian Judaism (i.e., inclusion of the Apocrypha). The LXX had been used in quoting the OT by NT writers. This became a significant issue later (e.g., for Jerome), but in the second-century church it was of little importance (except in dialogue with Jewish writers). For our purposes it has no direct bearing.

Though universally affirmed in the church, the place and authority of the OT for the Christian faith became a critical question as a result of objections by the heretic Marcion. Raised in a Christian home, Marcion eventually rejected the church's typological, often allegorical, exegesis of the OT, and so concluded that the OT was impossible to reconcile with the gospel of Christ. Legalism and rigid justice in the one, grace and redeeming love in the other were diametrically opposed views of religion. Marcion accepted the OT as literally true, but decided there must be two Gods. The "God" revealed in the OT, the God of Judaism, is the lower Demiurge who created the material universe. The supreme God was first made known by Jesus. While he did not link the God of the OT with the principle of evil, as did Gnosticism, Marcion's strong dualism, leading to the rejection of an authoritative OT for the Christian faith, moved him to canonize an alternative group of Scriptures for his church. What he took to be Paul's proper attitude to the Law made Paul, with modifications, Marcion's exemplar. His list of books, all "Judaizing" portions cut out, included Luke's Gospel and ten of Paul's epistles—all properly "modified."[9]

The powerful effects of Marcion's separation from the catholic church (144 A.D.) and his dualistic espousal of two gods have been misunderstood by Harnack who claimed Marcion originated the church's canon.[10] The church already had the canon collection, including the NT, *roughly* defined. Thus an *implicit Christian* canon was already "set" within the church's own convictions and practice (use of OT *and* NT as divinely authoritative, cf. below). But no major center of the church had officially delineated the authorized Christian books. But of *at least* equally great (and destructive) import was Marcion's attempt to sever the Christian faith from the redemptive, covenant history of Yahweh with the Jews. What was Christianity's relation to God's revelation in history and what about the NT canon and its relation to, its unity with, the OT.[11]

In principle, the Montanist movement was related to these concerns because Montanus and his two female prophets claimed to be fresh channels for the new outpouring of the Holy Spirit. The oracles of the Montanist prophets were understood to supplement the church's Scriptures.[12] The combination of Marcionism and Montanism created great concern in the church that, with a fresh defense of the OT, the NT (as it was coming to be called) should also be officially recognized as divinely authoritative, with the *right* books and *only* the right books included. Church concerns over these developments were tellingly reflected in Polycarp when he met Marcion in Rome: "Do you know me? I know you. You are the first-born of Satan."[13]

While Marcion's thought had affinities with Gnosticism, Gnosticism actually posed a different threat to the Christian faith, rooted in its claim(s) to a "secret apostolic tradition." Among the forms of "Gnosticism," the "Christian" Gnostics represent the "extreme Hellenization of Christianity." The mixture of fantasy, speculation and mysticism, with a scattering of scriptural references, was typical of Gnosticism.[14] Crucial to the claims of "Christian" Gnosticism and its use of Scripture was, again, the claim to possess an esoteric apostolic tradition. In fact, there was little that was truly Christian in Gnosticism. While willing to acknowledge some worth to portions of the OT allegorically interpreted, Christian Gnostics too placed a "chasm" between the old and new covenants. In reality, this was a facade of Christianity, whose patchwork speculations and belief that the human problem is "intellectual," denied the incarnation, while using Christian Scripture in fanciful interpretations to cover its true nature. This esoteric "secret apostolic tradition" was a hermeneutic, an interpretive "rule," that enabled one to attain to true gnosis/"knowledge" of God.[15]

These heresies found the catholic church initially unprepared, without much clear, expressed, explicit understanding of its divinely authoritative bases for doctrine. Again, much was assumed. Yet these unreflective beliefs about what the church received from Christ and the apostles proved to be of substantial use to the Christian leaders that immediately followed them, who would meet these crises with Holy Scripture and the ("apostolic") "rule of faith."

Sources of Divine, Authoritative Teaching: An Overview of Selected Early Second-Century Fathers

As noted, in the period we are studying, from the apostles to the early third century, the church was firm in its claim that its message, and so the sources of its message were of divine origin. All was centered in and from Jesus Christ. But early on, the accessible media whereby the revelation was preserved and handed down, were only implicitly understood. With the inherited OT Scriptures, everywhere recognized as the written Word of God and as the prophetic book of Christ, there was the "apostolic tradition" both oral and written. While the apostolic writings were not at first "officially" recognized to be on a par with the OT, they were immediately used in ways that reflected recognition of divine authority. On the one hand, as Kelly puts the matter,

> Throughout the whole patristic age, as indeed in all subsequent Christian centuries, the OT was accepted as the word of God, the unimpeachable source book of saving doctrine.[16]

While on the other hand, the recognition that

> a "New Testament" parallel to the Old . . . was inspired Scripture . . . [meant that] Paul's letters were placed on a level with the "other scriptures" . . . [and] "the gospel" was an equivalent authority to "the

prophets" . . . henceforth there could be no question that the Christian books belonged to what were called *hai hagiai graphai, sanctae scripturae,* or their numerous equivalents.[17]

The first writer to clearly refer to a "New Testament" was Irenaeus, but the apostolic writings had long been used as a corresponding source of divinely authoritative teaching.[18] But other sources, the oral tradition, church liturgy, the doctrine used to prepare catechumens for baptism, were also significant elements of "apostolic tradition." But, as the Fathers themselves state, there is nothing (variously) taught which is not found in the "holy" or "divine" Scriptures.[19] Apostolic tradition and written Scriptures were "twin," interrelated sources of authoritative teaching.

Again, clarification of the nature and importance of the two sources together in the catholic church was forced from implicit to explicit, and hence to clarity, by those second-century heresies, especially Marcionism and Gnosticism. The first necessitated the reaffirmation of the OT as Christian Scripture with Christ as its message, recognition of the all but finalized NT with the appropriate "inspired, apostolic books" and, so importantly, the unity of the two testaments. The one God was the ultimate author of both, with the one center and source, Jesus Christ. The second heresy, Gnosticism, with its claim to a "secret apostolic tradition" *beyond* that affirmed by the church, forced the church to articulate the core of apostolic teaching, especially in the *regula fidei*, the (apostolic) "rule of faith" (or "truth"). This "rule" gave hermeneutical regulation/guidance to those who would be faithful to the church's apostolic deposit. This is our concern here: the views of the early Fathers regarding the divine nature and authority of Holy Scriptures and the authoritative relation of the *regula fidei* to the prophetic-apostolic Scriptures. But from these bases we will ask the question: Is this combination, Scripture and a (traditional) hermeneutical rule viable within Protestant orthodoxy? Does this conflict with *sola scriptura*? As we sweep through the late first, second, and early third centuries, our special focus will be on Irenaeus and Tertullian.

Clement of Rome wrote to the Corinthians about their divisive or party spirit. It is noteworthy that Clement, as bishop, does not claim to be a source of authority. Scripture and tradition are important sources for Clement. What is the nature of each *and together* at this early stage of Christian thinking? For Clement the divine authority of the OT as Holy

Scripture is clear and direct. The term "Scripture" will not be applied to apostolic writings for one more generation. Clement refers to a body of teachings that present the Christian's responsibility to God. He refers to these as commands or ordinances of the Lord "written on the tables of your heart"[20] and as "the commands of Jesus."[21] As God teaches through Jesus, so Christ speaks by his Spirit in the words of the OT and in the message of the apostles.[22] The apostles founded the churches, he says, and

> Having therefore received their commands, and being fully assured by the resurrection of our Lord Jesus Christ, and with their faith confirmed by the word of God, they went forth in assurance of the Holy Spirit preaching the good news that the Kingdom of God is coming.[23]

Clement knows that in addition to preaching, the apostles wrote letters.[24] While he does not quote apostolic writings in a strict sense, Clement displays a thorough knowledge of them and refers to or "echoes" them freely. His usage reflects awareness of their authority, referring to passages with the words "remember the words of the Lord Jesus."[25] Clement's use of apostolic writings is modeled in chapter thirteen of his Letter to the Corinthians. He exhorts the Corinthians to humility of mind because of "that which stands written," then refers to Jeremiah, Matthew, and Luke. In chapter nineteen, Clement refers to previous generations who received God's oracles in fear and truth. In 53:1, he tells them they have good understanding of the Sacred Scriptures and have studied the oracles of God, and in 62:3 that he is writing to those who "had studied the oracles of God." These show Clement believed that God had revealed himself and his purposes, his Word, in an accessible written way that can be studied. God delivered this revelation by the inspiration of the biblical writers. The Holy Spirit was the ultimate author of Scripture, and speaks the words of Scripture.[26] Expressed differently, Clement says, "the ministers of the grace of God spoke though the Holy Spirit."[27] Hence, the Scriptures can be called "holy" and "true."[28]

Regarding "tradition" or a "rule of faith," Clement does use the verb *paradidomi* (to hand over) but not in the sense of "tradition" or handing over teaching. The noun form is combined with *kanon* once where he says: "Let us come to the glorious and venerable *rule* of our tradition." Lightfoot comments that "there seems to be no thought in Clement of a creed or rule of faith," as would soon develop because of heresy.[29] The context is more ethical than doctrinal. So while Clement makes much use of OT and apostolic tradition, especially the life of Christ, and uses a creedlike statement ("Have we not one God, and one Christ, and one Spirit of grace"[30]) which echoes Ephesians 4, there is no knowledge of a concrete rule or confession other than the Scriptures.

Ignatius, third bishop of Antioch, was condemned to face the beasts at Rome. En route, he wrote letters to churches of various cities. Together they show early second-century use of the gospel, of confession, as well as defense against heresy and the developing role of the bishop. Of Christ and the apostles, Ignatius says that Jesus brings knowledge (*gnosis*) as a teacher and lawgiver, but more, that Jesus is God's unerring mouthpiece.[31] Because the apostles followed him completely, he spoke through them and used their precepts as his own. Apostolic authority rests upon this apostolic obedience to Christ.[32] Further, against heresies Igantius made much use of the Scriptures, reflecting submission to their authority. One must "give heed to the prophets, and especially to the gospels."[33] For Ignatius, the two major sources of doctrine are the prophets (OT) and the gospels. The divine prophets lived according to Christ and were inspired by his grace to convince the disobedient there is one God, who manifested himself through Jesus Christ, his son. The OT prophets announced the gospel, hoped in Christ, waited for him and were united to him. Thus Christians must obey their word.[34] Yet more than the prophets, it is "canonically" significant that Ignatius' basic authority is "the gospel," a pointer to apostolic authority. Just as in the work of Clement, reference to the gospel is found in similar phrases and language use in Ignatius.[35] Here one can see much influence of Paul and John. Thus both OT Scriptures and apostolic writings (the emerging NT) *within* the "tradition" form the authoritative foundation of Ignatius' teaching. Both contain the gospel message, though regarding apostolic tradition it is not always clear whether his sources are oral or written. But, again, for the early Fathers there was no conflict between the two.

In Ignatius' letters, elements of the apostolic message are given in brief creedlike statements "designed" to protect believers from heresy—Ignatius' great concern. In one passage about Christ, the word "truly" is used four times and is aimed at docetism.[36] Other such statements occur, usually christological in focus. But sometimes they are "triadic" in character.[37]

While some have tried to assemble from these a "creed of Ignatius," C. H. Turner has said that we are not to think that Ignatius had any formal apostolic creed or code of canons in mind, yet he did believe in the apostolic authority of the Christian teaching of his day.[38] He presented the *essence* of that teaching, much like later writers (e.g., Irenaeus, et al.), as a "rule of faith" to be used as a doctrinal/hermeneutical norm against heresy.

As noted, the earliest Christian writings were for Christian edification. But as Christianity spread it faced both pagan opposition and heresy. The "Apologists" purposed to answer pagan accusations while making use of pagan culture (e.g., the Stoic "*logos* doctrine") to create common ground and to show that the Christian message was congruous with the highest pagan ethical and philosophical ideals. The most influential of these was Justin Martyr. Philosophically trained, his eager mind found no system that was satisfying until a stranger told him to find the true philosophy in the Hebrew prophets and in the gospel of Christ. As a Christian he taught philosophy at Rome until his martyrdom in about 165 A.D. In his dialogical/apologetic writings, Justin has much to say about "the Scriptures" (OT), the apostolic writings, the inspiration of both, and about interpretation, tradition, and a growing awareness of a "rule of faith."

Highlighting a few of the emphases from his many extant writings, Justin explains that his teaching is taken from Christ and the prophets who went before him. These, he says, had led him to God. This meant he was not following human notions but the truth of God.[39] By this he is referring to the OT as a whole, in keeping with universal Christian practice. But he relates Christ to OT authority by asserting that it was the pre-incarnate Christ who had taught the prophets. Thus for Justin to say "the Scripture says" is equivalent to "Christ says." And for Justin the *logos* was Christ. But further, Christ's teaching is accessible in the "memoirs of the apostles," which, unofficially and in terms of actual use and reverence, were by now held above the OT in many respects. By these memoirs he is relaying true Christian beliefs and practices.[40] The Christian believes these (OT) writings because he/she sees them fulfilled in events related by the "memoirs." Such evidence of divine approval induces belief in the prophets as heralds of Christian truth.[41] By this claim, Justin is clearly mindful of the apologetic value.

So it is, he says, with the "apostolic memoirs." Being aware of his readers, he does not quote these yet-unofficial writings directly as authoritative, but is willing to portray thereby the doctrines and precepts of the gospel. But Justin hardly depreciated gospel/apostolic authority. He explains that the apostles were sent by Christ to teach, that they and their disciples put their teachings into writing and these writings are placed *with* the prophets in *public* worship.[42] By Justin's time, "gospel" was often used to refer broadly to the apostolic writings. As noted, Justin sees these "memoirs" as divinely authoritative in their own right, especially when quoting Christ's words. As Westcott says, these writings "were now regarded as the sufficient and complete source of knowledge with regard to the facts of the gospel."[43] But almost invariably Justin's methodological use of Scripture was commanded by his apologetic concerns, especially fulfilled prophecy. Hence, the OT was very important to Justin's "pattern of authority." Apostolic writings were used where apologetically useful to corroborate the truth of his account.

The divine inspiration of Scripture was the basis for this authority. Directly and indirectly, Justin emphasizes that the voice behind the OT writers is the prophetic Spirit. The prophets were filled with and spoke by the divine Spirit; their statements were not finally their own but those of the *Logos* who moved them. Behind the Scriptures there is one divine Author.[44] Though less weighty for his apologetic purpose, Justin says the same of the inspiration of the apostles by the Spirit. They, too, were channels of God's message.[45] And as Christ taught the apostles the true meaning of the OT, the OT and the apostolic writings were mutually dependent. Therefore they cannot be rightly interpreted by the Jews; indeed, the OT belongs to Christians.[46] For Justin, the old and new covenant documents form one unified, harmonious whole.[47]

Justin knows of "apostolic tradition." In using a form of *paradosis* in this way, he explains that Scripture both "passes down" and "is passed down." That which is "passed down" is divinely authoritative and synonymous with revelation because it comes from Christ the Logos. Very significantly, Justin does not use apostolic "tradition" to refer to oral tradition, but consistently refers thereby to Scriptural teaching, to what is "written."[48]

In Justin, that which would come to be known as "the rule of faith" is not always clearly spelled out, but the elements are present. He is ready to point out that Christianity is grounded in essential doctrines that are given by God, rather than human opinion. These divine commands are ultimately summed up in Christ the Logos, and one's salvation depends on believing what God taught through Christ. Thus the Christian is really taught by Christ because Christian doctrines are his teaching.[49] Christ's teachings/doctrines came through the apostles. As the apostles "passed on" these dogmas from Christ to the church, so these are to be ever "passed on." To what do these essential teachings pertain? Justin says to Trypho that a Christian must believe in the crucified Jesus Christ, the Son of God, who received judgment over all humanity, and in Christ's eternal kingdom.[50] Faith in God is contextually assumed, given that Trypho, as a Jew, already believed in God. Some doctrines are said to be crucial for the Christian. Others, like Justin's belief in the earthly millennium, are secondary doctrines, and so not part of the doctrinal/hermeneutical heart of the Christian faith, the authoritative core of apostolic teaching termed "the rule."

Sources of Divinely Authoritative Teaching in the Face of Heresy: Irenaeus and Tertullian

The second half of the second century saw the church make needed clarification of its doctrinal norms and their relations. The Old Testament lost none of its authority as (written) divine revelation. But the apostolic writings were now officially "promoted" to canonical status, and so to a divinely authoritative level, which in fact they had possessed *practically* from the late first century. In the minds of Christians these writings possessed, under Christ, supreme authority.[51] Further, there was now a distinction between Holy Scripture (OT and NT) and the church's living tradition (valued especially for its effectiveness against heresy) as complementary sources of apostolic testimony. This distinction resulted from the church's struggle with Gnostic groups and their teachings, a struggle now fully engaged. As noted, the Gnostics not only misused Scripture to their own ends, but often did so by way of interpretive reference to and "support" from a "secret apostolic tradition" supposedly passed down to the enlightened. As a result, the church's more mature, nuanced position is excellently presented in the West by Irenaeus and Tertullian, and in the East by Clement and Origen from Alexandria (each duo reflecting the distinctive Western and Eastern/Alexandrian tendencies. For the sake of space, we will focus on Irenaeus and Tertullian.

Appendix

Irenaeus on the Nature of Scripture and the Authoritative "Rule of Truth"

Authoritative Scripture. Given Gnostic claims, which largely undercut the OT and made fanciful reference to a "secret apostolic tradition" and, thereby, an esoteric, speculative use of Scripture, it is appropriate that both Irenaeus and Tertullian charge the Gnostics with the misuse of Scripture, for their own distorted purposes. Irenaeus points out that the Gnostic twists Scripture out of all recognizable Christian sense. In the face of the potent Gnostic crisis, Irenaeus especially, then Tertullian, lead the way in maturing the church's understanding of the nature and proper use of Scripture in relation to the church's broader apostolic tradition, and in particular to the *regula fidei* or "rule of truth," as Irenaeus referred to it. For both, Christ is the ultimate source of doctrine, being the truth/Word by whom the Father was revealed. But he gave this revelation to his apostles, and only through them could that knowledge be acquired. "Through none other than those by whom the gospel reached us have we learned the plan of our salvation," wrote Irenaeus.[52]

But, again, the OT and NT were twisted by the Gnostics via their "secret apostolic tradition"; thus, they used the same authoritative books. For this reason the now distinctive nature of Christian tradition and particularly the "rule of faith," or "rule of truth," as condensed doctrinal summary, the "purport" of Scripture, and as authoritative hermeneutical guide, was brought necessarily to more precise form. This was crucial in the struggle for the historic Christian faith once delivered to the saints.[53]

By distinguishing the church's living tradition from its written Scriptures, Irenaeus could argue "against the heresies" (the Gnostics) that the Christ-given apostolic revelation has been preserved by them in and as written documents. "What the apostles first proclaimed they afterward, by God's will, conveyed to us in the Scriptures." Like the earlier Fathers, Irenaeus believed that every detail of the life, passion and teaching of Christ was foreshadowed throughout the OT, but for Irenaeus the now essentially canonical NT was the written formulation of the revealed apostolic message (cf. *engraphos*).

Despite the readiness of heretics to distort OT and NT Scripture, Irenaeus believed firmly that when taken as a whole, Scripture's teaching was self-evident (as reflected in the "rule of faith"). The heretics distorted Scripture out of evil intent and also because they ignored Scripture's underlying unity. Indeed, in the distinction-within-unity of the church's tradition in relation to Scripture, and the great polemic place Irenaeus gives to the church's public tradition against Gnostic "secret tradition" in his *Against Heresies*:

> [H]is real defense of orthodoxy was founded on Scripture. Indeed, tradition itself, on his view, was confirmed by Scripture, which was "the foundation and pillar of our faith."[54]

In the conflict with Marcion and the Gnostics, it was especially Irenaeus who first saw that the center of the struggle regarding Christian sources of authority revolved around two questions: (1) What are the Scriptures? and (2) How should they be interpreted? Irenaeus (and Tertullian) represent the close of the age that initially set the church upon the canonical principle of divinely inspired Christian writings. But further, it was Irenaeus (then Tertullian) who, in the case of biblical interpretation, gave the church a mature understanding of its tradition, especially the *regula fidei*, and the relation of such to Scripture.

Irenaeus refers to the apostolic Scriptures as well defined, fixed and divinely authoritative for doctrine.[55] Indeed, it is Irenaeus who first refers unequivocally to a "New" Testament having parallel divine authority, as "Scripture" and as canon, with the OT. As noted, his primary defense *of the authority* of orthodoxy was from Scripture. His approach can be observed when he explains that "it is easy to prove from the very words of the Lord" why the Catholic affirms *one* Father and Creator (to refer to just one doctrine).[56] It is foundational to his argument against Gnostic teachers that they are guilty of turning from the biblical bases of orthodox doctrine. And when shown to be in error from Scripture, the Gnostics suddenly turned on the text by accusing it "as if the Scriptures were not correct nor of (divine) authority."[57] Against the Gnostics, Irenaeus insists that there is no need to go beyond what the apostles have *openly* given in favor of some further "revelation," for the apostles were personally chosen by Christ to be his unique representatives and interpreters. These acquired "perfect knowledge."

For, after our Lord rose from the dead, the apostles were invested with power from on high when the Holy Spirit came down upon them, were filled from all his gifts and had perfect knowledge.[58]

The apostolic writings shared with the OT the authority inherent in writings inspired by the Spirit of God. In this, of course, Irenaeus was simply affirming as well as developing the church's universal belief that these books were the Word of Christ. Elsewhere, his proof of apostolic preaching is simply a series of biblical texts gathered for such support. Therein, he habitually attributes the words to "God"; "the Holy Spirit says" is his other regular way of referring to Scripture.[59] This method of reference is constantly used in *Against Heresies*, i.e., the Holy Spirit speaks through his prophets and the NT writers. As a result the Holy Scriptures are "divine" and "perfect."[60]

Irenaeus explains how this process of inspiration occurred: "It is not the man who utters the prophecy, but the Spirit of God, taking form and shape in the likeness of the person concerned, spoke in the prophets."[61] This explanation avoids "mechanical" notions of inspiration found in earlier writers, e.g., Athenagorus. Divine inspiration is not only basic to the divine authority of the prophetic-apostolic Scriptures but also explains the unity of the Scriptures. They are ultimately from one and the same Father.[62] The prophets spoke as they were moved by the Spirit, and so were less witnesses to their own day than to the coming of Christ. The apostles testified to the same Christ, though from first hand experience. Yet Irenaeus maintains that there is one difference. Though the one Spirit directs both OT and NT writers, the NT inspiration is of a higher order. This is because only from the clear revelation of Jesus Christ do the ambiguities of the OT become clear. Christ is the treasure hidden in the OT. Historical fulfillment was required before the prophecies could be understood.[63] In such ways, Irenaeus affirms, clarifies and develops the church's universal belief that the prophetic-apostolic writings are the written Word of God, inspired by the Spirit and "perfect" or "correct," not in error, contra Gnostic claims. Therefore one must be careful in approaching Scripture.

[One must have] a sound mind . . . that is devoted to piety and love of the truth, will eagerly meditate upon those things that God has placed within the power of mankind and has subjected to our knowledge [i.e., Scripture]. . . . I am referring to those things that fall under our observation and are clearly and unambiguously set forth in the sacred Scriptures in clear terms. . . .

For all the apostles taught that there were indeed two testaments among the two peoples, but that it was one and the same God who appointed both for the advantage of those men for whose sakes the testaments were given who were to believe in God.[64]

But these prophetic and apostolic writings which are, under Christ, the written Word of God, must not be twisted for illicit ends, but read in accord with "the rule of truth" (or, again, in most Fathers, "rule of faith," cf. Tertullian below).

The Authoritative Rule of Truth. Against the Gnostics and their "secret apostolic tradition," i.e. claims to special revelations and/or interpretations handed down secretly to the "enlightened," Irenaeus countered with the fact that apostolic teaching had always been public, open, accessible. It was absurd that the apostles had held anything back, as they themselves testify. They proclaimed "one God, not a hierarchy." The consistent teaching of those churches actually founded by the apostles (e.g., Rome, Antioch) testify to this open teaching of the apostles.

But of special polemical importance for Irenaeus was what he preferred to call "the rule of truth." The Gnostics forced these clarifications, first Scripture as distinct from the church's tradition (while the teachings were identical) and, therein, that the summary of the church's tradition/teaching from the apostles is found in the authoritative "rule of truth," to which he refers frequently.[65] This was a condensed doctrinal summary presenting key teachings/interpretive elements of the Christian revelation.

This "rule" stood within Irenaeus' "pattern of authority," the link between the Spirit-endowed prophets and apostles with Christ, and so with God the Father. Contra Gnostic secret tradition and its hierarchy of aeons, the "one God, Creator of heaven and earth," freely created that which is good, not evil. There is but one God, one Christ, the Son of God, and so one gospel. The Gnostics resisted this pattern of authority: the apostles, Christ and God the Father.[66]

Irenaeus usually understood by the "rule" an *authoritative* norm of doctrinal truth. It is literally "the rule that is the truth." But for greater precision regarding Irenaeus' sense of "the rule of truth," he says "the true believer retains in his heart the rule of truth which he received at baptism."[67] But Irenaeus' usage does not allow mere equation with the early baptismal confession. A number of his statements are triadic in structure and he clearly had specific key doctrines in mind.[68] Yet there is a degree of flexibility. There is clear relation to Scripture, notably when referring to Gnostics who twist Scripture out of its natural sense to apply it to alien subjects. But anyone who holds "the rule of truth" sees the error and refuses the blasphemous Gnostic system. In other contexts, Irenaeus refers to a doctrine which is an element of the rule of truth, and then cites Scripture passages in support of the doctrine.[69] Thus Scripture seems to be the *concrete* source of the doctrines of "the rule," hence his identification of the rule with, "the words of God."[70]

But, unlike some classic Reformation statements, Irenaeus is not equating Scripture and "the rule." The *regula* is both doctrinal and hermeneutical, i.e., it sets the interpretational boundaries beyond which Christian teachers must not go. And while the rule may be directly and indirectly extracted from the prophets and apostles, it is best to regard "the rule of truth" as the essence or purport of Scripture, the truth of God's revelation necessary for salvation and preached in the church.[71] It is the "apostolic" teaching set out in freely worded summaries, again, usually in "triadic" form, which emphasizes the foundational elements of salvation, and so the Christian view of God's program of redemption. Like Paul's summary in 1 Corinthians 15:1-5, and in response especially to the Gnostic challenge, Irenaeus' "rule of truth" sums up Christian teaching structured around the Father, the Son Jesus Christ, and the Holy Spirit. Hereby, the church could interpret Scripture by its underlying unity, rather than seizing on isolated passages. Scripture must be interpreted in light of God's ground plan. So correct interpretation of Scripture was the prerogative of the church alone, for *there* the apostolic doctrine, the rule of truth as the key to Holy Scripture, was kept faithfully (one example of Irenaeus' "rule of truth" is included here in endnote 73).[72]

Tertullian on Scripture and the Authoritative "Rule of Faith"

It is Irenaeus especially who, in conflict with heresies, gave initial rigor and concreteness to the church's thinking about the distinctive divine nature and role of Scripture, within the apostolic legacy, and to "the rule of truth" as he referred to it. Tertullian challenged the same heresies. Yet while on the whole Tertullian's views on Scripture and the *regula fidei* differ little from Irenaeus', Tertullian was an "innovator" of the faith as he too responded to heresies facing the church. Given his similarity to Irenaeus, we will be more concise with Tertullian's thought as representative of "the faith" and its authoritative elements.

Authoritative Scripture. Like Irenaeus and the earlier Fathers, as well as Christ and the apostles, Tertullian fully received "the prophets" (OT) as the written word of God. But Tertullian also resembles Irenaeus in making general appeal to "tradition" as the "message" delivered to the churches by the apostles. Yet beyond Irenaeus, Tertullian developed the term toward the meaning used today, i.e., that which has been in practice for generations.[73] For Tertullian, the relation of doctrinal development to fixed doctrine will become clearer under his view of the *regula fidei*. But, for Tertullian, too, Christ is the ultimate source of Christian teaching, being the truth and Word by whom the Father is revealed. But Christ has entrusted this revelation to his apostles, and only through the apostolically delivered revelation can knowledge of it be obtained.[74] That which was believed and preached in the churches was absolutely authoritative, for it was the same revelation received from the apostles, the apostles from Christ and Christ from God (following Irenaeus' "pattern of authority").[75] Christians cannot pick and choose doctrines they like because their only authorities were the apostles who faithfully "handed on" Christ's teaching, whether oral or written.[76] The whole of apostolic teaching, whether oral or written, Tertullian refers to as *apostolorum traditio or apostolica traditio*.[77]

Yet like Irenaeus, Tertullian's argument is ultimately grounded in Scripture, and tradition is confirmed by Scripture, though in content the two are considered identical deposits of apostolic revelation. While Tertullian was a developer of theological concepts (e.g., the Trinity) and the notion of "tradition" in the Western church, he says that "the faith" authoritatively proclaimed by the apostles was written and enshrined in the apostolic writings by the Holy Spirit. Thus Scripture is absolutely authoritative, whatever it teaches is true, and he warns against teachings not found in Scripture.[78]

Because Tertullian faced heresies that Irenaeus had responded to so successfully, he used many of the same arguments, but he did so with development, different emphases or in redirected form. He regards the apostolic writings to be part of the church's canon. As a whole, the Scriptures unite the apostles and evangelists with the Law and prophets. So combined, the books are authoritative, and from them the churches drink in their faith.[79] As one might expect, Tertullian is more "legalistic" than Irenaeus in his use of Scripture and to those who teach it. To Hermogenes he asserts, "If it is nowhere written, then let it fear the woe which impends on all who add to or take away from the written word."[80] The Scriptures are the divinely authoritative deposit from which Christian teachers and teaching must carefully partake. For one all too ready to develop the church's theological language, this is a strong point.

Tertullian, too, is incensed by heretical use of Scripture. Heretics falsely derive their arguments from "the records of the faith." Referring to the Scriptures as "the instruments of doctrine" or the "means by which doctrine is managed," he says that heretics rearrange contents and corrupt the text for their purposes. Yet he adds, "What is there in our Scriptures which is contrary to us? . . . Of them we have our being."[81] In all, Tertullian requires precise agreement between church teaching and the Scriptures. The Scriptures are the source and standard of Catholic teaching.

The basis for Tertullian's view of the nature of Scripture also paralleled that of Irenaeus, i.e., the Scriptures were produced by divine inspiration. In his polemics with heretics, his unconscious attribution of a biblical passage regularly slips from the writer to the Holy Spirit and back again.[82] And when interpretive difficulty or apparent contradiction between passages occurs he seeks harmony, for it is "unthinkable" that the apostle could contradict himself. Again, the reason is the textual unity given by the one ultimate Author.[83] Because God has thus given this written revelation, it is sufficient for all doctrinal purposes, or as he put it more forcefully, "What is written cannot but have been."[84]

The Authoritative "Rule of Faith." But as strong as Tertullian's emphasis was on the divine origin of prophetic-apostolic Scripture, and so its divine authority for church doctrine and preaching, the menace of the heretical mishandling of those same Scriptures required that Tertullian emphasize, even more than Irenaeus, the authoritative doctrinal-hermeneutical role of the *regula fidei*. Like Irenaeus' "rule of truth," Tertullian's "rule of faith" was somewhat flexible, though with essentially the same content throughout. Again, unlike Protestant vocabulary, he does not identify the regula with

Scripture, though he rejects any opposition between them. Like the church Fathers who preceded and followed, Tertullian understood the "rule" to refer to a series of core, formative doctrines which were thought traceable to the apostles. He presents the specific doctrines of the *regula* in three contexts: *The Prescription* 13, *Against Praxeas* 2, and *The Veiling of Virgins* 1. Though the shortest of the three, the last usefully portrays Tertullian's use of "the rule of faith."

> There is only one rule of faith, unchangeable and unalterable: that of believing in one only God, omnipotent, the creator of the world; and his Son Jesus Christ, born of the Virgin Mary, crucified under Pontius Pilate; on the third day raised again from the dead; received into heaven; now sitting at the Father's right hand; who will come to judge the living and the dead, through the resurrection also of the flesh.[85]

Similarity to "the Apostles' Creed" is clear. But then, while no reference to the "Holy Catholic Church" is expected from the now-Montanist Tertullian, lack of mention of the Holy Spirit is odd. Flexibility among the three in order and details shows that these are not the early baptismal formula. Tertullian does say that the "rule" was taught by Christ and given to the apostles, but the lack of fixity points essentially to several key "truths of God" committed to the church.[86]

Clearly, the doctrines of Tertullian's "rule" are found in Scripture, a point he makes in *Against Marcion*. It seems that his "rule," integral to his polemic against heretical misuse of Scripture, is a summary of the faith intended to guide the church's biblical hermeneutics, and so its teaching, and to make manifest false, destructive uses of Scripture. Like Irenaeus' "rule of truth," the *regula fidei* is doctrinally normative as it sets forth the essentials of the faith. The heretic is thereby marked for failure to adhere to this teaching.[87] Denial of one dogma is grounds for withdrawing the title "Christian,"[88] and, conversely, whoever knows the rule knows all one needs to know for the faith.[89]

As an authoritative summary, "the rule of faith" becomes synonymous with the faith, a body of doctrines immanent in the revelation brought by Jesus Christ and presented by the apostles, a set of formative revelatory truths which establish the *boundaries* of Christianity. Within these there is freedom for inquiry, but outside these lines there is exclusion from

Christianity because, says Tertullian, "faith has been deposited in the rule; it has a law and in the observance of it is salvation."[90] By the fourth and fifth centuries, "the rule of faith" came to include also the decisions of the first four ecumenical councils. One might say that such an authoritative, apostolic rule of faith, as doctrinal summary and as guide to faithful use of prophetic-apostolic Scripture, is "Mere Christianity."

The Rule of Faith and *Sola Scriptura*?
Martin Luther and John Calvin

"Protestant" is a term which is usually used, at least implicitly, in a "negative" way, i.e., in terms of what it is against. Early Protestantism had objections to elements of Roman Catholic teaching and practice, but the term, from the Latin "to bear witness" or "declare openly," originally centered on the "declaration" of positive principles. It did not and should not mean detachment from doctrinal standards, church authority or, importantly, from the core traditions of the past. It did not mean rejecting all developments of "the faith" prior to the Reformation. Even Bernard Ramm wrongly claimed that it was the rejection of Tradition that led the Reformers to the doctrine of *sola scriptura*.[91] It did not and cannot mean anti-Catholic. Early tradition, and notably "the rule of faith" was catholic, not Roman Catholic, from which originally (i.e., the oral preaching and teaching of the apostles) the apostolic Scriptures were then written and then recognized as canonical. The problem then with which we are dealing here is the modern Protestant, especially "evangelical," loss of firm connection between the first Protestants and their time and what had come before—and between Holy Scripture and the main tenets of the church's teaching. What then of *sola gratia*, *sola Christus*, *sola fidei* and, especially, *sola Scriptura*? We will focus briefly on the positions of Martin Luther and John Calvin. The sixteenth-century conflict was not primarily Scripture versus tradition. The Reformers showed no desire to overturn patristic conclusions about the faith of the church, but challenged Roman Catholic *use* of that authority. Rather they valued the tradition of the Fathers which resulted from their interpretation of Scripture.

Martin Luther: Scripture and "the Faith" of the Fathers

Protestant "mythology" portrays Luther's "breakthrough" or "rediscovery" as if it occurred in isolation from all preceding thought or teaching of the church. Very odd for an Augustinian monk. "Justification by faith" had a history among later Fathers.[92] Luther described his own theology as the desire that "the pure study of the Bible and the Holy Fathers might be returned to honor."[93] In 1518, Pope Leo X issued a proclamation that, as Luther understood it, had seized for the papacy the power to define Church teaching without submission to Scripture, the Fathers or ancient church canons.

From one side, Luther's reform was the cutting away of many medieval additions to Christianity that had altered the sacramental life of the Church. Church office did not guarantee authoritative interpretation of the faith. Like Irenaeus and Tertullian, Luther would not recognize dictates unless they were ultimately grounded in Scripture. He cites Hilary and Augustine, along with Scripture passages, to support his emphasis on the sufficiency of Scripture.[94]

From another side, Luther's reform was exactly that, internal reform of the Catholic Church, not a division from it. Luther eventually rejected papal authority, the magisterium and most of the councils, yet he never cast off the conclusions of the early Fathers. Hence, by emphasizing the sufficiency of Scripture, *sola scriptura*, Luther did not thereby believe that the Christian faith could discard the Fathers and the faith of the previous centuries. He did not espouse a sudden early "fall" of the church from its pristine origins.[95] Thus, Luther's view of the early church's "rule," the "Apostles' Creed" and the early ecumenical councils reflects recognition of their continuing authoritative, hermeneutical role in the church. Indeed, he asserts that the "Apostles' Creed" was written by the Holy Spirit, and perfectly expressed his own understanding.[96]

Luther showed much the same respect for the Nicene Creed and urged Christians to heed it as the best presentation of the Trinity. For Luther Nicaea was an authoritative doctrinal "rule," as it had been for over a thousand years. But further, Luther concluded that the first four ecumenical Creeds (Nicaea, Constantinople, Ephesus, Chalcedon) established no new doctrines, but simply showed and defended what the Holy Spirit had given the apostles at Pentecost.[97] Reform must occur by radical reception and submission to Holy Scripture, with the doctrinal conclusions of the Fathers as the authoritative prism by which Scripture is to be faithfully understood. As he put it in his *Appeal to the Ruling Classes*, the Fathers should be read as precursors to the reading of the Scriptures: "The intention of the early Fathers in their writing was to introduce us to the Bible; but we (wrongly) use them only to find a way of avoiding it."[98] The problem was not between the Fathers and Scripture, but in how they were used. Luther certainly did not put the patristic writings and conclusions on the same authoritative level as Scripture. He could point out their faults. But the faith hammered out by the Fathers (especially Augustine), because of great challenges, provided Luther with foundational elements for his *theologia crusis*, the hopelessness of the human situation, justification by grace through faith, etc. The Fathers were also ancient witnesses against papal domination. Unlike Leo, the Fathers never pitted councils and Fathers against Scripture; their conclusions were submitted to the authority of divine Scripture.[99] Thus Luther's reform was intended to be one with the early church-and not only that of the first century. The patristic conclusions, as trustworthy guardians of the truth of Christ, notably the "rule" of the first four councils, with the Apostles' Creed, must again, under Scripture, shape the church and so restore true catholicity.

John Calvin: Scripture and "the Faith" of the Fathers

John Calvin, likewise, had to deal with the weighty attack whereby "Romanists cite the ancient fathers against us" to support the claim to true Christian faith. In his *Reply to Cardinal Sadoleto*, he explains how the Reformation was more faithful to the teachings of the early church.

> You know, Sadoleto . . . that our agreement with antiquity is far closer than yours, but that all we have attempted has been to renew that ancient form of the church.[100]

Calvin affirms that the church founded by the apostles corresponds with the ancient form of the church reflected in the writings of, e.g., Chrysostom and Basil, of the Greek Fathers, and Cyprian, Ambrose and Augustine, of the Latin Fathers. This is in contrast to the "ruins of that church, as now surviving among yourselves." The Reformers have not toppled the church and its ministry, rather it is the Reform movement that truly embodies the writings of the Holy Fathers and is affirmed by the four ancient councils. Thus, Calvin challenges claims that "evangelical"[101] doctrines are of "recent origin" by asserting that Roman Catholic doctrines are contrary to the early church and that the Reformation message is faithful to that of the early Fathers. His opponents were guilty of altering the clear teaching of the divine Scriptures *and* the clear message of the early Fathers.

> All the Fathers . . . have abhorred and with one voice have detested the fact that God's Holy Word has been contaminated by the subtleties of sophists and involved in the squabbles of dialecticians.[102]

The same attitude is found throughout the *Institutes*. The Reformers alone justly lay claim to the ancient authorities. In his defense, Calvin reflects a strong knowledge of the Fathers. Many of his doctrinal arguments from Scripture are clearly filtered through the Fathers, the Apostles' Creed, and the four great councils. For an obvious example, Calvin's scriptural defense of the Trinity is very Nicene in form and content. As one would expect, Augustine is quoted more often than any other Father. The later "tyranny of human tradition," from arbitrary, extra-Scriptural decrees and canons, was not connected to the authoritative teaching of the great creeds of the church. As noted earlier, by the fourth- and fifth-century church, the content of these foundational Councils was regarded as "the rule of faith." For Calvin, the creeds of Nicaea, Constantinople, Ephesus and Chalcedon, are "simply expounding the real meaning of Scripture," and they are the work of the Holy Spirit.[103] Or as he says further on, these creeds teach nothing save "the pure and genuine exposition of Scripture" which the Holy Fathers faithfully applied against the enemies of "the faith."[104]

Yet, while venerating the faithful Fathers and ancient councils, affirming that they ought to have authority for the Christian faith, Calvin still called for *discernment* in the sense that not all councils are equal or authoritative. His guidelines for discernment include questions of time, issue, intent, persons involved, and finally comparison with Scripture. Only the four great ecumenical councils are received, and even these must not be esteemed infallible guides. As with Luther, Calvin is clear: only Holy Scripture is the written Word of God; all else is subject to it.[105]

Calvin's use of the Fathers was often polemically motivated. In the *Institutes* the Fathers are often used to counter Roman Catholic and scholastic views and practices, and to support Reformed theology and ministry. And just as clearly the patristic "rule of faith" had subordinate authority to the divine authority of Scripture. The early Fathers, the Apostles' Creed and the first four great councils are reckoned to be, by the Spirit, faithful expositors of Holy Scripture, in essential agreement with Scripture, and so the authoritative doctrinal and hermeneutical lense for the church's exposition of Scripture.

Recent Attempts to Appropriate "the Rule of Faith" into an Evangelical (and Free Church) "Pattern of Authority"

Stephen R. Holmes

Stephen Holmes is a lecturer in Christian doctrine at King's College at the University of London. He is a Baptist Union minister, a product of Spurgeon's College and of the University of London and an expert on Jonathan Edwards. In his recent work, *Listening to the Past: The Place of Tradition in Theology*, he begins with the common question, "Why can't we just read the Bible?" Thereby Holmes considers the question of the proper and, in some real sense, authoritative place of tradition in Christian theology. His own ecclesial tradition is impatient with "tradition"; it tends to conclude that because God has given us his truth in Scripture, we must simply proclaim it. What others have thought of Scripture is of little interest to us. Holmes is attempting to combat such conclusions and to outline a positive attitude to the Christian tradition *while accepting* the basic *sola scriptura* principle.[106] Listening to the church's "doctors," he says, is critical for theology now, for the theological task is irreducibly the task of the whole of God's people through the centuries.

Holmes is right that the question of divine authority in the church, and so the claimed sources for such authority, is always foundational to Christianity. Possible sources include, e.g., Scripture, tradition, reason and experience. But in fact these have different functions in theology. All agree that reason is an element in doing theology. All theological systems affirm that logic, if valid, has a place in theology, and thus incoherence is a flaw in any such formulation. But that function does not make reason a source of divine authority. It is also doubtful that any theological method can properly begin from our experience, except perhaps that which affirms or denies conclusions from elsewhere. But what of Scripture and "tradition" and their proper relation? Of the various ways one can relate Scripture and tradition, is there a truly Protestant, evangelical way whereby tradition, at least some aspect of it, is somehow normative alongside Scripture?[107]

Holmes begins by ascribing authority to a portion of Christian tradition because of what Jesus says about the revelatory work of the Holy Spirit in John 16:13-14.

> When the Spirit of truth comes he will guide you into all truth. He will not speak from himself but only what he hears, and he will announce to you what is to come. He will glorify me, taking what is mine and showing it to you.

Contra many classical Roman Catholic and Protestant conclusions about this passage, Holmes says this does not refer only or primarily to further revelation; Jesus Christ himself is the full and final revelation (15:15). Only after his death, resurrection and ascension will the disciples understand what he has revealed. The Spirit brings understanding into the words and works of Jesus. There is an eschatological flavor in the context, and the contextual look ahead looks to the second coming of Christ. But Holmes' point is ultimately that the work of the Spirit here described is the continuing interpretation and application of the once-for-all gospel into new places, situations and times. Thereby the church is to understand ever more fully the implications of Scripture until the eschaton.[108]

How then does Holmes relate this from a once-for-all written Scripture to at least some of "church tradition," and hence to an authoritative tradition? He points out that certain writers in the early church have long and generally been recognized as particularly effective in bringing forth the inner logic of the prophetic-apostolic Scriptures and so the message of Christ, with its implications for the context and needs of the church. By the working of the Spirit, these "doctors" of the church and the Fathers of the four great ecumenical councils were enabled to unfold doctrine that was essentially faithful to the logic and implications of the Word of Christ. Thus we have reason to affirm that certain writings are successful at this task. And where these documents agree, says Holmes, there is a presumption of the truth of these conclusions.[109] These documents of the church are said by Holmes to have "classic" status. The basic condition is that a work conforms to and explores the relevance of the gospel of Christ, i.e., Scripture presumably. Yet this is difficult to assess, and it is a difficult task to receive and apply Scripture to a different context. Success or failure can only be judged by other attempts at similar themes, themselves partial and capable of error. An example is the Arian dispute. However clear it seems to us that Alexander and Athanasius were right, it was not so then, and for many reasons.[110]

Hence, the need to discern the truth shows the need for "guides" within the larger tradition, however difficult these are to identify with certainty. Agreement becomes more weighty if extended across widely differing contexts and times. Individual contexts by themselves have unique presumptions and "blind spots." Again, it is broad and multicontextual agreement that "itself is evidence for the correctness of the theological position." Regarding generally acknowledged Fathers and doctrinal "classics" (e.g., the Nicene Creed, cf. below) that are judged to faithfully represent the gospel, Holmes adds that

> In these cases, while it is possible that such texts may be wrong on particular points, there must be a presumption that any position that is found in several such texts is correct, at least until a stronger counter-argument is offered.[111]

This process appears to be largely historical and sociological, but we must remember that for Holmes the hermeneutical authority of such "classic tradition" results from the continuing action of the Spirit (John 16:13-14). That the Spirit is at work in these processes "guarantees" effectiveness.

> [T]he role of the Spirit here is in ensuring that in and through confused, messy and ambiguous actions of creaturely agents the will of the Father still comes to pass.[112]

Thereby the Spirit works quietly in the minds of believers, and so the whole church, "leading us into all truth." This is no claim for infallibility or certainty. There can be "particular errors" in the documents, but, like prayer, we trust that despite great difficulties and lack of success the church's work and teaching has not been in vain—"into all the truth."[113]

This means that "tradition," particularly the main and universally recognized teachings of the Fathers and the four ecumenical creeds, possess a form of authority—relative, dependent (on the message of Christ in Scripture) and partial—but authority nonetheless. Again, the doctrinal success of a document, the acceptance of its teaching as correct, leaves it potentially open to yet stronger arguments to the contrary. As a test case, Holmes examines the Nicene Creed. He offers four *possible* forms of opposing argument by which to assess the Creed for efficacy: exegetical, (appeal to a *reading* of the text of Scripture), logical (the perceived logical implications or possible internal contradiction), experiential (claimed human experience), authoritative (appeal to a theological authority). Do these give reason to conclude that the Nicene Creed is a successful doctrinal statement? Giving special weight to exegesis of Scripture and logic, Holmes concludes, with the church through the centuries, that "it is so unlikely as to be virtually impossible" that the Nicene Creed would ever be rejected.[114] Such a central part of the tradition, then, becomes in effect an authoritative document. But its authority comes only from the church's recognition that it is a remarkably successful repetition of central truths found in the Bible. This is in keeping with Robert Jenson's conclusion that certain church decisions are irreversible: if they are wrong, faith has passed from the earth. The Nicene Creed is a clear example of this. Holmes allows that behind the leading early Fathers, e.g., Irenaeus, et al., and the four ecumenical creeds, that confessional points within particular strands of Christianity (e.g., the canons of the Synod of Dort) can have a further *relativized* authority in issues beyond the nature of God and Christ. But the point is that we cannot claim unmediated access to the Scriptures without acknowledging the authoritative place of "the rule of faith." But the test of truth will always be in the past in the person of Christ and the inspired prophetic-apostolic Scriptures which interpret his coming for us.[115]

Appendix

Daniel Harrison (D. H.) Williams

D. H. Williams, Baptist pastor and scholar, was, until recently, professor of patristics at Loyola University of Chicago. He now teaches at Baylor University. As one who stands, like Holmes, within evangelical Protestantism and the Free Church movement, Williams, too, has serious concerns, and calls evangelicals to emulate the Reformers and to heed the authority the early church Fathers.

Williams warns evangelicals, especially those in the free church heritage that such polity too often stresses autonomous congregations (which spills over to individuals) making these churches open to sectarianism. Churches and movements spring up around individuals with an experience or eloquence, governed only by the NT model of the apostolic age and the Spirit.[116] Evangelicals need to hear Philip Schaff's warning against the "poisonous plant of sectarianism." There remains within Reformational piety the impulse to retreat into subjective spiritualism and an ahistorical faith, seeking personal experience against ancient church authority. An experiential and voluntary foundation for any congregation, *detached from the "rule"* or "tradition" *of the ancient church*, makes such evangelicalism a fertile place for division. As Schaff says:

> The most dangerous foe . . . is not the church of Rome but the sect-plague in our midst; not the single pope . . . but the numberless popes, German, English, and American, who would enslave Protestants once more to human authority . . . mere private judgment and private will.[117]

The "tyranny" of the magisterium has fallen to the tyranny of individualism. Every evangelical conscience feels free to speak *ex cathedra*. This is not to argue against personal experience of God, much less against the central authoritative role of Holy Scripture as divinely given and so divinely authoritative in the church. But such experience is *not* self-authenticating and is problematic when set in *isolation* from the larger history of Christian truth.[118] Such sectarianism is a crude caricature of Reformation principles, providing false security for Christian truth.

> Without the external "check" of the church's theological history and [especially] ancient standards of doctrinal identity, the sectarian approach

will eclipse the congregation's ability to know its place within the larger Christian story.[119]

What then of the relation of divinely authoritative Scripture and "the rule of faith" of the early church? Williams emphasizes that the Reformers believed themselves to be *first* of all obedient to Holy Scripture, but *then* also to be following the practice of the patristic church. In preaching methods, discipline, liturgy, and government, the Reformation churches consciously used patristic models, regarding the patristic "rule" second only to Scripture in authority. And, *after* Scripture, it was the writings and documents of the Fathers by which these justified their views.

So while Scripture had, as the written Word of God, absolute and authoritative preeminence for the Reformers, the "center of gravity of the true faith," it did not and does not of itself set limits to proper reading of Scripture. Scriptural sufficiency, says Williams, was and should be reckoned *with* the interpretive authority of the early Church Fathers and great ecumenical creeds. Like the Reformers, we must read Scripture within the authoritative framework of the "rule of faith."[120]

Seeking to correct the course of the church, classical Protestantism did not endeavor to replace the church's faith, much less to create a new one. Rather, says Williams,

> When Luther argued that the faithful need to believe in the holy catholic church, exemplified in his discussion of the four ecumenical creeds, he meant not Protestantism . . . but a non-Roman Catholic church-one that is renewed after the orthodox teaching of historic catholicity. . . .
> If the Reformation tried to do anything, it tried to restore the ancient catholicity of the church—which arguably ought to be the goal of today's evangelical Protestants.[121]

Williams advocates an "evangelical catholicity" wherein one is called to think and believe (first) in accord with Scripture and so (second) via the patristic "rule" for interpreting the faith. Rather than religious individualism, evangelicals must maintain not only the *centrality* of "the Scripture Principle," for Christian individualists do the same (much like the heretics of the second century), but also "the power of history, and the idea of the church as the pillar and ground of the truth"-but with submission above all and thereby to the written word of God.[122]

Williams' point, then, is that we must regard the Reformation in continuity with the early church in the generations just after the apostolic era. That early church, too, is a valued part of our faith, providing for us now the critical basis for *how we should read* the Scriptures, understand the Trinity, or consider the meaning of the incarnation. Evangelical churches must see themselves as "standing under the authority of the confessional and doctrinal umbrella of the early church, i.e., "the rule of faith," which assumes the primacy of the prophetic-apostolic Scriptures.[123]

Conclusion

We have found that the second- and early third-century Fathers of the church were emphatic that the prophetic (OT) and apostolic (NT) Scriptures are, by revelation and inspiration, the written and authoritative Word of God, and are centered in, by and *under* Jesus Christ, the Word made flesh. As a result, this unitary collection of books, having "one (ultimate) Author," is authoritative for church doctrine, liturgy and Christian life. But the challenge of heresies forced the church to clarify its positions, not only in terms of the canon (Marcion, Montanists) but in terms of doctrine and interpretation (Gnostics). It was necessary to affirm, under and for the divinely inspired Scriptures, an authoritative "apostolic" summary of foundational Christian teachings, a *regula/kanon/*"rule of (truth) faith" to teach true doctrine and to guide interpretation of Scripture and thereby to exclude that which was not Christian. In the fourth and fifth centuries, this was by stages expanded to include the four ecumenical creeds describing the nature of the true God and of Christ.

The Reformation *sola*s, including *sola scriptura*, was in large measure a move back not only to the "sufficiency" of Scripture (properly understood) but to the early Fathers and great creeds, and so to the "classical" interpretation of Scripture. *Sola Scriptura* was not asserted at the expense of the Fathers but interpreted through "the rule" of the Fathers and first great creeds, these having a secondary and derivative authority under the primacy of Holy Scripture.

It is just this classical Christian asymmetrical complementarity, divinely authoritative Scripture and *then* the developed interpretation of Scripture which, I believe, Holmes and especially Williams correctly bring together. But for many contemporary evangelicals, this will reflect not only a modified but, I think, proper *sola scriptura*, and with that also a biblically balanced recognition of the promise of the Spirit in relation to the truth of God, as first of all church-related, and not in the first instance for individuals. Believers are related to the whole history of the church, especially to the paradigmatic first five centuries. In light of contemporary evangelical individualism and interpretive chaos, I would encourage evangelical churches to recognize what the early Fathers found necessary and the Reformers reaffirmed: first, the divinely authoritative Scriptures, and then the doctrinal-hermeneutical norm, the *regula fidei*, from the first five centuries of the church. Evangelicals already do this, e.g., the doctrine of the Trinity. But for the "health" of orthodoxy, the implicit must become explicit.

Endnotes

[1] Celsus, *On The True Doctrine: A Discourse Against the Christians*, trans. R. Joseph Hoffmann (Oxford: Oxford University Press, 1987).

[2] J. N. D. Kelly, *Early Christian Doctrines* (New York: Harper and Row, 1960) 29.

[3] Ibid., 29–30.

[4] Athanasius, *Against Serapion*, in *The Ante-Nicene Fathers* (Grand Rapids: Eerdmans, 1885, 1995) I, 28.

[5] Papias quoted in Eusebius, *Ecclesiastical History in The Ante-Nicene Fathers* (Grand Rapids: Eerdmans, 1885, 1995) III, 39.

[6] E.g., Clement (of Rome), *First Epistle to the Corinthians*, 7,2; Justin Martyr, *First Apology*, 12, 9; and *Dialogue with Trypho*, 80,3.

[7] Justin Martyr, *Dialogue with Trypho*, 81,1.

[8] Pseudo-Barnabas, 6,9; 9,8,10; 13,7.

[9] Irenaeus, *Against Heresies*, I, 27, 2; Tertullian, *Against Marcion*, 4–5; cf. Jaroslav Pelikan, *The Christian Tradition*, vol. 1, *The Emergence of the Catholic Tradition* (Chicago: University of Chicago Press, 1971) 57ff., 76–80; cf. Robert Wilken, The Spirit of Early Christian Thought (New Haven: Yale University Press, 2003) 62 f.

[10] Adolf von Harnack, *History of Dogma*, vol. II, trans. Neil Buchanan (Boston: Roberts Brothers, 1897) 25.

[11] Ibid., cf. Bruce Shelley, *By What Authority?* (Grand Rapids: Eerdmans, 1965) 85.

[12] Kelley, 59.

[13] Irenaeus, *Against Heresies*, III, 3, 4.

[14] Ibid., I, 1–8. The Valentinians taught of the supreme Father (*Bythos*) beyond the universe, unbegotten Monad, by him *Sige* (Silence) who is his thought. From these proceed successive emanations in pairs *Nous* (*Monogenes*) and *Aletheia* (Truth), *Logos* and *Zoe*, *Anthropos* and *Eccelesia*, etc. These and other aeons form the *Pleroma* or fullness of Godhead. But only *Nous* possesses that capability of knowing and revealing the Father. At the call of *Bythos* (Father), Nous and Aletheia produce a new pair of aeons, Christ and the Holy Spirit to teach the aeons of their proper relation to the Father. With true order restored they produce the Savior Jesus as the perfect fruit of the *Pleroma*. To move to the point, the spiritual element from the lower material elements with which it was united. This is accomplished by the Savior Jesus in the psychic and pneumatic classes of people by gnosis and imitation of Jesus, or by pure apprehension of the gnosis taught by Jesus.

[15] Shelley, 55, 93, 96, 102–3.

[16] Kelly, 53.

[17] Ibid., 56–57.

[18] Irenaeus, *Against Heresies*, IV, 9, 1.

[19] Kelly, 33.

[20] I Clement 1:3; 2:18; 3:4; 40:4; 58:2.

[21] I Clement 49:1.

[22] B. F. Westcott, *General Survey of the History of the Canon of the New Testament* (London: MacMillan, 1896) 25–26. Cf. I Clement 22:1; 59:3.

[23] I Clement 42:1-4.

[24] I Clement 47:1-3.

[25] E.g., I Clement 13:1, 46:7.

[26] I Clement 13:1; 16:2; 45:2.

[27] I Clement 8:1.

[28] I Clement 13:3; 45:2; 56:3.

[29] I Clement 7:2, and the discussion in J. B. Lightfoot, *The Apostolic Fathers*, vol. 1 (London: MacMillan, 1885–90) 60.

[30] I Clement 46:6.

[31] Ignatius, Epistle to the Romans 8:2.

[32] Ignatius, Epistle to the Magnesians, 7:1; 13:1-2.

[33] Ignatius, Epistle to the Smyrneans 7:2.

[34] Ignatius, Epistle to the Philadelphians 5:2; Magnesians 8:2; Smyrneans 7:2.

[35] Westcott, 33.

[36] Ignatius, Epistle to the Trallians ch. 9.

[37] Smyrneans 1, Magnesians 11 and 13; The Epistle to the Ephesians 18.

[38] C. H. Turner, "Apostolic Succession," in H. B. Swete, ed., *Essays on the History of the Church and the Ministry* (London: MacMillan, 1918) 114.

[39] Justin Martyr, *First Apology* 23:1; *Dialogue with Trypho the Jew* 134:1; 48:4; 80:3.

[40] *First Apology* 14:4; 23:1; 63:14; *Dialogue* 19:6; 48:4; 68:5; 80:3.

[41] Ibid., 30; 31:7.

[42] Ibid., 39:3; 66:3; *Dialogue* 100:1; 103:8.

[43] Westcott, p. 112.

[44] *Dialogue* 7:1; *I Apology* 35:5; 36:2; 40:5; 44:1.

[45] Ibid., 48:4; 119:6; *I Apology* 67:3.

[46] Ibid., 9:1; 136:3; *I Apology* 31:5; 32:2; 50:12.

[47] Ibid., 65:2, 105.

[48] *First Apology* 6:2; 53:6.

[49] Ibid., 16:8; 19:8; 21:1; 61:2; *Dialogue* 11:2.

[50] *Dialogue* 46:1.

[51] Kelly, 35.

[52] Irenaeus, *Against Heresies*, III, 1, 1.

[53] Ibid., III, 2–5; I, 22,1; V,20,1.

[54] Kelly, 38–39.

[55] Irenaeus, *Against Heresies*, V, 30, 1.

[56] Ibid., II, 11, 1.

[57] Ibid., III, 2, 1.

[58] Ibid., III, 1, 1.

[59] Irenaeus, *The Proof of Apostolic Preaching,* chapters 2, 24, 38, 42.

[60] Irenaeus, *Against Heresies*, IV, 20, 8; III, 16, 2; II, 27, 1; II; 28, 2.

[61] Ibid., IV, 32, 1–2.

[62] Ibid., II, 28, 2; IV, 10, 1.

[63] Ibid., IV, 26, 1.

[64] Ibid., XIV, 32, 1-2.

[65] Ibid., e.g., I, 10, 1f.; I, 22, 1; V, 20, 1.

[66] Ibid., III, 1, 2.

[67] Ibid., I, 9, 4.

[68] Ibid., I, 22, 1; III, 1, 1.

[69] Ibid., I, 22, 1.

[70] Ibid., IV, 35, 4.

[71] Ibid., III, 15,1; IV, 33,7.

[72] Ibid., IV, 26, 5; IV, 32, 1; V, 20, 2. Note here an example of Irenaeus' "rule of truth/ faith": "This then is the order of the rule of our faith. God the Father, not made, not material, invisible; one God, the creator of all things: this is the first point of our faith. The second point is this: the Word of God, Son of God, Christ Jesus our Lord, Who was manifested to the prophets according to the form of their prophesying and according to the method of the Father's dispensation; through Whom (i.e., the Word) all things were made; Who also, at the end of the age, to complete and gather up all things, was made man among men, visible and tangible, in order to abolish death and show forth life and produce perfect reconciliation between God and man. And the third point is: the Holy Spirit, through Whom the prophets prophesied, and the fathers learned the things of God, and the righteous were led into the way of righteousness; Who at the end of the age was poured out in a new way upon mankind in all the earth, renewing man to God."

[73] Tertullian, *Chaplet*, in *Ante-Nicene Fathers* vol. 3 (Grand Rapids: Eerdmans, 1885, 1995) 3.

[74] Tertullian, *Prescription*, 23, in ibid.

[75] Ibid., 21.

[76] Ibid., 6, 37.

[77] Ibid., 21; *Contra Marcion*, I 21; IV, 5.

[78] Tertullian, *Prescription*, 21; *The Flesh of Christ*, III, 6; *Against Praxeus*, 29.

[79] Ibid., 36.

[80] Tertullian, *Against Hermogenes*, 22.

[81] Tertullian, *Prescription*, 38.

[82] Tertullian, *To His Wife*, II, 2.

[83] Tertullian, *On Monogamy*, 11; *On Patience*, 17.

[84] Tertullian, *Against Praxeas*, 29; *The Flesh of Christ*, 3.

[85] Tertullian, *The Veiling of Virgins*, 1.

[86] Tertullian, *Prescription*, 13, 44.

[87] Ibid., 3; *Against Hermogenes*, 1.

[88] Tertullian, *The Resurrection of the Flesh*, 3.

[89] Tertullian, *Prescription*, 14.

[90] Ibid., 12, 14.

[91] Bernard Ramm, *The Evangelical Heritage* (Grand Rapids: Baker, 1973) 29–30.

[92] Cf. Augustine, Hilary of Portiers; cf. Stephen Strehle, *The Catholic Roots of the Protestant Gospel: Encounter Between the Middle Ages and the Reformation* (Leiden: Brill, 1995).

[93] Martin Luther, *Luther's Works* (St. Louis: Concordia) 1.170. Hereafter cited as *LW*.

[94] David Yeago, "The Catholic Luther," in *The Catholicity of the Reformation*, ed. C. Braaten and R. Jenson (Grand Rapids: Erdmans, 1996) 15.

[95] Ibid.

[96] Martin Luther, *Luther's Larger Catechism* (Minneapolis: Augsburg, 1967) chapters 165, 167.

[97] Martin Luther, *LW*, 50. 551, 607.

[98] Martin Luthers, *Appeal to the Ruling Class*, in *Martin Luther: Selections from His Writings*, ed. John Dillenberger (New York: Doubleday, 1958) III, 25.

[99] Martin Luther, *LW*, 41. 14, 27–29, 121–22, 131–36.

[100] John Calvin, *Reply to Cardinal Sadoleto*, in *John Calvin: Selections from His Writings*, ed. John Dillenberger (Missaula, Mont.: Scholars, 1975) 81.

[101] Ibid.

[102] John Calvin, *The Institutes of the Christian Religion*, trans. Ford Lewis Battles (Philadelphia: Westminster, 1960) preface, 4.

[103] Ibid. IV. 18, 23; IV, viii, 16.

[104] Ibid., IV. ix, 8.

[105] Ibid.

[106] Stephen R. Holmes, *Listening to the Past: The Place of Tradition in Theology* (Grand Rapids: Baker Academic, 2002) 154.

[107] Ibid., 153f.

[108] Ibid., 154–55. Here Holmes is especially influenced by notable interpreters of John's Gospel, i.e., George R. Beasley-Murray, Raymond Brown, and T. L. Brodie.

[109] Ibid., 156–57.

[110] Ibid., 157.

[111] Ibid., 158.

[112] Ibid., 158–59.

[113] Ibid.

[114] Ibid. This is in keeping with Robert Jenson's conclusion that certain Church decisions are irreversible: if they are wrong, faith has passed from the earth. The Nicene Creed is a clear example of this. Robert Jenson, *Systematic Theology* (Oxford: Oxford University Press, 1999) 1:23–41.

[115] Ibid., 162–64.

[116] D. H. Williams, *Retrieving the Tradition and Renewing Evangelicalism: A Primer for Suspicious Protestants* (Grand Rapids: Erdmans, 1999) 201–2.

[117] Philip Schaff, *The Principle of Protestantism*, trans. John Nevin (Chambersburg: Publication of the German Reformed Church, 1843) 121. As cited in Williams, *Retrieving*, 203.

[118] Williams, *Retrieving*, 201–2.

[119] Ibid., 204.

[120] Ibid., 199–200.

[121] Ibid, 201.

[122] Ibid., 202–3.

[123] Ibid., 203–4.

Bibliography

Abraham, William J. *Divine Revelation and the Limits of Historical Criticism.* Oxford: Oxford University Press, 1982.

Alston, William. *The Philosophy of Language.* Englewood Cliffs, N.J.: Prentice Hall, 1964.

———. *Illocutionary Acts and Sentence Meaning.* Ithaca, N.Y.: Cornell University Press, 2000.

Altaner, Berthold. *Patrology.* Translated by Hilda C. Graef. New York: Herder and Herder, 1960.

Altizer, Thomas J. J. *The Gospel of Christian Atheism.* Philadelphia: Westminster, 1966.

———. *The Descent into Hell: A Study of the Radical Reversal of the Christian Consciousness.* New York: Seabury, 1979.

———. *History as Apocalypse.* Albany: SUNY Press, 1985.

———. *The Self-Embodiment of God.* Lanham, Md.: University Press of America, 1987.

Anderson, Ray S. *Historical Transcendence and the Reality of God: A Christological Critique.* Grand Rapids: Eerdmans, 1972.

Austin, J. L. *How to Do Things with Words.* 2d ed. Cambridge, Mass.: Harvard University Press, 1975.

Baillie, John. *The Idea of Revelation in Recent Thought.* New York: Columbia University Press, 1956.

Barth, Karl. *Church Dogmatics.* Vols. 1 and 2. Translated by G. T. Thomson. Edinburgh: T. & T. Clark, 1936.

———. *The Word of God and the Word of Man.* Translated by Douglas Horton. New York: Harper, 1957.

———. *Karl Barth: Letters 1961–1968.* Translated by Geoffrey W. Bromiley. Grand Rapids: Eerdmans, 1981.

Berkhof, Hendrikus. *The Christian Faith: An Introduction to the Study of the Faith.* Translated by Sierd Woudstra. Grand Rapids: Eerdmans, 1979.

Bloesch, Donald G. *Wellsprings of Renewal: Promise in Christian Communal Life.* Grand Rapids: Eerdmans, 1974.

———. *The Struggle of Prayer.* Colorado Springs: Helmers and Howard, 1988.

Bibliography

————. *Holy Scripture: Revelation, Inspiration and Interpretation*. Downers Grove, Ill.: InterVarsity Press, 1994.

Bock, Darrell L. "The Words of Jesus in the Gospels: Live, Jive, or Memorex?" In *Jesus Under Fire*, edited by Michael J. Wilkins and J. P. Moreland. 73–99. Grand Rapids: Zondervan, 1995.

Bockmühl, Klaus. *The Unreal God of Modern Theology: Bultmann, Barth, and the Theology of Atheism: A Call to Recovering the Truth of God's Reality.* Translated by Geoffrey W, Bromiley. Colorado Springs: Helmers and Howard, 1988.

Bolich, Gregory G. *Karl Barth and Evangelicalism*. Downers Grove, Ill.: InterVarsity Press, 1980.

Bouwsma, William J. *John Calvin: A Sixteenth-Century Portrait*. New York: Oxford University Press, 1988.

Bray, Gerald L. *Biblical Interpretation: Past & Present*. Downers Grove, Ill.: InterVarsity Press, 1996.

Bromiley, Geoffrey W. "The Authority of Scripture." In *New Bible Commentary*, 2d ed., edited by Donald Guthrie and J. A. Motyer, 10–11. Downers Grove, Ill.: InterVarsity Press, 1970.

————. "The Church Fathers and Holy Scripture." In *Scripture and Truth*, edited by D. A. Carson and John D. Woodbridge 212–17. Grand Rapids: Zondervan, 1983.

————. "The Authority of Scripture in Karl Barth." In *Hermeneutics, Authority and Canon*, edited by D. A. Carson and John D. Woodbridge. 271–94. Grand Rapids: Zondervan, 1986.

Brown, Raymond E. "'And the Lord Said'? Biblical Reflections on Scripture as the Word of God." *Theological Studies* 42 (1981) 3–9.

Bruce, F. F. "(Biblical) Criticism." In *International Standard Bible Encyclopedia*, Vol. 1. Edited by Geoffrey W. Bromiley. 818ff. Grand Rapids: Eerdmans, 1979.

Brunner, Emil. *Reason and Revelation*. Translated by Olive Wyon. Philadelphia: Westminster, 1946.

Buber, Martin. *The Eclipse of God: Studies in the Relation Between Religion and Philosophy*. New York: Harper, 1952.

Bultmann, Rudolf. "The New Testament and Mythology." In *Kerygma and Myth*. Vol. 1. Edited by Hans Werner Bartsch, New York: Harper, 1953.

————. *Jesus Christ and Mythology*. New York: Scribner, 1958.

————. *Existence and Faith: Shorter Writings of Rudolf Bultmann*, selected, edited, and translated by Schubert M. Ogden. New York: Meridian, 1960.

Calvin, John. *Commentaries on the Epistle of Paul to the Hebrews*. Translated and edited by John Owen. Grand Rapids: Eerdmans, 1948.

————. *Commentaries on the First Twenty Chapters of Ezekiel the Prophet*. 2 vols. Edited and translated by Thomas Meyers. Grand Rapids: Eerdmans, 1948.

————. *The Gospel according to St. John 1–10*. Translated and edited by T. H. L. Parker. Edinburgh: Oliver and Boyd, 1959.

————. *The Gospel according to St. John 11–21 and the First Epistle of John*. Translated and edited by T. H. L. Parker. Grand Rapids: Eerdmans, 1961.

————. *Institutes of the Christian Religion*, edited by John T. McNeill and translated by Ford Lewis Battles, et al. 2 vols. Philadelphia: Westminster, 1960.

————. "Reply to Cardinal Sadoleto." In *John Calvin: Selections from His Writings* edited by John Dillenberger, AAR Aids for the Study of Religion. Missoula, Mont.: Scholars, 1975.

————. *Opera Selecta*. 5 vols. Edited by Petrus Barth, et al. Monachil, Spain: C. Kaiser, 1926–1963.

The Catechism of the Catholic Church. Washington, D.C.: United States Catholic Conference, 1994.

Bibliography

Carson, D. A. "Redaction Criticism: On the Legitimacy and Illegitimacy of a Literary Tool." In *Scripture and Truth*, edited by D. A. Carson and John D. Woodbridge. 115–42. Grand Rapids: Zondervan, 1983.

Celsus. *On the True Doctrine: A Discourse Against the Christians.* Translated by R. Joseph Hoffman. New York: Oxford University Press, 1987.

Clark, Gordon H. *Karl Barth's Theological Method.* Philadelphia: Presbyterian and Reformed, 1963.

Cobb, John B. *A Christian Natural Theology: Theology Based on the Thought of Alfred North Whitehead.* Philadelphia: Westminster, 1965.

Cobb, John B. and David Griffin. *Process Theology: An Introductory Exposition.* Philadelphia: Westminster, 1976.

Come, Arnold B. *An Introduction to Barth's Dogmatics for Preachers.* Philadelphia: Westminster, 1963.

Copleston, Frederick. *A History of Philosophy.* Vol. 4, *Modern Philosophy: Descartes to Leibniz.* New York: Doubleday, 1963.

Craig, William Lane. "A Classical Apologist's Closing Remarks." In *Five Views on Apologetics,* edited by Steven B. Cowan, 314–328. Grand Rapids: Zondervan, 2000.

Crehan, F. J. "The Bible in the Roman Catholic Church from Trent to the Present Day." In *The West from the Reformation to the Present Day,* edited by S. L. Greenslade, 199–237. Cambridge History of the Bible 3. Cambridge: Cambridge University Press, 1963.

Cullmann, Oscar. *Christology of the New Testament.* Translated by Shirley C. Guthrie and Charles A. M. Hall. Philadelphia: Westminster, 1959.

Day, Alan. "Bernard Ramm." In *Baptist Theologians,* edited by Timothy George and David S. Dockery, . Nashville: Broadman, 1990.

Dibelius, Martin. *From Tradition to Gospel.* Translated by Bertram Lee Woolf. Cambridge: James Clarke, 1971.

"Dei Verbum." In *The Documents of Vatican II.* London: Sheed and Ward, 1965.

Derrida, Jacques. *Of Grammatology.* Baltimore: Johns Hopkins University Press, 1976.

Dulles, Avery. *Models of Revelation.* New York: Doubleday, 1985.

———. "Faith and Revelation." In *Systematic Theology: Roman Catholic Perspectives.*Vol. 1, edited by Francis Schüssler Fiorenza and John P. Galvin, 89–128. Minneapolis: Fortress, 1991.

Einstein, Albert. "Physics and Reality." In *Ideas and Opinions,* edited by Carl Seelig, et al. Translated and revised by Sonja Bargmann, 290–323. New York: Crown, 1954.

Erickson, Millard J. *The Evangelical Left: Encountering Postconservative Evangelical Theology.* Grand Rapids: Baker, 1997.

Fackre, Gabriel J. *The Doctrine of Revelation: A Narrative Interpretation.* Edinburgh Studies in Constructive Theology. Grand Rapids: Eerdmans, 1997.

Feinberg, Paul D. "The Meaning of Inerrancy." In *Inerrancy,* edited by Norman L. Geisler. 265–304. Grand Rapids: Zondervan, 1979.

Frame, John. "God and Biblical Language: Transcendence and Immanence." *In God's Inerrant Word,* edited by John Warwick Montgomery, 159–77. Minneapolis: Bethany Fellowship, 1974.

Frei, Hans W. *The Eclipse of Biblical Narrative: A Study in Eighteenth- and Nineteenth-Century Hermeneutics.* New Haven: Yale University Press, 1974.

Gabler, Johann P. "An Oration on the Distinction between Biblical and Dogmatic Theology and the Specific Objectives of Each." In *The Flowering of Old Testament Theology: A Reader in Twentieth-Century Old Testament Theology, 1930–1990,* edited by Ben Ollenburger, et al., 497–507. Winona Lake, Ind.: Eisenbrauns, 1992.

Bibliography

Gadamer, Hans-Georg. *Truth and Method.* Translated by Garret Borden and John Cummings. New York: Crossroad, 1982.

Gasque, W. Ward. "Nineteenth-Century Roots of Contemporary New Testament Criticism." In *Scripture, Tradition and Interpretation*, edited by W. Ward Gasque and William S. LaSor. 146–56. Grand Rapids: Eerdmans, 1978.

Geisler, Norman L, editor. *Inerrancy.* Grand Rapids: Zondervan, 1980.

———. "Beware of Philosophy: A Warning to Biblical Scholars." *JETS* 42 (1999) 3–19.

Griffin, David R. *A Process Christology.* Philadelphia: Westminster, 1973.

Goldingay, John. *Approaches to Old Testament Interpretation.* Downers Grove, Ill.: InterVarsity Press, 1981.

Hamilton, Kenneth. *The System and the Gospel.* Grand Rapids: Eerdmans, 1963.

Harnack, Adolf von. *History of Dogma.* Translated by Neil Buchanan. 7 vols. New York: Dover, 1961.

Harrison, Everett F. "The Phenomena of Scripture." In *Revelation and the Bible: Contemporary Evangelical Thought*, edited by Carl F. H. Henry. 235–50. Grand Rapids: Baker, 1958.

Hasel, Gerhard F. "The Future of Old Testament Theology: Prospects and Trends," In *The Flowering of Old Testament Theology: A Reader of Twentieth-Century Old Testament Theology, 1930–1990*, edited by Ben Ollenburger et al. 21ff Winnona Lake, Ind.: Eisenbruans, 1992.

Helm, Paul. *The Divine Revelation: The Basic Issues.* Westchester, Ill.: Crossway, 1982.

Henry, Carl F. H. *The Protestant Dilemma.* Grand Rapids: Eerdmans, 1948.

———. *God, Revelation and Authority.* 6 vols. Waco, Tex.: Word, 1976–1983.

Heschel, Abraham. *God in Search of Man.* London: Jason Aronson, 1987.

Jenson, Robert W. *Systematic Theology.* 2 vols. New York: Oxford University Press, 1997–1999.

Jüngel, Eberhard. *The Doctrine of the Trinity: God's Being is in Becoming.* Translated by Horton Harris. Grand Rapids: Eerdmans, 1976.

———. *God as the Mystery of the World.* Translated by Darrell Guder. Grand Rapids: Eerdmans, 1984.

Kant, Immanuel. *The Critique of Pure Reason.* Translated by Norman Kemp Smith. New York: Macmillan, 1929.

Kelly, J. N. D. *Early Christian Doctrines.* New York: Harper and Row, 1960.

Kelsey, David H. *The Fabric of Paul Tillich's Theology.* New Haven: Yale University Press, 1967

———. *Proving Doctrine: Uses of Scripture in Modern Theology.* Harrisburg, Penn.: Trinity, 1999.

Kierkegaard, Søren. *Philosophical Fragments, Johannes Climacus.* Translated by Howard V. Hong and Edna H. Hong. Kierkegaard's Writings. Princeton: Princeton University Press, 1985.

Kümmel, Werner Georg. *The New Testament: The History of the Investigation of Its Problems.* Translated by S. McLean Gilmour and Howard C. Kee. Nashville: Abingdon, 1972.

Lash, Nicholas. *Easter in Ordinary: Reflections on Human Experience and the Knowledge of God.* Notre Dame, Ind.: University of Notre Dame Press, 1990,

Lewis, C. S. "Fern-Seed and Elephants." In *Fern-Seed and Elephants, and Other Essays on Christianity*, edited by Walter Hooper, 106–13. Glasgow: William Collins Sons, 1975.

Lightfoot, J. B. *The Apostolic Fathers.* Vol. 1, *St. Clement of Rome.* London: Macmillan 1885–1890.

Lindbeck, George A. *The Nature of Doctrine: Religion and Theology in a Postliberal Age.* Philadelphia: Westminster, 1984.

Longman, Tremper. *Literary Approaches to Biblical Interpretation.* Grand Rapids: Zondervan, 1987.

Bibliography

Luther, Martin. *Works*. Edited by Jaroslov Pelikan, et al. 55 vols. St. Louis: Concordia, 1955–1986.

———. "Appeal to the Ruling Class of German Nationality." In *Martin Luther: Selections from His Writings*, edited by John Dillenberger, 403–88. New York: Doubleday, 1961.

Machen, G. Gresham. *Christianity and Liberalism*. Grand Rapids: Eerdmans, 1923.

McCormack, Bruce L. "The Being of Holy Scripture is in Becoming: Karl Barth in Conversation with American Evangelical Criticism." Paper, tenth annual Wheaton College Theology Conference, Wheaton, Ill. April 5, 2001.

———. "The Being of Holy Scripture is in Becoming: Karl Barth in Conversation with American Evangelical Criticism." In *Evangelicals and Scripture: Tradition, Authority and Hermeneutics*, edited by Vincent E. Bacote, et al., 55–75. Downers Grove, Ill.: InterVarsity Press, 2004.

McInerny, Ralph M. *Characters in Search of Their Author*. Notre Dame, Ind.: University of Notre Dame Press, 2001.

McKim, Donald K. *What Christians Believe About the Bible*. Nashville, Tenn.: Thomas Nelson, 1985.

McKinnon, Donald M. *Borderlands of Theology*. Philadelphia: Lippencott, 1968.

Migliore, Daniel L. *Faith Seeking Understanding*. Grand Rapids: Eerdmans, 1991.

Moltmann, Jürgen. *Theology of Hope*. London: SCM Press, 1967.

Morrison, John D. "John Calvin's Christological Assertion of Word Authority in the Context of Sixteenth-Century Ecclesiological Polemics." *Scottish Journal of Theology* 45 (1992) 465–86.

———. *Knowledge of the Self-Revealing God in the Thought of Thomas Forsyth Torrance*. Issues in Systematic Theology 2. Geneva, Switzerland: Peter Lang, 1997.

———. "Scripture as Word of God: Evangelical Assumption or Evangelical Question?" *Trinity Journal* 20 (1999) 165–90.

———. "Spinoza, Semler and Gabler: Headwaters of the Modern Disjunction of Holy Scripture from the Word of God." Forthcoming.

Mueller, David L. *Karl Barth*. Waco, Tex.: Word, 1972.

Neil, William. "The Criticism and Theological Use of the Bible, 1700–1950." In *The West from the Reformation to the Present Day*, edited by S. L. Greenslade, 238–93. Cambridge History of the Bible 3. Cambridge: Cambridge University Press, 1963.

Osborne, Grant R. "The Evangelical and Redaction Criticism Critique and Methodology." *JETS* 22 (1979) 305ff.

———. *The Hermeneutical Spiral*. Downers Grove, Ill.: InterVarsity Press, 1991.

———. "Historical Criticism and the Evangelical." *JETS* 42 (1999) 193–210.

Packer, J. I. "The Adequacy of Human Language." In *Inerrancy*, edited by Norman L. Geisler, 197–228. Grand Rapids: Zondervan, 1980.

Pannenberg, Wolfhart. *Jesus, God and Man*. Philadelphia: Westminster, 1968.

———. *Revelation as History*. New York: Macmillan, 1968.

———. *Systematic Theology*. Vol. 1. Grand Rapids: Eerdmans, 1991.

Parker, T. H. L. *John Calvin: A Biography*. Philadelphia: Westminster, 1975.

Pelikan, Jaroslov. *The Christian Tradition: A History of the Development of Doctrine*. Vol. 1, *The Emergence of the Catholic Tradition*. Chicago: University of Chicago Press, 1971.

Perrin, Norman. *Rediscovering the Teachings of Jesus*. New York: Harper, and Row 1967.

———. *What Is Redaction Criticism?* Philadelphia: Fortress, 1969.

Pinnock, Clark H. *The Scripture Principle*. San Francisco: Harper and Row, 1984.

Pinnock, Clark H. and Delwin Brown. *Theological Crossfire: An Evangelical–Liberal Dialogue*. Grand Rapids: Zondervan, 1990.

Pittinger, W. Norman. *The Word Incarnate: A Study of the Person of Christ.* Library of Constructive Theology. New York: Harper, 1959.

Rahner, Karl. "Revelation." In *The Encyclopedia of Theology: The Concise Sacrementum Mundi*, edited by Karl Rahner. 14–61. New York: Seabury, 1975.

―――. *Foundations of Christian Faith: An Introduction to the Idea of Christianity.* Translated by William V. Dych. New York: Seabury, 1978.

Ramm, Bernard L. *Special Revelation and the Word of God.* Grand Rapids: Eerdmans, 1961.

―――. *Protestant Biblical Interpretation.* 3d revised ed. Grand Rapids: Baker, 1970.

―――. *The Evangelical Heritage.* Waco, Tex.: Word, 1973.

―――. *After Fundamentalism: The Future of Evangelical Theology.* San Francisco: Harper and Row, 1983.

Roberts, Alexander and James Donaldson, editors. *The Ante-Nicene Fathers: Translations of the Writings of the Fathers Down to 325.* 10 vols. Grand Rapids: Eerdmans, 1965–1968.

Robinson, James M., editor. *The Beginnings of Dialectical Theology.* 2 vols. Richmond, Va.: John Knox, 1968.

Runia, Klaas. *Karl Barth's Doctrine of Holy Scripture.* Grand Rapids: Eerdmans, 1962.

Sandys-Wunsch, John and Laurence Eldredge. "J. P. Gabler and the Distinction between Biblical and Dogmatic Theology: Translation, Commentary and Discussion of His Originality." *Scottish Journal of Theology* 33 (1980) 133–58.

Schaff, Phillip. *The Creeds of Christendom.* Grand Rapids: Baker, 1977

Schleiermacher, Friedrich, D. E. *The Christian Faith.* Translated by H. R. Mackintosh and James S. Stewart. Edinburgh: T. & T. Clark, 1928.

Scholem, Gershom. *On the Kabbala and Its Symbolism.* London: Routledge, Kegan, Paul 1965.

Seynaeve, Jaak, editor. *Cardinal Newman's Doctrine on Holy Scripture.* Louvain, Belgium: Publications Universitaires, 1953.

Searle, John. *Expression and Meaning: Studies in the Theory of Speech-Acts.* Cambridge: Cambridge University Press, 1979.

Shelley, Bruce L. *By What Authority?: The Standards of Truth in the Early Church.* Grand Rapids, Eerdmans, 1965.

Silva, Moisés. *God, Language and Scripture.* Grand Rapids: Zondervan, 1990.

―――. "Can Two Walk Together Unless They Be Agreed? Evangelical Theology and Biblical Scholarship." *JETS* 41 (1998) 3–16.

Spinoza, Baruch. *Ethics.* Translated by R. H. M. Elwes. New York: Aladdin, 1901.

―――. *A Theologico-Political Treatise.* Translated with an introduction by R. H. M. Elwes. New York: Dover, 1951.

Stanton, G. N. "Presuppositions of New Testament Criticism." In *New Testament Interpretation*, edited by I. Howard Marshall. 60–72. Grand Rapids: Eerdmans, 1978.

Stein, Robert H. "Authentic or Authoritative Sayings: What's the Difference?" In *Gospels and Tradition*, edited by Robert H. Stein. 147–52. Grand Rapids: Baker, 1991.

―――. "What Is Redaction Criticism?" In *Gospels and Tradition*, edited by Robert H. Stein. 21–34. Grand Rapids: Baker, 1991.

Steiner, George. *Real Presences.* Chicago: University of Chicago Press, 1989.

Stonehouse, Ned. "The Infallibility of Scripture and Evangelical Progress." *BETS* 1 (1958) 9ff.

Strehle, Stephen. *The Catholic Roots of the Protestant Gospel: Encounter Between the Middle Ages and the Reformation.* Studies in the History of Christian Thought 60. Leiden, Netherlands: Brill, 1995.

Stump, Eleonore. "Medieval Biblical Exegesis: Augustine, Aquinas, and Swinburne." In *Reason and the Christian Religion: Essays in Honor of Richard Swinburne*, edited by Alan G. Padgett (Oxford: Clarendon, 1994) 161–97.

Bibliography

Turner, C. H. "Apostolic Succession." In *Essays on the Early History of the Church and the Ministry*, edited by H. B. Swete, n.p. London: Macmillan, 1918.

Swinburne, Richard. *Revelation: From Metaphor to Analogy*. Oxford: Clarendon, 1992.

Tavard, George H. *Paul Tillich and the Christian Message*. New York: Scribner, 1962

Thatcher, Adrian. *The Ontology of Paul Tillich*. Oxford: Oxford University Press, 1978

Thiselton, Anthony C. *The Two Horizons: New Testament Hermeneutics and Philosophical Description*. Grand Rapids: Eerdmans, 1980.

———. *The Promise of Hermeneutics*. Grand Rapids: Eerdmans, 1999.

Tillich, Paul. *Systematic Theology*. Vol. 1. Chicago: University of Chicago Press, 1951.

———. *Systematic Theology*. Vol. 2. Chicago: University of Chicago Press, 1957.

———. *Theology of Culture*. Edited by Robert C. Kimball. New York: Oxford University Press, 1959.

———. *Christianity and the Encounter of the World Religions*. New York: Columbia University Press, 1963.

———. *Ultimate Concern: Paul Tillich in Dialogue*. Edited by D. Mackenzie Brown. New York: Harper, 1965.

———. *On the Boundary: An Autobiographical Sketch*. New York: Scribner, 1966

Torrance, Thomas Forsyth. *Space, Time, and Incarnation*. London: Oxford University Press, 1969.

———. *Theological Science*. London: Oxford University Press, 1969.

———. *God and Rationality*. London: Oxford University Press, 1971.

———. *Theology in Reconciliation: Essays Toward Evangelical and Catholic Unity in East and West*. Grand Rapids: Eerdmans, 1975.

———. *Space, Time, and Resurrection*. Grand Rapids: Eerdmans, 1976.

———. *Christian Theology and Scientific Culture*. New York: Oxford University Press, 1981.

———. *The Ground and Grammar of Theology*. Charlottesville: University Press of Virginia, 1980.

———. *The Mediation of Christ*. Grand Rapids: Eerdmans, 1984.

———. *Transformation and Convergence in the Frame of Knowledge: Interrelations of Scientific and Theological Enterprise*. Grand Rapids: Eerdmans, 1984.

———. *Reality and Scientific Theology*. Edinburgh: Scottish Academic Press, 1985.

———. *The Trinitarian Faith*. Edinburgh: T. & T. Clark, 1988.

———. "The Doctrine of the Holy Trinity according to St. Athanasius." *Anglican Theological Review* 71 (1991) 395–405.

———. *Theology in Reconstruction*. Eugene, Ore.: Wipf & Stock, 1996.

Vanhoozer, Kevin J. "The Semantics of Biblical Literature." In *Hermeneutics, Authority and Canon,* edited by D. A. Carson and John D, Woodbridge, 85–92. Grand Rapids: Academie Books, 1986.

———. *Is There a Meaning in this Text?: The Bible, the Reader, and the Morality of Literary Knowledge*. Grand Rapids: Zondervan, 1998.

———. *First Theology: God, Scripture and Hermeneutics*. Downers Grove, Ill.: InterVarsity Press, 2002.

Van Til, Cornelius. *The New Modernism: An Appraisal of the Theology of Barth and Brunner*. Philadelphia: Presbyterian and Reformed, 1946.

———. *Christianity and Barthianism*. Philadelphia: Presbyterian and Reformed, 1962.

Wallace, Ronald S. *Calvin's Doctrine of the Word and Sacrament*. Grand Rapids: Eerdmans, 1957.

Warfield, B. B. *Inspiration and Authority*. Philipsburg, N.J.: Presbyterian and Reformed, 1979.

Bibliography

Weber, Otto. *Karl Barth's Church Dogmatics: An Introductory Report.* Translated by Arthur C. Cochrane. Philadelphia: Westminster, 1953.

————. *Foundations of Dogmatics.* Vol. 1. Translated by Darrell L. Guder. Grand Rapids: Eerdmans, 1981.

Westcott, B. F. *General Survey of the History of the Canon of the New Testament.* London: Macmillan, 1896.

Wheat, Leonard F. *Paul Tillich's Dialectical Humanism.* Baltimore: Johns Hopkins University Press, 1970.

Wilken, Robert. *The Spirit of Early Christian Thought.* New Haven: Yale University Press, 2003.

Williams, D. H. *Retrieving the Tradition and Renewing Evangelicalism: A Primer for Suspicious Protestants.* Grand Rapids: Eerdmans, 1999.

Wolterstorff, Nicholas. *Divine Discourse: Philosophical Reflections on the Claim that God Speaks.* Cambridge, England: Cambridge University Press, 1996.

Woodbridge, John D. *Biblical Authority: A Critique of the Rogers/McKim Proposal.* Grand Rapids: Zondervan, 1982.

Work, Telford. *Living and Active: Scripture in the Economy of Salvation.* Grand Rapids: Eerdmans, 2001.

Wright, G. Ernest. *God Who Acts: Biblical Theology as Recital.* London: SCM Press, 1954.

————. "Archaeology, History and Theology." *Harvard Divinity Bulletin* 28 (1964) 85–96.

————. *Theology and the Old Testament.* New York: Harper and Row, 1969.

Yeago, David S. "The Catholic Luther." In *The Catholicity of the Reformation*, edited by Carl E. Braaten and Robert W. Jenson, 13–34. Grand Rapids: Eerdmans, 1996.

Young, Norman J. *History and Existential Theology: The Role of History in the Thought of Rudolf Bultmann.* Philadelphia: Westminster, 1969.

Index

G